The InDesign 1.5 Tools Palette

- Keyboard shortcuts in parentheses
- Shift+shortcut cycles through hidden tools

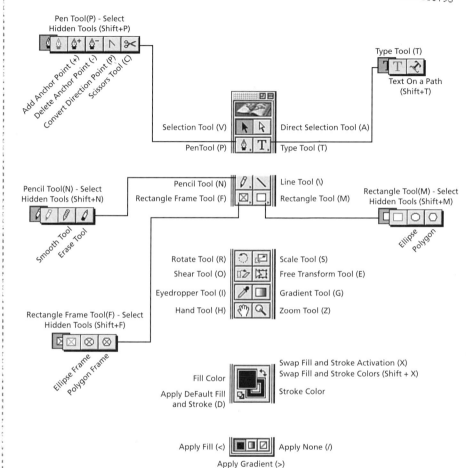

Pen Tool(P) - Select
Hidden Tools (Shift+P)

Add Anchor Point (+)
Delete Anchor Point (-)
Convert Direction Point (P)
Scissors Tool (C)

Type Tool (T)

Text On a Path
(Shift+T)

Selection Tool (V) Direct Selection Tool (A)

PenTool (P) Type Tool (T)

Pencil Tool(N) - Select
Hidden Tools (Shift+N)

Smooth Tool
Erase Tool

Pencil Tool (N) Line Tool (\)

Rectangle Frame Tool (F) Rectangle Tool (M)

Rectangle Tool(M) - Select
Hidden Tools (Shift+M)

Ellipse
Polygon

Rotate Tool (R) Scale Tool (S)

Shear Tool (O) Free Transform Tool (E)

Eyedropper Tool (I) Gradient Tool (G)

Hand Tool (H) Zoom Tool (Z)

Rectangle Frame Tool(F) - Select
Hidden Tools (Shift+F)

Ellipse Frame
Polygon Frame

Swap Fill and Stroke Activation (X)
Swap Fill and Stroke Colors (Shift + X)

Fill Color

Apply DeFault Fill
and Stroke (D)

Stroke Color

Apply Fill (<) Apply None (/)

Apply Gradient (>)

MMS

Teach Yourself Adobe® InDesign™

in Hours

InDesign 1.5 Keyboard Shortcut Quick Reference

Windows users should use the Alt key instead of Opt, and Ctrl instead of Cmd.

FILE MENU

New	Cmd+N
Open	Cmd+O
Close	Cmd+W
Save	Cmd+S
Save As	Shift+Cmd+S
Save a Copy	Opt+Cmd+S
Place	Cmd+D
Links	Shift+Cmd+D
Export	Cmd+E
Document Setup	Opt+Cmd+P
Page Setup	Shift+Cmd+P
Preflight	Opt+Shift+Cmd+F
Package	Opt+Shift+Cmd+P
Print	Cmd+P
Quit	Cmd+Q

EDIT MENU

Undo	Cmd+Z
Redo	Shift+Cmd+Z
Cut	Cmd+X
Copy	Cmd+C
Paste	Cmd+V
Paste Into	Opt+Cmd+V
Paste In Place	Opt+Shift+Cmd+V
Duplicate	Opt+Cmd+D
Step and Repeat	Shift+Cmd+V
Select All	Cmd+A
Deselect All	Shift+Cmd+A
Find/Change	Cmd+F
Find Next	Opt+Cmd+F
Check Spelling	Cmd+I
Preferences, General	Cmd+K

LAYOUT MENU

First Page Up	Shift+Cmd+Page
Previous Page	Shift+Page Up
Next Page	Shift+Page Down
Last Page Down	Shift+Cmd+Page
Go Back	Cmd+Page Up
Go Forward	Cmd+Page Down
Insert Page Number	Opt+Cmd+N

TYPE MENU

Character	Cmd+T
Paragraph	Cmd+M
Tabs	Shift+Cmd+T
Character Styles	Shift+F11
Paragraph Styles	F11
Create Outlines	Shift+Cmd+O
Show Hidden Characters	Opt+Cmd+I

OBJECT MENU

Arrange, Bring To Front	Shift+Cmd+]
Arrange, Bring Forward	Cmd+]
Arrange, Send To Back	Shift+Cmd+[
Arrange, Send Backward	Cmd+[
Group	Cmd+G
Ungroup	Shift+Cmd+G
Lock Position	Cmd+L
Unlock Position	Opt+Cmd+L
Text Frame Options	Cmd+B
Fitting, Fit Content to Frame	Opt+Cmd+E
Fitting, Fit Frame to Content	Opt+Cmd+C
Fitting: Center Content	Shift+Cmd+E
Fitting: Fit Content Proportionally	Opt+Shift+Cmd+E
Text Wrap	Opt+Cmd+W
Corner Effects	Opt+Cmd+R
Clipping Path	Opt+Shift+Cmd+K
Image Color Settings	Opt+Shift+Cmd+D
Compound Paths, Make	Cmd+8
Compound Paths, Release	Opt+Cmd+8

VIEW MENU

Zoom In	Cmd++
Zoom Out	Cmd+-
Fit Page In Window	Cmd+0
Fit Spread In Window	Opt+Cmd+0
Actual Size	Cmd+1
Entire Pasteboard	Opt+Shift+Cmd+0
Display Master Items	Cmd+Y
Show/Hide Text	Opt+Cmd+Y
Show/Hide Frame Edges	Cmd+H
Show/Hide Rulers	Cmd+R
Show/Hide Guides	Cmd+;
Lock Guides	Opt+Cmd+;
Snap to Guides	Shift+Cmd+;
Show/Hide Baseline Grid	Opt+Cmd+'
Show/Hide Document Grid	Cmd+'
Snap to Document Grid	Shift+Cmd+'

WINDOW MENU

Transform Palette	F9
Align Palette	F8
Pages Palette	F12
Layers Palette	F7
Swatches Palette	F5
Stroke Palette	F10
Color Palette	F6

HELP MENU (WINDOWS ONLY)

Contents	F1

NAVIGATION

100% size	Cmd+1
200% size	Cmd+2
400% size	Cmd+4
50% size	Cmd+5
Access page number box	Cmd+J
Access zoom percentage box	Opt+Cmd+5
Change Image Display preference	Shift+Cmd+F5
First spread	Opt+Shift+Page Up
Fit selection in window	Opt+Cmd++
Force redraw	Shift+F5
Go to first frame	Opt+Shift+Cmd+Page Up
Go to last frame	Opt+Shift+Cmd+Page Down
Go to next frame	Opt+Cmd+Page Down
Go to previous frame	Opt+Cmd+Page Up
Last spread	Opt+Shift+Page Down
Next spread	Opt+Page Down
Previous spread	Opt+Page Up
Scroll down one screen	Page Down
Scroll up one screen	Page Up

Richard Romano

SAMS
Teach Yourself

Adobe®
InDesign™ 1.5
in 24 Hours

SAMS

A Division of Macmillan USA
201 West 103rd St., Indianapolis, Indiana, 46290

Sams Teach Yourself Adobe InDesign 1.5 in 24 Hours

Copyright © 2000 by Sams Publishing

International Standard Book Number: 0-672-31905-5

Library of Congress Catalog Card Number: 99-69832

Printed in the United States of America

First Printing: September 2000

02   01   00   4   3   2   1

Trademarks

Warning and Disclaimer

ACQUISITIONS EDITORS
Randi Roger
Jeff Schultz

DEVELOPMENT EDITOR
Jonathan Steever

MANAGING EDITOR
Charlotte Clapp

PROJECT EDITOR
Carol Bowers

COPY EDITOR
Kezia Endsley

INDEXER
Rebecca Salerno

PROOFREADER
Daniel Ponder

TECHNICAL EDITOR
Paul Rosenberg

INTERIOR DESIGNER
Gary Adair

COVER DESIGNER
Aren Howell

PRODUCTION
Brandon Allen
Steve Geiselman

Contents at a Glance

Contents

Part II Working with Text   105

Hour 6 Creating Text   107

Part III Working with Graphics 165

About the Author

RICHARD ROMANO is managing editor of *Micro Publishing News*, a newsmonthly in the Cygnus Graphics Network that provides industry news, product information, and hardware and software news and reviews for content creators, electronic designers, and print buyers. Romano writes news items and features on new technologies and coordinates and writes hardware and software reviews for such graphics-related products as digital cameras, scanners, printers, large-format output devices, and a wide variety of graphics software—including InDesign. From 1997 to 1999, Romano was also a product reviewer and coordinator for *Digital Imaging*, a then-sister publication of *Micro Publishing News*. He is the author of *Digital Photography Pocket Primer: Capturing and Optimizing Images for Print- and Web-based Publishing*, published in June 2000 by Windsor Publishing, and is the editor-in-chief of *The GATF Encyclopedia of Graphic Communications*, published in 1998 by The Graphic Arts Technical Foundation, as well as the *Yearbook 2000* supplement. Romano is a graduate of Syracuse University's Newhouse School of Public Communications and has a certificate in multimedia technology from New York University. Originally from New York City, he now lives in Los Angeles.

Acknowledgments

Big thank yous to everyone involved in this project, especially the fine and at times beleaguered folks at Macmillan: Randi Roger, who originally approached me for this project and endured my many noodgy emails, and her successor Jeff Schultz; development editor Jon Steever, who has a sharp eye and can whip even someone as verbose as me into coherent shape; copy editor Kezia Endsley—who I think only exists as pink text in a Word document—also has a terrific eye and somehow seemed to know what I was getting at better than I did; and technical editor Paul Rosenberg, who also raised some great points. Thanks to everyone else on the Macmillan team.

I was not the first to work on this project, and I would like to thank John San Filippo and Sarah O'Keefe for laying down much of groundwork for this project, which I hope I have only improved on.

I would also like to thank Becky Ross, Dave Evans, and the rest of the InDesign team at Adobe Systems—and the PR folks at Eastwick Communications—for keeping me in the loop on new developments with InDesign, and for answering my panicked questions. Oh, and I guess I should also say thanks for InDesign, without which this book would not exist.

I would also like to thank my colleagues at *Micro Publishing News*—Ken Spears, David Griffith, Wendy Quintanilla, Alison Blasko, Chuck Ward, and Joe LiPetri—just for existing, really. Special thanks to Christopher Simmons, president of Mindset Communications, and Andy Shalat of Shalat Design for other crucial feedback, opinions, and advice. Extra special thanks to MPN's founding publisher James Cavuoto for getting me involved in all this to begin with (and for the Giants' tickets). Thanks also to Ken Aniolek, who keeps me sane.

And finally, thanks to you for buying this book. And if you stole it, I'm flattered that you would risk jail time for it.

Tell Us What You Think

As the reader of this book, *you* are the most important critic and commentator. We value your opinion and want to know what we're doing right, what we could do better, what areas you'd like to see us publish in, and any other words of wisdom you're willing to pass our way.

You can email or write me directly to let me know what you did or didn't like about this book—as well as what we can do to make our books stronger.

Please note that I cannot help you with technical problems related to the topic of this book, and due to the high volume of mail I receive, I might not be able to reply to every message.

When you write, please be sure to include this book's title and author as well as your name and phone number. I will carefully review your comments and share them with the author and editors who worked on the book.

email: graphics_sams@mcp.com
Mail: Mark Taber
          Associate Publisher
          Sams Publishing
          201 West 103rd Street
          Indianapolis, Indiana 46290 USA

Introduction

In the fall of 1998, at Seybold Seminars San Francisco, one of the publishing industry's biggest and most important trade shows, the graphics industry got the first sneak peek of a new page layout application from Adobe Systems, then code-named "K2." Until that point, word of the program's existence proliferated as nothing but rumor and innuendo. Getting any information out of Adobe was like scaling the peak for which the project was named. Hype proliferated.

If you don't come from the professional publishing industry, it's hard to describe the excitement that the existence of K2 (later renamed InDesign) engendered.

Users of the de facto standard for page layout, QuarkXPress, disliked the company (Quark) and were eager for a more customer-friendly company (like Adobe) to give them a powerful tool in its stead. The time was right for a twenty-first century publishing application. Is InDesign that program? That's a very good question. InDesign appeared at the same time as the movie "*Star Wars: Episode I, The Phantom Menace*," and in my original review of InDesign in *Micro Publishing News*, I had stated that, like that movie, InDesign could never be as good as the hype that preceded it. Which is not to say that it was a bad program at all; it's not. I gave the program a very good review at the time, and I have come to like it even more in the months since. Have I completely abandoned QuarkXPress? No; I still use Quark for many things, and since I don't work in a vacuum, I often need to keep using Quark for projects that involve other people.

InDesign did not take the industry by storm, and even though service bureaus reported that they weren't getting very many InDesign jobs, many users have at least picked it up for fact-finding and reconnaissance purposes. There's always a stigma attached to version-1.0 software (often for good reason), so I suspect most people are waiting for a few revs before signing on wholeheartedly.

User feedback was voluble, and Adobe quickly came out with version 1.5, which attempts to fix many of the shortcomings in version 1.0. As you'll see throughout this book, many tools have been added to version 1.5.

Which brings us to the present. If InDesign is your first page layout application, you're in great shape. You bring no baggage to the program. One of the problems that so many people have with InDesign is that they bemoan the fact that it's not QuarkXPress or PageMaker. They have grown comfortable with Quark (or PageMaker, as the case may be) and are resistant to change.

If you do come with the baggage of knowing another program such as QuarkXPress or PageMaker, some of InDesign's conventions will take you by surprise and you might get frustrated at first. Learning new software is always frustrating at first. However, if you've used any graphics applications in the past five years, you won't have a problem with InDesign.

So, fire up the computer, put on a pot of coffee, and let's get started.

Is This The Book For You?

This book is intended for everyone: from beginners who have never created a single layout, to intermediate level graphic artists looking to learn a new software package. Although this book covers some basic concepts of "electronic publishing," the focus is on learning the software quickly. Stepping through each lesson, beginners will learn basic design concepts while learning the software, whereas the accomplished artist can quickly learn by example how to use the tools.

How This Book Is Organized

- Part I, "Getting Started with Adobe InDesign" (Hours 1–5), pretty much, as you would expect, starts at the beginning. What are the tools that InDesign puts at your disposal? How are the menus organized? What do the palettes do? How do you go about creating a new document? How do you create and manage pages?

- Part II, "Working with Text" (Hours 6–8), explores the wealth of typesetting tools that InDesign has given would-be (and will-be) typesetters. How are fonts and type sizes applied? How does InDesign let you create great-looking type?

- Part III, "Working with Graphics" (Hours 9–12), kicks it up a notch, to coin a phrase. In this section, you'll learn how to create your own graphics using InDesign's extensive array of professional drawing tools. You'll also learn how to import graphic files that were created with other programs, and how text and graphics work together to make pages dynamic.

- Part IV, "Working with Color" (Hours 13–16), begins with simply applying colors to objects and continues through the more crucial considerations of professional color output. What is CMYK? What is RGB? Should you do your own trapping? You'll also be able to answer that age-old question, "Why doesn't my printed output match what I see on the screen?"

- Part V, "InDesign Output" (Hours 17–21), What goes in must come out—and here is where you'll explore all the things you can do with your InDesign documents, from setting up a desktop printer, to preparing files for service bureau output. You'll also learn how to export your files as PDFs, and even how to repurpose your pages as Web pages.

- Part VI, "Advanced InDesign" (Hours 22–24), takes InDesign outside the box, so to speak. How can you customize InDesign so that it provides a comfortable work environment? How can you share files and resources with others in workgroups? How does InDesign function in a cross-platform environment?

Conventions Used in This Book

This book uses the following conventions:

Text that you type and text that you see on-screen appear in `monospace type`.

> A **Note** presents interesting information related to the discussion.

> A **Tip** offers advice or shows you an easier way to do something.

> A **Caution** alerts you to a possible problem, and gives you advice on how to avoid it.

What's On the Web Site?

On the Web site, you will find downloadable, compressed archives containing the files that are occasionally called for to complete certain exercises in this book. All files are organized by chapter numbers for ease in locating. To get to the Web site, point your Web browser to:

`http://www.mcp.com/sams/detail_sams.cfm?item=0672319055`

Once the main book page has loaded, click on the `Downloads` link to get to the files.

PART I

Getting Started with Adobe InDesign

Hour

HOUR 1

Introducing Adobe InDesign

Reader, InDesign. InDesign, Reader. Greetings to you both. Let's get on with it, shall we?

We have a lot of work cut out for ourselves in the next 24 hours, so let's start off a little slowly and passively before we stampede straight to the exercises.

One of the missions of this book in general— and this chapter in particular— is to get you familiar with the InDesign way of doing things.

So in this hour you'll learn:

- How InDesign came to be
- How InDesign's toolbox is set up
- How to work with InDesign's palettes

In other words, we'll take it a bit easy in this hour and leap into the fray with both feet starting with Hour 2, "Preparing to Work in InDesign."

The Birth of InDesign from the Spirit of PageMaker

When Adobe announced the program that was eventually to become InDesign (at the time, it was code-named "K2"), there was a great deal of buzz in the graphics and publishing industry. Designers and page layout specialists were initially optimistic; QuarkXPress, the de facto standard for page layout in the graphics industry, has a large installed base of users, and many of them reported that they love the program, but have had bad experiences with the company, and therefore would be willing to entertain the notion of a competitive application.

Putting the Puzzle Together

Meanwhile, Adobe's own page layout program, PageMaker— now seemingly frozen in time at version 6.5, which has remained essentially unchanged since 1996— is not really Adobe's baby. It's more of a changeling. PageMaker first appeared in 1985, developed by Aldus Corporation, and was the program that originally made desktop publishing possible. When Adobe Systems acquired Aldus in 1994, PageMaker came as part of the package, and Adobe began to put out its own updates of PageMaker. The two Adobe versions, 6.0 and 6.5, were solid updates, and Adobe's marketing team tried to cast PageMaker, with Photoshop and Illustrator, as one of the trinity of essential graphics and publishing tools. Yet this grande dame of desktop publishing was beginning to show its age. Service bureau support began to wane, and users were migrating en masse to QuarkXPress.

Meanwhile, Adobe's own Acrobat, a suite of programs for creating, editing, and reading Portable Document Format (PDF) files, was catching on in myriad markets. Especially in the graphic arts and prepress, PDF was (and continues to be) looked to as a cure-all file format for many prepress and printing workflow ills. More and more workflow "solutions" (notice that we now have more solutions than problems) are using PDF as a means of supplying files to printers. We'll look at PDF in more detail in Hour 19, "Preparing Acrobat Output with InDesign."

So Adobe has great success with Photoshop, the industry standard for image editing and manipulation; with Illustrator which, although sharing the market with Macromedia's FreeHand, is a very popular vector illustration tool; with PostScript, the standard page description language that makes consistent output of documents possible; and with Acrobat, which is an increasingly popular means of proofing documents, as well as an increasingly viable means of providing documents to service providers and/or printers.

1

Adobe has most of the pieces of the graphic arts puzzle. So what's missing? A compelling and popular page layout program.

Enter InDesign

So Adobe decided to build its own "from-the-ground-up" page layout program which could act as the bridge between the creative end of the process (Photoshop and Illustrator) and the output end (Acrobat and PostScript).

So why is any of this important for you? Well, an understanding of why InDesign exists is a good way to start to understand its features. Knowing what it was designed to do is a good way to start to learn what you can do with it.

InDesign— especially version 1.5— has many of the same tools that Photoshop and Illustrator have. This is a boon to those who may be proficient in either or both of those other programs and want a reasonably seamless way to add a layout application to their toolbox without having to learn a whole new interface.

InDesign is reminiscent enough of PageMaker that users who are familiar with PageMaker will not likely find themselves floundering.

Whither PageMaker? Is our old friend being wished into the cornfield by Adobe? Not at all. In fact, PageMaker has remained unchanged and unscathed. Its only difference really is in marketing. About the same time that InDesign appeared, PageMaker 6.5 Plus was unveiled, which is the same old PageMaker repositioned as a high-quality alternative to Microsoft Publisher. Add a bunch of document templates, and you've got a tool targeted to corporate publishers and other lower-end graphics users.

Similarly, InDesign is also reminiscent of QuarkXPress that Quark users will also not find themselves too far at sea.

What is interesting to see is that all the folks who said initially that they would abandon Quark for InDesign didn't put their money where their mouths were. InDesign has taken a while to catch on, but the word on the street is that with version 1.5, more and more user— and service bureau— acceptance is on the way. Many folks simply avoid 1.0 products like the plague— and probably for good reason. Adobe realized that 1.0 didn't spring full-grown from the head of Zeus, and version 1.5 has gone a long way to answer a good many of user complaints and requests. But as we all know you can't please all the people all the time.

That said, there are a few areas where Adobe still has some work to do, and from what I have read in various user forums and heard through the grapevine, those areas that still need work include support for "long documents." Long documents are things such as books, which typically comprise several different files (chapters, for example) that are grouped together and treated as a single unit. Part of this long document support is the ability to automatically create tables of contents and indices. InDesign lacks long document support, even though PageMaker has it.

Another area that users are complaining is that InDesign lacks a story editor. A story editor is an alternate mode you can use that displays text in a word processor-like format, making onscreen proofing and editing easier than trying to read WYSIWYG (what-you-see-is-what-you-get) type, which can be very hard to read on screen. Needless to say, Adobe is aware of these limitations and, well, Christmas is coming...

To Switch or Not to Switch

We'll look at this issue— converting from Quark/PageMaker to InDesign in Hour 24, "Deploying InDesign in the Real World," but for now let's just say that converting to another layout program is rife with issues beyond simply plunking down a few hundred bucks for a new program, picking up this book, and getting on with it. Depending on your environment, there may be site license fees involved, there may be issues of converting documents and templates, there may be issues of retraining, there may be issues of service bureau and printer support. If you've been in the graphics game for a while, you may have invested a great deal of time, money, and labor in your current workflow. Is it in your best advantage to switch? I can't answer that for you. Personally, I like InDesign. Personally, I would like to switch over completely, but I don't work in a vacuum.

So my goal is not to make a case for converting your workflow. Besides, if you've bought this book and the program, you've likely at least entertained the notion of adopting InDesign, so all I can do is explain how to use the program and let you go from there.

If you're a savvy graphics and software person, you may be wondering why I've omitted any mention of Adobe's FrameMaker, which is a page layout program that has existed for many years. FrameMaker's main claim to fame is its support for long documents. FrameMaker, for reasons known only to the fickle finger of fate, never really caught on save for a few niche markets, such as technical writing and documentation. There is a new version of FrameMaker, released concurrently with InDesign 1.5, yet you rarely see any mention of it.

Understanding the InDesign Interface

When you first launch InDesign, you'll get a tableau not unlike Figure 1.1.

FIGURE 1.1

InDesign, right after launch time.

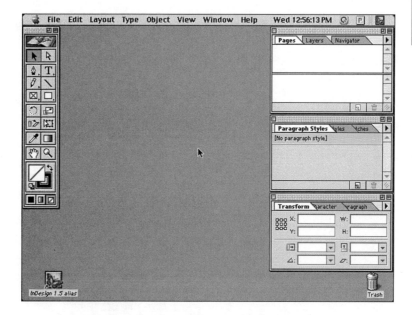

Frames, Handles, Paths, and Anchor Points

Before we leap into the tools, we need to understand what we mean by certain page objects, as these are the things we will be manipulating with the various tools. Many elements in InDesign are added via *frames*. Frames are simply empty boxes that you put things in, be it text or a picture. Text appears in text frames. Pictures appear in picture frames.

Each frame has a number of different *handles*. By clicking and dragging handles, objects are resized. If you've used other graphics programs, this won't be foreign to you. If this *is* foreign to you, don't worry. Working with frames and handles will be second nature by the time we're through with you.

In some graphic objects, specifically vector objects, or those graphics that you draw using InDesign's drawing tools, you have what are known as *anchor points*. Anchor points are like frame handles, except insofar as they define the *path* that comprises the drawn object. The path is simply the line and/or curve that connects the anchor points to make up a shape. We'll look at anchor points and paths in more detail in Hour 10, "Using InDesign's Drawing Tools."

Know Your Tools

The most conspicuous element on the screen right now is perhaps the Tools palette, also called the toolbox.

The Tools palette, isolated in Figure 1.2, is command central for InDesign.

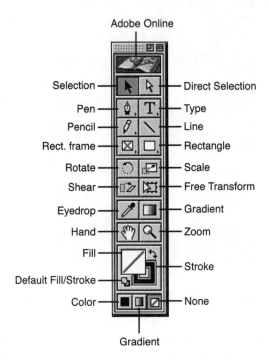

We'll cover each of these tools in much greater detail in subsequent hours, but a few one-liners about each will stand us in good stead for some of the exercises to come.

Each tool is selected by clicking on it in the Tools palette. Alternately, each tool can also be selected using a keyboard shortcut (indicated in parentheses after each tool name in the list below). Simply hit the indicated key, and that tool is made active. With one exception: If you have the Type tool active and you hit a key, you will actually type that letter rather than select the tool to which it corresponds.

Adobe Online—If you have an Internet connection, you can set up InDesign to automatically access Adobe's Web site (www.adobe.com) to receive tips, news, and updates on InDesign, as well as technical support.

Selection (V)—Lets you select page objects and move or resize them.

Direct Selection (A)—Lets you adjust the content of a picture frame or edit the anchor points that comprise a path.

Pen (P)—Lets you draw and edit paths. If you click and hold down the Pen tool icon for a few seconds, you will see that there are additional tools hidden beneath it (see Figure 1.3).

FIGURE 1.3

Additional variations of the Pen tool.

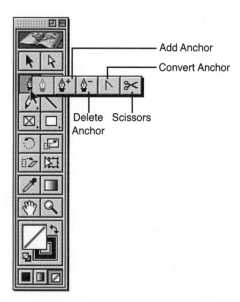

Add and Delete Anchor Point are pretty straightforward. Convert Direction Point lets you change an anchor point from a smooth point to a corner point. (We'll see what that means in Hour 10.) The Scissors tool is used to snip a path into two.

Type (T)—Lets you add a text frame and, ergo, add text. If you click and hold on the Type tool, you get another option (see Figure 1.4).

FIGURE **1.4**

The hidden Path
Type tool.

Path Type

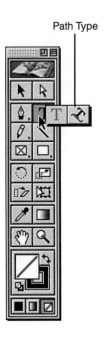

The Path Type tool, a new feature introduced in version 1.5, lets you add text on a path, which we will look at in greater detail in Hour 11, "Combining Text and Graphics."

Pencil (N)—Another new tool added in version 1.5, the Pencil tool lets you draw freeform paths, just like you would using a pencil on paper. If you click and hold on the Pencil tool icon, you will see a few hidden tools (see Figure 1.5).

Since many of us find it hard to draw a smooth line with the Pencil tool using a mouse, InDesign gives us a Smooth tool that removes some of the bumps. The Erase tool, not surprisingly, lets us erase what we've drawn.

Line (\)—Lets us draw lines, the color, thickness, and other aspects of which we can control using various palettes.

Rectangle Frame (F)—Lets us draw a rectangular picture frame on a page, which we can then import a picture into. If you click and hold on the Rectangle Frame tool, you will get other options (see Figure 1.6).

FIGURE 1.5

Some hidden Pencil tool variations.

Smooth

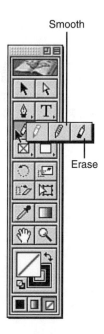

Erase

FIGURE 1.6

Rectangle Frame options include other shapes.

Ellipse Frame

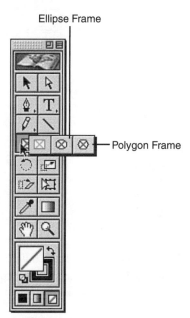

Polygon Frame

Our other options are essentially different-shaped frames, namely an ellipse and a polygon.

Rectangle (M)—This tool is like the Rectangle Frame tool, except insofar as it creates a simple rectangle shape that can be filled with a color or gradient. The difference between this and the previous tool is that you cannot import a picture into it. Clicking and holding on the Rectangle tool gives us similar options (Figure 1.7)—an ellipse and a polygon shape.

Figure 1.7

Rectangle tool options include other shapes.

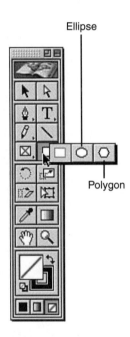

Ellipse

Polygon

Rotate (R)—Lets you rotate page objects.

Scale (S)—Lets you proportionally enlarge or reduce the size of a page object.

Shear (O)—This is more of a skew than a shear, but it essentially lets you slant an object along its horizontal axis.

Free Transform (E)—A new tool in version 1.5, based on Photoshop's similar tool. The Free Transform tool lets you perform a variety of actions—resizing, scaling, moving, rotating, shearing, and more, all from the comfort of one tool.

Eyedropper (I)—A wonderful new addition to version 1.5, and a tool I refer to as the Turkey Baster. This lets you suck up colors or paragraph and character styles and apply them elsewhere in your document. We'll look at the Eyedropper in more detail in Hour 11, "Combining Text and Graphics."

Gradient (G)—Lets you apply a gradient to a page object. We will look at gradients and the Gradient tool in detail in Hour 14, "Advanced Color Work."

Hand (H)—This tool lets you move the document around your screen, which is useful if your screen is not large enough to display all of a page, or if you have zoomed in very far.

If you have the Selection tool active, you can automatically get a page-grabbing Hand tool by holding down the spacebar. But be careful if you have the Type tool active, otherwise you'll add a bunch of word spaces to your text!

Zoom (Z)—Lets you zoom in or zoom out. Selecting this tool and clicking zooms in. Selecting this tool and holding down the Option (on the Macintosh) or Alt (on PCs) key zooms out.

Fill (X)—This color chip tells you what your current fill color is.

Stroke (X)—This color chip tells you what your current stroke color is.

Swap Fill/Stroke (Shift+X)—This makes the stroke color the fill color and vice versa.

Default Fill/Stroke (D)—This lets you revert to whatever you have set up as your default fill and stroke colors.

Color (<)—This lets you apply the last used fill color.

Gradient (>)—This lets you apply the last used gradient.

None (/)—This lets you clear the fill or stroke colors.

These last few tools—fills, strokes, and gradients—will be covered in more detail in Hour 13, "Simple Coloring with InDesign," as well as Hour 14.

If you find that your Tools palette doesn't look exactly like what we've outlined above, then chances are you are using version 1.0, which had fewer tools, and had other tools "out in the open" rather than hidden. I've indicated which tools are new in 1.5 above, but for the sake of keeping this chapter at a reasonable length, I haven't noted all the changes.

Know Your Palettes

Most of InDesign's features exist in palettes. Palettes are small windows-cum-dialog boxes in which you add, delete, set up, and manage pages (the Pages palette), adjust your typographic specifications (the Character and Paragraph palettes), create and apply colors (the Swatches and Color palettes), and so on. Palettes tend to be grouped in sets as, for example, Figure 1.8, which comprises the Pages, Layers, and Navigator palettes.

You can get from palette to palette in this set by clicking on the respective tab. Other palettes can be accessed through the menus and/or via keyboard shortcuts. Each palette will be discussed in detail in its appropriate hour.

Most palettes in InDesign have some items in common. Most notably, they all have a palette menu, which is accessed by clicking on the arrow at the top right of each palette. See Figure 1.9 for an example.

A palette menu is a set of commands and functions that let you perform various tasks. In the case of the Pages palette, you can add pages, delete pages, set up spreads, add master pages, and so forth. (Don't worry if that doesn't mean much to you right now; we'll look at the Pages palette in excruciating detail in Hour 4, "Managing Pages.")

Know Your Dialog Boxes

Like most programs, InDesign lets the user communicate with it via dialog boxes. These are places where InDesign asks you what you want to do and you reply. Many of the dialog boxes in InDesign comprise several panes. As we go through the lessons that follow in subsequent hours, you'll see that dialog boxes can have many panes indeed.

There are usually two ways to getting from pane to pane in a particular dialog box, as you can see in Figure 1.10.

FIGURE 1.10

To get from pane to pane of a dialog box, you can click and scroll through the pop-up menu, or use the Prev and Next buttons.

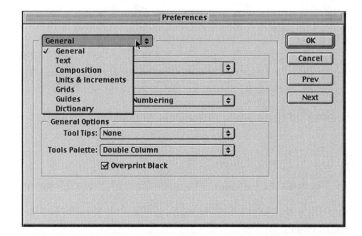

Take the Preferences dialog (found in the Edit menu). It comprises seven different panes: General, Text, Composition, Units & Increments, Grids, Guides, and Dictionary. If you click on the pop-up menu at the top of the dialog box, you can see that you can scroll to each one individually. Or, you can use the Prev and Next buttons on the right side of the dialog box. If you click Prev, you'll go to the pane that preceded the one you are now in. If you click Next, you'll go to the next pane in the sequence.

Hitting OK applies any changes you may have made and returns you to your document. Hitting Cancel returns you to your document without making any changes. And many dialog boxes and panes therein have a Preview button which lets you see the effects of any changes you are making on your document live, so you can decide if you like the effect before you are committed to it.

Looking Forward

If you have never used a page layout program before, you'll take to InDesign quite easily. If you have grown up with QuarkXPress or PageMaker— well, initially it will be like learning a second language. And you'll probably grouse that things aren't as intuitive as in Quark, blah blah blah. I know; I groused. But as I started to think about it, the only reason why things didn't seem as intuitive in InDesign is that I had been using Quark for 10 years! Of course InDesign is not going to seem intuitive right off the bat. It's like those tedious debates over which is better: the Macintosh or Windows— or, even whether the Beatles were better than the Stones, or Bach better than Beethoven.

It's all a matter of what you are comfortable with and are used to. And as I got used to InDesign, I discovered things about it that I liked better than Quark and PageMaker. I like its superior typographic control, and the seamless integration with other graphics products, in particular Photoshop, Illustrator, and Acrobat.

So, open your mind, relax, and float downstream…

Q&A

Q I heard that InDesign will open QuarkXPress documents. Is this true?

A Yes, and it works better than you'd think it would. We'll cover this in more detail in Hour 24.

Q I don't see the point of putting Photoshop and Illustrator tools in InDesign. I already have Photoshop and Illustrator. Why do I want to pay twice for the same toolset?

A There are things you can do in Illustrator and Photoshop that you will never be able to do in InDesign. And vice versa. The crossover tools make sense for a number of reasons. The first is the on-the-fly nature of a lot of design and publishing. Adding simple drawing tools to InDesign allows designers who may need to add spot art or a graphic element to do so natively, without needing to open up Illustrator, create a file, save it out, then import it into InDesign. Obviously, you're not going to want to create an entire illustration in InDesign natively, but for small, last-minute crisis work (which a lot of design and publishing can be, believe me), having these tools in the layout program can save time.

Q Why didn't Adobe just put everything that's in InDesign into PageMaker? Wouldn't it make more sense to build on an established brand than create a new one from scratch?

A Not necessarily, and remember that PageMaker was losing a great deal of market share. Although this isn't supposed to be *Teach Yourself Software Marketing in 24 Hours*, it made more sense to try to create the page layout tool for the twenty-first century rather than keep an old dinosaur alive. Whether InDesign is indeed the page layout tool for the twenty-first century remains to be seen, however.

Exercises

Spend some time getting used to the interface. Open a blank document and try each of the tools out. You probably won't know exactly what you're doing, but don't worry: You can't break anything. Also, check out some of the palettes that InDesign by default shows on the screen at launch time. You may not know what everything means, but spend some time becoming familiar with commands and common features. And when we come to the pertinent sections later on in this book, there will be a spark of recognition in your eyes and a frisson of excitement down your spine as you realize you have seen some of these things before. Well, okay, maybe not, but you get the idea.

HOUR 2

Preparing to Work in InDesign

It doesn't matter how experienced you are as a driver. If you get into a car you've never driven, it only makes sense to take a few minutes to look around and figure out where all the controls are—how to do this and that.

The same holds true for software. You may be an experienced veteran in PageMaker, QuarkXPress, or some other page layout program, but InDesign is still going to take some getting used to.

During this hour, you'll learn:

- How InDesign's menus are organized
- How to use the functions of some of the more important menu options
- How to use the keyboard shortcuts for common menu options
- How to set your InDesign preferences

InDesign's Menu Structure

Generally speaking, InDesign's menu structure is not unlike that of most other programs. After all, that's the point of having a GUI like Windows or the Macintosh OS. InDesign's eight menus are

- File
- Edit
- Layout
- Type
- Object
- View
- Window
- Help

The File Menu

InDesign's File menu contains all the options you'd expect—Open, Save, Print, and so on. However, as you can see in Figure 2.1, it also contains a few options with which you might not be familiar.

FIGURE 2.1

The File menu presents you with a variety of choices for bringing files into InDesign, as well as outputting them in a variety of ways.

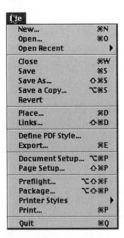

Various items are grouped together according to similar functionality using solid lines. There are two noteworthy sections on this menu. The first is the section that includes various output controls and tools. These are Preflight, Package, and Print (covered in Hour 17, "Printing from InDesign," and Hour 18, "Getting Ready for the Service Bureau").

When you're ready to either print your document or send it somewhere else for final output, you'll find these tools invaluable.

InDesign 1.5 has a new field at the top called Open Recent…, which is where you can get a list of your recent InDesign documents, providing useful shortcuts if you want to reopen projects you have been working on. (In 1.0 these files simply appeared in the middle of the File Menu, which tended to make the menu very long.)

InDesign 1.5 also gives you the ability in this menu to define and apply PDF Styles, which we will cover in greater detail in Hour 19, "Preparing Acrobat Output with InDesign."

The Preferences and Color Settings, which were in the File Menu in 1.0 have been moved to the Edit Menu in 1.5.

The Edit Menu

InDesign's Edit menu, shown in Figure 2.2, is largely unremarkable—with one important exception. I'd like to draw your attention to the Undo and Redo commands.

FIGURE 2.2

The Undo and Redo commands are more powerful than they appear.

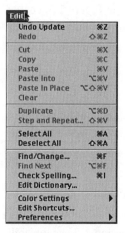

We've all seen Undo and Redo commands in our programs. The true strength of these commands in InDesign is that the program is capable of multiple Undos and Redos. In other words, if you realize that you made a mistake 10 steps ago, you can simply back your way out of it.

How far back can you go? Up to 300 actions, if your computer has enough memory available to track that many.

Photoshop users may be used to that program's History palette, which lets you select a single action to undo without stepping back through all the interim actions. In other words, Photoshop doesn't force you to undo actions consecutively. Unfortunately, a similar feature hasn't found its way into InDesign—at least not yet.

If you're in a hurry and have several steps to undo or redo, InDesign has what I call express undo and redo. If you simply press and hold the keyboard shortcut for either action (covered later this hour), InDesign will step through multiple actions automatically.

Another important section in the Edit menu is the one that includes various options for controlling InDesign's settings. These are Preferences, Color Settings, and Edit Shortcuts. You'll learn more about Preferences later this Hour. Color Settings are covered in Hour 13, "Simple Coloring with InDesign," and Hour 16, "Color Management with InDesign," and Edit Shortcuts are addressed in Hour 22, "Customizing InDesign."

InDesign's Other Menus

The commands in the Layout menu, shown in Figure 2.3, control the overall visual appearance of your document, and also help you navigate around your document.

FIGURE 2.3

You can change the general appearance of your document with tools in the Layout menu.

Layout
Margins and Columns...
Ruler Guides...
Create Guides...
Layout Adjustment...
First Page ⇧⌘↑
Previous Page ⇧↑
Next Page ⇧↓
Last Page ⇧⌘↓
Go Back ⌘↑
Go Forward ⌘↓
Insert Page Number ⌥⌘N

The Type menu, shown in Figure 2.4, gives you access to all the tools you need to control your type with exacting precision. InDesign 1.5 has the ability to find fonts and make font substitutions. One cool new feature is the ability to fill a text frame with greek (placeholder) text, if you are just doing comps or sample layouts and don't want to come up with actual text.

The Object menu, shown in Figure 2.5, is like the flip side of the Type menu. The commands on the Object menu are used primarily to control the look and attributes of graphical elements in your document. However, text frames—if not the text within those frames—can also be considered as graphical objects. InDesign 1.5 has a Transform feature, much like that found in Photoshop and Illustrator.

FIGURE 2.4

The Type menu covers all things typographic.

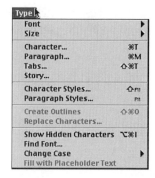

FIGURE 2.5

InDesign's Object menu gives you control over various aspects of graphical objects.

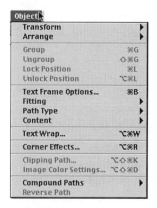

The controls in the View menu, shown in Figure 2.6, enable you to see your document and its various characteristics from different perspectives.

FIGURE 2.6

InDesign's View menu lets you control how you view your document on-screen, including what sets of guides and grids are visible.

InDesign tries to give you the tools you need, when you need them, without ever getting in your way. For that reason, a good number of InDesign's tools are available through various floating palettes, which you can display and hide at will. The Window menu, shown in Figure 2.7, gives you access to all of these palettes, as well as to specific "tabs" on those palettes. These palettes are covered during the appropriate hours later on in the book.

FIGURE 2.7

InDesign's Window menu lets you toggle various palettes on and off.

Finally, the Help menu, shown in Figure 2.8, gives you access to InDesign's help features, both within the program and on the Internet. The Windows version of the Help menu differs slightly; there are no Balloon Help options, and it includes the About InDesign option, which is located under the apple menu on Macs.

FIGURE 2.8

Help is just a mouse click away.

10 Most Important Keyboard Shortcuts

The quick reference card at the front of this book provides you with a complete list of InDesign's keyboard shortcuts. However, what a card can't tell you is which keyboard shortcuts you're likely to use most. I figured I'd take care of that here. Table 2.1 shows my top-10 list of InDesign keyboard shortcuts, excluding the simple ones, such as copy and paste.

TABLE 2.1 Top 10 Keyboard Shortcuts

Function	Windows	Mac
Place (Import)	Ctrl+D	Command+D
Redo	Ctrl+Shift+Z	Command+Shift+Z
Spell-Check	Ctrl+I	Command+I
Bold	Ctrl+Shift+B	Command+Shift+B
Italic	Ctrl+Shift+I	Command+Shift+I
Underline	Ctrl+Shift+U	Command+Shift+U
Flush Left	Ctrl+Shift+L	Command+Shift+L
Center	Ctrl+Shift+C	Command+Shift+C
Justify	Ctrl+Shift+J	Command+Shift+J
Pan	Spacebar+drag	Spacebar+drag

The Pan function is not available when the Type tool is active and a text frame is selected. In fact, if you try it, you will inadvertently end up with lots of wordspaces in your text.

If you're a PageMaker user, you may be familiar with many of these shortcuts; InDesign borrows heavily from PageMaker in that respect. However, if you're used to simply pressing Ctrl+B (Command+B on the Macintosh) to switch to bold type in your word processor, you may find these keyboard shortcuts frustrating at first.

Although these shortcuts might seem odd at first, I suggest you get to know them. As you'll learn during Hour 22, you can always change the shortcuts to your liking. However, you need to be careful of the ripple effect. For example, you might decide you want the shortcut for bold type to be Ctrl+B just like your word processor. However, InDesign uses Ctrl+B to bring up the Text Frame Options dialog box. That means you'd also have to change that shortcut to something else.

Setting Your Application Preferences

As you might expect, a program as sophisticated as InDesign gives you plenty of choices when it comes to specifying application preferences. In fact, InDesign has eight different categories of preferences. You can access any of these by selecting the Preferences submenu from the Edit menu, as shown in Figure 2.9.

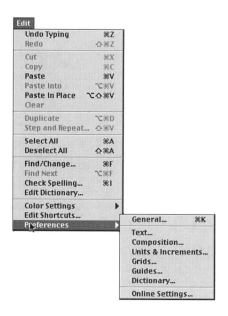

FIGURE 2.9

Access Preferences from the Edit menu.

General Preferences

When you select General from the Preferences submenu, the program displays a Preferences dialog box (see Figure 2.10).

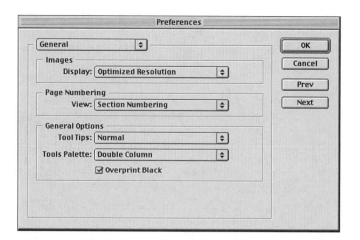

FIGURE 2.10

There are only a few General preferences.

Before I cover the specifics of this dialog box, I want to point out some of the features common to all Preferences dialog boxes. First, note that you can switch from one category of preferences to another by using the pull-down menu where you now see the word General. You can also cycle through each category using the Prev and Next buttons.

> The Online Settings category of preferences is not available in this grouping. As explained later, you need to specifically select this option from the Preferences submenu.

The Display pull-down menu gives you four options for controlling how images are displayed on your monitor: Full Resolution Images, Optimized Resolution Images, Proxy Images, and Gray Out Images. The default is Proxy Images. With this setting, you'll see low-resolution representations of your bitmapped graphics. This is the equivalent of an FPO (for position only). Proxy Images will let you accurately position images, but you will not be able to make out much detail within them. This can be a problem, especially if you need to see detail within an image (as when writing captions, for example). So you can select Full Resolution to get a truer representation and see more detail, but it will slow down your screen display. Selecting Gray Out Images will give you the fastest video performance.

InDesign 1.5 has an Optimized Resolution option. With this Preference selected, InDesign will downsample imported images until the downsampled version reaches a minimum of 72 dpi, or fit into 15 percent of the RAM available—whichever comes first. Basically, this option streams enough data to the screen that you can see it at the highest resolution the monitor will allow, which is usually about 72 dpi.

> InDesign also lets you change your display preferences on an image-by-image basis. If you right-click (on PCs) or Ctrl-click (on the Mac) an image, you will get a pop-up menu that lets you set individual display preferences.

As we'll explain in Hour 5, "Using Layers and the Layout and Formatting Tools," InDesign lets you break document page numbering up into sections if you want. The View pull-down menu controls how the page numbers are displayed on the Pages Palette (also covered in Hour 5). You can display them according to your section numbering, or you can have the pages numbered consecutively on this Palette. Don't worry if this doesn't make sense now; it'll be clear by the time you finish Hour 5.

The three General Options control whether a description is displayed when you pass your mouse over a specific tool, how the Tools palette is displayed (single row, single column, or the default double column—we'll look at this in a bit more detail in Hour 22), and whether black ink is always overprinted. What this means is that when you type black text or place a black object on top of another object, the black ink will cover but not replace what is beneath it. With this option unchecked, when you type black text, it will knock out the object beneath it. This will become an issue with regard to trapping, which we will cover—along with a closer look at overprinting—in more detail in Hour 15, "Trapping and Other Prepress Considerations."

Text Preferences

The Text Preferences dialog box, shown in Figure 2.11, gives you several options for controlling how your type appears on a page.

FIGURE 2.11

Text preferences control the appearance of your type.

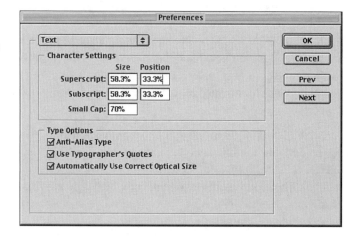

The various Character Settings options control the appearance of superscript and subscript type, as well as InDesign-induced small caps. (In other words, this Small Caps setting has no impact on fonts specifically designed to have small caps.) You can change these numbers at will. However, I suggest you accept the defaults unless you have a very compelling reason to do otherwise.

This dialog box also gives you three Type Options. If selected, Anti-Alias Type will have InDesign anti-alias type that appears on-screen. Anti-aliasing is a technique that slightly blurs the edges of the text to give it a smoother appearance onscreen. This setting has no effect on actual output.

The Use Typographers Quotes option controls whether InDesign automatically changes your straight quotes to "curly" quotes.

NEW TERM Some multiple master fonts include variations according to the selecting font size. This is called *optical sizing*. The Automatically Use Correct Optical Size controls whether InDesign automatically takes advantage of this option in multiple master fonts where it's available.

Composition Preferences

Composition preferences, the dialog box shown in Figure 2.12, controls various ways that InDesign handles hyphenation and justification issues.

FIGURE 2.12

You control how InDesign handles hyphenation issues.

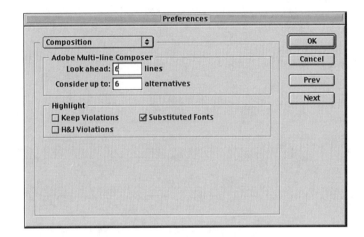

2

InDesign's Multi-line Composer, covered in Hour 7, "Basic Typesetting with InDesign," lets the program consider the appearance of the previous lines of text when determining the line break and hyphenation for the current line. Contrary to what the name implies, the Look Ahead setting actually controls how many lines the program looks back when considering the current line. Consider Up To controls how many different line-break options the program considers before making its final choice. While increasing either of these numbers may produce better overall results, it may also slow down system performance.

Composing a line of text can get pretty complicated from InDesign's point of view. For that reason, it can't always follow the composition that rules the way you define them. To help you spot potential problems, you can automatically have InDesign highlight in yellow any violations by checking the Keep Violations and H&J Violations checkboxes. There are three possible shades of yellow; the darker the yellow, the more serious the violation.

When you open a document for which an included font is not installed on your system, InDesign lets you substitute a font that you do have installed. Checking the Substituted Font checkbox here allows you to easily spot any occurrences of substituted fonts.

Units & Increments Preferences

As shown in Figure 2.13, the Units & Increments preferences determine which units of measurement InDesign uses when displaying rulers, as well as increments for various functions.

FIGURE 2.13

InDesign lets you control various measurements.

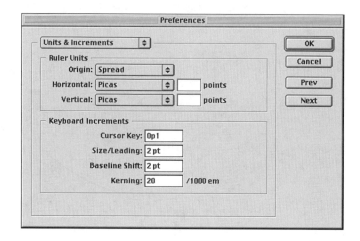

The Horizontal and Vertical pull-down menus allow you to specify any standard unit of measurement (all of which are covered in Hour 3, "Creating, Saving, and Opening Documents"). You can also select Custom. If you do, you'll need to enter a number into the corresponding Points field. This field is grayed out when Custom is not selected.

InDesign 1.5 allows you to set the Origin—where the zero point on the ruler is. You can either set it at the top left corner of a spread, at the top left corner of an individual page, or at the binding spine.

InDesign lets you "nudge" elements using your arrow keys. The Cursor Key controls how far each nudge pushes an element.

InDesign also provides keyboard shortcuts for adjusting type size, leading, baseline shift, and manual kerning. Each of these is covered in the appropriate hour, or you can check the keyboard shortcut quick reference to see them all together. The point here is that each of the remaining fields in this dialog box controls the amount of change that occurs when you use the corresponding keyboard shortcut.

Grids Preferences

The Grids preferences, shown in Figure 2.14, control the appearance of both baseline and document grids. Grids are covered fully in Hour 5.

FIGURE 2.14

InDesign offers two types of grids: baseline and document.

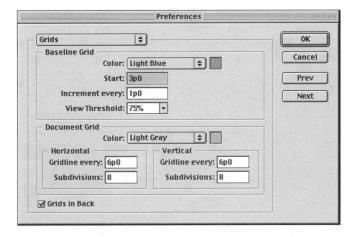

The purpose of a baseline grid is to help you align columns of text by aligning the baselines of the text in each column. It includes only horizontal lines. New in 1.5 is the ability to set both a horizontal and vertical document grid for enhanced accuracy in placing elements on the page. Also new and convenient in 1.5 is the ability (via a checkbox) to have the gridlines appear behind all your other page elements. If you need them brought to the fore, you can simply uncheck this option, align your objects, and then recheck this option. (We'll see what this specifically means in more detail in Hour 5.)

Color is fairly obvious. In the Start field, you specify how far from the top of the document you want the baseline grid to begin. Use the Increment field to specify the distance between grid lines. The View Threshold field determines the magnification level below which the grid will no longer be displayed.

To be most effective, the Increment field should be set the same as the leading for the type used most often in your document. Otherwise, if your grid increment varies significantly from your leading, the chances of keeping your text aligned to the grid become slim, becoming worse and worse as you move down a column of type. As a result, you can have "bottoming out" problems, especially with adjacent columns.

Document grids are used to help you align objects on the page. They include both horizontal and vertical lines. The Gridline Every field determines the distance between gridlines. If you specify a number in the Subdivisions field, the grid will visually be broken up into larger squares according to that number.

Guides Preferences

The options in this dialog box, shown in Figure 2.15, control the characteristics of your document's visual guides.

FIGURE 2.15

You have complete control over your guides.

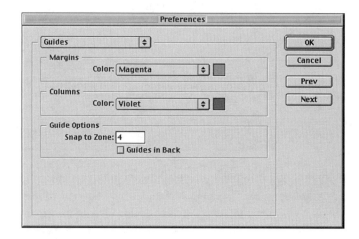

Strangely, while you control the color of the guides you create manually (called ruler guides) by selecting Ruler Guides from the Layout menu, you control the colors of the guides displayed for your document margins, as well as for columns, here.

You also have two Guide Options. The snap zone is the distance, in points, at which InDesign will invoke its Snap to Grid feature. This is covered more in Hour 5.

For the sake of selecting an item, ruler guides are normally on top. That means that if a page element and a ruler guide intersect at some point, and you click on that point, you'll select the ruler guide, not the page element. If you find this inconvenient for any reason, just check the Guides in Back checkbox.

Dictionary Preferences

The Dictionary preferences, shown in Figure 2.16, allow you to select various dictionaries for use in spell checking your document.

You select a dictionary using the Language pull-down menu. Besides English:USA, the two most useful dictionaries for most people will likely be English:USA Legal and English:USA Medical.

One new feature in 1.5 that users clamored for was the ability to embed hyphenation exceptions in individual documents, rather than in InDesign preferences that remained on a single system. The problem that could result was, if you created custom hyphenation rules (such as proper names or technical terms), and someone else opened your document on another system, text could be reflowed according to a different set of hyphenation rules. Thus, you can determine here if you want to use just the document, just the built-in dictionary, or a combination of both (the latter is the default and best option) to determine how words are hyphenated. You can also determine if you want to store hyphenation exceptions in the document (always best) or in the dictionary. Remember, you may not always want to have the same hyphenation exceptions carried from document to document.

FIGURE 2.16

Just pick a dictionary.

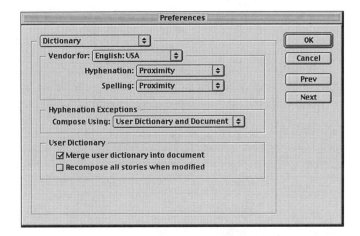

InDesign's open architecture also allows you to add spelling and hyphenation components from other vendors. If you purchase such a component, you must first install it according to the vendor's directions, and then select it here.

Online Settings

Adobe Online is a convenient feature that allows you to obtain product updates and other information over the Internet. You control the settings for this service by selecting Online Settings from the Preferences submenu in the File menu. The resulting dialog box is shown in Figure 2.17 (Mac) and Figure 2.18 (Windows).

Rather than go through all these settings, I'd like to draw your attention to the Setup button on the right side of this dialog box. Click this button and a setup wizard will guide you step-by-step to get these settings exactly the way you want them.

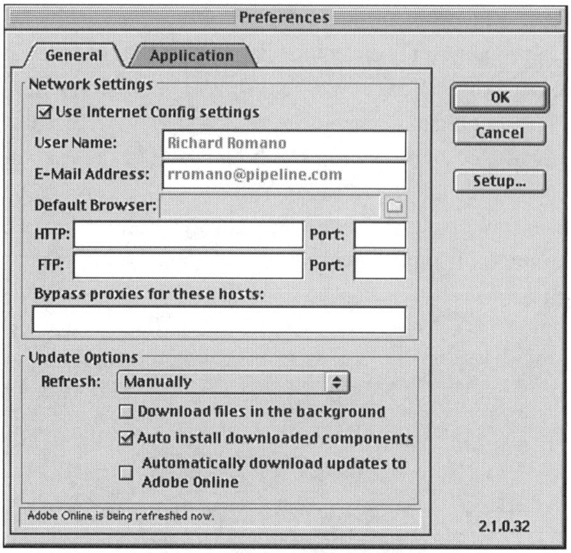

FIGURE **2.17**

These Mac settings (gleaned from the Internet Config file; they probably do not need to be noodled with) might seem complicated, but they're not.

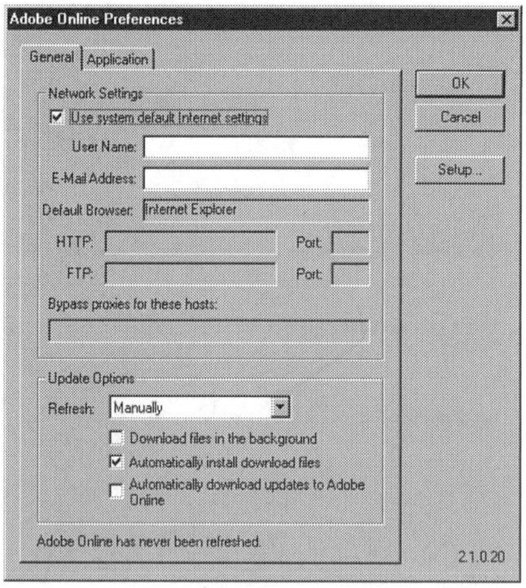

FIGURE **2.18**

The corresponding Windows settings.

Restoring Default Preferences

Whether you use Macintosh or Windows, all of the settings you specify for various preferences are stored in a file called InDesign Defaults. If you find that you've totally messed up your preferences and want to go back to the stock factory settings, all you need to do is delete this file while InDesign is closed.

The down side to this is that when you delete this file, you delete *all* of your preferences, as well as the defaults described in the next section. Instead of completely deleting the InDesign Defaults file, you may want to start by simply moving the file to a different location. If the results aren't what you expected, you can move it back. If they are, you can then delete the file. Keep in mind, though, that InDesign must be closed each time you take any action with this file.

2

Other Defaults

In addition to the preferences described earlier this hour, InDesign lets you specify a wide variety of other program defaults. For example, suppose that you use Adobe Garamond for the primary font 99 percent of the time when you create a new document. Or suppose that having Helvetica or Arial always appear when you type in a text frame is getting annoying. Instead of changing the font after you create each new document, you can simply make Adobe Garamond your default font.

To Do: Creating a Default Font

To create a default font, do the following:

1. Make sure InDesign is running and no documents are currently open.

2. Go to the Font submenu in the Type menu and select the font to use as a default. I've chosen Adobe Garamond Regular, but select whatever font you would like to use and have loaded. See Figure 2.19.

3. Although we haven't covered creating new documents or using the Type tool yet, you can get a sneak preview of upcoming hours to see the effect of what you just did. Under the File menu, select New, and just hit OK to accept the default page specs.

4. Select the Type tool (the tool with a big "T" on it) from the Tools palette, and start typing anywhere on the page. The font that is typed will be the default you just set.

▼

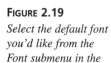

FIGURE 2.19
*Select the default font
you'd like from the
Font submenu in the
Type menu.*

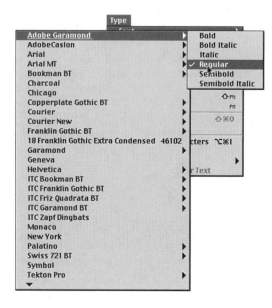

If you decide at a later date that you want to switch the default font, you can repeat the above with any font you have loaded on your system.

To see all the items that you can set as defaults, simply close all your documents and start exploring InDesign's menus. If you can select it and set it, you can create a default setting.

Summary

InDesign gives you complete control over how you work, and part of that means giving you numerous preference options. By fine-tuning the preferences, as well as changing the program defaults, you can tweak InDesign into exactly the program you need it to be.

Don't be concerned if certain parts of this don't make complete sense right now. Depending on your page layout experience, some of it may require the context found in later hours. That's one of the great things about preferences and defaults: You can change them whenever you learn that the current settings aren't what you need.

Workshop

Sometimes, changing a particular preference can produce an unintended result. Although problems aren't generally too tough to fix, you'll come out ahead in the long run, if you exercise some caution at the front end.

Read through the following Q&A to get some helpful tips. Then hit the exercises to broaden your experience using InDesign's Preferences dialog boxes.

Q&A

Q I deleted my InDesign Defaults file and now everything is messed up. What should I do?

A Hopefully, the file is still sitting in the trash can/recycle bin. If so, you can just drag it back to its original location, which is simply in the first level of the InDesign application folder. If not, I'm afraid you'll have to start over.

Q I have different needs for different types of projects. Is there any way to create different sets of preferences?

A Not directly, but it is possible. All you'd need to do is set the preferences the way you want them and move the InDesign Defaults file to a new location. Then repeat the process. Keep in mind, though, that each version must be stored in a different location because the filename needs to be exact. To use a particular version, just copy it back to the correct location. Also, be aware that some preferences can be overridden while you're using the program. These instances are described where appropriate later in the book.

Exercises

The exercises are easy for this hour: Go back through the Preferences dialog boxes we have explored in this chapter, and experiment with different settings, especially as you go through the exercises later on in this book. It's a good way of getting a sense of what these settings actually do.

Hour **3**

Creating, Saving, and Opening Documents

If you've used a personal computer for more than 15 minutes, you already know the basics of creating, saving, and opening documents within an application program. For example, no matter what program you're using, pressing Ctrl+N (or Command+N if you're a Mac user) will probably result in the creation of a new document.

The things that vary from one application to the next are the options you have as you create, save, and then reopen your documents. As you perform these operations in InDesign, you have various decisions to make, each of which affects the ultimate outcome of your action. During this hour, you learn how to reach the right decisions according to your specific needs.

To be more precise, in this hour, you learn the following:

- How to create a new document with InDesign
- How to save your new document
- How to open a saved InDesign document
- How to open a document created in PageMaker
- How to open a document created in QuarkXPress

Creating Your First Document

In general terms, creating a new InDesign document is just like creating a new document in any other application program. However, when you're using InDesign, it's in the New Document dialog box that you define the basic layout of your document—its dimensions, margins, and so on.

To create a new InDesign document, you launch the program and then either press Ctrl+N (Command+N on the Mac) or select New from the File menu. The choice is yours. After you've done either of these, InDesign displays the New Document dialog box, as shown in Figure 3.1.

FIGURE 3.1

You have many options for defining your new document.

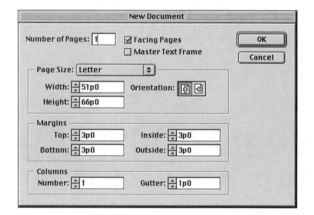

The idea here is to define your document as accurately as possible so that, by the time you see the blank document on your screen, it's ready for you to start adding content. However, don't be too worried about making a mistake in this dialog box. With the exception of the Master Text Frame checkbox, all these settings can be readjusted after you've created the document. Getting it right the first time around just saves you the extra hassle.

Selecting the Right Unit of Measurement

As you can see from Figure 3.1, creating a new document means specifying many different measurements. Instead of forcing you to work with one specific unit of measurement, InDesign gives you a choice of several. Specifically, you can define measurements in InDesign using the following units (illustrated in Figure 3.2):

- *Picas*—There are six picas in one inch.
- *Points*—There are 72 points in one inch, and there are 12 points in a pica.

- *Picas and Points Together*—This is the most common form of measurement in typography and is the default system for InDesign.

- *Inches*—Probably most commonly used in non-professional desktop publishing environments, such as a corporate marketing department.

- *Millimeters*—Used when you need to be metric.

- *Ciceros*—The *cicero* is the European answer to the pica. There are 15 ciceros in 16 picas. Note that the *didot point*, which is not supported by InDesign, is typically used in conjunction with the cicero. There 15 didot points in 16 "normal" points.

In Hour 4, "Managing Pages," you'll learn how to change InDesign's settings so that all the measurements in the New Document dialog box are displayed in units of your liking. However, at this point you're free to use any units you want. For example, even though the dialog box uses points and picas, you can specify measurements in inches. Later in this hour, I explain the New Document dialog box on a field-by-field basis. Table 3.1 shows you the proper format for typing values into any of the measurement fields in this dialog box.

TABLE 3.1 Formats for Different Units of Measurement

Unit	Letter to Type	Example
Picas	p (after number)	12p
Points	p (before number)	p5
Picas and Points	p (between picas and points)	12p5
Inches	i (after number)	8.5i
Millimeters	mm (after number)	60mm
Ciceros	c (after number)	10c

Defining Your New Document

Let's get back to the New Document dialog box. The first thing you need to decide is how many pages you want to start with (remember that you can add and delete pages later). InDesign lets you create documents with up to 9,999 pages, which is probably more than you'll ever need—unless you're James A. Michener.

There are two checkboxes next to the Number of Pages field. If you leave the Facing Pages checkbox checked (which is the default), InDesign lays out your document with both right and left pages. If you uncheck this box, you'll get right-sided pages only. Leave the box checked if you want to print two-sided documents, or uncheck it if you want to print on only one side of each page.

When you uncheck the Facing Pages checkbox, notice that the Inside and Outside fields in the Margins section change to Left and Right, respectively. That's because Inside and Outside are relative terms that describe facing pages. On a left-facing page, the inside is on the right and the outside is on the left. On a right-facing page, the inside is on the left and the outside is on the right. Figure 3.2 demonstrates this point.

FIGURE 3.2

The inside and outside of the page are relative to which side you're talking about.

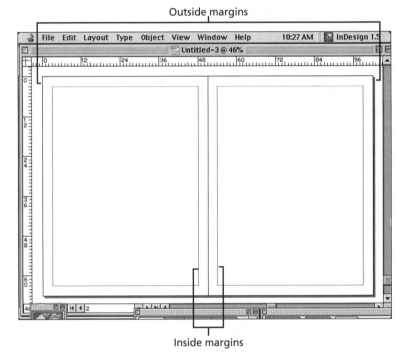

If you check the Master Text Frame checkbox, InDesign creates a text frame to fill the space inside the area defined by your margins. This text frame is added to your document's primary master page. A *master page* is where you add elements that are displayed on all subsequent pages. You learn all about master pages in Hour 4. Text frames are covered during Hour 6, "Creating Text."

For most projects, you probably can specify your document's physical dimensions by choosing a paper size from the Page Size drop-down menu. InDesign's built-in paper sizes are as follows:

- Letter
- Legal
- Tabloid
- Letter-Half
- Legal-Half
- A4
- A3
- A5
- B5
- Compact Disc (for creating a jewel-box insert)

If you're using some non-standard paper size, you can also specify a custom width and height. You can either type the appropriate measurements into the Width and Height fields, or you can use the up and down arrows to the left of these fields to change the corresponding measurement incrementally.

> Check Table 3.1 if you're unsure of the correct format for manually entering values in these fields.

The Orientation area of the New Document dialog box offers you two buttons—one to indicate portrait orientation (up and down), the other to indicate landscape orientation (sideways).

> The default orientation is portrait. The active Orientation button is the one that's white and is pressed. The inactive Orientation button is grayed out and slightly protruding.

To specify any of the four margins, use the same technique you use for defining a custom page size. In other words, you can type a value into each field, or you can use the corresponding up and down arrows to change each value incrementally.

Using either of these techniques, you can also change the value in the Number field under the Columns heading. InDesign enables you to specify up to 20 columns per page. If you specify multiple columns (any number other than 1 in the Number field), the Gutter field specifies the amount of space between each column.

After you have everything set the way you want, click the OK button to create the document you've just specified.

To Do: Create a New Document

It's time to get down to business and actually create a new document:

1. Either press Ctrl+N (Command+N on the Mac) or select New from the File menu to display the New Document dialog box.

2. Play around with the various settings until you get a feel for them. Try using different units of measurement in different fields.

> You can move forward from field to field by pressing the Tab key, or backward from field to field by holding down the Shift key and pressing Tab.

3. Click the OK button to see exactly what you've created. Your final product should look something like Figure 3.3.

FIGURE 3.3
Here's one example of a brand new document.

Saving a Document

Most of the remainder of this book is devoted to helping you learn how to add various sorts of content to your InDesign documents. However, no matter how creative you get with your documents, you still need to save them at some point.

Three Options for Saving

InDesign provides three ways to save your document in native InDesign format. (You'll learn about other ways to save your documents—as Web pages, as PDF files, and more—during Hours 19, "Preparing Acrobat Output with InDesign," 20, "Creating Web Content with InDesign," and 21, "Exploring Other Export Options.") Table 3.2 describes the native save options.

TABLE 3.2 How to Save Your Documents

File Menu Option	Keystroke (Win/Mac)	Purpose
Save	Ctrl+S/Command+S	Used to save a new document for the first time, and to save revisions to an existing document using the same filename and location
Save As	Shift+Ctrl+S Shift+Command+S	Used to save the current document with a different filename or location
Save a Copy	Ctrl+Alt+S Command+Option+S	Used to save a copy of the current document with a different filename or location

Be careful when you're using the Save a Copy option. Even though you've saved the document to a different name or location, you continue to work on the original document after the save is complete.

I provided Table 3.2 to help you decide which save option to choose. No matter which of these options you choose, the ensuing dialog box is nearly identical.

Although there's no corresponding option in the File menu, InDesign does provide a keyboard shortcut for saving all your open documents at the same time. (As you discover later in this hour, you can have more than one InDesign document open at the same time.) The key combination for Windows is Ctrl+Alt+Shift+S, and the key combination for the Mac is Command+Option+Shift+S. Using one of these key combinations has the same effect as using the Save command for each open document. It's just a heck of a lot faster.

Making the Save

When you save a new document for the first time, as well as when you use Save As or Save a Copy, you're presented with a fairly standard dialog box. If you're a Mac user, it'll look just like the one in Figure 3.4. If you're a Windows user, you'll see the dialog box shown in Figure 3.5.

FIGURE 3.4

On the Mac, InDesign uses a new style of Save As dialog box—a departure from the "traditional" look.

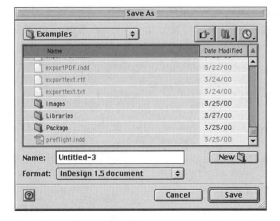

FIGURE 3.5

On a Windows machine, InDesign displays the typical Save As dialog box.

As with any other application, you navigate through your hard drive or network to determine where you want to keep the document, give the file a name, and then click the Save button.

As you might already know, when you save a file using any Windows program, an extension (a period and a couple of letters) is added to the end of the filename. Each program creates a unique extension. This is how your Windows programs can tell their own files from those belonging to other programs. When you save an InDesign document in Windows, the filename includes an `.indd` extension.

If you're creating InDesign documents on a Macintosh and those documents will eventually be used with InDesign for Windows, consider this trick. When you're naming the file on your Mac, tack an `.indd` extension onto the end of the filename, even though you don't have to. That way, when the document finally makes its way to the Windows system, InDesign can recognize it as one of its own files. If you're saving a document template (a discussion of which follows), use an `.indt` extension instead.

The one thing that's unique about InDesign's Save As dialog box (in the Windows version) is the field marked Save as type. If you click the arrow to the right of that field, you see that you have two options: InDesign Document or InDesign Template. If you choose to save your document as a template, the only thing that changes is how InDesign treats that document the next time you open it. By default, instead of opening the original document, InDesign opens a copy of the document template.

Macintosh users who want to save an InDesign document as a template need to select Stationery Option from the Format pop-up menu at the bottom of the Save As dialog box. This brings up another box with two radio buttons, one for Document, one for Stationery. You need to click the one that says Stationery to save a template.

In Hour 7, "Basic Typesetting with InDesign," you'll learn how to create custom styles. A *style* is a collection of formatting rules that you can apply to whole paragraphs or selections of text. For example, when I was typing this Note in Microsoft Word, I used a different style than I used for the previous paragraph. The most common use of a document template is to save a collection of custom styles that you can use again and again in document after document.

For example, suppose you need to create a series of product sheets for your company. You can design the first one and then save a copy of it as an InDesign template. Each time you need to create a new product sheet, you can start with that template instead of starting from scratch. That way, all the paragraph formatting is done for you.

To Do: Save a Document

After you're done working on a new document, saving it is easy:

1. Either press Ctrl+S (Command+S on the Mac) or select Save from the File menu. (This assumes it's still Untitled; if it has already been saved once, you will get no dialog box.)

2. In the resulting dialog box, navigate through your system to find the folder where you want to store the document.

3. Give the file a unique name.

4. If you want to save the document as a template, select InDesign Template in the Save as type pull-down menu (on Windows) or select Stationery from the Format pop-up menu (on the Macintosh).

5. Click the Save button.

Opening InDesign Documents

As you should expect, InDesign can easily open documents created with InDesign. InDesign for Windows can even open documents created with InDesign for the Macintosh, and vice versa. That only makes sense.

However, there's a pretty good chance that InDesign isn't your first page layout program. In developing InDesign, the folks at Adobe rightly assumed that many new InDesign users are coming from either Adobe's own PageMaker or QuarkXPress. For that reason, InDesign can open and convert documents created in PageMaker 6.5 or QuarkXPress 3.3 and later into InDesign format.

Opening an InDesign document isn't much different from opening any other document in its corresponding application program. If you're perusing your files in My Computer or Windows Explorer, or in the Finder on your Mac, you can double-click any InDesign file to automatically launch the program and open that file.

One convenient alternate way of opening InDesign documents is by simply dragging an InDesign file onto the application icon, and it will open automatically. You can even create an alias of the InDesign application and keep it on the desktop, providing an easy drag-and-droppable file opener.

Likewise, opening a document from within InDesign is pretty standard. You can either press Ctrl+O (Command+O on the Mac), or select Open from the File menu. When you do either of these, Mac users will be presented with an Open a File dialog box like the one shown in Figure 3.6, and Windows users will see the dialog box in Figure 3.7.

FIGURE 3.6

You have several choices when opening InDesign files.

FIGURE 3.7

Windows users will see a slightly different version.

When you see this dialog box, you can find the InDesign document you want, double-click it, and you're off to the races. (I discuss opening PageMaker and Quark documents in a few minutes.)

> If you're opening in Windows an InDesign document created on a Mac, and the Mac user didn't heed my previous tip about adding the appropriate extension to the filename, select All Files from the Files of type pull-down menu. Otherwise, you won't be able to see the file in this dialog box.

The one area I want to bring to your attention is the Open As area of this dialog box. You might go your whole life without having to select anything other than Normal, but you should still understand these options just in case.

When you open an InDesign document, InDesign opens the original document. That's considered the normal action for that type of document. On the other hand, when you open an InDesign template, the normal action is to open a copy of that template.

However, suppose you want to either open and edit a document template directly, or use a regular InDesign document as a template for a new document. To open and edit a document template directly, select the document template and then click the Original radio button before clicking the Open button. To use a regular InDesign document as a template for a new document, select the document and then click the Copy radio button before clicking the Open button.

You can actually open more than one document at a time by using this dialog box, as long as all the documents you want to open are in the same folder. In Windows, simply hold down the Ctrl key as you click each document. On a Mac, hold down the Shift key while clicking each document.

Reverting to the Last Saved Version

There's one other option in the File menu that qualifies as a way to open an InDesign document. It's called the Revert command. If you open an existing document, make a bunch of changes, and then decide they all stink, the easiest way to undo them all is to use the Revert command by choosing File, Revert. This simply reverts the document to its last saved version.

Recovering from a System Crash

Like many programs do these days, InDesign is constantly saving a separate version of your file as you work just in case of emergency. If InDesign is shut down abnormally for any reason—a crash, a power outage, the reset button being pressed—all might not be lost. The next time you launch InDesign, the program automatically opens the auto-saved version of the document you were working on as an untitled document. You then have the option to use it.

Converting PageMaker and QuarkXPress Documents

The InDesign documentation claims that you can open PageMaker and QuarkXPress documents using InDesign. Although you can access these document types using the Open command, I think "convert" is a more accurate term. That's because InDesign doesn't really open these document types—it converts them to untitled InDesign documents without modifying the originals.

Regardless of what you call it, this is a very powerful feature for anyone who's coming to InDesign from either of these software packages.

As I mentioned a moment ago, you convert documents of these types using the Open command. You start out just as if you were opening any other InDesign document. The only real difference is that you need to select the appropriate document type in the Files of type pull-down menu in the Open a File dialog box.

Keep in mind, though, that you're converting a document, not really opening it. In other words, InDesign has to analyze the document and figure out how to change its innards to something that InDesign can understand. The interim result is that, depending on the size and complexity of the original document as well as the speed of your computer, it might take InDesign a few seconds to figure everything out. In short, converting one of these documents isn't as fast as opening a native InDesign document.

The result is that InDesign attempts to match your new document as closely as possible to the original. For example, all your styles from the original should be converted to the new document—that is, as long as you still have the right fonts on your system. However, just as in almost any other document-conversion scheme, the conversion is rarely perfect. Here are a few of the shortcomings of opening a PageMaker or QuarkXPress document:

- Although InDesign converts *linked graphics* (graphics placed or imported into the original), it cannot convert graphics that were pasted into the original.
- InDesign cannot import OLE graphics. OLE, short for Object Linking and Embedding, refers to Windows-based graphics (such as Excel spreadsheets, tables, or graphs) that can be embedded in various applications' data files and can thus be shared by different documents and applications. That said, InDesign does not support OLE.
- InDesign also cannot import graphics created by third-party Quark XTensions.
- InDesign cannot import QuarkXPress color profiles.
- Although most of your colors are converted exactly, there are a few exceptions. It's best to check all your colors after the conversion is done.
- Lines drawn in the original might not have the same style after conversion.

We will look at the QuarkXPress/PageMaker to InDesign conversion process in more detail in Hour 24, "Deploying InDesign in the Real World."

As I stated earlier, any type of document conversion is a complex and imperfect process. Whenever you convert any document from one format to another, give the new document a good once-over as soon as the conversion is complete. Check the characteristics that are most important to you. That way, you won't be surprised and frustrated later.

Summary

For the most part, creating, saving, and opening documents with InDesign is very similar to doing so in any other program. However, there are choices to be made each step of the way. And although you can always fix any mistakes you make in any of these operations, you'll save plenty of time if you get it right the first time.

It's also important to remember that Adobe has made special provisions for PageMaker and QuarkXPress users. If you're using PageMaker 6.5 or QuarkXPress 3.3 or later, you can easily convert your existing documents to InDesign documents.

Workshop

Sure, most of this is simple stuff. As I've said before, the key is making the right decisions about your documents. In this Workshop section, you can review some of the finer points of creating, saving, and opening documents. I promise it'll save you time in the long run.

Q&A

Q Help! I just created a new document with Master Text Frame checked, and I can't type in or get rid of the text frame. Is there a bug in the program?

A Not at all. We haven't covered Master pages yet, but suffice it to say here, the Master Text Frame option puts the text frame on the master page. To enter text in it, you need to go to the master page (in the Pages palette) and enter text there. Similarly, to delete it, you need to go to the master page and delete it from there.

Q What's the difference between saving as an InDesign document and saving as an InDesign template?

A Generally, InDesign documents are final works—the finished product, so to speak. You save a document as a template when you want to use it as a model for future documents. When you open a template, you're really opening an untitled copy.

Q Can I open a PDF in InDesign?

A Not as such, no. You can place a PDF file like any other graphic file (we'll cover that in Hour 9, "Using Graphics from Other Programs"), but you cannot convert it to an InDesign document the way you can a QuarkXPress or PageMaker document. Sorry.

Quiz

1. What is the maximum number of pages that can exist in an InDesign document?

   a. 99 pages

   b. 999 pages

   c. 9,999 pages

2. You need to convert inches to picas and points. Which of the following conversions is a correct statement?

   a. There are six picas in an inch and 12 points in a pica.

   b. There are 12 picas in an inch and six points in a pica.

   c. First you have to convert the points to ciceros.

3. What happens when you uncheck the Facing Pages checkbox in the New Document dialog box?

   a. The Outside and Inside margins change to Right and Left.

   b. You create a document meant to be printed on only one side of the paper.

   c. Both a and b.

4. You have a regular InDesign document (not a template) that you want to use as a model for another document. What's the easiest way to accomplish this?

   a. When you open the document, make sure you check the Copy radio button.

   b. Open the original document, save a copy as a template, and then open the template.

   c. Open the original and save it with a new filename.

Quiz Answers

1. c. You can have as many as 9,999 pages—probably more than you will ever need.

2. b. There are 12 picas in an inch and six points in a pica. This means that there are 72 points in an inch. Trust me, knowing this will come in handy at some point in your electronic publishing career.

3. c. Both a and b. The immediate effect is that two changes are made to the Margins section of the dialog box. However, the ultimate result is that you've created a one-sided document.

4. a. When you open the document, make sure you check the Copy radio button. Although all these eventually achieve the desired result, the fastest way is to simply open a copy of the document. However, if you want to use one document as the model for *several* other documents, you should go with option b. That will save you time in the long run.

Exercises

The exercises are once again easy for this hour: Simply practice creating, saving, and then reopening documents. Save them as both documents and templates. If you have PageMaker or QuarkXPress files to work with, try converting a few of them, too. Make sure to scour the converted documents for any subtle changes from the original.

HOUR 4

Managing Pages

The page is to a desktop publishing project what lumber is to a construction project. Documents are constructed from pages. Construction projects are built from lumber. More importantly, if you can use better technology to get the lumber where it needs to be more efficiently, you can increase quality and reduce construction time. The same goes for pages. The more efficiently you're able to manipulate them, the better off you'll be in the long run.

During this hour, you learn the following:

- How to navigate and view your document
- How to manipulate pages with the Pages palette
- How to work with spreads
- How to create and use master pages

Finding Your Way Around Your Document

InDesign offers several ways to get from point A to point B in your document. The reason this is so helpful is that you typically don't have to break stride to move around in your document. No matter what you're doing, there's probably some sort of navigational tool nearby.

InDesign also gives you virtually unlimited control over the magnification of your document on the screen—think of it as layout at the atomic level.

Moving from Page to Page

The easiest way to display a different page or spread in the document window is to double-click the desired page or spread in the Pages palette. (We'll look more closely at the Pages palette later this hour.) You can also use the scroll bar on the right side of the document window to scroll from spread to spread, similar to the way you would scroll in a word processor.

The Navigator palette, an example of which is shown in Figure 4.1, provides another convenient way to move around in your document.

FIGURE **4.1**

The Navigator palette helps you move from one page to another.

Red box

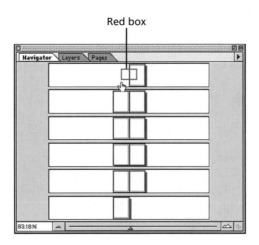

The Navigator palette shows a thumbnail of every spread in your document. The red box, which undoubtedly looks gray in this figure, represents the area currently displayed in the document window.

To display a different portion of the document in the document window, you can either drag the red box to any location, or click any location outside the red box. When you do the latter, the red box (and thus the view in the document window) is centered where you clicked.

Using the Navigator palette menu, you can toggle between View All Spreads and View Active Spread. If you choose View All Spreads (which I find more useful), no matter how many pages you add to your document, and no matter how big or small you make the Navigator palette, it always displays *all* of your spreads. The more pages you add, the smaller each spread appears in the Navigator palette. If you have more than a couple of pages in your document, I suggest you enlarge the Navigator palette. To do this, simply click and drag its lower-right corner down and right.

Note that if the currently displayed page is a master, only that master spread appears in the Navigator palette.

The Layout menu also provides six options to help you navigate through your document. They're described in Table 4.1.

TABLE 4.1 Navigating from the Layout Menu

Command	Windows Shortcut	Mac Shortcut	Description
First Page	Shift+Ctrl+ PageUp	Shift+ Command+ PageUp	Displays the first page in your document
Previous Page	Shift+ PageUp	Shift+ PageUp	Displays the page that precedes the currently displayed page
Next Page	Shift+ PageDown	Shift+ PageDown	Displays the page that follows the currently displayed page
Last Page	Shift+Ctrl+ PageDown	Shift+ Command+ PageDown	Displays the last page in the document
Go Back	Ctrl+PageUp	Command+ PageUp	Like your Web browser's Back button; displays the page you were viewing prior to the current page
Go Forward	Ctrl+ PageDown	Command+ PageDown	Like your Web browser's Forward button; enables you to move forward after you've used the Go Back command

4

Another navigational keyboard shortcut not found in the Layout menu is Option-PageUp and Option-PageDown (on the Mac), and Alt-PageUp and Alt-PageDown (in Windows), which jumps to the next/previous spread.

 Notice that some of the keyboard shortcuts in Table 4.1 use the Ctrl key (in Windows) or the Command key (on the Mac). If you substitute the Ctrl key with the Alt key, or the Command key with the Option key, all commands are performed on spreads instead of pages. For example, in Windows, pressing Shift+Alt+PageDown displays the last spread, which of course includes the last page.

The first four commands are also represented by four buttons in the bottom left of the document window, as shown in Figure 4.2.

FIGURE 4.2

Each button corresponds to a navigational menu command.

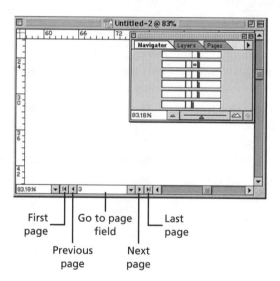

First page | Go to page field | Last page
Previous page | Next page

In between these buttons is a Go to Page field that displays the current page number. If you know the exact page number you want to display, you can type it in this field and press Enter or Return. You can also type the prefix to any master page to display that master.

You can click your cursor in the Go to Page field, highlight the current page number, and then type the new one. However, you can also complete the first two of these three steps with a keyboard shortcut. In Windows, it's Ctrl+J; on the Mac, it's Command+J. This is the same as the equivalent command in QuarkXPress, and you can think of the "J" standing for "jump to," a useful mnemonic for this most useful of keyboard shortcuts.

Zooming In and Out

InDesign offers magnification from 5% to 4,000%. Wow! What's more, you have precision control over the magnification down to .01%.

You access the Zoom In and Zoom Out commands from the View menu. The keyboard shortcuts for these commands are Ctrl++ (plus sign) or Command++ (for Zoom In), and Ctrl+- (minus sign) or Command+- (for Zoom Out). When you use these commands, the zoom percentage is changed incrementally. Depending on the current zoom percentage, these commands produce one of the following results: 5%, 12.5%, 25%, 50%, 75%, 100%, 200%, 400%, 800%, 1200%, 1600%, 2400%, 3200%, or 4000%.

The View menu also offers four other magnification options that are relative to your screen resolution. These are shown in Table 4.2.

4

TABLE 4.2 Magnification and View Shortcuts

Command	Win Keys	Mac Keys	Description
Fit Page in Window	Ctrl+0	Command+0	Centers the current page in the document window
Fit Spread in Window	Ctrl+Alt+0	Option+ Command+0	Centers the current spread in the document window
Actual Size	Ctrl+1	Command+1	Shows as much of the current spread as possible at its actual size
Entire Pasteboard	Shift+Ctrl+ Alt+0	Shift+ Option+ Command+0	Displays the entire pasteboard for the current spread

Other "stealth" keyboard shortcuts not listed under the View menu are Ctrl/Command+2 (zooms to 200%), Ctrl/Command+4 (zooms to 400%), and Ctrl/Command+5 (zooms to 50%).

Alas, for those who like Macintosh extended keyboards and prefer to enter numbers via the numeric keypad, these relative zoom values cannot be entered that way; you need to use the number keys on the main keyboard. And attempting to change this setting by customizing the shortcuts does not work.

Two important points here. First of all, I doubt you'll memorize the keyboard shortcut for the last command, so plan on selecting it from the View menu. Second, just so you know, the pasteboard is the area outside the page boundaries. As you'll learn in later hours, you can store page elements on the pasteboard and drag them onto your pages when you need them.

No matter what magnification you use, the percentage is always displayed in two places: in the lower-left corner of the Navigator palette and in the lower-left corner of the document window. You can change the magnification by typing a new percentage into either of these boxes and pressing Enter or Return.

 When typing a magnification percentage, you can type a value with up to two decimal places. For example, you can specify 72.14%. If you type more than two decimal places, the value is rounded to two decimal places.

Just to the right of the magnification field, in the lower-left corner of the document window, there's a small button that looks like a down arrow. Click there and you'll see a pop-up that displays all the increments available using the Zoom commands. You can select any magnification from this list.

Finally, there's the good old Zoom tool, which looks like a magnifying glass on the Tools palette. To zoom in, select the Zoom tool and click where you want to zoom. To zoom out, select the Zoom tool, hold down the Alt or Option key, and click where you want to zoom out from.

 And let's not forget one keyboard shortcut that is common to all Adobe applications. If you hold down Command+spacebar (on the Mac) or Ctrl+spacebar (in Windows), you can switch to the Zoom tool and zoom in from any other tool. If you wish to zoom out, the key combination is Option+Command+spacebar (on the Mac) and Alt+Ctrl+spacebar (on Windows).

The Pages/Layers/Navigator Palette(s)

Your InDesign documentation refers to separate Pages, Layers, and Navigator palettes. In reality, though, these are really just separate tabs on one common "megapalette," as shown in Figure 4.3. Each tab can be "ripped" off, and each palette can stand alone, if you want.

FIGURE 4.3

The Pages, Layers, and Navigator palettes are basically three tabs in a larger "megapalette."

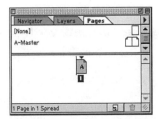

You hide this palette using standard Windows or Mac conventions. In other words, you just click the close box on the palette—whichever one is appropriate for your platform.

To display the palette again, choose Pages, Layers, or Navigator from the Window menu. The keyboard shortcut for the Pages palette is F12, whereas the keyboard shortcut for the Layers palette is F7. (There is no keyboard shortcut for the Navigator palette.) You can also use these shortcuts to toggle between the Pages and Layers palettes. Finally, you can click the appropriate tab to select the desired palette.

You can easily resize any of these palettes by clicking and dragging the lower-right corner of the dialog box. Each palette can also be collapsed by double-clicking on its tab; this helps to conserve screen real estate. Each tab can also be torn off, and any one palette can be docked with any other palette. We cover this in more detail in Hour 22, "Customizing InDesign."

The Layers and Navigator palettes are covered in the next hour, "Using Layers and the Layout and Formatting Tools." This chapter focuses on the Pages palette.

Anatomy of the Pages Palette

The Pages palette is split into two halves. The bottom of the palette shows a representation of all the pages and spreads you've created for the current document. As you add more pages and spreads, they also appear on this palette. You'll learn more about spreads later this hour. For now, all you need to know is that when you create a new document using the Facing Pages option (see Hour 3, "Creating, Saving, and Opening Documents"), the two pages that make up one set of facing pages are referred to as a *spread*.

The top half of the Pages palette shows all of the master pages you've created for the current document. Master pages are also covered later this hour.

Manipulating Pages in the Pages Palette

To really get a feel for the Pages palette, you need to be working in a document that has multiple pages and uses the Facing Pages option. So here's a little exercise to get you going.

To Do: Creating a Multipage Document with Spreads

To create a multi-page document with spreads, follow these steps:

1. Create a new document, making sure that the Facing Pages checkbox is checked. Specify 10 pages in the document.

2. Make sure that the Pages palette is displayed. If it's not, press F12. The Pages palette should look something like the one shown in Figure 4.4.

FIGURE 4.4

Your Pages palette should look like this.

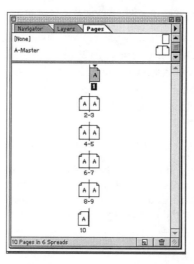

It's that easy. You can also add and remove pages and spreads one by one, as we'll see, but if you know in advance that your document is going to have 10 pages, this is a quick way of getting all your pages into place. All that remains is to fill the pages with text and graphics.

Selecting Pages and Spreads

To select a particular page in the Pages palette, simply click its icon. To select the entire spread, click the page numbers under the icons. For example, to select page 3, click the icon that represents the third page. Figure 4.5 shows the Pages palette with page 3 selected.

FIGURE 4.5

The selected page is highlighted.

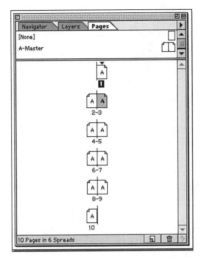

To select the entire 2-3 spread, click 2-3 under the page icons. Figure 4.6 shows this entire spread selected.

FIGURE 4.6

The selected spread is highlighted.

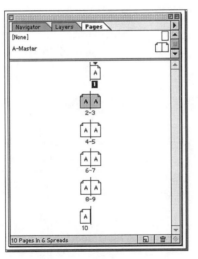

You can use the Shift and Ctrl (or Command) keys while clicking to select multiple pages or spreads, just like selecting multiple items in other Windows and Mac applications. For example, if you hold down the Shift key while clicking on pages, you will select a contiguous set of pages. If you hold the Ctrl (in Windows) or Command (on the Mac) key while clicking, you can select non-contiguous pages one at a time.

Notice that in Figure 4.6, 1 is highlighted even though the 2–3 spread is selected. That's because page 1 is displayed in the document window. This brings up a very important point. Simply selecting a page or spread doesn't cause it to be displayed in the document window. To actually switch to a page or spread, you need to double-click its icon instead of the single click used to select it. In other words, double-clicking a page icon displays that page; double-clicking the page numbers of a spread displays that spread.

Moving Pages and Spreads

InDesign makes short work of rearranging pages and spreads. If you're familiar with the Document Layout palette in QuarkXPress, this will all seem very familiar. Pages are inserted, deleted, and moved in much the same way. Using the Pages palette, rearranging pages is simply a drag-and-drop operation.

To Do: Moving a Page

To move a page or spread, do the following:

1. If you still have the 10-page document you created in the previous To Do, open it, if it is not already opened. If you didn't save it, create a new one. It's okay, I'll wait.

2. Let's assume that for whatever nefarious reason, we want to put page 3 between pages 5 and 6. Select page 3 with a single click, and then drag it to the left edge of page 6. A vertical black line shows you where the page will be moved to as shown in Figure 4.7.

FIGURE 4.7

The black vertical line marks the insertion point.

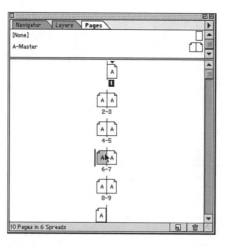

Spreads can be moved in the same way. Simply select the spread by clicking on the page numbers and drag to a new location.

Needless to say (but I'll say it anyway) you probably won't need to rearrange a document comprising only blank pages—I mean, what's the point of putting a blank page 3 before a blank page 6? Once we start putting text and objects on pages, you can revisit this To Do and see what the effects are of moving pages and spreads around.

Inserting Pages and Copying Spreads

Just to the left of the Pages palette's trash button is another button that looks like a little page (see Figure 4.8). That's an appropriate icon because it's the New Page button. However, don't let the name fool you. This button actually serves two purposes: to create new pages and to copy existing spreads.

FIGURE 4.8

The New Page button at the bottom of the Pages palette.

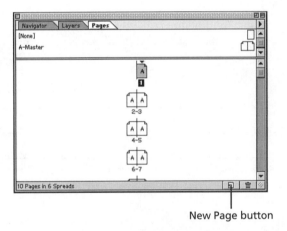

New Page button

The New Page button is at the bottom of the Pages palette. To create a new page using the New Page button, click it. InDesign automatically adds a new page to your document.

 It's important to know *where* InDesign is inserting your new page. You might expect it to be following the *selected* page or spread, but that's not the case. When you click the New Page button, the page is inserted after the page or spread that's currently *displayed* in the document window.

This is a good time to introduce the idea of palette menus. Each InDesign palette has a corresponding palette menu. For example, the Pages palette has a corresponding Pages palette menu. To display any palette menu, just click the arrow to the far right of the palette name. Figure 4.9 shows the Pages palette with the Pages palette menu displayed.

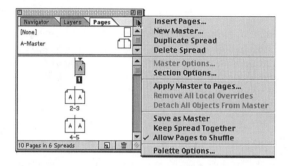

The reason I bring this up now is that choosing Insert Pages from the Pages palette menu gives you more control over the operation than simply clicking the New Page button. When you choose Insert Pages from the Pages palette menu, the Insert Pages dialog box is displayed, as shown in Figure 4.10.

FIGURE 4.10

*Using the Insert Pages
command gives you
several options.*

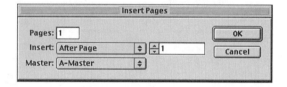

Pressing Alt (in Windows) or Option (on the Mac) while clicking the New Page button has the same effect as choosing Insert Pages from the palette menu.

By choosing Insert Pages from the Pages palette menu, you can specify how many pages you want to add. You can also specify where to insert the new pages. Your choices are After Page, Before Page, At Start of Document, or At End of Document. If you select one of the first two options, you also need to specify a page number.

Finally, you can select which master page to apply to the new pages. Master pages are covered later this hour. After you've specified the desired options, click OK.

To insert a spread using the New Page button, select the desired spread and drag and drop it onto the New Page button. When you release the mouse button, InDesign places a copy of the spread at the end of your document. You can then move it wherever you want.

Perhaps you noticed the Duplicate Spread option in the Pages palette menu. This option is available only when an entire spread is selected. Selecting this option has the same effect as dragging a spread to the New Page button.

There's a third way to copy a spread. It may be the method you use most, because it places the spread right where you want it and you can use the same basic technique to copy pages. To copy a spread or page to a new location, press and hold the Alt key (Windows) or Option key (Mac), click the spread or page to select it, and then drag it where you want within the Pages palette.

Deleting Pages and Spreads

To delete a page or spread, select the appropriate page or spread and then choose Delete Page or Delete Spread from the Pages palette menu. (The palette menu displays the appropriate choice depending on what you've selected.) Optionally, you can select the page or spread, and then click the Trash button next to the New Page button. Finally, you can drag and drop any selected item onto the Trash button to delete it.

Spreads with Three or More Pages

For most of your documents, traditional spreads—those with right and left facing pages—will probably do the trick. However, you're still likely to encounter projects that require something a little out of the ordinary.

The most common is the classic tri-fold brochure. In my PageMaker days, laying out a tri-fold brochure meant creating a two-page document and laying out three panels on each side of the page. However, InDesign enables you to lay out each panel of a tri-fold brochure as a separate page, which gives you more flexibility.

A tri-fold brochure that uses a three-page spread throughout the entire document is one thing. But what if you need to create an unusual spread right in the middle of your document? For example, what if you're working on an annual report that has a fold-out in the middle? Thanks to InDesign, this sort of thing is no problem.

No matter what the purpose, a spread that uses more than two pages is called an *island spread*.

4

Users who are familiar with the Create Island Spread command in version 1.0 may be somewhat at sea (as it were) in version 1.5, as the term "island spread" has been removed from the Pages palette. As the product manager for InDesign just told me as I was frantically trying to find the Create Island Spreads command, "No one knew what the heck an island spread was." So, basically, in InDesign 1.5, the Create Island Spread command has been replaced by the Keep Spread Together command. It works the same way.

To Do: Creating an Island Spread

To create an island spread (or keep your spread together, if you prefer…) in your InDesign document, do the following:

1. Hopefully, you still have the 10-page document you have been using for the past couple of To Dos. If not (sigh)…create a new one. I'll wait.

2. Select a spread in the Pages palette—say, 2–3.

3. Choose Keep Spread Together from the Pages palette menu (see Figure 4.11). This simply tells InDesign that you want to add additional pages to this spread. You will notice that brackets appear around the spread in the center of the palette. These mark the boundaries of your "island."

FIGURE 4.11

Select Keep Spread Together to create an island spread.

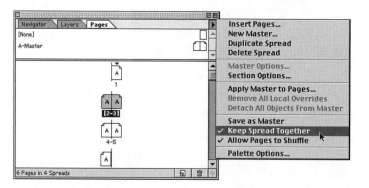

4. Select Insert Pages from the Pages palette menu and insert one page after page 2 or, in other words, in the middle of the island. You'll notice that you now have a three-page spread. See Figure 4.12.

FIGURE 4.12

They say no man is an island, but this spread is.

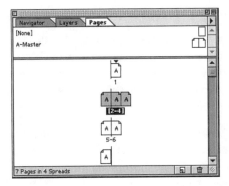

The vertical line dividing two of the pages tells you where your binding spine is, and you can use the left/right page icons at the top of the Pages palette to determine which pages in your island are left-hand or right-hand pages or, in other words, how they will get bound.

You can add more and more pages to your spread by using the Insert Pages command.

To eliminate the island spread and revert back to simple two-page spreads, go back to the Pages palette menu and deselect Keep Spread Together. Also make sure that Allow Pages to Shuffle is selected, and you will be back to your humdrum two-page spreads. However, deselecting Keep Spread Together redistributes all the pages of the island spread into the main spread and is therefore likely to affect the other spreads in your document. You can add pages to an island spread using any of the techniques you learned earlier this hour. However, there are a couple of differences.

First of all, if you add a page between two other pages in a traditional spread, each page after the inserted page is bumped one spread position to the right. For example, if you add a page between pages 2 and 3, the former page 3 becomes page 4 in the 4-5 spread, and so on.

However, when you add a page to an island spread, you simply increase the number of pages in the island spread. In other words, no pages are bumped to the next spread.

The same holds true when you delete pages from an island spread. This action renumbers pages only from within the spread without affecting any pages in other spreads.

In the next hour, you learn about automatic page numbering, including how to restart page numbering for a new section in the same document. This can be handy when you're working with island spreads because you may not want each page in the island spread to have its own page number. In that case, you display the page number on the first page in the island spread, and then use section numbering to number the first page after the island spread with the next page number.

4

Mastering Master Pages

Master pages, or simply *masters*, contain collections of page elements that you want to appear in the same positions on multiple pages or spreads. For example, if the company president wants the company logo to appear on the upper corner of every page in your document (despite your strenuous objections), you can simply position the logo in the appropriate locations on both the right and left master pages and be done with it.

Former PageMaker and QuarkXPress users will welcome the fact that InDesign enables you to create multiple master pages in the same document and apply them to individual pages and spreads as necessary. What's more, you can selectively apply right and left masters to individual pages. About the only thing you can't do is apply a right master to a left page, or vice versa.

Like document pages, you manage masters from the Pages palette. You may recall that master pages are displayed in the upper portion of this palette, as shown in Figure 4.13.

FIGURE 4.13

Masters are displayed in the upper portion of the Pages palette.

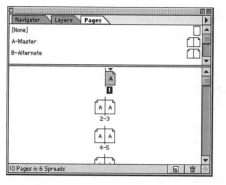

You can give each master spread a name, as well as a one-character prefix. The default prefix/name combination for the default master is A-Master. In the Pages palette, the master prefix is included in each page icon. That explains why in the previous figure, every page icon has an A in it. Any page to which the B-Alternate master is applied would have a B on its icon.

You can apply different names and prefixes when you create a new master page with the New master command in the Pages palette. For example, you could call it B-Master, B-Alternate, or 2-Moist, if you wanted to. And each master page is given an Options command that lets you change its name and prefix, as well as other aspects, which we'll cover in a moment.

Adding Elements to a Master

You add elements to a master just as you add elements to any other InDesign page. It's really that simple. In the Hours to follow, you learn about text and graphics and all the other goodies you can put on a page. The same rules apply to masters. To add elements to a master, just display the master in the document window by double-clicking it in the Pages palette. Then start adding stuff by drawing, typing, or importing them on to the master. The elements you add will appear on any page to which you apply that master.

Creating and Modifying Masters

InDesign makes short work of creating and editing master pages. It is all handled via the Pages palette.

To Do: Creating and Editing Master Pages

To create a master page, do the following:

1. If you still have your 10-page document from previous To Dos, you're catching on. Open it, if it is not already open. If you discarded it yet again... what am I going to do with you? Anyway, create another new document, although it doesn't need to have 10 pages. One will be sufficient.

2. Make sure the pages palette is open by selecting it from the Window menu or hitting F12.

3. Choose New Master from the Pages palette menu. Doing so displays the New Master dialog box shown in Figure 4.14.

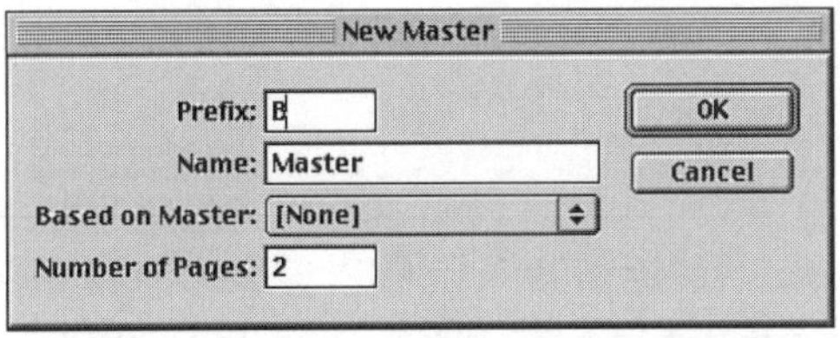

FIGURE 4.14

You have several options when creating a new master.

4. In the prefix field, type a single character. This character will appear in the page icon of any page to which that master has been applied. You can enter as many as four characters in the prefix field, but the idea is to make it easy for you to see at a glance which pages use which masters. You can also use numbers and symbols (like #, @, &, etc.) if you'd like.

5. In the Name field, type a short, descriptive name that helps you identify that master.

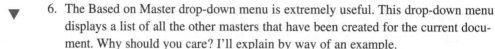

6. The Based on Master drop-down menu is extremely useful. This drop-down menu displays a list of all the other masters that have been created for the current document. Why should you care? I'll explain by way of an example.

   Suppose you're creating a document in which all the pages can use the same master, except for the fact that the first page of each section needs a watermark. First, you create a master for all the common elements. Next, you create a new master based on the first one, and add the watermark to the new one. Now when you make changes to the first master, those changes are also made to the second master, but *not* vice versa. When you use this option, the prefix for the "based on" master appears in the page icon for the new master.

   However, since we don't have any other masters yet defined, it's a moot point at this stage.

7. In most cases, you can leave the Number of Pages set with the default value of 2. The only time you need to enter a different number is when you're using island spreads in your document. You can create a master for your island spreads by entering the appropriate number in the Number of Pages field.

8. Define a few more master pages.

9. When you're done, click OK.

> Suppose you create a regular spread and then realize that it would make an ideal master for your document. No problem. Just select the spread and drag it down to the masters portion of the Pages palette. Doing so copies the selected spread to a new master. If the original spread used a different master, the new master will be based on that one.

10. Uh oh. We goofed. We need to edit a master page. Select any one of the masters you just created and then choose Master Options for from the Pages palette menu. This brings up a dialog box just like the one we just saw in Figure 4.14 above.

11. You can change the prefix, the name, the master upon which it is based, or the page count. When you're done, hit OK.

Once your masters are created, you can duplicate a master by clicking it, and then choosing Duplicate Master Spread from the Pages palette menu.

You can copy a master to another open InDesign document by dragging the master to the document window of the other document. InDesign is smart enough to know what you want to do and automatically adds the master to the other document. Obviously, this is easier with a larger monitor.

You can also delete a master by clicking it and choosing Delete Master Spread from the Pages palette menu.

 When you delete a master, all master elements are removed from any page to which that master was applied. In other words, the page is rendered "masterless." It's the equivalent of applying the None master (described shortly) to a page or spread. Use the techniques you're about to learn to apply a different master to those pages.

Applying Masters

Applying a master to a page or spread is a simple drag-and-drop operation. Select the master you want to apply and drag it to the page or spread you want to apply it to. It doesn't even matter whether you select one page in the master or the whole spread. What does matter is exactly where you drag it.

If you drag the master over a spread such that a box appears around the entire spread (see Figure 4.15), both the right and left masters will be applied to the right and left pages in the spread. If you drag the master so that only one page is boxed (see Figure 4.16), the corresponding master page will be applied only to the boxed page. In other words, if you highlight the right page of a spread, the right master will be applied to that page. If you drag the master to the left page, the left master will be applied to that page.

Figure 4.15

To apply a master to a whole spread, make sure the whole spread is boxed.

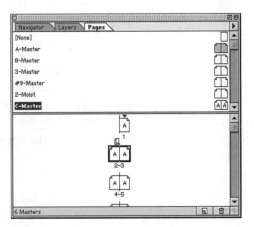

FIGURE 4.16

FIGURE 4.16

To apply a master to only one page, make sure only that page is boxed.

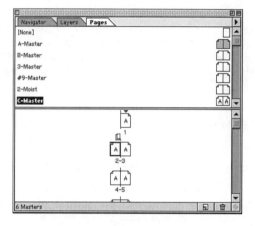

You can also apply the same master to any combination of multiple pages and spreads. To do this, select all the pages to which you want to apply a master, using either Shift (to select a set of contiguous pages), Ctrl (on the PC), or Command (on the Mac) to select a noncontiguous set of pages. Then choose Apply Master to Pages from the Pages palette menu. This displays the Apply Master dialog box, shown in Figure 4.17.

FIGURE 4.17

Choose which master to apply and which pages to apply it to.

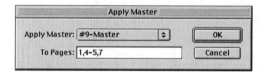

The next step is to select the appropriate master from the drop-down menu. The To Pages field lists all of the pages you selected. If you realize that you've made an error, you can edit this list now. Use commas to separate individual pages and hyphens to designate page ranges.

If you have pages and/or spreads to which you don't want any masters applied, apply the None master to those pages.

Master Overrides

If you have several pages that need to vary from the current master, your best bet is to create a new master using the techniques you've already learned. However, from time to time, you may come across a single page that needs to vary just slightly from the master. Instead of going to all the trouble to create a new master, you can selectively override each master element on any page.

To do this, first display the page (not the master) to which you want to make the overrides. Then, while pressing Ctrl+Shift (Windows) or Command+Shift (Mac), select the master item you want to change. From there on out, that element will behave as though it were placed on that page instead of on the master. You can change it at will.

To change the element back to its original master form, click it and choose Remove Selected Local Overrides from the Pages palette menu. If you want to remove all overrides at once, make sure nothing is selected and then choose Remove All Local Overrides (which replaces Remove Selected Local Overrides) from the Pages palette menu.

If you don't want to display any master items on the currently displayed spread, you can also disable Display Master Items in the View menu. Note that this affects the entire spread, but only the currently displayed spread. The keyboard shortcut to toggle this option is Ctrl+Y in Windows (and Command+Y on the Mac).

Summary

Being able to both easily control how your page looks and easily navigate around your documents is essential to effective, efficient electronic page layout. Fortunately, InDesign provides you with extremely advanced and powerful tools in this area.

4

Workshop

InDesign offers so many ways to accomplish the same thing; sometimes presenting them all may raise more questions than it answers. Just remember that nobody expects you to use every technique. The whole idea is to give users a variety of choices so they can work their own way.

Q&A

Q It seems that for so many functions, there's a menu command, a keyboard shortcut, a drag-and-drop method, and maybe even a button. Which is the best method?

A I'm a visual person, so I generally prefer drag-and-drop. However, I know a number of speed demons who swear by keyboard shortcuts. It's really a matter of personal preference.

Q Zooming is especially confusing. How do I know which method is best?

A Again, it's a matter of personal preference. My suggestion—and this goes for everything you do in InDesign—is to find the techniques that you are most comfortable with and use them, knowing all the time that you have the others to fall back on if necessary.

Q I removed one of the master elements as a local override. Now there's no way to select it so I can bring it back. What do I do?

A You need to remove all the local overrides. If this is the only local override you have, you're in luck. However, if you have others that you don't want to remove, you have a little work ahead of you. First, you have to remove all the local overrides to bring back the deleted element. Then you have to redo the overrides that you didn't want to remove.

Quiz

1. What's the relationship between pages and spreads?

    a. A page usually consists of two spreads.

    b. A spread usually consists of two pages.

    c. You combine pages and spreads to create masters.

2. An island spread is which of the following?

    a. A tropical feast or luau.

    b. A spread that has no master applied.

    c. A spread with more than two pages.

3. How many characters can the prefix for each master page have?

    a. 4

    b. 5

    c. 7

4. How many magnification levels are available in InDesign?

    a. 2

    b. 14

    c. More than I care to count

Quiz Answers

1. b. When you use the Facing Pages option, the combination of a left and right page makes up a spread. In most documents, the only spreads that include one page are the first page and any even-numbered last page.

2. c. An island spread has more than two pages. You can create an island spread in the middle of a "regular" document if necessary.

3. a. The prefix can have as many as four characters, although one or two is most preferable. The prefix has to fit on the page icon for each page to which the master has been applied.

4. c. This is kind of a trick question. There are 14 preset zooms. However, don't forget that you can manually type a zoom percentage with up to two decimal places. That means that there are 99 possibilities between 5% and 6%. Because values can range from 5% to 4000%, there are close to 400,000 possibilities.

Exercises

In many ways, the techniques you learned this hour really form the backbone for all your electronic page layout projects. Go pour yourself a cup of coffee. Then come back and experiment with these techniques. Create a new document with all sorts of pages. Move them around. Create different masters. Zoom in. Zoom out. In short, don't be afraid to go crazy. It's only when you do that you'll discover both the power and the limits of InDesign.

4

HOUR 5

Using Layers and the Layout and Formatting Tools

In a broad sense, laying out a page with InDesign is no different than cutting different page elements out from hard copy and manually pasting them onto a pasteboard. Where these two page layout techniques drastically diverge is in ease of use and precision.

During this hour, you'll learn the following:

- How to perform precision alignment using grids, guides, and rulers
- How to manage document layers
- How to let InDesign adjust your layout automatically

Guides, Grids, and Rulers

A *guide* is a nonprinting horizontal or vertical line that you create to help you align objects. For example, if you have several graphics that need to be aligned on their left sides, you can create a vertical guide at the alignment point. Then it's easy to place the graphics along the guide.

A *grid* is a series of evenly spaced guides that you create to further ease the alignment process. InDesign can create two kinds of grids on command: document and baseline grids. A *document grid*, having both horizontal and vertical lines, makes the document window look like a sheet of graph paper, whereas a *baseline grid,* having only horizontal lines, makes the document window look like a sheet of notebook paper. The document grid makes aligning objects easy, whereas the baseline grid simplifies the task of aligning multiple columns of text.

You can also create your own grids from rulers, and even copy and paste your custom grids to other pages.

Finally, rulers are what the name implies. They look like real rulers and, depending on your preference, they appear along the left and top sides of the document window. They help position guides and other objects on your page.

Working with Ruler Guides

When you create a new document, the page margins you set serve as your document's first official guides. These are called *margin guides*. As I mentioned earlier, a guide is just a nonprinting horizontal or vertical line that helps you align the elements of your document.

For a simple document—say, a flyer—the margins may be all the guides you need. However, if you find you need a guide anywhere else on the page, creating it is easy.

To create this type of guide (called a *ruler guide*), you must be sure that the document window displays its rulers. If you don't see any rulers along the top and left sides, press Ctrl+R (Windows) or Command+R (Mac). Alternately, you can select Show Rulers from the View menu. Your document window should look something like the one shown in Figure 5.1.

Rulers

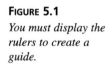

FIGURE 5.1

You must display the rulers to create a guide.

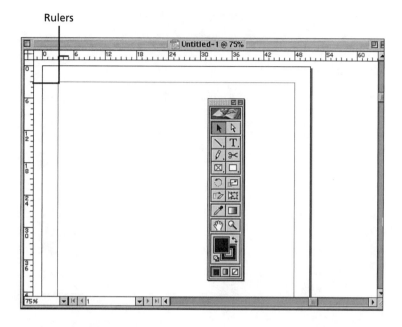

To Do: Creating a Ruler Guide

To create a ruler guide, do the following:

1. Create a new document in InDesign. The default size and margins will do. Make sure you are displaying the rulers (as mentioned above).

2. Position your selection tool over one of the rulers, let's say the one running along the left side of the document. (If you want to create a horizontal ruler guide, position the pointer over the top ruler.)

3. When you click, the cursor will turn into a double-headed arrow. Drag onto the page or spread where you want the guide to appear.

   As long as you keep the mouse button clicked, you can continue to move the ruler guide anywhere you want. If you release the mouse button, you can click the ruler guide again to move it farther.

   Notice too that as you move the vertical ruler guide, its position is marked on the top ruler. (Similarly, if you were dragging a horizontal ruler, its position would be marked along the side ruler.) So drag your guide to the position of your choosing, depending on what units you have set for your ruler. For example, in Figure 5.2, I have created a vertical ruler and have dragged it to the 12 pica position. The dotted line on the top ruler indicates the guide's position.

5

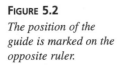

Ruler guide position marker

FIGURE 5.2

The position of the guide is marked on the opposite ruler.

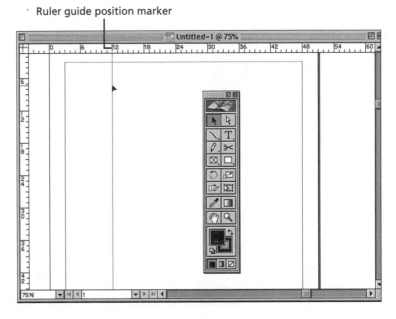

You can create as many guides as you'd like, both vertical and horizontal. You can also zoom in (using techniques you learned in Hour 4, "Managing Pages") to position your guides with almost molecular accuracy.

Here are a couple of guidelines for creating guides:

- If you release the mouse button over a page, the ruler guide you created appears only on that page.
- If you release the mouse button over the pasteboard, the ruler guide appears across the entire spread and out onto the pasteboard.
- If you press and hold the Ctrl key (Windows) or Command key (Mac) while creating your ruler guide, the guide appears across the entire spread no matter where you happen to release the mouse button.
- To delete a ruler guide, select it and press the Delete key. You can select multiple guides just as you select any other multiple. To select all ruler guides on the current spread, press Ctrl+Alt+G (Windows) or Command+Option+G (Mac).
- If you create a series of ruler guides that you want to apply to other pages (such as when you use ruler guides to create a custom grid), you can select those guides and copy and paste them to other pages. If you need those ruler guides on several pages, consider copying and pasting them onto a master page instead, which will save time since you only have to copy or create them once to have them appear on all the pages on which you want them.

- The Ruler Guides option in the Layout menu enables you to change the appearance of your ruler guides. You can adjust the color, as well as the magnification threshold. The default threshold is 5%, which means at 5% magnification, InDesign automatically hides your ruler guides.

Creating Margins and Columns

As you learned earlier, your page margins also represent a special kind of guide. When you flow text into your document, the margin guides control how far your text can extend. In other words, these guides define your page borders.

Another type of guide that works hand in hand with your margin guides is the column guide. If you need to create a multicolumn page, you simply define the necessary column guides. These column guides then appear on the page to help control the flow of text. You can create column guides on a regular page or spread, or on a master page.

The margin and column guides are both controlled through the same dialog box. That means you can use the same basic technique to adjust either.

To Do: Creating Margin and Column Guides

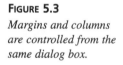

To create margin and column guides, do the following:

1. If you still have the document from the last To Do open, keep it open. If you do not have an open document, create a new blank document in InDesign. Don't worry about setting margins and columns in the New Document dialog box. Just hit OK.
2. Select Margins and Columns from the Layout menu. You'll see the dialog box shown in Figure 5.3.

FIGURE 5.3

*Margins and columns
are controlled from the
same dialog box.*

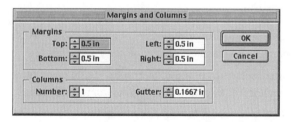

5

3. The Margins area provides four fields that identify the bounds of the margins. Each field represents a measurement from the edge of the page. You can change these to your liking. Notice in Figure 5.3 that the default is .5 inches all around. For fun, change all margins (say, to 1 inch). You can enter numbers manually, or use the up and down arrows to the left of each field to respectively increase or decrease the margins. You can move from field to field by hitting the Tab key.

▼

▼ 4. When you're done, hit OK. Notice the effect on the page. The colored lines mark-
      ing your margins have now moved to the new dimensions you just set.

> You may not be displaying your margins, rulers, and guides in inches. You
> can go to the Units & Increments Preferences dialog box (under Edit,
> Preferences) and change your measurement units to inches, millimeters, or
> whatever you'd like using techniques you learned in Hour 2, "Preparing to
> Work in InDesign."

   5. Okay, go back to Layout, Margins and Columns… The Columns area provides two
      fields. In the Number field, type the number of columns you want to create, in this
      case, say, 2.

   6. In the Gutter field, type the amount of space you want between each column.
      Usually the default works well. (For a refresher on entering measurements, refer to
      Hour 3, "Creating, Saving, and Opening Documents.")

▲ 7. Finally, click OK. Your new column guides appear as you specified.

> When you create column guides, the columns are evenly spaced. However, if
> you need unevenly spaced columns, you can click and drag any column
> guide pair to move it where you want.

Here are a couple of other points you need to consider when changing margins and creating column guides:

- Any changes you make in the Margins and Columns dialog box affect only the
  pages or spreads currently selected in the Pages palette.

- If you want to create column guides for a single page, make sure only that page is
  selected in the Pages palette before you create the guides.

- If you want to create column guides on both pages in a spread, make sure the
  whole spread is selected in the Pages palette.

- If you want changes to apply to any combination of multiple pages and spreads,
  make sure they're all selected in the Pages palette.

- If you want changes to apply to all the pages in a document (or all left or right
  pages), the appropriate Master Pages should be selected in the Pages palette.

Creating Evenly Spaced Ruler Guides

InDesign also provides a way to create a series of evenly spaced horizontal and or vertical ruler guides. That means you can create what appear to be rows and columns on your page. The reason I say *appear to be* is that unlike column guides, these guides don't do anything to control the flow of text. This is just a shortcut to creating a series of ruler guides for positioning graphics or other page elements at regular intervals.

To Do: Creating Evenly Spaced Ruler Guides

To create a series of evenly spaced ruler guides, do the following:

1. With a blank document open, select Create Guides from the Layout menu. The Create Guides dialog box appears, as shown in Figure 5.4.

FIGURE 5.4

The Create Guides dialog box.

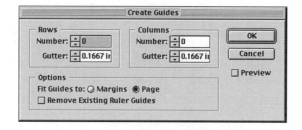

2. The fields in the Rows and Columns areas are identical. Rows creates horizontal ruler guides, while Columns creates vertical ruler guides. In the Number field under Rows, type the number of rows you want to create. Let's say, 3. Leave Columns at 0 for now. In the Gutter field, indicate the amount of space between each row. The default will be fine.

3. In the Options area, you can control whether the rows and columns fit into the page margins, or are evenly spread across the entire page. Select Page. (Also notice that you can remove all existing guides if you'd like. Leave that unchecked for now.)

4. Hit OK. Your page should resemble Figure 5.5.

5. Now, go back to the Create Guides dialog box. Enter 3 in the Rows field, but this time select Fit Guides to Margin. And this time, check the Remove Existing Guides box. Hit OK. You should now have a page that resembles Figure 5.6.

5

FIGURE 5.5

The rows span the page.

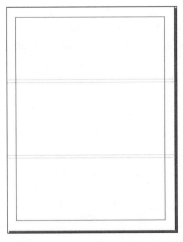

FIGURE 5.6

The rows fit between the margins.

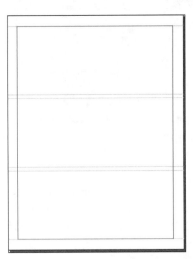

As you have no doubt surmised, the Remove Existing Ruler Guides checkbox has your new rows and columns replace the existing ruler guides. Leave it unchecked if you want the new guides to appear in addition to any others you have created.

The most useful feature in this dialog box is the Preview checkbox. With this box checked, you'll see changes in the background as you make them. If something doesn't look right, just change it. If your changes look too hideous and you want to start over, you can always click Cancel.

Rows and columns you create in this manner are applied to all pages on the currently displayed spread, regardless of what's selected in the Pages palette. No other pages or spreads are affected. If you want to add the same rows or columns to another page, use the copy and paste method to do so.

Controlling Your Guides

The View menu provides three options for controlling your various guides. Here's a description of each option:

- Hide Guides (Ctrl+; or Command+;) hides (but doesn't delete) all the guides in the current document. This is useful when you want to see exactly what your document looks like without all the guides cluttering the page. You can use the keyboard shortcut to toggle back and forth.

- When you have several objects on a page, it's easy to accidentally select and do something to a guide instead of to the intended object. After the guides are set the way you want, you may want to use the Lock Guides command (Ctrl+Alt+; or Command+Option+;) to lock them in place. You unlock them the same way.

- The Snap to Guides option (Shift+Ctrl+; or Shift+Command+;) controls whether snap zones have any effect. (Snap zones were discussed in Hour 2.) With this option checked, objects you drag around the page will snap to the guides according to the preferences you set. Snapping to guides is useful when positioning objects, but sometimes it can be annoying when you want to position something *near* a guide but not necessarily aligned with it. So you can turn Snap To Guides off and on easily.

Using Grids

As I mentioned earlier, you can create custom grids with ruler guides and copy and paste them around as needed. However, for most of your grid needs, InDesign's two built-in grids may prove quite adequate.

The document grid makes your page look like a sheet of graph paper, as shown in Figure 5.7.

The baseline grid makes your page look like a sheet of notebook paper, as shown in Figure 5.8.

5

FIGURE 5.7

The document grid is helpful in positioning objects.

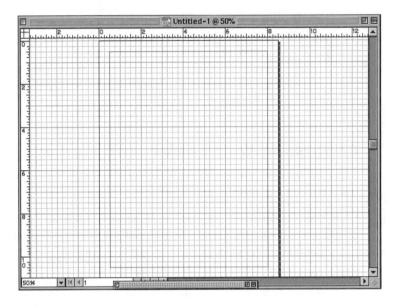

FIGURE 5.8

The baseline grid helps to align columns of text.

The key to success when using either of these grids is in how you set the preferences, which you already learned in Hour 2. To display the baseline grid, select Show Baseline Grid (Ctrl+Alt+' in Windows or Command+Option+' on the Mac) from the View menu. To display the document grid, select Show Document Grid (Ctrl+' in Windows or Command+' on the Mac) from the View menu.

> The View menu also includes a Snap to Document Grid option (Shift+Ctrl+'
> in Windows or Shift+Command+' on the Mac). Be aware that when you
> select this option, objects will snap to the document grid even when the
> document grid is not displayed.

Ruler Basics

You've already learned how to hide and display your document rulers, and you've
learned their purpose in helping you create ruler guides. Rulers are also very useful when
you're positioning objects on a page. Notice the *hash marks* (the small vertical lines) on
each ruler in Figure 5.9. They mark the outside boundaries of any object as you drag it
around the page. You'll learn more about positioning graphical objects in Hour 11,
"Combining Text and Graphics," and Hour 12, "Managing Objects on a Page."

FIGURE 5.9

*Ruler hash marks show
the position of a
selected object.*

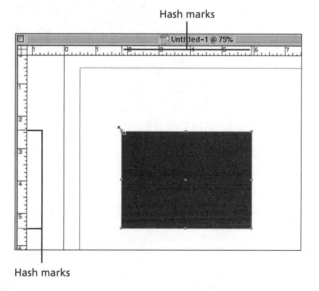

The one thing you can actually *do* with your rulers is change what's called the *zero point*.
By default, the upper-left corner of the left page is marked as 0 (zero) on both the horizontal and vertical rulers. That means this is the default zero point.

So why would you want to change the zero point? You can do this to measure an object
without moving it. You can move the zero point to the upper-left corner of the object and
instantly determine its dimensions.

To change the zero point, click and drag the small box where the two rulers intersect. As you drag across the screen, two lines appear to indicate the new position of the zero point, as shown in Figure 5.10. Release the mouse to set the zero point.

FIGURE 5.10

Drag from the ruler intersection to change the zero point.

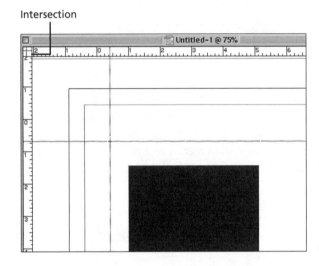

To restore the zero point to its normal position, double-click the box where the two rulers intersect. You can also lock and unlock the position of the zero point by right-clicking (Windows) or Ctrl-clicking (Mac) the intersection box.

You can also right-click (Windows) or Ctrl-click (Mac) on either the horizontal or vertical ruler to change its units of measurement on-the-fly.

Working with Document Layers

Some time during junior-high science class, you probably saw a series of overlaid transparencies that represented the human body. The bottom one had a picture of the skeletal system, the next one showed internal organs, the one after that showed connective tissue, and so on. Put them all together and you could see the entire picture.

With InDesign, you can work on the same premise—that sometimes it's more convenient to place different elements on different layers in the same document.

One of the best uses of layering, at least in my opinion, is to store multiple versions of the same document without creating multiple documents.

Suppose for example that you need to create both an English and Spanish version of the same print advertisement. Except for the language, the two ads are identical.

Instead of creating two separate documents, you can put the English text on one layer and the Spanish text on another layer. Then, when you make changes to nontext elements, both versions are updated simultaneously. When it comes time to output the file, just display the appropriate text layer and go.

The more you work with layers, the more you'll come to appreciate the extra flexibility they bring to your page layout projects. Other possibilities include placing text and graphics on separate layers so it's easy to output a text-only copy for your copy editor, or placing different variations of a design on different layers so it's easier to experiment.

Document layers are managed primarily through a combination of options available directly on the Layers palette and through the Layers palette menu. The Layers palette shares the same physical palette with the Pages and Navigator palettes. To display the Layers palette, you can either click its tab (if one of the other two palettes is currently displayed), or press F7.

Basics of the Layers Palette

Figure 5.11 shows the Layers palette as it looks in any new document. As you can see, a new document contains only one layer by default. We'll take a look at multiple layers later this hour. For now, I just want you to become familiar with the various parts of this palette.

FIGURE 5.11

A new document contains only one layer.

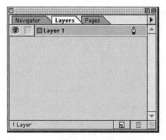

5

To the left of every layer are two buttons. The left-most button (the Visibility toggle) controls whether the corresponding layer is displayed. If the eyeball is displayed, the layer is visible. If you click the eyeball, it disappears—and so does the layer. Click the button to bring back the eyeball and the layer.

This button controls both the screen and output display. In other words, if you hide a layer, you don't see it on the screen and it isn't printed, either.

The other button is the Lock toggle. When it's off (as shown in Figure 5.11), you can make changes to the selected layer. If you click this button, a pencil with a red line through it appears, and you can no longer make changes to any elements on that layer.

Moving right, there's a colored box next to the layer name. Each time you create a new layer, a different color is assigned to that layer. When you add graphics, text boxes, and other elements to a page, the handles and bounding boxes for the element are displayed in the color corresponding to the layer on which the element is located. This makes it easy to tell at a glance which layer any given element is on. Later this hour, you'll learn how to change both the color and the layer name.

To the far right of the layer name, notice what appears to be the tip of a fountain pen. This marker indicates on which layer the next element will be placed. For example, if you have multiple layers and draw a square, that square will be located on whichever layer was marked with the fountain pen at the time. The layer marked with the fountain pen is called the *target layer*.

The New Layer button (which looks just like the New Page button on the Pages palette) and the Trash button work just like the corresponding buttons on the Pages palette. When you click the New Layer button, a new layer appears in the list just above the currently selected layer.

The order in which layers are listed in the Layers palette controls the order in which they're "stacked" in your document. In Hour 9, "Using Graphics from Other Programs," you learn about the Object menu's Arrange commands. However, those commands only affect objects on the same layer. When two objects from different layers overlap, the object on the higher layer always appears in front of the other object.

To change the stacking order of your layers, simply drag the appropriate layer to its new location in the Layers palette.

To Do: Creating New Layers

Now that you are familiar with the basics of the Layers palette, you need to create a couple of new layers if you want to follow along.

1. With a blank document open, make sure the Layers palette is open (hit F7 or select Window, Layers).

2. Click the New Layer button to create a new layer. The result should look something like Figure 5.12.

FIGURE 5.12

This document now has two layers.

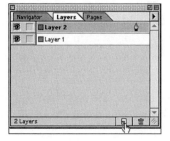

3. Repeat step 2 to add a third layer to the document.

The Layers Palette Menu

The Layers palette menu, shown in Figure 5.13, provides several options for managing your layers.

FIGURE 5.13

You manage layers from the Layers palette menu.

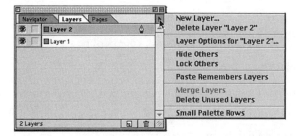

Selecting New Layer from the Layers palette menu brings up a dialog box like the one shown in Figure 5.14.

You can achieve this same result by holding down the Alt or Option key while clicking the New Layer button.

FIGURE 5.14

Change the settings of a layer here.

5

Modifying Layers

You can type a descriptive name in the Name field to name your layer. The Color pull-down menu enables you to select one of 20 colors to represent this layer. Being able to change the color comes in handy, for example, when you're working with a dark background and thus want the bounding box for various page elements to be displayed in lighter colors.

The Show Layer and Lock Layer checkboxes are pretty straightforward. No matter how you set these now, you can easily change them using the Lock button on the Layers palette.

Earlier this hour, you learned how to hide and lock guides throughout your entire document. The Show Guides and Lock Guides checkboxes in the New Layer dialog box bring this same control to the layer level. The options you select here affect only the current layer.

> So what happens when the document guide settings conflict with the layer guide settings? The more restrictive of the two options takes precedence. In other words, if either is set to hide guides, the guides will be hidden. For the guides to be displayed, both must be set to show guides.

When you're done, click OK. If you need to make changes to any of these settings, click the layer in the Layers palette and select Layer Options for the Layers palette menu.

To delete a layer, click it, and then select Delete Layer from the Layers palette menu.

> Deleting a layer deletes *everything* on that layer. If there are page elements that you want to keep, you need to move them to different layers before you delete the layer.

Other Layers Palette Menu Options

The Hide Others and Lock Others options on the Layers palette menu enable you to perform those operations on all but the selected layer or layers.

I think Adobe could have come up with a catchier name than *Paste Remembers Layers*, but this Layers palette menu option is very useful anyway. Here's how pasting works when this option is off (the default): When you copy or cut an object from any layer and then paste it somewhere else, it's pasted into the current target layer.

If you turn this option on and paste an object, it is pasted into the same layer as it origi-
nated from, regardless of the current target layer. This is useful in a number of situations,
such as when you are moving several things around and moving from layer to layer. You
want to cut and paste, but have everything remember where it came from.

> When you're copying and pasting between two InDesign documents, the
> settings of the *originating* document control the operation. If you have
> Paste Remembers Layers turned on in the originating document when you
> copy (or cut) something, the object is pasted into the same layer in the desti-
> nation document. If a layer with the same name doesn't exist in the destina-
> tion document, a new layer with that name is created when you perform
> the paste.

If you have more than one layer selected in the Layers palette, you can merge them into a
single layer using the Merge Layers command from the Layers palette menu. When you
do this, all selected layers are merged into the selected layer that's highest on the list.
This is useful for consolidating objects on different layers into one place, typically for
reasons of output.

> Merging all layers into a single layer is referred to as *flattening* your docu-
> ment.

Use the Delete Unused Layers command to permanently delete all layers on which no
objects currently exist.

Moving an Object from One Layer to Another

Suppose you put an object on one layer and then decide it should really be on a different
layer. The long way to address this problem is to cut the object from the current layer and
then paste it onto the desired layer. Fortunately, InDesign provides a much easier way.

When you select an object on your page, a small box appears in the Layers palette to the
right of the layer on which the object currently resides. See Figure 5.15 for an example.

To move an object from one layer to another, all you have to do is drag that little box
from its current location to the layer where you want it. It's that easy. And option-
dragging the little box copies the selected object(s) to the target layer.

5

FIGURE 5.15

The little box shows which layer the object is on.

Automatic Layout Adjustments

In the past couple of years, repurposing content has become a popular activity in many businesses. Most often, it entails taking printed material and adapting it for the Web. However, electronic page layout pros have been repurposing content since the beginning of time—or at least since the beginning of desktop publishing.

How many times have you had to convert a tabloid-sized ad into a little insert, or a full-size brochure into a trifold, or a three-column document into a two-column document? Each time, by my definition anyway, you repurposed your original content.

In the old days, changing the basic layout of a document entailed a lot of tedious work. With InDesign, however, you have at your disposal a feature called *Layout Adjustment*.

When you make certain layout changes with this feature enabled—specifically when you use Document Setup from the Page menu or Margins and Columns from the Layout menu—InDesign automatically adjusts various page elements to accommodate your changes. The results may not be exactly what you want, but chances are, they'll be very close.

To enable or modify the settings for Layout Adjustment, select Layout Adjustment from the Layout menu. This displays a dialog box like the one shown in Figure 5.16.

FIGURE 5.16

InDesign can adjust your layout according to your specifications.

At the top of this dialog box is an Enable Layout Adjustment checkbox that, as you would expect, allows you to enable and disable Layout Adjustment. With this box unchecked, all other options in this dialog box are grayed out.

Here's a description of the other options in this dialog box:

- The Snap Zone setting works just like the snap zones you already learned about in Hour 2. The only difference is that this snap zone only affects changes made as the result of Layout Adjustment.
- Selecting the Allow Graphics and Groups to Resize checkbox allows InDesign to resize graphical elements in proportion to any changes you make to the physical dimensions of your document.
- If you check the Allow Ruler Guides to Move checkbox, InDesign will move your ruler guides according to your layout changes.
- If you check the Ignore Ruler Guide Alignments checkbox, InDesign will still align text and objects to margin and column guides, but ignores your ruler guides.
- Select the Ignore Object and Layer Locks checkbox when you want InDesign to adjust locked page elements. With this option unchecked, all locked items stay in their original locations.

Because every layout is different from every other layout, the results you get from using Layout Adjustment will vary from project to project. The best way to become accustomed to this particular feature is to use it and see what happens.

In general, you should leave Layout Adjustment disabled unless you specifically need it. Otherwise, you may get unintended results from doing something as simple as adding a column guide.

Summary

Automation is the name of the game in electronic page layout. The more a page layout program can do for you, the more you can get done in any given period of time. InDesign's formatting and layout tools push layout automation to a whole new level.

Workshop

Sure, most of this is simple stuff. The key, as I've said before, is being able to make the right decisions about your documents. In this Workshop section, you'll go over some of the finer points of using Layers and InDesign's layout and formatting tools. I promise that becoming proficient with these steps will save you time in the long run.

Q&A

Q **Can I make changes to the settings for more than one layer at a time?**

A Yes. You can select multiple layers in the Layers palette and then select Layer Options from the palette menu. The Name field is understandably grayed out in the resulting dialog box. Oddly, you can assign the same color to more than one layer. Doing so, however, renders the concept of color-coding your layers useless.

Q **When I drag items around on my page, they move in short jumps instead of a smooth motion. What's wrong?**

A Chances are that you selected the Snap to Document Grid option from the View menu. Remember that this option causes objects to snap to the grid even when the grid isn't visible. To correct the problem, disable this option from the View menu.

Q **When I copied and pasted an object from one document to another, I had Paste Remembers Layers selected in the new document, but the object still pasted into the target layer. What went wrong?**

A Remember that when copying (or cutting) and pasting between two InDesign documents, it's the Paste Remembers Layers setting in the originating document that controls the operation.

Q **How many layers can I have in a document?**

A Theoretically, you can have as many as you want. However, there are two limiting factors. First, each new layer requires additional system memory. Therefore, you can run out of memory trying to add too many layers. Also, because you have only 20 layer colors to choose from, having more than 20 layers defeats the purpose of using different colors. However, the chances needing anywhere close to 20 layers is *very* slim.

Quiz

1. Ruler guides do which of the following?

    a. Help control the flow of text.

    b. Override column guides in terms of flowing text.

    c. Have no impact on the flow of text.

2. When you create column guides, you can do which of the following?

    a. Move pairs independently of each other.

    b. Move all the pairs at the same time.

    c. Never move pairs without going back to the Margins and Columns command.

3. What's the optimum spacing for baseline rules?

    a. The same as the most common font size in the document.

    b. The same as the most common leading in the document.

    c. It doesn't really matter.

4. The Layout Adjustment feature can adjust which of the following?

    a. The size of graphical elements.

    b. The positions of page elements.

    c. Both a and b.

Quiz Answers

1. c. Although you can use the Create Guides command to make what *appear to be* columns from ruler guides, these columns have no effect on text flow.

2. a. When you first create column guides, they're evenly spaced across the page. However, you can reposition each pair any way you want.

3. b. When the baseline grid and the leading are the same, it's easy to align two columns of text by aligning any two text lines.

4. c. Layout Adjustment has the potential to affect both the size and position of graphical objects and page elements.

Exercises

I hate to sound like a broken record (if anyone in this age of CDs remembers what a broken record sounds like), but just like the techniques you learned in Hour 4, you can master the techniques learned this hour only through extensive experimentation. Practice creating and editing margins and guides. Experiment with column guides and creating layers. Draw simple objects on different layers and experiment with cutting and pasting them from layer to layer.

If you plan to do a lot of document repurposing, you should pay particular attention to the Layout Adjustment feature. Try making some extreme adjustments with Layout Adjustment enabled and see what happens. Such practice will better prepare you when you have Layout Adjustment enabled in a real production environment.

5

PART II
Working with Text

Hour

HOUR 6

Creating Text

When you think of page layout software, you probably think of electronic typesetting—making the text look pretty. But before you can make text look pretty, you obviously need to get that text into your page layout software. That's what this hour is all about.

During this hour, you'll learn:

- How to create and manipulate text frames
- How to thread text through multiple frames
- How to add text to your documents
- How to insert special characters into your text
- How to use word-processor-like features such as spell checking and find and replace
- How to automatically number pages and sections

Learning Text Frame Basics

All editable text in your InDesign documents must be contained in a text frame. Stated another way, a text frame is simply a container into which you can place text. There are four ways to create text frames with InDesign:

- By including master frames on your master pages
- By creating a new frame with the Text tool
- By creating a new frame while flowing text
- By auto-creating a new frame while importing text from another application

No matter how you create a text frame, it works the same way as any other text frame. When text frames are not selected on your page, they appear as simple (non-printing) boxes so you know where they are. After you click a text frame, it takes on an appearance similar to the one shown in Figure 6.1.

FIGURE 6.1

A selected text frame includes handles and borders.

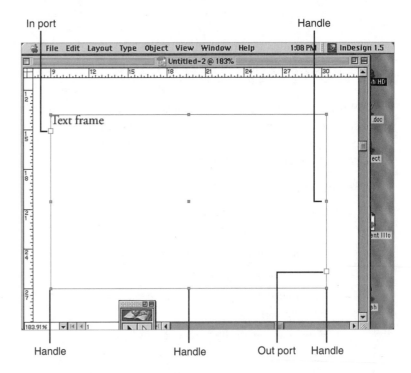

First, notice that a selected text frame includes eight handles. You can use these handles to resize the text frame just as you resize objects in any other application.

The two items that might be unfamiliar are the *in port* and *out port* boxes. The in port is the box near the upper-left corner of the text frame, and the out port is the box near the lower-right corner of the text frame. These ports help you identify and control *text threading* (which you'll learn more about later this hour). For now, here's what you need to know about threading and its relationship with the in and out ports:

- Text threading involves making continuous text flow from one frame to another.

- Continuous text that occupies one or more frames is called a *story*.

- If the in port contains a tiny right arrow, text is threading into that frame from some other frame.

- If the in port is empty, that frame represents the start of the story.

- If the out port contains a tiny right arrow, text is threading out of that frame into some other frame.

- If the out port is empty, that frame represents the end of the story.

- If the out port is red and contains a tiny plus sign (+), the story continues beyond the physical boundaries of the frame, but has not been threaded into another frame. In other words, you can't currently see the end of the story.

- If you get confused by multiple stories threaded to various frames, select the Show Text Threads option from the View menu. This option enables you to see the complete flow of any story when you click any of its text frames.

Text Frames and Master Pages

The easiest way to create a text frame is to have InDesign create it for you as you're opening a new document. However, before you continue, be sure that you remember certain concepts from previous lessons. First, in Hour 3, "Creating, Saving, and Opening Documents," you learned about the Master Text Frame option when you create a new document. This is where that option comes into play. In Hour 4, "Managing Pages," you also learned about *master overrides*—another important concept for this lesson. Be sure to review those hours if you don't feel comfortable with those concepts yet.

6

After you've created a text frame, you can select the Text tool, click in the text frame, and start typing just as you would in a word processor. However, if you used the Master Text Frame option when you created your document, there's one extra step. The reason for this step is that using this option simply creates text frames on the master; these text frames are not directly accessible from your document page.

To use the master text frame, you need to apply the same technique described for master overrides. In other words, you need to actually move that text frame from the master to your document page. This should make more sense when you try a little experiment, as follows.

To Do: Moving a Master Text Frame

To move a master text frame, do the following:

1. Create a new document, making sure to check the Master Text Frame option.

2. With the selection tool, click anywhere within the page margins. Note that nothing becomes selected.

3. Next, using the Text tool, click (but don't drag) anywhere within the page margins. Note again that nothing happens.

4. Now using the selection tool again, press Ctrl+Shift (in Windows) or Command+Shift (on the Mac) and click anywhere within the page margins. Suddenly a text frame appears.

5. Finally, using the Text tool, click anywhere in the text frame and start typing.

What you've done here, as stated earlier, is move the master text frame from the master to the current page.

>
>
> Even if you have two facing pages in a spread, this action affects only one page at a time. If you want to use the master frame on both pages in a spread, you have to repeat the process for each page.

Creating New Text Frames

As you learned earlier this hour, if you click an existing text frame using the Text tool, a cursor appears in the frame and you can start typing and editing. You can also use the Text tool to create a new text frame wherever you need one. To do this, simply click and drag the Text tool anywhere on the document page to define the boundaries of your text frame.

> The one exception when creating text frames is that you can't create a text frame inside another text frame. If you click and drag within an existing text frame, you'll simply select the text in that frame, just as you would when clicking and dragging in your word processor. However, you can create a new text frame elsewhere in the page, then cut and paste it into a previously existing text frame.

Frames and Threading

Suppose your story is bigger than your text frame. In other words, the out port on your text frame has a red plus sign on it. Then what? No problem. Your next step depends on whether you've already created another frame into which you want the text to flow.

To Do: Threading Text Into a New Frame

Let's create some text frames and thread some text throughout them. This will also be a good way of also introducing a new feature added in version 1.5—Fill With Placeholder Text.

So, to thread text from one frame to another, do the following:

1. Create a new document. The default size and margins will be fine.

2. Select the Text tool from the Tools palette and, as you just learned, drag out a text frame anywhere on the page.

3. After you release the mouse, you should have a frame and an insertion point. At this stage, you could start typing, or you could place some text that existed in a word processing or text file. But, for this exercise, we're going to use what is known as "greek" text.

> Despite its name, "greek" text is not actual Greek (it's vaguely Latin, but let's not go there…). It is simply nonsensical text that designers often use when creating sample designs without having actual text on hand. Oh, sure, you could make up some text (which could be fun, admittedly) but time is money. InDesign now has a feature that automatically streams in nonsense greek text to a text frame.

So, under the Type menu, select the Fill With Placeholder Text command. Your text frame should now be filled with text, not unlike Figure 6.2.

4. Now, you'll notice that the greek text fills the frame exactly. (It's easy to precisely fill a frame with placeholder text. Actual text requires more noodling and copyfitting, but we'll save that for the next hour, "Basic Typesetting with InDesign.") To see how threading works, select the Selection Tool from the Tools palette and click anywhere in the frame to select it.

5. Click the text frame handle at the bottom center of the frame, and drag it up to the center of the text frame, and release. There should now be a red "+" in the out port, indicating that there is more text than the frame can hold (see Figure 6.3).

6

FIGURE 6.2

A text frame filled with placeholder text.

Lorper adip endreetum velis niamcorem vulputpat.
Lore doloborti iscidunt ulputem verci blandrem ing euipsum incipis nosto
do core tatum iriure del doloboreet wissi exercipsum zzrilit, velit praesto
odo del et luptatio od doleniam velit ip exerat. Ut lamet nibh ea faci
blandre veliscill mconummy nibh el ex et, veliquatue molorero odolorting
ercilit at atis adiamet dipit ute magnim zzriliquisl eugiatie enim ver in
vulputet praesequam dolut at.
Lorperil el ulla cor susto odipisl irit nim dolenit doloret alissis nonul-
putem zzril ing euiscidunt wis nonsequi esent ullam quam ver at, vul-
landit nullandipisim dunt ver at alit, consed eugiamcor susto core delenit
vero conullut am, cor senis ad tationulputpatie mod tem deliquamconum
quissi.
Duip eum dolor summodit pratio ero do ex enis ea facilis accumsandigna
commolore do ea feu feu feugiam, commodolum ex ex elit prate min

FIGURE 6.3

After resizing our text frame, all the text no longer fits.

Lorper adip endreetum velis niamcorem vulputpat.
Lore doloborti iscidunt ulputem verci blandrem ing euipsum incipis nosto
do core tatum iriure del doloboreet wissi exercipsum zzrilit, velit praesto
odo del et luptatio od doleniam velit ip exerat. Ut lamet nibh ea faci
blandre veliscill mconummy nibh el ex et, veliquatue molorero odolorting
ercilit at atis adiamet dipit ute magnim zzriliquisl eugiatie enim ver in
vulputet praesequam dolut at.

6. We now need to create a new frame to accommodate the rest of the story. So, use the selection tool to click the current frame's out port. The pointer turns into what's called a *loaded text icon*, and looks like a tiny page of text.

> For keyboard shortcut lovers out there, hold the Command (on the Mac) or Ctrl (on Windows) key to temporarily switch to the selection tool without clicking on the Tools palette icon.

7. Now position the cursor anywhere on the page (except over an empty text frame). Click and drag to mark the boundaries of a new text frame. The result should look like Figure 6.4.

   If you click without dragging, you'll still create a new text frame. Its top boundary will be even with the point where you click; its sides and bottom will extend to the page margins.

> Sometimes as you are resizing text frames, you'll inadvertently click the out port and the pointer will change to the loaded text icon, even though you don't want it to. To "unload" the loaded text icon, simply click on the Select Tool in the Tools palette.

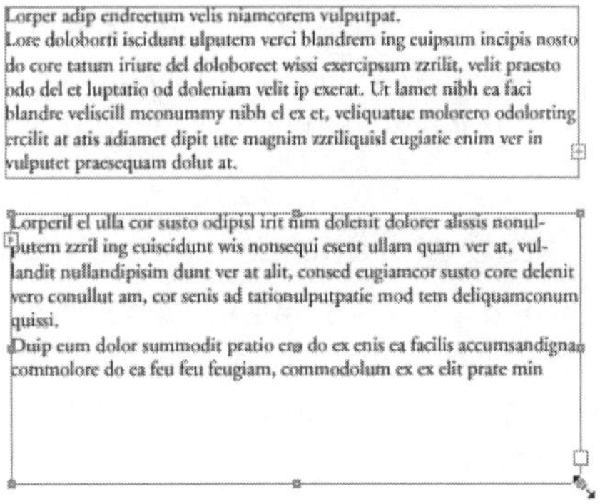

FIGURE 6.4

We have now created a second text frame into which the text from our first frame is continued.

Threading Into an Existing Frame

Another option for your oversized story is to create a new text frame first, and then thread the story into it. To do this, create a text frame as described earlier, but don't type anything into it. Once again, use the selection tool to click the out port of the frame that contains the story. Once again, the pointer changes to the loaded text icon. However, when you move the pointer over your empty frame, it turns into a chain links icon known as the *thread icon*.

When the thread icon appears, click once to thread the story into the new frame.

When you're following these steps, InDesign recognizes any master frames, even if you haven't yet moved the master text frame to your document page. When you move the pointer over a master frame, the thread icon still appears. When you click, the master frame automatically moves to the document page and the story threads into it—all in one easy step.

Threading Options

After you've clicked an out port and the pointer has changed into the loaded text icon, you have two other options for controlling how text flows.

Normally, if the story length exceeds the frame into which it has been threaded, you have to select the second text frame, and click the new out port to "reload" the loaded text icon to continue the threading. However, if you hold down the Alt key (in Windows) or the Option key (on the Mac) while clicking, the loaded text icon remains active when the story exceeds the size of the frame. In other words, you can continue threading without clicking another out port.

6

Holding down the Shift key while clicking goes one step further. If you do so, InDesign creates a new text frame according to any margins and columns you've established, and adds new pages and frames to your document until all the text in the story has been threaded. This is handy when you're importing large text files, as described later this hour.

Creating Frames Ahead of Time

From time to time, you might find yourself in a situation where you need to get going on a project, but a client or copywriter is still working on the text. In this case, you can create empty text frames as placeholders, and even thread them together according to how you expect the text to eventually flow.

To do this, follow the previous procedures for threading text into an existing frame. Even though the out port on the first frame will be empty, you can still click it and thread it into another frame. This will give you a set of empty, linked text frames ready for what-ever text you see fit to deposit into them. At this point, if you select Fill With Placeholder Text from the Type menu, the placeholder text will fill all the linked frames, which is a quick and easy way of generating comps.

Text Frame Options

Like most features in InDesign, you can change certain characteristics of a text frame. To do this, select a text frame and then choose Text Frame Options from the Object menu. (You can also right-click [in Windows] or Ctrl-click [on the Mac] the frame and choose Text Frame Options from the resulting context-sensitive menu.) The Text Frame Options dialog box appears, as shown in Figure 6.5.

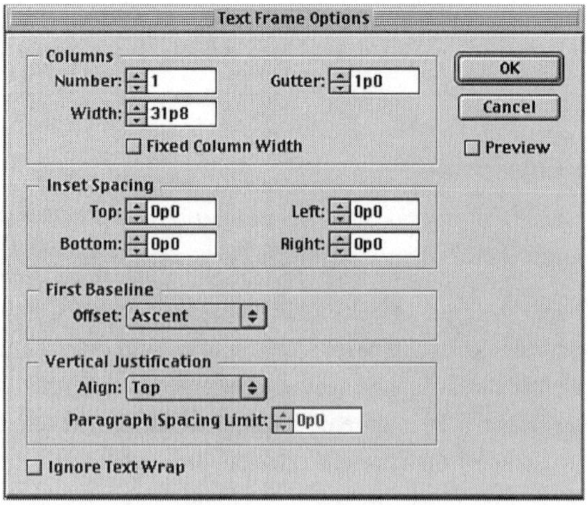

FIGURE 6.5

You can set the text frame options on a frame-by-frame basis.

First, you can create columns within frames, just as you learned to do with pages in Hour 5, "Using Layers and the Layout and Formatting Tools." The one difference here is the Fixed Column Width checkbox. If you leave this box unchecked, columns are automatically resized as you resize the frame. However, if you check this box, InDesign automatically adds or deletes columns as you resize the frame.

You can use the Inset Spacing controls to essentially create outer margins for the frame.

The Offset pull-down menu gives you three options for positioning the baseline of the first line of text in relation to the top of the frame:

- If you choose Ascent (the default), the top of the tallest character will fall slightly below the top of the frame.

- If you choose Cap Height, uppercase letters will touch the top of the frame.

- If you choose Leading, the distance between the top of the frame and the baseline will be equal to the leading for that line of text.

Figure 6.6 illustrates the differences among these Offset options.

FIGURE 6.6

This example shows (from left to right) Ascent, Cap Height, and Leading offsets.

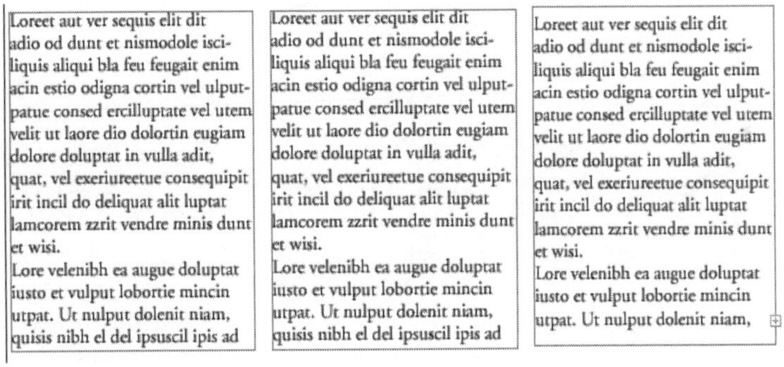

New in version 1.5 is another feature that users of 1.0 clamored for: vertical justification of text within frames. This lets you align your text either at the top of the frame, at the bottom of the frame, in the center of the frame, or "justify" your text vertically from top to bottom. Figure 6.7 illustrates these differences.

There are two more checkboxes in this dialog box. If you check the Ignore Text Wrap checkbox, text in that frame ignores the text-wrapping settings for any graphic it encounters. (You'll learn about text wrapping in Hour 11, "Combining Text and Graphics.") The Preview checkbox enables you to see the results of your changes before you accept them.

6

FIGURE 6.7

This example shows (from left to right) Top, Center, Bottom, and Justify options for vertical justification.

Lore commy nullandip euguerature magna augait augiam, susto odit praesequat wis nissecte conulla feumsandionum ver iurem vel er augue euis ad essit iriure dolup-tat lum iusci blaore facid-unt alit vent vel iuscinisit num irit illum dionsectem venis do esequis

Lore commy nullandip euguerature magna augait augiam, susto odit praesequat wis nissecte conulla feumsandionum ver iurem vel er augue euis ad essit iriure dolup-tat lum iusci blaore facid-unt alit vent vel iuscinisit num irit illum dionsectem venis do esequis

Lore commy nullandip euguerature magna augait augiam, susto odit praesequat wis nissecte conulla feumsandionum ver iurem vel er augue euis ad essit iriure dolup-tat lum iusci blaore facid-unt alit vent vel iuscinisit num irit illum dionsectem venis do esequis

Lore commy nullandip euguerature magna augait augiam, susto odit praesequat wis nissecte conulla feumsandionum ver iurem vel er augue euis ad essit iriure dolup-tat lum iusci blaore facid-unt alit vent vel iuscinisit num irit illum dionsectem venis do esequis

Removing a Frame from a Thread

You can remove a frame from a thread in two ways, depending on your intended out-come. If you want to completely remove the frame, just delete it. Although doing so deletes the frame, the story itself is unharmed. Text in the deleted frame flows into the next frame in that thread, or, if there is no frame after the deleted one, it is stored unseen in the previous frame, and that frame will have a red "+" in the out port, indicating that there is more text available.

Unthreading two frames is nearly as easy as deleting a frame from a thread. Simply double-click the out port of the first frame to unthread it.

Be particularly careful when your story threads through more than two frames. Double-clicking the out port causes the link between the clicked frame and all subsequent frames to be broken.

For example, suppose a story is threaded through three frames. If you unthread frames 1 and 2, the story is also removed from frame 3, and the empty frames 2 and 3 remain threaded together.

Importing Text from Other Applications

Although you can create all your text within InDesign, the program was designed with the thought that you're more likely to do your writing in some other application (such as a word processor) and then bring it into InDesign for layout. InDesign provides three ways to import text—you can use the Place command from the File menu, or you can employ either of two drag-and-drop methods.

The Place Command

Before I describe the particulars of the Place command, I need to explain exactly where your "placed" or imported text will appear. If you position the text cursor in a text frame when you use this command, the imported text is inserted where the cursor is positioned. If you're not in typing mode, so to speak, importing a text document turns the pointer into a loaded text icon, at which point you can click and drag to create a new frame for your text.

When you choose Place from the File menu, you see the Place dialog box, shown in Figure 6.8.

FIGURE 6.8

Select the file you want to import.

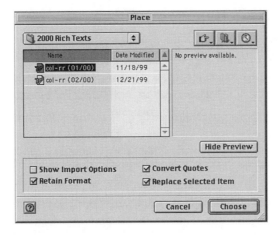

For the most part, this dialog box works just like an Open dialog box in any other application. However, you do have a couple of options.

Checking the Convert Quotes checkbox converts any straight quotes and apostrophes to typographer's (curly) quotes and apostrophes. Checking the Retain Format checkbox retains the formatting specified in the original document.

Show Import Options is the most important checkbox in this dialog box. If you check this box and then click Choose (on the Mac) or Open (in Windows), InDesign displays another checkbox with additional options unique to the specific type of document you're importing. In other words, you'll see one set of options when you import a Word file, and a different set when you import a text file. It's a good idea to become familiar with the options of whatever type of document you're most likely to import.

6

Drag and Drop

When you have a document open in another application that supports drag and drop (such as Microsoft Word), you can select a range of text and drag it right into your InDesign document. When you do so, InDesign creates a new text frame to hold the text.

However, if you want to drag and drop an entire document, you can drag that document into InDesign directly from its folder or directory. This enables you to have slightly better control over where the dragged document ends up.

To Do: Drag a Text File into InDesign

To drag and drop an entire document into InDesign, do the following:

1. Find a suitable text or word processing file on your hard disk. It can be any Word document up to Word 97/98, a generic text file, or something similar. (If you have no such file, you can just follow along.)

2. Open the folder that contains the file using My Computer (in Windows) or the Finder (on the Mac). Then, with an open, blank InDesign document visible in the background, drag and drop the document's icon over any point on the InDesign page.

The reason this method gives you a little better control is that you can create a frame in advance and if you drag the document over that empty text frame, the text is imported into it. If you drag the document anywhere else on the page, InDesign creates a new frame, just like when you drag and drop from an open document.

Inserting Special Characters

A *special character* is any text character that you can't insert by pressing a single key on your keyboard. Examples include bullet characters (•) and trademark symbols (×). InDesign gives you three ways to create these characters. In any case, the text cursor needs to be active in a text frame. In other words, you need to be at a point where you're ready to type the character.

The slowest way to insert special characters is to choose Insert Character from the Type menu. This pops up the Insert Character dialog box, shown in Figure 6.9.

The Insert Character dialog box shows a scrollable chart of all the characters available in any font and style. To insert one of these characters, click it, and then click the Insert button. You can make the characters in the chart larger or smaller by using the two buttons in the lower-right corner of the dialog box. When you're through, click Done.

FIGURE **6.9**

You can insert any character available in the selected font.

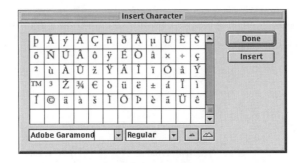

A quicker way to do this is to right-click (in Windows) or Ctrl-click (on the Mac) the point in the text frame where you want the character to appear. From the resulting context-sensitive menu, choose Insert Special Character. This displays a submenu, as shown in Figure 6.10.

FIGURE **6.10**

You can choose from a list of common special characters.

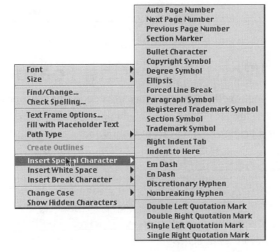

From here, just click the character you want to insert.

Now for the quickest way. Although special characters don't have single-key assignments on your keyboard, many of the most common ones are available through keyboard combinations. If you find yourself inserting special characters on a regular basis, it pays to learn the appropriate keyboard combinations.

Table 6.1 shows my top-10 list of common special characters and their keyboard combinations. If you're a Windows user, note that the keyboard combinations containing numbers require you to hold down the Alt key until you've typed all the numbers for that character. You also must use the numeric keypad to type those numbers.

6

TABLE 6.1   Keyboard Combinations for Special Characters

Character	Windows	Mac
Bullet	Alt+8	Option+8
Trademark	Alt+2	Option+2
Registered trademark	Alt+0174	Option+R
Copyright	Alt+0169	Option+G
Ellipsis	Alt+semicolon	Option+semicolon
Cent sign	Alt+0162	Option+4
Degree sign	Alt+0176	Shift+Option+8
Em dash	Shift+Alt+hyphen	Shift+Option+hyphen
En dash	Alt+hyphen	Option+hyphen
Plus or minus (±)	Alt+(0177)	Shift+Option+equals sign
Division sign (÷)	Alt+(0247)	Option+slash

InDesign's Word Processing Features

As I've already mentioned, InDesign is not intended to be your primary tool for creating new text. However, the program does include both a spellchecker and a find-and-replace feature. They aren't much different from similar features in your favorite word processor.

Using the Spellchecker

To check your spelling, choose Check Spelling from the Edit menu. (If the text cursor is active in a text frame, you can also right-click [in Windows] or Ctrl-click [on the Mac] and choose Check Spelling from the contextual menu.) You'll see the Check Spelling dialog box, shown in Figure 6.11.

With the exception of the Search pull-down menu, there's nothing especially noteworthy about InDesign's spellchecker. If you've spell checked a word processing document, you know just about all you need to know.

You use the Search pull-down menu to specify the range of text that InDesign should check. The reason this menu can get tricky is that the options that appear in this pull-down menu change according to the text you selected when you start the spellchecker. First I'll give you the possible scenarios, and then I'll give you the options to which each scenario applies.

*The spellchecker is
pretty standard fare.
Some choices, as in
all spellcheckers, are
kind of amusing.*

You can start the spellchecker with any of the following:

- Nothing selected
- A single frame selected
- Multiple frames containing multiple stories selected
- The insertion point active in a text frame
- A range of text selected in a text frame

Here are the options you might see in the Search pull-down menu. Note that not all of these options are available in every situation. It depends on what text you have selected.

- Document—Checks all stories in the active document
- All Documents—Checks all stories in all open documents
- Story—Checks the selected story, if indeed a text frame has been selected
- Stories—Checks stories associated with all selected frames
- To End of Story—Checks the selected story starting where the text cursor is positioned
- Selection—Checks the selected text

If the spellchecker comes across a word that InDesign doesn't identify but you know is a legitimate word—this happens often in technical documents, or documents with proper names—you can add that word to the dictionary. InDesign doesn't have the best way of handling this. Essentially you click the Add button, which brings up the Dictionary dialog box. You then need to hit Add again to add the word to the dictionary. Then hit Done, and then hit Ignore back in the main pane of the spellchecker. It's functional but a tad unwieldy. See Figure 6.12.

6

FIGURE 6.12
There are a bit too many steps to go through to add a word to the dictionary.

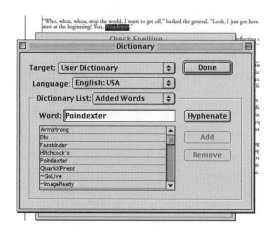

Using Find and Replace

To find and replace any text in your document, choose Find/Change from the Edit menu. (If the text cursor is active in a text frame, you can also right-click (in Windows) or Ctrl-click (on the Mac) and choose Find/Change from the contextual menu.) Doing so displays the Find/Change dialog box, shown in Figure 6.13.

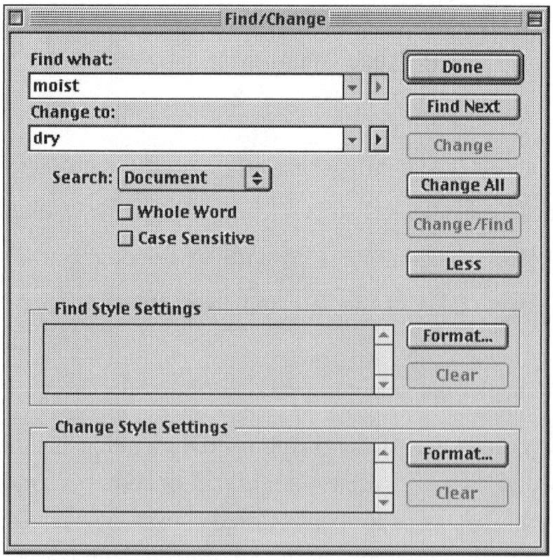

FIGURE 6.13
You have many options for finding and changing text.

This feature works pretty much like the corresponding feature in a word processor.

You can use the pull-down menus to the immediate right of the Find What and Change To fields (the ones with the down arrows) to display text you've previously typed in either of those fields.

If your Find/Change operation involves special characters, typing them in can prove to be a real hassle. Instead, you can use the other pull-down menus a little further to the right (the ones with the right arrows) to access all the special characters shown in the special character contextual menu.

The Search pull-down menu here works just like the one found in the spellchecker. The Whole Word and Case Sensitive checkboxes work just like those found in word processors.

Clicking the More button brings up more options, seen at the bottom of Figure 6.13 above. Click either Format button and you're presented with a new dialog box containing a wide variety of options. Another pull-down menu breaks these up into several categories. You can also search and replace basic Character Formats.

When you're done specifying any options in this dialog box, click OK to return to the previous dialog box. Any changes you made are reflected in the appropriate Settings field. To clear any changes, click the appropriate Clear button.

Automatic Page and Section Numbering

InDesign enables you to automatically number document pages, and then goes one better by enabling you to perform custom section numbering within your document.

Page Numbering

Automatically creating a visible page number on each page in your document is a simple task. With the text cursor active in a text frame, right-click (in Windows) or Ctrl-click (on the Mac) and choose Auto Page Numbering from the Insert Special Character submenu.

Most of the time, it's best to do this on a master page so that the numbering appears on all pages associated with the master. When you do this on a master, InDesign inserts an A as a marker on a left master and a B as a marker on a right master.

You can also do this on a document page if you need to add the current page number in a specific location. In this case, you'll see the actual page number. And if the true page number changes, so does the visible number on the page.

6

After you add a page number, you can modify its appearance (font, style, and so on) using procedures you'll learn during Hour 7, "Basic Typesetting with InDesign." You can also change the numbering format (such as to Roman numerals) using the section numbering technique that you're about to learn.

Section Numbering

Word processors force you to start page numbering at a certain point and continue through to the end. However, the documents you create might not conform to that limitation. For example, it's not uncommon to see the front matter in a document numbered using lowercase Roman numerals, and then have the primary content begin at page 1. InDesign enables you to do just that by creating unique sections within your document.

By design, all documents contain at least one section. Any page that begins a new section is marked in the Pages palette by a small black arrow, as shown in Figure 6.14.

FIGURE 6.14

A black arrow marks the start of each new section.

New section indicator

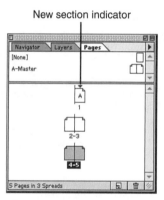

To Do: Creating a New Section

To create a new section, do the following:

1. Create a new document in InDesign. Default size and margins are fine. Give it, say, five pages.

2. Open the Pages palette by hitting F7, or selecting Window, Pages.

3. Select any page in the Pages palette—except one that already starts a section. Let's make it page 4. Choose Section Options from the Pages palette menu. This displays the Section Options dialog box, shown in Figure 6.15.

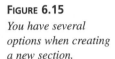

FIGURE 6.15

*You have several
options when creating
a new section.*

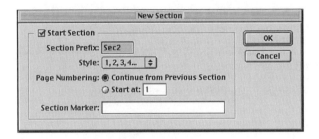

4. First, make sure Start Section is checked. If it's not, you'll simply be making changes to the current section instead of creating a new one.

5. The Section Prefix box serves a purpose similar to the master prefix. The Section Prefix appears along with the current page number near the lower-left corner of the document screen, and also appears when you move the mouse over the black section arrow in the Pages palette. The prefix can be up to five characters long, with no spaces or punctuation. You can leave the prefix as is, or give it something a bit more to your liking. You make the call.

6. The Style pull-down menu enables you to format any automatically generated page numbers as regular numbers, upper- or lowercase Roman numerals, or upper- or lowercase letters. Just for fun, select lowercase Roman numerals.

7. The Page Numbering radio buttons enable you to either continue numbering based on the previous section, or restart numbering with any number you specify. Click on Start at 1.

8. Remember how you insert a page number by making a selection from the Insert Special Character contextual submenu? If you type any text into the Section Marker field, you can automatically make that text appear anywhere you want using a similar technique. The only difference is that instead of choosing Automatic Page numbering from the submenu, you choose Section Marker. Most of the time, you'll probably use section markers and automatic page numbering together on master pages. For now, leave it blank.

9. When you're done, click OK.

You should immediately see the changes in your pages palette. For starters, you'll notice that there is now a black arrow over the former 4. And since it is now page i, it is a standalone righthand page.

6

If you ever need to change any of these section attributes, you can do one of two things:

- Select any page in that section in the Pages palette and then choose Section Options from the Pages palette menu.

- Double-click the black arrow in the Pages palette that marks the start of the section.

Either of these actions will redisplay this dialog box.

When you're making changes to section attributes, make sure the Start Section checkbox is *not* checked. Otherwise, you'll start a new section instead of making changes to the old one.

Summary

InDesign wasn't designed as a text-creation tool. However, the program gives you many options for bringing in text from other programs. After you get that text into your InDesign document, there's no end to what you can do with it.

Workshop

Text frames and threading might seem complicated at first glance. However, after you've used them a little, flowing text around your document will become second nature. The goal of this workshop section is to make you more comfortable with these procedures.

Q&A

Q When I try to enter text on a right master, the cursor jumps over to the left master. What's wrong?

A There's nothing really wrong. When you created the document, you selected the Master Text Frame option. Although these frames are treated separately on document pages, they're threaded together on the master. If you need to type text into the right master frame, just unthread the two frames.

Q Can I use drag and drop to insert text into the middle of an existing story?

A Unfortunately, no. If you need to insert an entire document, use the Place command. Otherwise, you can use the standard copy-and-paste procedures.

Q Are there keyboard combinations for other special characters?

A Yes. I included only the most common special characters. A more complete list is available on the Quick Reference Card located in the front of the book.

Q **How can I change the page numbering style if my document doesn't use sections?**

A Every document contains at least one section, even if you don't define any. That means you can use the procedures you already learned for changing section attributes to change the numbering style for your whole document.

Quiz

1. All InDesign text is contained in a text frame.

   a. True

   b. False

   c. Most of the time

2. What are the in and out ports?

   a. Small buttons that control where imported text is placed

   b. Small buttons that help you control the threading of text

   c. Menu commands that control the threading of text

3. What options exist when importing a file from another program?

   a. There are none.

   b. You can control the conversion of curly quotes and document formatting.

   c. It depends on what type of document you're importing.

4. Where can you put an automatic page number?

   a. Only on a master page

   b. Anywhere

   c. Only on a document page

Quiz Answers

1. a. This is true. If you want to get technical, text that's part of a graphic doesn't need to be in a *text* frame. However, for all practical purposes, this statement is true.

2. b. The in and out ports enable you to easily thread a story from one text frame to another.

3. c. As long as you check the Show Import Options checkbox, InDesign presents you with options based on the type of document you're importing.

4. b. Although it's most common to put a page marker on a master, you can put one anywhere.

6

Exercises

Start by importing one of your existing word processing documents into an empty InDesign document. Import your files in several ways: using the Place command (and be sure to check out all your import options), dragging and dropping highlighted text, and dragging and dropping document files right onto an InDesign page. Start with a single frame, and create additional frames on successive pages in which to thread your story.

Be sure to try out various text frame options. Duplicate the same frame on a single page (as we did earlier in this hour), and apply different vertical justification and baseline options.

And while you're experimenting, make sure you're using the Show Text Threads option. That way you can really see exactly what's going as you take various actions.

HOUR 7

Basic Typesetting with InDesign

Getting text onto a page is one thing. Getting it to look pretty—via typesetting—is quite another. Nearly all InDesign's typesetting tools are available from two palettes. One is the Character palette, and the other is the Character Styles palette. Thus, mastering the basics of InDesign typesetting is really a matter of mastering these two palettes.

During this hour, you learn:

- How to select fonts and type styles
- How to change font size and leading
- How to adjust kerning and tracking
- How to scale type
- How to skew type
- How to create baseline shifts
- How to change the language for spelling and hyphenation
- How to use the Character palette menu
- How to create and use character styles

The Character Palette

You can make most of your typesetting choices using the Character palette, which is accessed under the Type menu, or by hitting Command+T (on the Macintosh) or Ctrl+T (in Windows). The Character palette is shown in Figure 7.1. It shows what each of the items in the Character palette does.

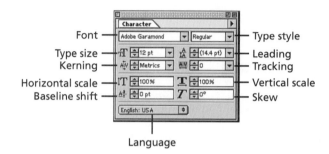

You can view the Character palette any time the Text tool is active and the text cursor is active in a text box. You can also view this palette using the Selection tool, in which case you'll see the default type settings for the current document. You can, at that point, change those default settings.

Character Basics

The four most basic attributes of type are the font family (such as Adobe Caslon), the type style (such as semi-bold), the size (such as 14 pts.), and the leading (or space between lines). As you might expect, InDesign provides you with more than one way to specify any of these type characteristics.

Fonts and Type Styles

The most straightforward way to select a font family is to click the Font pull-down menu in the Character palette. However, as shown in Figure 7.2, if you have a lot of fonts installed on your computer, this can make for a lot of scrolling.

To select a font, you can scroll through this list and click the font you want. This is useful when you're not quite sure which font you want and you need to see the complete list.

FIGURE 7.2

Too many fonts make for too much scrolling.

✓   Adobe Garamond
AdobeCaslon
Arial
Arial MT
Bookman BT
Charcoal
Chicago
Copperplate Gothic BT
Courier
Courier New
Dorchester Script MT
Franklin Gothic BT
FranklinGothic
Garamond
Geneva
Helvetica
ITC Bookman BT
ITC Franklin Gothic BT
ITC Friz Quadrata BT
ITC Garamond BT
ITC Korinna
ITC Zapf Dingbats
Monaco
New York
Palatino
Star Trek Next BT
Swiss 721 BT
Symbol
Tekton Pro
Times
Times New Roman PS

If you work with a lot of fonts, you may want to think about investing in a font management program, which will allow you to activate and deactivate fonts on-the-fly. You can customize font sets for different jobs and only activate those that you need at any one time. Common font management programs include Suitcase from Extensis (www.extensis.com), Adobe Type Manager Deluxe from Adobe (www.adobe.com), and my personal favorite, (Macintosh only) Font Reserve from DiamondSoft (www.fontreserve.com).

However, if you already know the name of the desired font, there's an easier way. Simply double-click the first word in the font name and then start typing the name of the new font. As you type, InDesign automatically fills in the name of the font. The more characters you type, the more InDesign narrows the search down. For example, to use Adobe Garamond, you might have to type **adobe g** to get past Adobe Caslon. This same technique works for specifying the type style.

You can also scroll through the list of fonts by clicking in the font field and using the up and down arrow keys.

When you change the font from the Character palette, there's a chance that the font won't match the type style. For example, suppose the font starts out as Adobe Garamond and the type style starts out as semibold. Then you change the font to Arial. There's no such thing as Arial semibold.

7

The good news is that InDesign spots these problems for you. The program puts invalid type styles in brackets, so it's easy to see that there is no such thing as Arial Semibold. On the page, the invalid style will be indicated by red highlighting.

One way to select both the font and the type style at the same time is to choose Font from the Type menu. When you do so, you see a complete list of all available fonts, with their available type styles shown as submenus. However, as you can see from Figure 7.3, depending on the name of the font, you can have plenty of menus to navigate through.

FIGURE 7.3

Lots of fonts mean lots of menus.

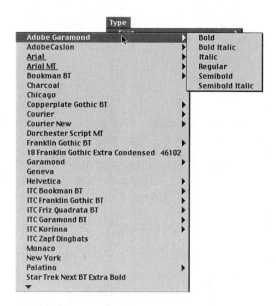

One great feature—actually, it's a great lack of a feature—in InDesign is that you don't have the ability to create "false" italics and bolds from a Style menu or palette. For example, in Word—or even in other layout programs such as QuarkXPress and PageMaker—you could select a font, then simply click on a Bold or Italic button and your type would be boldfaced and/or italicized. When you did this, the program simply made type strokes thicker (in the case of bold) or slanted (in the case of italic), and was different than the "real" bolds and italics that came with the font. Using "faux" bolds and italics was always a bad idea, especially because when you sent a file to a service bureau, any type styles applied in that way rarely output properly. Fortunately, InDesign only lets you apply the real styles that are provided with the font.

Sizing and Leading

InDesign offers you four ways to change the type size. You can:

- Select a type size from the pull-down menu in the Character palette.
- Double-click the current type size in the Character palette and type a new value. You can specify anywhere from .1 to 1296 points, in .001-point increments.
- Select Size from the type menu, which gives you the same options as the pull-down menu in the Character palette.
- Right-click (Windows) or Ctrl-click (Mac) the text you're editing and select Size from the contextual menu. Again, this gives you the same options as the pull-down menu in the Character palette.

Selecting Other in any of these size menus simply highlights the current size in the Character palette. As stated previously, just type the value you want.

The term *leading* refers to the amount of vertical space between lines. Leading is measured from baseline to baseline (see Figure 7.4). There are two ways to adjust the leading in InDesign.

FIGURE 7.4

Leading is the amount of vertical space as measured from baseline to baseline.

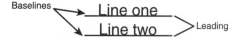

The first way is to select a leading value from the pull-down menu in the Character palette. This pull-down menu presents you with several common leading values, as well as the Auto option. When you select Auto, the leading is set according to the auto-leading percentage value for that paragraph. The default auto-leading value is 120 percent of the type size. You learn how to change that value in Hour 8, "Working with Paragraphs."

The second way to adjust the leading is to double-click the current value in the Character palette and type a new value. This is handy when you're working with unusually small or large type, or any time you need a very precise leading value. You can specify leading from 0 to 5000 points, again in .001-point increments.

Controlling Letter Spacing

There are two ways to control the spacing between letters. First there's *kerning*, which controls the spacing between specific letter pairs. The other is *tracking*, which controls the "tightness" of type across a range of characters.

7

Three Kerning Options

Again, kerning refers to the spacing between letter pairs. For example, the letter combination WA is normally kerned so that if you were to draw a vertical line between the two, you'd see that they overlap. This makes this particular letter combination more pleasing to the eye than if there were a noticeable space between the two.

Fontographers have the ability to put precise kerning pairs into their fonts, and many of them choose to do so. To take advantage of these built-in kerning pairs, Metrics (the default) needs to be selected from the Kerning pull-down menu.

The problem is that quality, including the sophistication of kerning pairs, can vary from font to font. In the old days, if you needed to use a font that included inadequate kerning pairs, you might find yourself spending an inordinate amount of time manually kerning different character pairs.

InDesign largely eliminates the need for manual kerning with a feature called *optical kerning*. Select Optical from the kerning pull-down menu and InDesign will adjust the kerning as best it can, based on the visual appearance of the letters.

To Do: Changing Kern Settings

To see the difference among different kerning options, do the following:

1. Open a blank InDesign document.

2. Select the Type tool and drag out a text frame anywhere on the page.

3. Type "Washington, D.C." This isn't for political reasons; rather, "Wa" is a letter combination that is often a prime candidate for kerning.

4. Select the text you just typed, and copy it. Paste a copy on the next line. Repeat. You should now have "Washington, D.C." written three times.

5. Open the Character palette. With the first "Washington, D.C." selected, make sure that the kern field in the Character palette says Metrics.

6. Select the second line. In the kern field, select Optical.

7. Select the third line. Select "0" (in other words, "none") from the kern field.

Figure 7.5 shows the difference between metrics kerning, optical kerning, and no kerning, from top to bottom. Notice the big gap between the first two letters in the last example. Select all three lines and apply different fonts. See how more or less egregious the gap becomes in different fonts.

FIGURE 7.5

Kerning controls the spacing between letter pairs.

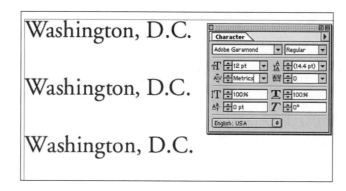

FIGURE 7.5

Kerning controls the spacing between letter pairs.

Of course, if for some reason you need to manually kern a pair of letters, you can do that, too. Simply click the text cursor between the two letters you want to kern and then do any of the following:

- Select a value from the Kerning pull-down menu.
- Double-click the current value and type a new one.
- Press Alt+right/left arrow (Windows) or Option+right/left arrow (Mac).

Kerning is measured in 1/1000th of an em space. An em space is relative to the point size of the type, and is equivalent to that point size. For example, in 14-point type, an em space equals 14 points.

Tracking

At first, the difference between kerning and tracking might not be entirely clear. The key difference is that kerning controls letter spacing by adjusting specific letter pairs. Tracking, on the other hand, applies uniform spacing across a range of text, regardless of any specific letter pairs that might be present. In other words, you can use tracking to control the "tightness" or "looseness" of text.

Like kerning, tracking is measured in 1/1000 em space. And like kerning, you can specify tracking from a pull-down menu, or manually type a value. For most instances, I suggest you leave tracking set to 0. Figure 7.6 shows the same sentence with no tracking, with a tracking value of –10, and with a tracking value of 10, from top to bottom.

FIGURE 7.6

Tracking controls the "tightness" of your type.

I didn't see the giant squid.
I didn't see the giant squid.
I didn't see the giant squid.

7

The amount of tracking will depend on how you think the text looks. If a line or paragraph looks loose and gappy (or tight and dense), then you may want to adjust the tracking accordingly. In magazine publishing, it is not uncommon to adjust the tracking to fit copy in a column, rather than add or cut text. If done judiciously, it is scarcely visible, and no one is any the wiser.

Scaling and Skewing Type

You can customize the look of a range of text by adjusting its horizontal or vertical scale, or by skewing (slanting) it. To do so, simply double-click the appropriate field on the Character palette and type the desired value.

Scaling is measured as a percentage of the current type size, with 100 percent as the true size. You can adjust either the horizontal or vertical scaling anywhere from 1 percent to 1000 percent, in .01 percent increments.

The Skew setting determines the angle of the slant and can be set anywhere from 85 degrees to –85 degrees. Using a positive number slants the text to the left; using a negative number slants the text to the right.

Baseline Shifts

From time to time, you might need to apply a baseline shift to one or more characters. This means moving the character above or below its normal baseline. The most common use of this feature is when you're manually typesetting a fraction. To apply a baseline shift, select the text you want to shift and do one of the following:

- Double-click the current value (normally 0) and type a new one. You can type a value anywhere from –5000 to 5000 points (assuming you haven't changed your units and measurements preferences, as described in Hour 2, "Preparing to Work in InDesign").
- Click the current value and then press the up or down arrow.
- Click the current value, hold down the Shift key, and press the up or down arrow to change the baseline shift in larger increments.

Choosing a Dictionary

In Hour 2, you learned how to specify a default dictionary. Using the Dictionary pull-down menu on the Character palette, you can choose a different dictionary for a selected range of text. This can be useful, for example, if you're creating a document in English, but it has a passage written in French. In this case, you select the French text and then select French from the Dictionary pull-down menu.

The Character Palette Menu

The Character palette menu, shown in Figure 7.7, provides various other options.

FIGURE 7.7

You have a few more options for fine-tuning your type.

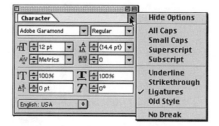

The first option controls how the Character palette is displayed. Selecting Hide Options hides everything to the below the kerning and tracking controls. When those items are hidden, this menu option becomes Show Options.

The other menu options affect selected text as follows:

- All Caps changes all selected text to uppercase.

- Small Caps changes the selected text to the look of uppercase, but the size of lowercase. If a font includes its own "small cap" characters, InDesign uses them. Otherwise, the program creates small caps based on that font's uppercase characters.

- Superscript and Subscript create those types of characters, respectively.

- Underline and Strikethrough perform the obvious styling functions.

- Ligatures controls whether InDesign uses ligatures for certain letter pairs. A ligature is two or more typographic characters designed as a single, distinct unit for reasons of aesthetics. In InDesign, each character in the ligature is fully editable, yet prints as if it were a single character. The top row in Figure 7.8 shows two common ligatures—"fi" and "fl"—and the bottom row shows what they look like if the Ligatures command is deactivated. The Ligatures option is selected by default.

- If you're using an OpenType font, selecting Old Style causes numerals to be displayed slightly descended.

- No Break means the selected text won't break at the end of a line. For example, if my name were something like Richard Von Hindenberg or Dennis Staten Island, I could set it so that the two words comprising my last name did not break at the end of a line.

7

FIGURE 7.8
Two common ligatures.

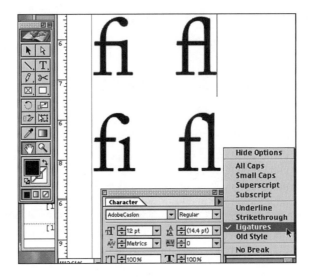

Character Styles

Suppose that you're working on a project for a company that always wants its name to appear in Helvetica bold-italic. Normally, this is a lot of work for a relatively useless effect. But the customer's always right, right?

To make short order of this sort of thing, InDesign lets you create character styles. A *character style* is simply a collection of user-defined text attributes that you can apply to selected text in one mouse-click or keystroke.

You work with character styles in the Character Styles palette, which shares space with the Paragraph Styles and Swatches palettes (see Figure 7.9). To display the Character Styles palette, select Character Styles from the Type menu, or press Shift+F11.

FIGURE 7.9
You control character styles from this palette.

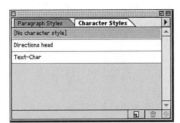

To Do: Creating Character Styles

To create a new character style, do the following:

1. Open a blank InDesign document, if you do not have one open already.

2. Open the Character Styles palette by going to Type, Character Styles or hitting Shift+F11.

3. Either click the New Character Style button in the lower-right corner of the Character Styles palette and then double-click the new style when it appears in the list, or select New Style from the Character Styles palette menu. In either case, you're presented with a dialog box like the one shown in Figure 7.10.

FIGURE 7.10

The New Character Style dialog box.

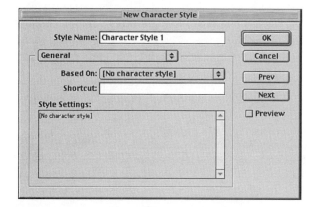

In this opening box, you can name your new style. For example, if you are creating this style to apply to a corporate logo, you can name it "Logo." So give it a distinctive name. You can also base a style on a previous style. For example, if this new style is simply a bold version of another character style, you can base the style on the older one. This will apply all the specifications of the previous style to the new one, and you can simply change those specs you want different—in this case, make it bold.

You can also add a keyboard shortcut to the style, if it is a style you think you'll be using a lot.

When you're assigning a shortcut to a character style, it's easy to confuse yourself. For example, in Windows, holding down the Ctrl key and pressing 0 (zero) on the regular keyboard causes the view to change to Fit Page in Windows. However, you can also assign Ctrl+(keypad zero) to a style. Whenever possible, try to avoid these types of shortcut combinations.

▼

7

▼   4. Click the Next button, or select Basic Character Formats from the pop-up menu.
       You'll see a dialog box like that in Figure 7.11.

FIGURE 7.11

*The Basic Character
Formats options in the
New Character Style
dialog box.*

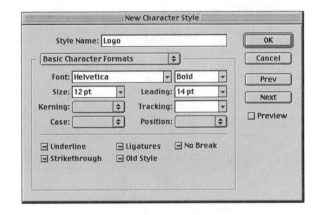

5. Enter the type specs you want. For example, in this case, we made it Helvetica
   Bold, with a point size of 12 and 14 points of leading. Add any other options
   you'd like.

6. Click Next or select Advanced Character Formats from the pop-up menu. You'll
   get the Advanced Character Formats options (see Figure 7.12).

FIGURE 7.12

*The Advanced
Character Formats
options in the New
Character Style
dialog box.*

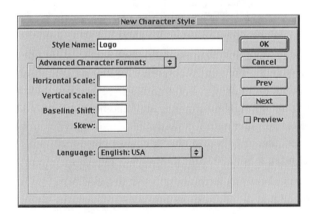

Here is where you can add any horizontal and/or vertical scaling, baseline shifts, or
skewing to your character style. You can also select your default dictionary in this
dialog box. So, change any of these settings that you wish.

7. Click Next or select Character Color from the pop-up menu. You'll get the
▼   Character Color options as seen in Figure 7.13.

FIGURE 7.13

The Character Color options in the New Character Style dialog box.

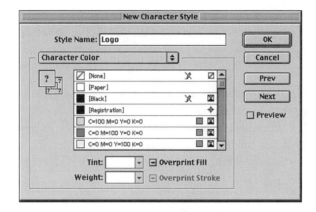

This is where you can change the color of text, if you would like. For example, you may need to use a corporate logo color, if this style is in fact designed to be used for a logo. We'll cover this in more detail in Hour 13, "Simple Coloring with InDesign."

8. When you're done defining your new character style, you can click the Preview checkbox to see the results. You can use the Prev and Next buttons (or the pop-up menu) to scroll through the dialog boxes we were just in and make any further changes. When you're done, click OK.

To edit an existing style, either double-click it in the Character Styles palette, or select Style Options from the Character Styles palette menu.

Other Character Style Options

Some of the options in the Character Styles palette menu (shown in Figure 7.14) are obvious—for example, Delete Styles. Others aren't.

FIGURE 7.14

Use the Character Styles palette menu to manage your character styles.

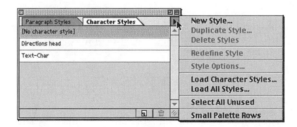

The Redefine Style option (grayed out in the figure) can be particularly confusing. I'll explain it by way of example. Suppose you're working and realize you need to make a change to a character style. One way to do this is to edit the style as described earlier.

7

However, a possibly quicker way is to simply make the desired changes to the text in your document and, with that text still selected, choose Redefine Style from the palette menu. Whatever changes you made to the text are automatically copied over to that character style.

The Load Character Styles and Load All Styles options enable you to import character styles from other InDesign documents, as we'll explore in more detail in Hour 23, "Using InDesign in a Mixed Environment." So what's the difference? As you'll discover during Hour 8, you can also create paragraph styles. When you use the Load All Styles option, InDesign copies both character and paragraph styles from the selected document.

The down side to importing styles from other documents is that you cannot decide which styles to import. If you select a document to import styles from, all that document's styles are imported. This can be a problem when a style from your current document has the same name as, but different attributes than, a style in the other document. When you import styles from the other document, the style with the same name will overwrite the style in your document.

You can avoid this problem by steering clear of generic styles names—such as "Text," "Normal," or "Head"—and using document-specific names, such as "Report-Head," "Resume-Text," and so on.

Summary

Typesetting is the art of making type look attractive, and InDesign enables you to approach the task with scientific precision and efficiency.

Workshop

Making text look good is largely a matter of sizing, scaling, and spacing. After you've mastered the different ways to do this, you'll be a master of InDesign typesetting.

Q&A

Q Which kerning option is best?

A As they say, beauty is in the eye of the beholder. In other words, the best kerning option is the one that makes your type look the way you want it to. Personally, I tend to favor InDesign's optical kerning.

Q **What happens when I assign a shortcut to a character style and that keystroke combination is already assigned to another function within the program?**

A Fortunately, that's impossible. InDesign has very few shortcuts that rely on the number keys, and those that do use the numbers on the actual keyboard. Style shortcuts use numbers from the keyboard.

Q **What happens when I assign the same shortcut to two different styles?**

A InDesign won't let you do that, either. If you try, the program will tell you that the shortcut is already in use.

Q **What happens when I apply kerning and tracking to the same text?**

A As the text is loosened or tightened by the tracking setting, kern pairs will retain their same relative distance.

Quiz

1. The default auto-leading value is which of the following?

    a. 12 pts

    b. 120 percent of the type size

    c. 120 percent of the horizontal scaling

2. Kerning and tracking control which of the following?

    a. The spacing between characters

    b. The spacing between lines

    c. The spacing between paragraphs

3. What text attributes can you define in a character style?

    a. Font and size

    b. Leading and scaling

    c. Both a and b

4. What happens when you import a style with the same name as an existing style in your current document?

    a. The existing style take precedence.

    b. The imported style overwrites the existing style.

    c. A second style is created with a (1) after the style name.

Quiz Answers

1. b. 120 percent of the type size. Auto-leading is determined by the size of the type.

2. a. The spacing between characters. Kerning controls the spacing between letter pairs, whereas tracking controls spacing across a range of characters.

7

3. c. Both a and b (font and size, as well as leading and scaling). You can define these, as well as many other type attributes, in a character style.

4. b. The imported style overwrites the existing style. Imported styles always overwrite existing styles with the same name.

Exercises

Selecting fonts and type sizes is old hat, I'm sure. However, working with InDesign's optical kerning definitely isn't. I suggest you spend some time experimenting with different kerning options on the fonts you use most. Also, make sure you're comfortable creating character styles. They will save you loads of time down the road.

HOUR **8**

Working with Paragraphs

It was probably in second-grade English class that you learned how written documents are broken into individual paragraphs. Paragraphs are important, because they help separate distinct ideas. However, the text formatting in paragraphs can be important for another reason.

For example, if you've made it this far in this book, you've undoubtedly noticed different formatting for different types of paragraphs. A series of bullet characters represents a list. Sans serif type in a rectangular box marks some sort of special note. You don't necessarily need to read the actual text to have some idea of what lies ahead.

Just like typesetting, most paragraph formatting in InDesign is done from one of two palettes: the Paragraph palette and the Paragraph Styles palette.

During this hour, you'll learn:

- How to align type in several ways
- How to create indents
- How to control various aspects of paragraph spacing

- How to easily create drop caps
- How to control hyphenation and justification
- How to create horizontal rules
- How to create tabs
- How to create and use paragraph styles

Working with the Paragraph Palette

Most paragraph formatting is handled from the Paragraph palette, which is shown in Figure 8.1.

FIGURE 8.1

The Paragraph palette controls the look of paragraphs.

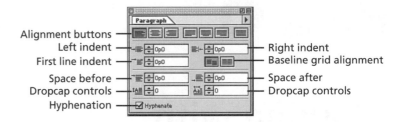

You can view the Paragraph palette any time by pressing Ctrl+M (in Windows) or Command+M (on the Mac), or by selecting Paragraph from the Text menu. If you make changes while the text cursor is inserted in a paragraph or while a range of text is selected, those changes affect only paragraphs included in the selected text. Changes made any other time affect the default paragraph characteristics for the entire document.

Alignment Options

There's nothing mysterious about text alignment. It's a feature that's included in even the most basic word processors. To change the alignment of one paragraph, click the Text tool in the paragraph you want to change, and then click the appropriate alignment button on the paragraph palette. Likewise, if you want to change the alignment in more than one paragraph, select a range of text that includes all the paragraphs you want to change, and then click the appropriate button.

InDesign differs from most other programs in terms of text alignment because it provides several extra options. For example, I'm actually writing this book in Microsoft Word, which has four alignment options: ragged right, centered, ragged left, and justified. InDesign's Paragraph palette includes those four standard buttons, along with these three additional options:

- Justifies the paragraph just like the Justified button, except that the final line of the paragraph is centered instead of flush left.

- Justifies the paragraph just like the Justified button, except that the final line of the paragraph is flush right instead of flush left.

- Justifies all lines in the paragraph, including the last line. If there aren't enough characters to fill the last line, extra space is added between characters to stretch the text.

Creating Indents

InDesign enables you to create three types of indents: left indents, right indents, and first-line indents. As the name implies, the first-line indent controls only the first line in the paragraph. You can type the indent in any unit of measurement supported by InDesign. Check Hour 2, "Preparing to Work in InDesign," if you need a little refresher on how to do this.

One important point to remember about first-line indents is that you can specify a negative measurement, as long as it doesn't exceed the setting of the left indent. For example, if you set a left indent of 1p6, you can set a first-line indent as low as –1p6.

For those who don't recall the nomenclature of typographic measurements, "1p6" means "1 pica, six points." As you recall, 12 points equal one pica. So 1p6 is equal to 1 1/2 picas.

To Do: Creating a Bulleted List

The first-line indent is important when you need to set hanging indents, such as when you want to create a bulleted list. To create a bulleted list, follow these steps:

1. Open a blank InDesign document. Select the Text tool and drag out a text frame anywhere on the page.

2. Open the Paragraph palette. Set the left indent to the value you want to indent. Let's say, 0p6, or half a pica.

3. Set the first-line indent to the negative value of your left indent. For example, if you set the left indent to 0p6, make the first-line indent -0p6.

4. You'll also need to set a tab. We'll look at tabs in greater detail later this hour, but let's learn enough now to be dangerous. Open the Tabs palette by selecting Type, Tabs or by hitting Shift+Command+T (on the Macintosh) or Shift+Ctrl+T (in Windows).

▼   5. You'll notice that the indent and first line are indicated by two tiny black triangles at the top left of the ruler at the top of the Tabs palette. To add a tab, click anywhere to the right of those little triangles in the white space above the ruler. A tab stop marker will appear under the pointer. Drag it left and release the mouse when the tab stop is over the left indent marker. The X dimension field should tell you that the tab stop is at position 0p6.

6. Now, click the Text tool in the text frame and type a bullet character (Option+8 on the Macintosh, or Alt+8 in Windows), and then press the Tab key.

7. Start typing some text—enough to drop down to the second line. It should all resemble Figure 8.2.

FIGURE 8.2

Setting up a bulleted list.

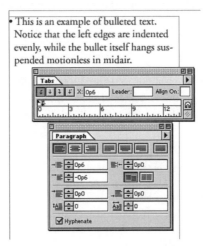

▲

Vertical Alignment to the Baseline Grid

Two buttons control whether each line of text in a paragraph is aligned to the baseline grid. By default, this feature is disabled.

Figure 8.3 shows a paragraph with this feature disabled. Figure 8.4 shows this same paragraph with baseline grid alignment on. Finally, Figure 8.5 shows why figure 8.4 looks the way it does.

FIGURE 8.3

Baseline grid alignment is off.

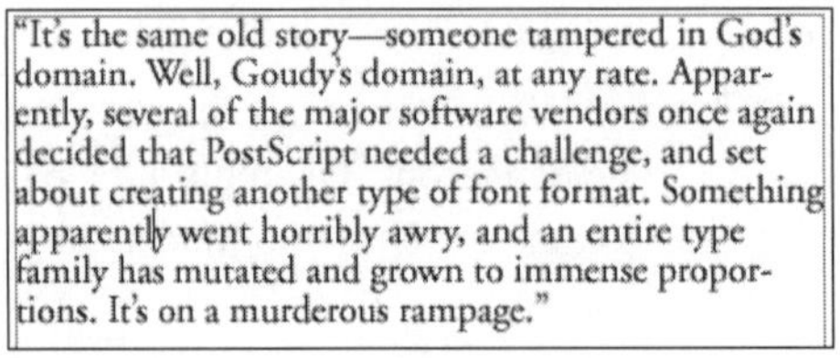

"It's the same old story—someone tampered in God's domain. Well, Goudy's domain, at any rate. Apparently, several of the major software vendors once again decided that PostScript needed a challenge, and set about creating another type of font format. Something apparently went horribly awry, and an entire type family has mutated and grown to immense proportions. It's on a murderous rampage."

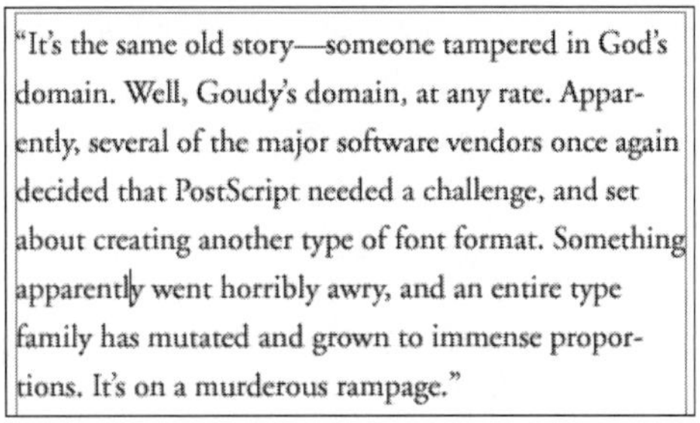

FIGURE **8.4**
Baseline grid align-ment is on.

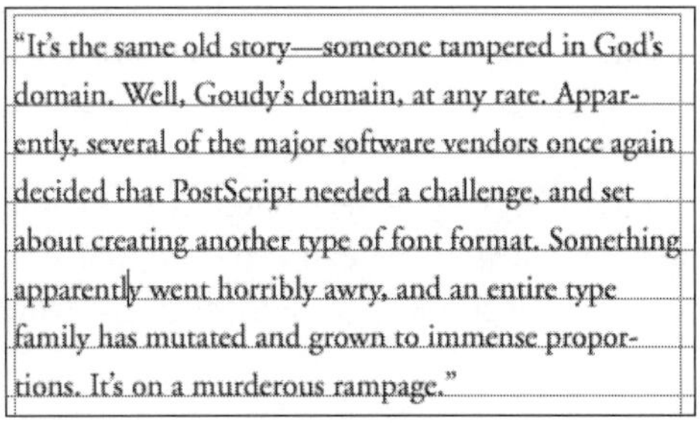

"It's the same old story—someone tampered in God's domain. Well, Goudy's domain, at any rate. Apparently, several of the major software vendors once again decided that PostScript needed a challenge, and set about creating another type of font format. Something apparently went horribly awry, and an entire type family has mutated and grown to immense proportions. It's on a murderous rampage."

FIGURE **8.5**
The baseline grid is displayed.

"It's the same old story—someone tampered in God's domain. Well, Goudy's domain, at any rate. Apparently, several of the major software vendors once again decided that PostScript needed a challenge, and set about creating another type of font format. Something apparently went horribly awry, and an entire type family has mutated and grown to immense proportions. It's on a murderous rampage."

The important point to remember is that when you apply baseline grid alignment to one paragraph, any subsequent paragraphs in the same story are bumped down. Also, if you move the text frame, lines snap to the nearest baseline grid.

You may recall from Hour 2 that you set your baseline grid increments in the Grids Preferences under the Edit menu. We had mentioned at the time that your grid increment should be equal to your most common leading. You can see why that would be in Figures 8.3 and 8.4 above. If you align to baseline grid, the grid increment will override your leading setting and may give your text an "overleaded" look.

Spacing Between Paragraphs

If you want to create spacing between paragraphs, you may be inclined to add paragraph returns at the end of a paragraph. This technique doesn't give you precise control over the spacing between paragraphs; you're stuck with one full line of space whether you want it or not.

The better, more precise, way is to use either the Space Before or Space After option on the Paragraph palette. By using one of these options, you eliminate the need for those extra returns, and you have more precise control over how much space appears between each paragraph.

> Chances are that you create your original text in a word processor. When you do, remember to leave out those extra paragraph returns. It might look funny in your word processor, but after you apply one of these options in InDesign, everything will look just right. Modern word processing programs, such as Word, now have similar Space Before and Space After options, so you really don't need to be adding extraneous paragraph spaces anyway.

Generally speaking, I prefer the Space After option. If you apply the Space Before option to the first paragraph in a story, an extra space is added to the top of the story, which might not be desirable. Experiment with these to see which one suits your needs best.

Deciding Whether to Hyphenate

The Hyphenate checkbox controls whether InDesign inserts line breaks mid-word in the specified paragraph. In my opinion, whether or not you hyphenate depends on the mood you're trying to create. Hyphenation is normally used in most business documents. However, no hyphenation, along with a ragged right margin, creates a warmer, more personal feel. This is the option I use in almost all correspondence—even business-related correspondence.

However, hyphenation may be dictated by the business in question, or by the client. If you are using InDesign for these kinds of documents, be sure to check with the client as to the policy on hyphenation.

In publishing, depending on the publication, most text is justified, and hyphenation is acceptable—but within reason. Typically, no more than two hyphens in a row is considered typographically acceptable. This can be set using the Paragraph palette menu options, which we will cover shortly.

Using the Paragraph Palette Menu

At this point, I'm sure it comes as no surprise that the Paragraph palette includes a corresponding Paragraph palette menu. The first option in this menu controls how the Paragraph palette is displayed. Selecting Hide Options hides everything on the palette below the first-line indent. When those items are hidden, this menu option becomes Show Options.

Justification Options

When you select Justification from the Paragraph palette menu, you're presented with the Justification dialog box, shown in Figure 8.6.

FIGURE 8.6

Justification affects words and characters.

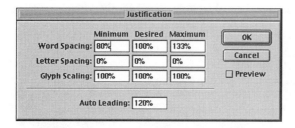

For each option—Word Spacing, Letter Spacing, and Glyph (or character) Scaling—you can specify a minimum, desired, and maximum value, each expressed as a percentage. The big question is: a percentage of what? Here's the rundown:

- Word spacing refers to the amount of space that is added or removed between words to make a line of text justified. A value of 100% indicates "normal" word spacing—the spacing you see in nonjustified text. Because InDesign relies primarily on adding or removing space between words to justify text, you need to give the program some leeway with the minimum and maximum values. The default values of 80% and 133% are fairly standard.

- Letter spacing (or more accurately, character spacing) refers to the spacing between letters in the same word. The odd part here is the 0% is the "normal" setting. When you change values in these settings, it's as a percentage of variance from the normal. Positive numbers increase letter spacing. Negative numbers decrease letter spacing.

- Glyph is just another word for character. So glyph scaling simply refers to InDesign's ability to horizontally scale individual characters while justifying a line. With glyph scaling, like word spacing, 100% is the "normal" setting.

I haven't quite figured out why the designers at Adobe stuck the Auto-Leading field in this dialog box. As you might recall from the previous hour, auto-leading controls the space between one line and the next, and really has nothing to do with justification. In any event, this is where you go to change the percentage of the point size by which auto-leading is calculated. The default Auto-Leading value is 120% of the point size. This means that if your point size is set at 12 points, the leading will be 14.4 pts.

Widows and Orphans

When you're flowing text from page to page or column to column, it's generally considered unattractive to have a single line separated from the other lines in the same paragraph. The common terms for these separated lines are *widows* and *orphans*.

Specifically, a widow is a line of text at the end of the paragraph that, because of a page or column break, is separated from the rest of the paragraph. An orphan is a first line of a paragraph that is separated from its mates for the same reason.

> ### Widows and Orphans
>
> There is some debate over what constitutes a widow or an orphan. According to "The GATF Encyclopedia of Graphic Communication," the term widow is used to refer to the last line of a paragraph that is much shorter than the line length. An orphan is often used to describe a widow that appears at the top of a column. See Figure 8.7.

FIGURE 8.7

A widow and orphan.

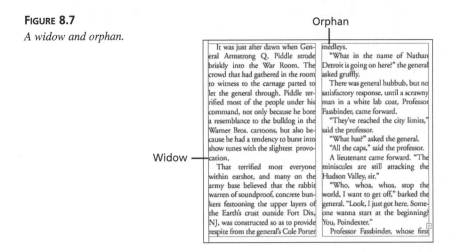

Fortunately, InDesign (like most page layout programs) can automatically prevent widows and orphans from appearing on your page. You control this feature by selecting Keep Options from the Paragraph palette menu. When you select this option, you're presented with the Keep Options dialog box, shown in Figure 8.8.

The Keep With Next field controls how many lines from the next paragraph stay with the current paragraph. For example, suppose the current paragraph is some sort of heading. You don't want that heading to appear at the bottom of a page by itself. By entering a value here, you can make sure that a few lines of the next paragraph always stay with the heading. Keep this in mind whenever you create a paragraph style for a heading. (Paragraph styles are covered later this hour.)

FIGURE 8.8

You control how InDesign treats widows and orphans in your document.

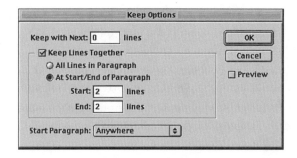

The Keep Lines Together checkbox gives you two options. You can make sure that the entire paragraph stays intact with no breaks, or you can specify a number of lines to preserve at the beginning or end of the paragraph to prevent widows and orphans.

Finally, if you're auto-flowing text into your document, the Start Paragraph options—Anywhere, Next Column, Next Frame, Next Page, Next Odd Page, or Next Even Page—control where a text flows after a break.

Hyphenation

Assuming you have hyphenation on for the current paragraph, selecting Hyphenation from the Paragraph palette menu enables you to control exactly how InDesign handles hyphenation. Selecting this option displays the Hyphenation dialog box, shown in Figure 8.9.

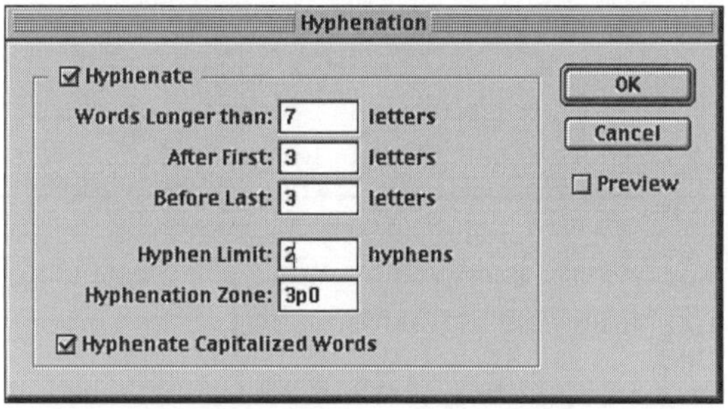

FIGURE 8.9

InDesign gives you precise control over hyphenation.

Here's a rundown of the various options in this dialog box:

- The value you enter for Words Longer Than determines the minimum length of a word that InDesign will hyphenate. For example, with the default value of 7, InDesign will only hyphenate words that are eight characters or longer.

- The After First field controls the minimum number of letters InDesign will leave at the beginning of a word before it considers hyphenating that word. For example, with the default value of 3, the program will not hyphenate between the first and second or second and third letters of a word.

- The Before Last field controls the same minimum number of letters at the other end of the word.

- The Hyphen Limit field controls how many consecutive lines can end with hyphenated words. In traditional typography, two hyphens in a row is the limit.

- The Hyphenation Zone is the distance from the right margin within which InDesign begins considering whether to hyphenate a word.

- If you leave the Hyphenate Capitalized Words checkbox unselected, InDesign won't hyphenate such words. This is handy when your text includes a lot of proper nouns that you want kept together.

Creating Paragraph Rules

You can use the Paragraph Rules option in the Paragraph palette menu to create *rules*, which are horizontal lines attached to a paragraph. (This means that rules become a part of the paragraph and move with it.) When you select Paragraph Rules from the Paragraph palette menu, you're presented with the Paragraph Rules dialog box, shown in Figure 8.10.

FIGURE 8.10

You can create rules that are "attached" to any paragraph.

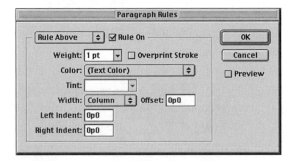

There are any number of reasons you might want to create these sorts of rules. However, the most common reasons are as follows:

- To set a paragraph off from others by adding a rule both above and below it.

- To create a shaded bar behind a single-line paragraph, for elements such as a paragraph heading or for alternating rows in some tabular information.

Therefore, I'll teach you how to do these two things, and in the process, you'll become a paragraph rule expert and can apply the technique however you need it.

To Do: Creating Rules Above and Below a Paragraph

▼ To Do

To create rules both above and below a paragraph, follow these steps:

1. With the text cursor positioned in the paragraph to which you want to add the rules, select Paragraph Rules from the Paragraph palette menu. InDesign displays the Paragraph Rules dialog box. Select Rule Below from the drop-down menu at the top of this dialog box.

2. Check the Preview checkbox so you can instantly see and evaluate the results of the various steps. Then check the Rule On checkbox. This checkbox turns the rule on and off. Notice that a rule now appears along the baseline of the last line in the paragraph.

3. For the time being, leave the line weight as 1 point and the color as text color. If your page has a colored background, you might want to consider checking the Overprint Stroke checkbox. (You'll learn more about overprinting in Hour 15, "Trapping and Other Prepress Considerations.")

4. For your rule's width, select Column from the Width drop-down menu. Doing this makes the rule extend to the edges of the column. (The other option, Text, has the rule extend only as far as the text extends. Of course, if your text has no indents, it really doesn't matter which option you choose here.)

5. Set the Offset to 1p0. This moves the rule down one pica. Note that you can move a lower rule up by entering a negative value in this field. You can also set left and right indents for the rule independent of any indents you've set for the text.

6. Click the drop-down menu next to Rule Below and select Rule Above. Then check the Rule On checkbox.

▲ 7. Set the Offset of the top rule to 1p6.

There are two important points to be aware of here. First, setting the offset of an upper rule works just the opposite of a lower rule. For a lower rule, you enter a positive value to move the rule down, and a negative value to move it up. Conversely, with an upper rule, you enter a positive value to move it up, and a negative value to move it down. Finally, note that you have to enter a greater value for the upper rule offset to compensate for the fact that the upper rule always starts on the baseline.

When you're finished, your paragraph should look similar to the one shown in Figure 8.11.

8

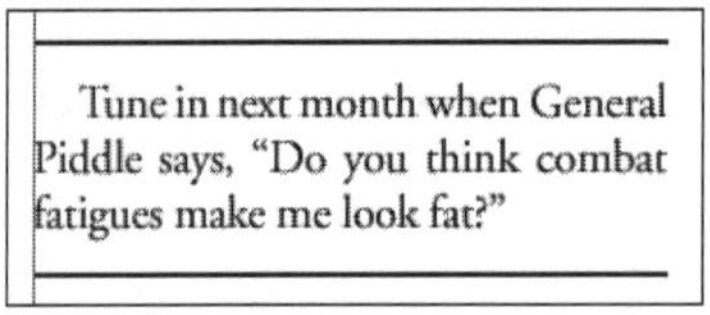

Figure 8.11

This paragraph has a rule both above and below it.

Tune in next month when General Piddle says, "Do you think combat fatigues make me look fat?"

To Do: Creating a Shaded Background Rule

To perform this operation, you first need to create a color to use with the rule. Creating colors is covered thoroughly during Hour 13, "Simple Coloring with InDesign." Therefore, you can consider these steps a partial preview to that lesson. Anyhow, to create a shaded bar behind a single-line paragraph, follow these steps:

1. Press F5 to display the Swatches palette. This palette shares the same space with the Paragraph and Character palettes.

2. Click Black in the Swatches palette and then select New Tint Swatch from the Swatches palette menu.

3. In the resulting dialog box, you have only one option: entering a percentage value for the tint. Type **20** and then click OK.

4. Using the Text tool, click the paragraph to which you want to add the rule.

5. Select Paragraph Rules from the Paragraph palette menu and make sure you're creating a Rule Above by selecting it from the drop-down menu.

6. Select a line weight that's larger than the size of the type in the paragraph. For example, in Figure 8.12, I used 24-point type and a line weight of 36 points.

Figure 8.12

The shaded area is just a paragraph rule.

7. Select the tint you just created as the color.

8. Experiment with the offset to move the rule down an appropriate amount. This is where the Preview checkbox comes in very handy. Just remember that to move an upper rule down, you need to type a negative value. In the case of this example, I had the best results with –0p10.

To noodle with the Offset, you can also use the up and down arrow keys to change the offset in one-point increments.

You are now officially a paragraph rule expert.

Composition Options

The final two options on the Paragraph palette menu enable you to choose between the Single-Line Composer and the Multi-Line Composer. These two composition methods determine how InDesign applies line breaks.

The Single-Line Composer considers only the current line when determining line breaks. This is how virtually all other programs work. However, the Multi-Line Composer considers previous lines as well, and can therefore make better decisions about where to break a line. The Multi-Line Composer adjusts previous lines as new lines are added. This might seem confusing, but essentially the Multi-Line Composer produces a better look. It's selected by default, and you'll probably want to leave it that way for most every project you undertake.

Using Other Paragraph Options

There are two paragraph attributes that you don't control from the Paragraph palette. The first is the creation and management of tabs. The second is the use of optical margin alignment.

Setting Tabs

You manage tabs from the Tabs palette. To display this palette, you can either select Tabs from the Text menu, or press Shift+Ctrl+T (in Windows) or Shift+Command+T (on the Mac). The Tabs palette is shown in Figure 8.13.

FIGURE 8.13
The Tabs palette.

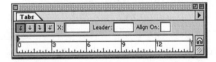

When you have the text cursor inserted in a paragraph when you display the Tabs palette, the palette appears directly above and aligned with the active text frame. This is similar to the way it's done in PageMaker, but superior in one important way. In PageMaker, the equivalent of the Tabs palette appears directly over the line of text where the cursor is positioned, thereby obstructing your view of the lines that precede that point. InDesign gives you the advantage of being able to see all the text in the text frame.

One other great feature of this palette is the Position Palette button. This is the button that looks like a little horseshoe magnet on the right side of the palette. Suppose you're working away and have moved the Tabs palette off to the side. To realign and resize the Tabs palette to the current text frame, just click the Position Palette button.

The group of buttons in the upper-left side of the Tabs palette controls the type of tab you create. For the most part, these are standard tab types, and are described here from left to right:

- A left tab is a "normal" tab. With this type of tab, text you type after the tab appears to the right of the tab.

- When you use a center tab, any text you type after the tab, but before the next tab, is centered on that tab stop.

- A right tab works just the opposite of a left tab. Any text you type after a right tab appears to the left of the tab stop.

- You can use a decimal tab to align multiple rows of numerical information, such as financial figures. InDesign does one better, though, in that when you select decimal tab in this palette, the Align On field is also made available. This field defaults to a period (decimal), which means that rows are aligned on their decimal points. You can, however, enter any character to suit your needs.

Before you create your new tab stop, you can also specify a *leader character* in the Leader field. The most common leader character, of course, is a period (used to create a "dot leader"), but InDesign enables you to use any character you want. Your leader character fills the space between the point where you pressed the Tab key and the tab stop. Dot leaders are often used in tables of contents to aid in matching up a chapter or subchapter with its corresponding page number.

As for actually creating the tab, you have two options. You can type a value into the X field. This value corresponds to the ruler on the Tabs palette, not your regular document rulers. However, the easier way is to simply click and hold the mouse somewhere in the white area just above the Tabs palette ruler. With the mouse button still down, move back and forth in this area. As you do this, you'll see the X value change accordingly. When you have the tab just where you want it, release the mouse button.

To select any tab you've created, just click it. To remove a tab, drag it off the Tabs palette and release; the tab disappears.

After you've created at least one tab, the two options in the Tabs palette menu—Repeat Tab and Clear All Tabs—are available. The Clear All Tabs button is pretty obvious.

If you select a tab and then choose Repeat Tab from the Tabs palette menu, InDesign measures the distance between that tab and the previous tab (or from the left margin if the selected tab is the first one). It then places another tab at that interval.

Here's a little tab trick that comes in handy now and then. Suppose you want part of a line flush left and part of it flush right. This is common in document headers and footers. You don't have to set any special tabs to achieve this effect. Just press the Tab key between the two parts, and then right justify that text. InDesign automatically pops each half over to its given margin.

8

If you position the mouse directly over the Tabs palette ruler, the pointer turns into a hand. By clicking and holding, you can then drag the ruler left and right according to your needs. To return the ruler to its normal position, click the Position Palette button.

Finally, you can also use the Tabs palette to visually adjust the left, right, and first-line indents of the current paragraph. The black left-pointing arrow on the right side of the ruler controls the right indent.

The right-pointing arrow on the left side of the ruler is split into the two little triangles we saw earlier this hour. The bottom one controls the left indent. The top one controls the first-line indent. You can move either of these by dragging it along the ruler, or by selecting it and entering an X value.

Optical Margin Alignment

There's one obscure palette called the Story palette and it does one thing: It controls the optical margin alignment. To display this palette, select Story from the Text menu; there is no built-in keyboard shortcut. The Story palette is shown in Figure 8.14.

FIGURE 8.14

The Story palette serves a single purpose—optical margin alignment control.

When you turn optical margin alignment on, any punctuation at the beginning of a line (such as quotation marks) hang outside of the left margin. (This explains why optical margin alignment is also called hanging punctuation.) This can create a visually pleasing effect.

The font size field on this palette controls the amount of overhang. This particular function is a little quirky. The InDesign documentation suggests that you specify a point size equal to the size of the type in your story. However, I've found that to hang the punctuation entirely outside the margin, you need to double the point size. Furthermore, if you go much past double, the results become unpredictable. If you want to use optical margin alignment, I suggest you do a little experimentation.

 The reason this palette is called the Story palette is because the changes you make here affect all paragraphs in the selected story. You can't apply optical margin alignment on a paragraph-by-paragraph basis.

Working with Paragraph Styles

Remember learning character styles from the previous lesson? Paragraph styles work with the same basic concept, except they are applied to entire paragraphs. If you've already mastered character styles, paragraph styles are a snap.

As you might have guessed, you control paragraph styles from the Paragraph Styles palette. You can display this palette any time by pressing F11 or selecting Paragraph Styles from the Type menu. The Paragraph Styles palette is shown in Figure 8.15.

FIGURE 8.15

The Paragraph Styles palette is similar to the Character Styles palette.

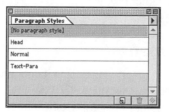

Similar to character styles, any formatting that you apply to a paragraph can be specified as part of a paragraph style. As you've learned this hour, that's a lot of options.

To Do: Making a Paragraph Style from an Existing Paragraph

Instead of starting from scratch when creating a paragraph style, try this little shortcut.

1. Open a blank InDesign document, create a text frame, and type a paragraph's worth of text. (Or, if you're feeling uninspired, you can use the Fill With Placeholder Text feature you learned about in Hour 6, "Creating Text.")

2. Highlight the paragraph and format the text. Give it a new font, point size, custom leading, and so forth.

3. Make sure you have the Paragraph Styles palette open. Select New Style from the Paragraph Styles palette menu. When you do, all the formatting you specified for the current paragraph is copied into the new style. Give the new style a unique name and you're done.

The one last change you should consider is the use of the Next Style option—an option that's not available with character styles. You can use this option to specify the style of a paragraph that follows a paragraph of the current style. Sound a little confusing? Here's an example.

Suppose you have one paragraph style called Heading 1 and another paragraph style called Body Text. And suppose that you find that every time you place a return at the end of a Heading 1 paragraph, you always change the paragraph style of the next paragraph to Body Text. If you select Body Text as the next style in the Heading 1 settings, InDesign does this automatically.

Summary

Unless you subscribe to the *Wired* magazine school of thought, creating a professional document includes attention to uniformity. The key to a clean, uniform document are paragraphs that are properly formatted. In short, paragraph formatting is every bit as important as character formatting.

Workshop

Although the character can be considered the basic building block of typography, the paragraph is the most conspicuous unit on a page. Formatting paragraphs so they look good is the most basic goal of typography. Therefore, spend some time reading through the Q&A and Quiz that follows, and then tackle the exercises at the end of the Hour to build your paragraph formatting proficiency.

Q&A

Q I want to create a document with double-spaced type, like in my old term-paper days. How do I do this?

A InDesign gives you two options. The first is to adjust the leading to approximately twice the type size. The second is to adjust the line spacing on the baseline grid and then align the text to the baseline grid.

Q Okay, I forgot. How do I change the baseline grid?

A You control the characteristics of the baseline grid in Grid Preferences. Refer to Hour 2 if you need a refresher.

Q Is there any time I'd want to use the Single-Line Composer instead of the Multi-Line Composer?

A If you're used to creating a lot of manual line breaks and want to continue doing so, you might want to use the Single-Line Composer. However, I personally view it as a big time-waster.

Quiz

1. Which of the following is true of a first-line indent?

    a. It must be a positive value.

    b. It can be positive or negative.

    c. It must be a negative value.

2. Instead of placing double returns at the ends of paragraphs, you can do which of the following?

    a. Add space above each paragraph.

    b. Add space below each paragraph.

    c. Do either of the above.

3. How do you create a drop cap?

    a. Set the two drop-cap options.

    b. Run the built-in drop cap macro.

    c. Set the drop cap as a separate story.

4. When you create a paragraph rule, what does a positive offset do?

    a. It moves the rule up.

    b. It moves the rule down.

    c. It depends on the type of rule.

Quiz Answers

1. b. A negative value moves the first-line indent to the left. A positive value moves it toward the right.

2. c. Although I prefer adding space below the paragraph, both A and B are valid options.

3. a. Set two options and InDesign automatically creates your drop caps.

4. c. For an upper rule, a positive offset moves the rule up. For a lower rule, a positive offset moves the rule down.

Exercises

In my opinion, paragraph styles are one of the most powerful formatting tools that InDesign has. They enable you to apply many formatting attributes with a single mouse click. If you want to save yourself many hours down the road, spend some time now getting comfortable with paragraph styles. Create some, change some, apply some, and delete some. Make the use of paragraph styles second nature. Import some text—or create it natively—and create some stock paragraph styles you can apply to various blocks of text. Come up with a body text style, a headline style, a subhead style, and perhaps a few other styles that you can use in upcoming lessons when we start assembling documents.

Also spend some time understanding justification and hyphenation settings.

8

PART III
Working with Graphics

Hour

Hour 9

Using Graphics from Other Programs

Now that you're comfortable creating files and manipulating text in your files, it's time to move on to graphics. In addition to the graphics you create in InDesign (discussed in Hour 10, "Using InDesign's Drawing Tools"), InDesign enables you to incorporate graphics from other applications, and you can use this power to create exciting, visually appealing documents.

Before you jump in and start adding graphics, it's a good idea to take a look at the formats that InDesign supports and learn how to choose a format that's right for your requirements. Once you pick a format, you can insert the graphic into InDesign in several ways.

In this hour, you learn the following:

- What formats are supported by InDesign and how to choose a format and resolution
- When to import a graphic by placing it, copying and pasting it, or dragging and dropping it

- The difference between linked and embedded graphics and how to use both
- How to save frequently used items in object libraries

Choosing a Graphic Format

InDesign supports a wide variety of graphics formats. Some of the more common ones include TIFF, EPS, PDF, AI, PSD, BMP, GIF, JPEG, WMF, and PCX. If you're not sure whether your file's format is supported, just try importing it (or check InDesign's online help for a complete list of supported formats).

If you're working in Adobe Illustrator or Photoshop, you can save your graphics in their native formats (.ai and .psd, respectively) and import them directly into InDesign.

Choosing the Right Format

Given all these choices, which format is best for your graphics? It depends on how you're planning to output your InDesign file and on the contents of your graphic. In general, you first choose between the two major graphic types: bitmap and vector.

A bitmap image is a graphic that represents information as a series of dots (or pixels). Bitmaps formats include BMP, PCX, TIFF, GIF, WMF, and PSD. They are most often used for photographs and screen captures. A vector image represents the graphic as a group of mathematical statements that describe lines and shapes.

Vector formats include EPS and PDF. They make sense for graphics that include drawings and text, such as diagrams, flow charts, and graphs.

Aside from the gruesome details of how the graphics are described under the covers, the biggest difference between bitmap and vector images is *scalability*. Because the line in a vector image is described mathematically, you can make the line bigger or smaller by scaling, and the line will remain smooth and clean. In a bitmap image, though, scaling often produces jaggy, unattractive lines. This is because in a bitmap image, the line is described as a series of pixels. When you make the line bigger, you simply make the pixels bigger, instead of recalculating what the line should look like.

Once you choose a graphic format, you'll need to make some decisions about the graphic's resolution and size in InDesign. For vector images (such as EPS files), this is easy. You can resize them as much as you want and the graphic will be just as sharp and clear as the original.

But with bitmap images, things are a little more complicated. For a bitmap, you must specify a resolution when you import the graphic. The resolution is the number of pixels per inch. For example, if you have a bitmap that measures 300 by 300 pixels, then importing that bitmap at a resolution of 150 dots per inch (dpi) will result in a bitmap that measures 2 inches by 2 inches. Increasing the dpi setting makes the graphic smaller (because you jam more pixels into each inch).

Most office laser printers output at 600 dpi, so if you're planning to print something at the office, you'll get the best quality if you import your bitmaps at 600 dpi. If you can't get resolution that high, try a number that divides evenly into 600, like 300 or 150 dpi. If you're planning to have your document printed professionally, the printer may use a resolution of 1200 or 2400 dpi. Check with the printer to find out what the best resolution is for your bitmaps.

Importing Graphics

InDesign offers several ways to import graphics—you can place a graphic, copy and paste it, or drag and drop it. Placing a graphic is the most powerful and flexible way to add a graphic to your documents. It lets you review the import options and change them before dropping the graphic into the document. Copying and pasting from another application or dragging and dropping a file is often faster, though.

For some applications, copying and pasting lets you import an editable object. Placing or dragging and dropping always imports a non-editable object. This is discussed further later in this chapter.

To Do: Placing a Graphic

Here's how to place a graphic in your document:

1. Using the Selection tool, click the pasteboard (outside the page area). This ensures that nothing is selected when you place the graphic.

2. Select File, Place to display a directory navigation dialog box. The Windows version is shown in Figure 9.1.

3. Make sure that Show Import Options is checked.

4. Select the graphic that you want to use and click Open.

5. Because you checked Show Import Options, the Image Import Options dialog box is displayed (Figure 9.2). The options shown depend on the format of the graphic that you're importing.

FIGURE 9.1

InDesign shows you all the available graphics.

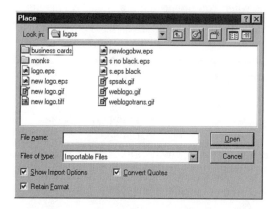

FIGURE 9.2

You can set options for the image as you place it.

One of the most important options is the Proxy Image Resolution option. When you import a graphic, InDesign creates a low-resolution preview, or *proxy image*. You determine the resolution of this preview when you import the graphic. A low resolution (such as 72 dpi) creates a preview that displays quickly but is not very sharp. A higher resolution (such as 300 dpi) creates a preview that takes longer to display but is more clear.

If you have lots of graphics and a relatively slow computer, use low-resolution previews. If you have only a few graphics or a very fast computer, use high-resolution previews.

The preview's resolution does not affect the graphic itself. The preview is used on-screen only. When you create output from your InDesign file (for example, by printing it or creating a PDF file), the original graphic is used.

▼   6. Choose the appropriate graphic import options, and then click OK.

▲   7. Your regular cursor is replaced by a graphic icon. This is called the "loaded graph-
           ics icon." Click on your page to place the graphic.

Using Place versus Copy and Paste or Drag and Drop

Instead of placing your graphics, you can insert them by copying and pasting them from
most graphics applications or by dragging and dropping them. So why go to the trouble
of placing them?

Placing gives you the most control over your graphics. When you copy and paste or drag
and drop graphics, you do not see the Image Import Options dialog box (Figure 9.2).
Instead, InDesign uses the settings from the last graphic you imported. If you want to be
able to check and modify the import settings, use the Place command.

In some cases, copying and pasting produces a lower-resolution graphic than placing.

If you're working with Illustrator files, copying and pasting does have a benefit—the
graphic is imported as a grouped, editable object. If you want to change your Illustrator
graphics using InDesign's drawing tools, make sure that you drag and drop or copy and
paste them instead of using the Place command.

> If your Illustrator drawing is complex, it's probably best to place it and mod-
> ify the original in Illustrator because InDesign's drawing tools are less pow-
> erful than Illustrator's. If your graphic contains gradients or colors, I
> recommend that you place it.

Setting Borders with Clipping Paths

When you place a graphic, it's surrounded by a rectangular border. But for some graphics, you'll want a border that follows the edges of the graphic instead. To do this, you
need to set up a *clipping path,* which is an outline around the graphic (see Figure 9.3).

Some imported graphics already contain clipping paths (usually set up in Illustrator or
Photoshop). When you place these graphics, the Image Import Options dialog box
(Figure 9.2) includes a Create Frame from Clipping Path checkbox. Make sure that
option is selected and then import the graphic as usual.

You can also add a clipping path (or replace the one included with the graphic). InDesign
provides an easy way to do this, discussed in the next section.

FIGURE 9.3

A clipping path lets the surrounding text follow the shape of the graphic.

To Do: Creating a Clipping Path in InDesign

If your graphic needs a clipping path or if you want to replace the one provided in the graphic, you can create a new clipping path in InDesign. Here's how to do it:

1. Place the graphic in InDesign using the steps discussed previously.
2. Select Object, Clipping Path to display the clipping path options (see Figure 9.4).

FIGURE 9.4

Clipping path options control how your clipping path looks.

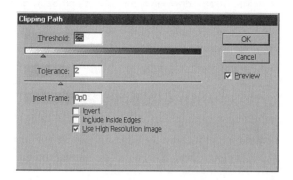

3. Set the clipping options you want and click OK to create the clipping path. Table 9.1 lists the options available in the Clipping Path dialog box.

TABLE 9.1   Options in the Clipping Path Dialog Box

Option	How It Affects the Clipping Path
Threshold	A threshold of 0 means that the clipping path excludes all white areas. Increase the threshold to exclude darker areas.

Option	How It Affects the Clipping Path
Tolerance	A higher tolerance value makes a smoother, less jagged clipping path. A lower tolerance makes a tighter path with more corners.
Inset Frame	To shrink the clipping path closer to the object, type a value here. Type a negative value to make the clipping path looser.
Invert	Use this to switch the areas excluded by the clipping path.
Include Inside Edges	Use this to set up additional clipping paths to carve out any gaps in the graphic.
Use High Resolution Image	If checked, InDesign calculates the clipping path based on the original, high-resolution graphic, which gives you the most accurate clipping path but takes more time. If not checked, InDesign uses the preview image instead.

9

Setting Up Inline Graphics

When you placed a graphic earlier in this hour, I told you to click the pasteboard area to ensure that nothing was selected before you placed the graphic. This step is important when you insert a *free-standing* graphic—one that is independent of the surrounding text. But InDesign also lets you insert *inline* graphics. An inline graphic is a graphic that's placed into your text and moves with the text.

Inline graphics are especially useful for small graphics that are used as part of your text, such as graphic "bugs" to indicate the end of an article or a section break.

To Do: Placing an Inline Graphic

Here's how to place an inline graphic in your document:

1. Position your cursor in your text where you want the graphic. Make sure that the blinking I-beam cursor is displayed.

2. From this point on, the process is identical to the process of inserting a regular, free-standing graphic (see "To Do: Placing a Graphic," earlier in this chapter). You place the graphic and then can modify the graphic's frame. But, with an inline graphic, the frame is considered part of the text and thus will move with the text.

▼ To Do

▲

Managing Links

When you insert a graphic into your document (by placing, copying and pasting, or dragging and dropping), the graphic is either embedded or linked. A graphic is embedded if the InDesign document contains a complete copy of the graphic. A graphic is linked if the InDesign document contains only a reference to an external graphic file.

Embedding is convenient because it consolidates all your graphics and your InDesign content into a single file, but every time you embed a file, the InDesign file gets bigger.

Linking has the advantage that you only insert a pointer to the original graphic. This means that your InDesign file does not get bigger with each graphic you insert. But the disadvantage of linking is that you have to keep track of all of the graphics that are linked because InDesign needs them. Fortunately, InDesign provides some handy features to manage links.

By default, InDesign sets up all graphics over 48K as *links* instead of embedding them. All your linked graphics are listed in the Links palette (Figure 9.5), which you can display by selecting File, Links.

You can choose to embed larger graphics when you import them.

FIGURE 9.5

The Links palette gives you complete control over linked graphics.

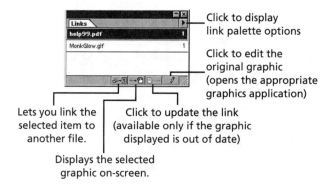

Click to display link palette options

Click to edit the original graphic (opens the appropriate graphics application)

Lets you link the selected item to another file.

Click to update the link (available only if the graphic displayed is out of date)

Displays the selected graphic on-screen.

From the Links palette, you can update graphics, view information about embedded graphics, and change a linked graphic to an embedded graphic.

Updating Graphics

If you change a graphic file that's linked into your document, the Links palette displays a "needs updating" icon (see Figure 9.6).

FIGURE 9.6

The warning triangle indicates that the graphic needs to be updated.

"Needs updating" icon

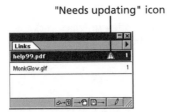

To Do: Updating a Graphic

Here's how to update a graphic:

1. Select the graphic (or graphics) in the Links palette.
2. Click the Update Link button. InDesign updates the graphic that's displayed with the latest information from the graphic file.

> Make sure that the new graphic is the same shape as the old one; otherwise, InDesign will squeeze (or stretch) the new graphic to make it fit!

Viewing Information About Linked Graphics

InDesign provides a dialog box that displays information about linked graphics.

To Do: Viewing Information About a Linked Graphic

Here's how to display information about a linked graphic:

1. Select the graphic in the Links palette.
2. Click the arrow at the top right to display the pop-up menu and select Link Information. A dialog box is displayed with information about the selected graphic (see Figure 9.7).

FIGURE 9.7

You can review all information about the linked graphic in this dialog box.

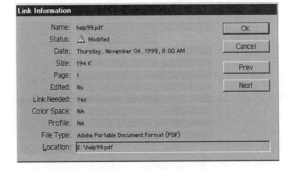

To view link information for other graphics, click the Next or Prev buttons. The graphics are listed in the order they appear in your document, starting on the first page.

Changing Linked Graphics to Embedded Graphics

Linked graphics are useful because they keep your publication small and because you can update the external graphics and have the changes appear in InDesign. But working with linked graphics requires you to keep track of external files. In some cases, you might start out with linked graphics and later change your mind and want embedded graphics. Fortunately, InDesign makes it easy to change from linked to embedded graphics.

To Do: Changing a Graphic from Linked to Embedded

Here's how to change a graphic from linked to embedded:

1. Select the graphic (or graphics) in the Links palette.

2. Click the arrow at the top right to display the pop-up menu and select Embed.

3. InDesign warns you that embedding destroys the link and tells you how much the publication size will increase. Click OK.

   The graphic disappears from the Links palette. (The graphic displayed in your document stays the same.)

▲

Using Object Libraries

InDesign's object libraries provide a convenient way to store text, graphics, and other document components that you use frequently. For example, if you're a freelancer, you can create an object library for each of your clients and store logos, graphics, and boiler-plate text in each library. Every time you start a new project for a specific client, you can open the appropriate object library so that you have all the bits and pieces you need in one location.

To Do: Creating a Library

Before you can work with object libraries, you need to create them. Here's how to do it:

1. Select Window, Libraries, New. Doing so displays a directory navigation box.

2. Navigate to the directory where you want to save the library, give the library a name, and click Save.

   The new, empty library is displayed in a palette (see Figure 9.8 for an example of a library palette containing objects).

To Do: Opening a Library

When you create a new library, the library's palette is displayed automatically. But if you want to display an existing library, you need to open it. Here's how to do it:

1. Select Window, Libraries, Open to display a directory navigation box.

2. Navigate to the directory where the library was saved, select the file, and click Open. Another palette is displayed with that library's contents (see Figure 9.8).

9

FIGURE 9.8

The Library palette helps you manage frequently used items.

▲

Once you've opened a library, you can show or hide it using the Window, Library menu. This is faster than opening and closing the library.

Adding Items to a Library

To add an item to a library, select a graphic or other object and drag it onto the library. Once inside the library, the cursor changes to a gray rectangle with a plus sign (Windows) or a closed hand with a plus sign on it (Mac). Drop the item to add it to the library.

To add text, select the frame that contains the text, then drag it to the library.

Using Items in a Library

To reuse an item stored in a library, select it in the library, and then drag and drop it to the location on your page where you want it.

Summary

In this hour, you learned how to import graphics, control your graphics options, work with clipping paths, link and embed graphics, and use object libraries. These features give you complete control over graphics that you create in other applications. In the next hour, you learn how to create your own graphics using InDesign's built-in tools.

Workshop

In this hour, you've learned about different graphic formats, how to import graphics into InDesign, and how to manage the graphics after you've imported them. In this workshop, we'll take you through all of those techniques and give you a chance to put your new graphic prowess to work.

Q&A

Q Can I use scanned graphics in InDesign?

A Yes, but InDesign does not provide direct support for scanning (there's no support for TWAIN). If you want to scan a graphic for use in InDesign, you need to use another graphics tool to scan the graphic (such as Photoshop or the software that came with your scanner). Once you've scanned the image, you can save it as a graphic and import that graphic into InDesign.

Q My graphic uses a format that's not supported by InDesign. How can I place it in my document?

A Use a graphics tool such as Photoshop or Illustrator to convert the file to a format that is supported by InDesign. Or, convert the file to PDF format and import the PDF.

Q Should I crop my graphic in a graphics application or inside InDesign?

A It depends. If the graphic contains extraneous material around the edges that you'll never need, crop it in your graphics application. But if you plan to use different parts of the graphic in different locations, it might make sense to crop it inside InDesign. Keep in mind that when you crop the graphic in InDesign, the entire graphic is still stored in InDesign, whereas cropping it in your graphic applications leads to a smaller graphic being imported.

Quiz

1. Why is placing a bitmap graphic better than copying and pasting it?

    a. Copying and pasting sometimes results in a lower-quality graphic.

    b. Placing lets you set import options.

    c. Both a and b.

2. If text flows around a graphic and follows the shape of the object in the graphic, which of the following is true?

    a. The graphic was cropped.

    b. The graphic has a clipping path.

    c. The graphic is corrupted.

3. Embedding a graphic means what?

    a. The graphic is linked to an external file.

    b. The total InDesign file size is smaller than it would be if the graphic were linked.

    c. The source file is not required to produce final output.

4. An object library is which of the following?

    a. The room in your house where you keep books.

    b. A file in which you store graphics and other objects for reuse.

    c. A programming term that isn't relevant in InDesign.

Quiz Answers

1. c. Copying and pasting imports the graphic using default settings. Depending on the source application, you might lose some of the graphic's information, which results in a lower-quality graphic.

2. b. A clipping path enables text to flow around an irregular shape.

3. c. The advantage of embedding graphics is that you have all your content in one location. But if you embed large files, your InDesign file will get very big. Linking enables you to avoid big files by referencing external files.

4. b. Use object libraries to store collections of graphics that you need to use frequently. This might include logos, standard copyright statements, and a set of elements from a page.

Exercises

Now is the time to try out all those graphics that you have lying around. Try this:

- Import various graphics that use different formats. Check out how the import options change depending on the format of the graphic you're inserting.

- Import a graphic by placing, copying and pasting, and dragging and dropping. If you have Illustrator files, try copying and pasting them and verify that they are editable in InDesign.

- Import a linked graphic, then change it to an embedded graphic. Check out the options on the Links palette.

- Add one of the graphics you've placed in your document to an object library.

- Pick an interesting graphic with irregular edges and create a clipping path for it.

Import them, try the different import options, move things around, and build clipping paths. InDesign's support for external graphics is strong, so take advantage of it and make some fun files!

Hour 10

Using InDesign's Drawing Tools

Like many page layout applications these days, InDesign includes a comprehensive set of drawing tools. If you're already using Adobe Illustrator, these tools are going to look very familiar. Why would you want the same tools as Illustrator in another program? Isn't that like paying for the same stuff twice? Not really. Very often you'll need to add quickie graphics to a page and it is just quicker and more convenient to be able to do it natively.

So, in this hour, you learn the following:

- How to use InDesign's drawing tools
- How to use the new Free Transform Tool
- How to work with paths

Using InDesign's Drawing Tools

You'll find InDesign's drawing tools in the Tools palette, which we took a tour of a while ago in Hour 1, "Introducing Adobe InDesign." By default, the Tools palette is displayed as a two-column set of tools, which usually appears on the left side of the screen, though you can move it anywhere you'd like (see Figure 10.1). You've been using the various tools on this palette over the course of the last nine hours, so you and the Tools palette should be old friends by now.

FIGURE 10.1

The Tools palette and InDesign's drawing tools.

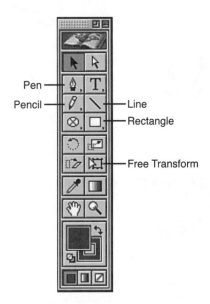

Pen
Pencil
Line
Rectangle
Free Transform

The Pencil Tool

If you select the Pencil tool from the Tools palette (or hit N on the keyboard) you access the Pencil Tool, which lets you draw freeform lines and curves. (The Pencil Tool is a new addition to version 1.5 of InDesign.)

If you double-click on the Pencil Tool, you will get the Pencil Tool Preferences, which let you set how sensitive the tool is to movements of the mouse (see Figure 10.2).

If you use this tool a lot, adjust the tolerance settings until drawing is comfortable. You may also want to consider purchasing a graphics tablet and stylus (from the likes of Wacom and others) that feel and function more like pens and pencils than does a mouse.

FIGURE **10.2**

The Pencil Tool
Preferences.

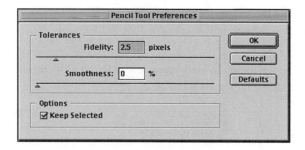

If you click and hold on the Pencil Tool on the Tools palette, you will see two additional tools. The first is the Smooth Tool which lets you flatten out any bumps and other aberrations that can occur when you try to use a mouse as a drawing tool. The Erase Tool lets you erase portions of a shape you have drawn. The Erase Tool works not only with shapes you have drawn with the Pencil Tool, but also with those created with other drawing tools as well.

To Do: Drawing with the Pencil Tool

Let's see how this actually works. To draw a simple shape with the Pencil Tool, do the following:

1. Open a blank page in InDesign and select the Pencil Tool, either by clicking on the tool in the Tools palette or by hitting N.

2. By clicking on the page and dragging the mouse, draw a simple shape—be it a circle, square, triangle, or what have you. I have no artistic ability whatsoever, so I just did a simple, very sick looking wave.

3. Depending on how smooth your shape is, you may need to further smooth it. To do that, select the Direct Selection Tool from the Tools palette, and click anywhere on your shape.

   You will see that it turns light blue and comprises a set of blue squares. These are the *anchor points* that define the shape. The blue line is the *path*. Think of a curve created in this way as being akin to a connect-the-dots puzzle. The more points that there are, the more precise the path, and the smoother the shape or line will be. (We'll look at paths, curves, and anchor points in excruciating detail later this hour.)

4. If you're good at editing paths, then you know how you can use the Direct Selection Tool and/or the Pen Tool to smooth out your shape. For now, let's just run the Smooth Tool over various bits of it.

10

▲ To Do

▼

▼　　5. Make sure the shape is selected with the Direct Selection Tool and click and hold
on the Pencil Tool until you can see the hidden tools. Select the middle tool—the
Smooth Tool.

　　6. Find a bumpy patch in your shape and drag the Smooth Tool across that segment of
the path. See Figures 10.3 and 10.4.

FIGURE **10.3**

*A bumpy path before
using the Smooth
Tool...*

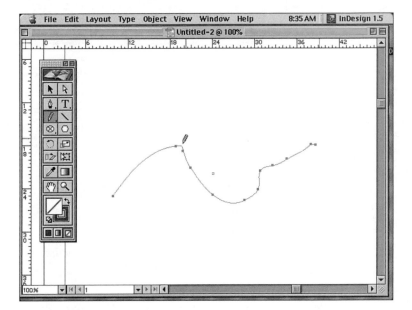

FIGURE **10.4**

*...becomes less bumpy
after dragging the
Smooth Tool across
the path.*

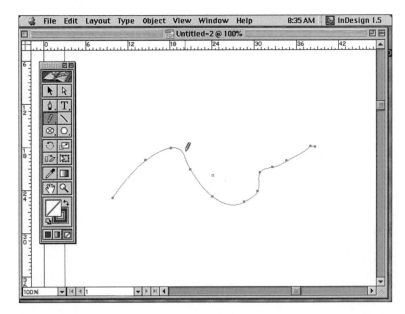

▼

▼   7. Finally, if you go back under the Pencil/Smooth Tool (depending which one you
        have selected at the moment), you will see the Eraser Tool. Use that to erase
▲   portions of your path.

The Line Tool

Surprisingly, the Line Tool lets you draw…lines. Select it, and then click and drag to
create a line. (If you hold down the Shift key, the line will snap to the nearest 45-degree
angle.)

To Do: Drawing a Line

Okay, this may seem like a "well-duh" sort of exercise, but let's look at how we can
adjust the attributes of our lines:

1. Open a blank InDesign document and select the Line Tool, either by clicking it on
   the Tools palette or by hitting \ on the keyboard. Bear in mind that that's the
   backslash (\) not the forward slash (/). The pointer will then turn to a cross hairs.

2. Click and drag a line. When you release the mouse, your line will be surrounded
   by its bounding box, and you can click and drag its handles to make the line longer
   or change its direction. See Figure 10.5.

FIGURE 10.5

*A line drawn in
InDesign. Dragging
the handles on the
bounding box will
resize the line or
change its direction.*

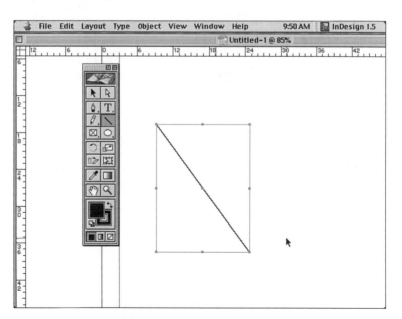

10

▼

NEW TERM A *bounding box* is a rectangle that surrounds a page object—be it a line, a curve, or a shape. A bounding box has eight *handles* that you click and drag to resize the object. If you click on a page object with the Selection Tool, you select the bounding box. If you click the object with the Direct Selection Tool, you select the object's path, or the content of that bounding box.

3. Now, there are two aspects of a line that you may want to change. The first is its Stroke, or how thick it is. Open the Stroke palette by going to Window, Stroke, or by hitting F10. The Stroke palette is seen in Figure 10.6.

FIGURE 10.6

The Stroke palette lets you change the characteristics of your line.

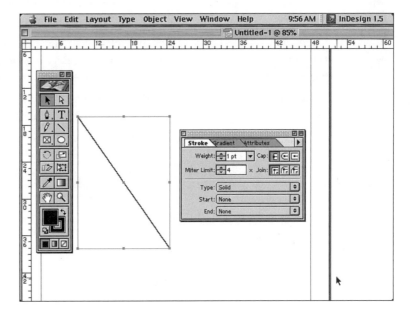

4. To change the thickness, simply enter a different number in the Weight field, or click the small up and down arrows to its left to change the weight in one-point increments. Or, you can click on the larger arrow to the right of the Weight field to pop up a list of common weights.

5. The three Cap options determine if you want your line to have square ends or rounded ends.

6. Note the three pop-up menus at the bottom of the Stroke palette. This lets you
▼   determine how you want your line to look. *Type* lets you determine if you want

▼   your line solid, or if you want it to comprise several smaller lines. You can also choose a dashed line here. You will need to increase the weight of a line to see how these options work.

7. *Start* and *End* let you choose what shape you want at the beginning and/or end of your line. You can choose a solid circle, an open circle, a bar, or a square. Somewhat counterintuitively, if you want arrow heads on your line, you need to choose either Curved, Barbed, TriangleWide, Triangle, SimpleWide, or Simple.

▲   See Figure 10.7 for an "Arrow Gallery."

FIGURE 10.7

Arrows galore! From top to bottom: Curved, Barbed, TriangleWide, Triangle, SimpleWide, Simple. The difference between Curved and Barbed is very subtle. Can you spot it? I can't...

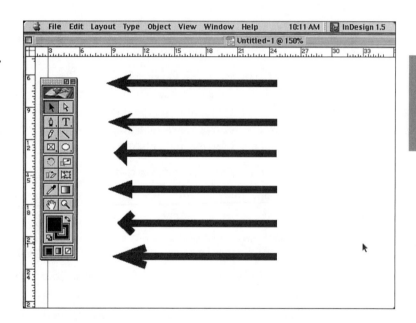

Spend some time adjusting these options to get a sense of what effects the various options have on your line.

Rectangle Tool

To draw a rectangle or a square, select the Rectangle Tool, or hit M on the keyboard, and then click and drag to create a rectangle. Shift-click and drag to create a square.

If you click and hold the Rectangle Tool on the Tools palette, there are two additional tools—the Ellipse Tool and the Polygon Tool, which work just like the Rectangle Tool. The Ellipse tool draws ellipses. Shift-click and drag to create a perfect circle.

After you have drawn a shape, you can modify it in any number of ways, from basic resizing (accomplished by clicking and dragging the shape's handles) to rotating to shearing.

After you create a shape and keep the Ellipse or Rectangle Tool selected and then click on a drawn shape, a dialog will pop up and tell you the dimensions of your object. You can resize it using the dialog box, as well, if you'd like precise numerical control over resizing.

Free Transform Tool

You can also modify page objects with the Free Transform Tool, which can be selected on the Tools palette, or by hitting E on the keyboard.

A new tool added in InDesign 1.5, the Free Transform Tool comes from Photoshop and Illustrator, and if you've used it in those programs it works exactly the same here. Basically, it's a shortcut tool, letting you perform multiple transformations—rotating, resizing, and skewing—with one tool, rather than having to select, say, the Rotate Tool, the Shear Tool, and the Selection Tool, respectively.

To Do: Using the Free Transform Tool

Let's quickly see how this tool works, because it can save some steps when you are editing page objects.

1. Open a blank InDesign document, and using the Rectangle Tool, draw a rectangle anywhere on the page.

2. With the object selected, click the Free Transform Tool in the Tools palette, or hit E.

3. Move the pointer over the rectangle. The pointer will turn to a stemless arrowhead. This lets you move the object around the page.

4. Move the cursor off the object. You'll see the pointer turn into a curved, double-headed arrow. If you now click and drag, the object will be rotated.

5. Move the pointer over one of the object's handles. The pointer will turn into a straight, double-headed arrow. If you click and drag, the object will be resized, either larger or smaller, depending on the direction you drag it. If you Shift-drag while resizing, the object's height and width will be resized proportionally.

6. Click and drag a side handle (not a corner). *After* you start dragging, hold down the Option+Command keys (on the Mac) or the Alt+Ctrl keys (on PCs). This skews the object. You can also hold down Shift+Option+Command (or Shift+Alt+Ctrl on PCs) to skew proportionally.

You can use the Free Transform Tool on any page object.

Polygon Tool

Anyway, back to our drawing tools. Also hidden under the Rectangle Tool (next to the Ellipse Tool) the Polygon Tool lets you create many-sided shapes, like pentagons, hexagons, and the ever-popular dodecahedron. You can also use it to create stars.

By default, the Polygon Tool creates a hexagon. Select the Polygon Tool, and then click and drag to create the shape.

 You can create a polygon with as few as three sides (a triangle); less than three violates some laws of geometry, at least in this dimension. Your polygon can have as many as 100 sides. But remember that the more sides you add the closer you come to having a circle.

To change the number of sides for the next polygon, double-click the Polygon Tool in the tools palette. This displays the Polygon Settings dialog box shown in Figure 10.8.

10

FIGURE 10.8

You can create many shapes, including stars, using the Polygon Tool.

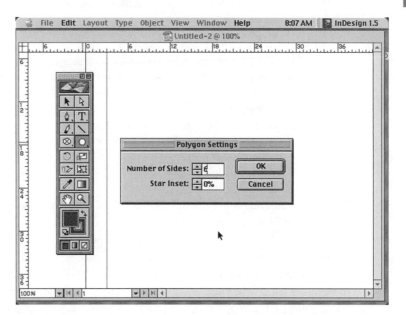

Type in or click the arrows to select the number of sides you want. To create a regular polygon, make sure that the Star Inset value is 0%. If you want to create a star, the number of sides you have set will determine how many points the star has. The Star Inset percentage you select will determine how pronounced the points are. The greater the percentage, the "starrier" it will look.

Pen Tool

We've saved the best for last. The Pen Tool is the most interesting—and can be the most complicated—of the drawing tools. You can use it to create simple lines, just like the Line Tool or the Pencil Tool, but you can also create curves and closed paths with the Pen Tool. The Pen Tool and the creation of paths requires a more in depth discussion than a few one-liners about the Pen Tool. So let's enter the wonderful world of paths.

Creating Paths

A path is essentially a line that describes a shape. A simple straight line is a path. A curve is a path. The outline of a circle or square is a shape. The outline of a silhouette of Abraham Lincoln is a path. Paths are the most basic elements of what are known as "vector graphics," which is essentially what we are creating.

In programs such as InDesign, as well as Illustrator, FreeHand, and other programs, lines and shapes exist as *vectors*, or what are known as *Bézier curves*. (Pierre Bézier was a French mathematician whose name lives on in graphics programs.) Essentially, these shapes are defined by mathematical equations, and exist in contrast to bitmap images, which simply comprise a grid of pixels. The primary difference is that vectors can be scaled to any size and will reproduce at the highest resolution supported by the output device it is sent to, unlike bitmaps which will only reproduce as smoothly as its number of pixels allows.

What does this mean for us now? The drawing tools we have been looking at essentially create Bézier curves—or paths. A curve or line is called an *open path*; a shape such as a circle or a rectangle is a *closed path*.

When we create shapes in InDesign, we are creating paths. Tools such as the Line Tool, the Rectangle Tool, and so on are simply preset paths that let us quickly create a shape. We can use the Pen Tool, though, to create a shape—a path—from scratch. Think of it as the difference between opening a can of soup or making it from the scratch. You throw a can of chicken soup in a pot and it's already made. You don't worry about what's in it. On the other hand, when you make chicken soup from scratch, you know exactly what's in it. It's more laborious, but you have more control over the contents.

That's probably a labored example (it's getting on to lunchtime as I write this), but the preset shape tools are the canned soup. You can pop them on the page and not worry too much about editing them. But you can use the Pen Tool to create the path from scratch.

Creating Simple Open Paths

Paths come in two types: open and closed. An *open path* is a line or curve. A *closed path* is a shape such as a rectangle, circle, etc., in which the last path segment hooks back up with the first path segment, kind of like a snake eating its own tail. Let's start with open paths.

Even though we can use the Line Tool to draw a line, we can also use the Pen Tool to create a line. To draw a straight line, click at the beginning of the line to create an anchor point, and then click again at the end of the line. InDesign creates a line that connects the two anchor points. See Figure 10.9.

Figure 10.9

A straight line created with the Pen Tool.

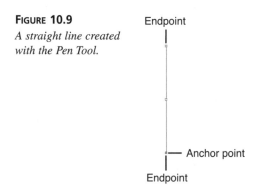

10

Straightforward, right? Well, now things get a bit more complicated. To draw a curved line, click and drag at the beginning of the line to create an anchor point for a curve, and then click and drag again at the end of the line to create another curved anchor point. See Figure 10.10.

Figure 10.10

A curved line created with the Pen Tool.

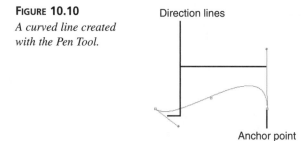

Let's dissect these lines and curves and check out their anatomy.

An *anchor point* is any of the points that comprise the path. Think of them as the "dots" in the connect the dots. In an open path—such as a line—the beginning and end anchor points are also called *endpoints*. A *path segment* is the line that connects one anchor point to another.

When we deal with curves, we also have what are known as *direction lines*. Direction lines extend out from anchor points. Dragging the direction lines changes the shape of a curve.

Think of it this way, and here's a simple non-computer exercise that will help illustrate paths and direction lines. Take a rubber band and snip it so that you have a straight line. Place it on the desk or table in front of you and tape it down at either end—or, better yet, pin both ends to a bulletin board. These pieces of tape or push pins are the anchor points for the path defined by the rubber band. Now, take a pen, and place the point of it under the rubber band right next to the rightmost pushpin or piece of tape. Drag the pen upward. The rubber band will bow out, forming a curve, but if your tape or pin is strong enough, the anchor point won't move.

It's not a perfect example, but that's the basic principle. Back in InDesign, two basic physical rules apply to direction lines: the longer the direction line, the more the path segment is affected by the curve; and the greater the angle of the direction line with respect to the path, the more pronounced the curve.

Okay, that's a simple path, be it straight or curved. But paths can have more than two anchor points, and thus more than one segment. The anchor points at which two segments meet can be one of two types: a corner point or a smooth point. At a *corner point*, a path changes direction rather abruptly. At a *smooth point*, one path segment is segued into the next via a continuous curve. Figure 10.11 illustrates these two types of points.

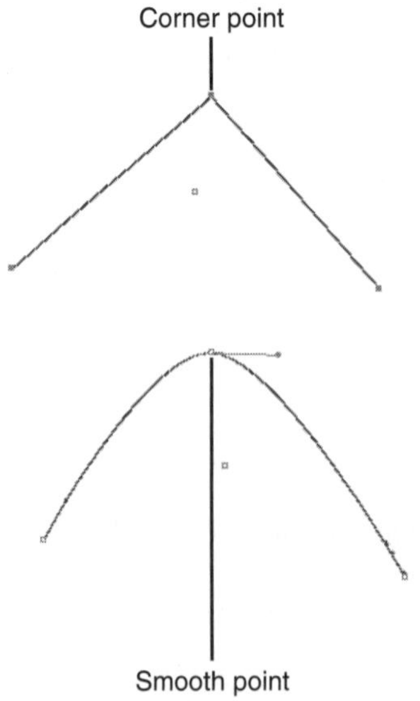

FIGURE **10.11**

The top figure shows two path segments connected via a corner point. The bottom figure shows the two segments connected via a smooth point.

Corner point

Smooth point

To Do: Creating a Curve

I know what you're saying: "What the heck is he on about?" Well, let's have a look. Here's how to create a curve. Try experimenting with the Pen Tool to figure out how curves really work:

1. Select the Pen Tool, either by clicking it on the Tools palette or by hitting P on the keyboard.

2. Click and drag to create the first curved anchor point.

3. Click and drag to create the second curved anchor point.

> When drawing with the Pen Tool, unlike the Pencil or Line Tool, you do not drag out the line or curve itself. You cannot drag the Pen Tool to create a line; dragging changes the anchor point into an endpoint for a curve.

10

Creating Closed Paths

What we've looked at so far have been open paths—lines, curves, and the like. Closed paths have the same basic anatomy as open paths—anchor points, path segments, direction lines, and so on. Figure 10.12 shows an open path versus a closed path.

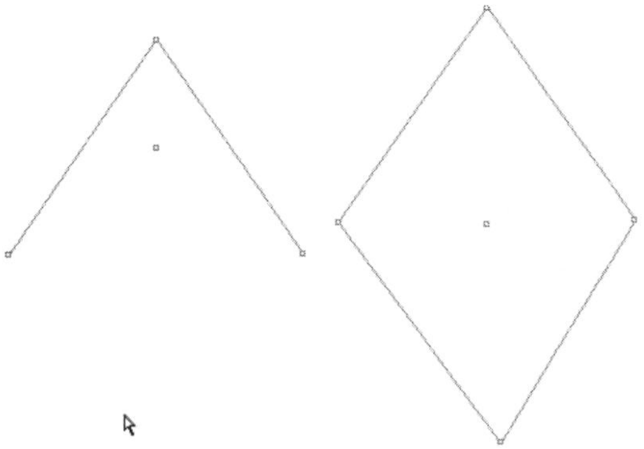

FIGURE 10.12

The figure on the left is an open path. The figure on the right is a closed path.

To Do: Creating a Closed Path

You can use the Pen Tool to create a closed path. To create a closed path, follow these steps:

1. Select the Pen Tool.

2. Click to create two or three straight anchor points, or click and drag to create curved anchor points. I'll leave it up to you.

3. To connect the line to the first anchor point and close it, click the first anchor point. Notice that the cursor changes from a standard pen to a pen with a tiny "o" next to it (which means that that you can close the path by clicking there). See Figure 10.13.

FIGURE 10.13

The cursor changes to show that you can close the path by clicking here.

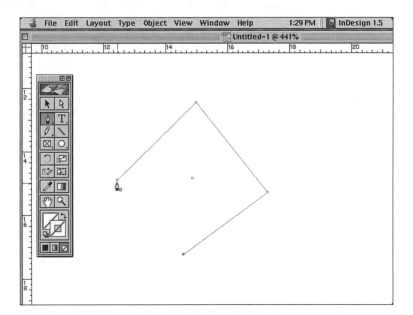

Closed paths can be used to create customized shapes beyond the simple circles, rectangle, and so on that InDesign gives you. You can use paths as picture frames (you can create a closed path and import an image into it), or use it as part of an illustration. The options are limitless.

Well, okay, not limitless, but suffice it to say there are quite a lot of them. You can also color your paths and shapes, which we will cover in Hour 13, "Simple Coloring with InDesign" and Hour 14, "Advanced Color Work."

What we're getting at is that these drawing tools are for exactly that: drawing. Depending on your illustration skills, you can use the tools to create original artwork. Many of the things you can do in Illustrator or FreeHand you can now do in InDesign.

Editing Paths

To reiterate: Any object you draw in InDesign is made up of one or more paths. Paths are made of anchor points. Paths—and therefore shapes—are modified by editing the anchor points.

You can select an entire path, which enables you to move the path or change it in other ways. You can also select a single anchor point and modify it. To do this, you need to use the Selection Tool and the Direct Selection Tool as follows:

- To select an entire path, click the Selection Tool, and then click anywhere on the path. The entire bounding box will be selected, as in Figure 10.14.

10

FIGURE 10.14

Selecting a shape with the Selection Tool selects the entire path en masse.

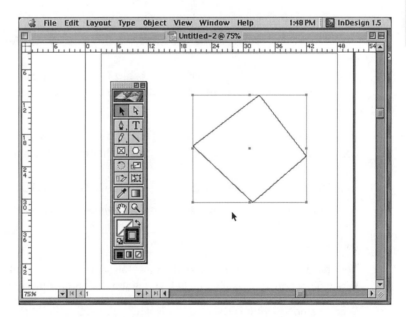

- To select an anchor point, click the Direct Selection Tool. The path itself, replete with anchor points, will be selected, and individual anchor points can be modified, as in Figure 10.15. (For keyboard shortcut fans, you can toggle between these two tools by hitting V to select the Selection Tool and A to select the Direct Selection Tool.)

Figure **10.15**

*Selecting a shape with
the Direct Selection
Tool selects the path
and its individual
anchor points.*

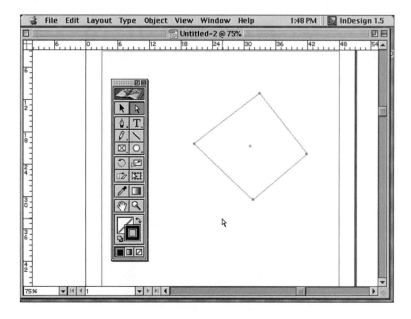

When you select a path, a bounding box is displayed around the path. When you select an anchor point, it appears filled in. (All the anchor points except the selected one stay hollow.)

If the path is selected, clicking and dragging moves the entire path. But if just an anchor point is selected, clicking and dragging that anchor point moves the anchor point.

Using Corner Points and Smooth Points

As we've seen, there are two types of anchor points—corner points and smooth points. Straight paths, like straight lines or the corners on a rectangle, use corner points. Curved paths, like arcs and ellipses, use smooth points.

You move corner points and smooth points the same way—just select the point with the Direct Selection Tool, and then click and drag it to the new location.

When a smooth point is selected, it displays its direction lines. (We looked at direction lines briefly earlier.)

To change the shape of a curve, you change the length and angle of the direction lines attached to the smooth point.

To Do: Changing a Corner Point to a Smooth Point

You can change a point from a corner point to a smooth point, and vice versa. There's a tool hiding under the Pen Tool just for this purpose.

1. Open a blank InDesign document. Create a painfully angular path having a corner point, like the one in Figure 10.16.

FIGURE **10.16**

A path having a corner point.

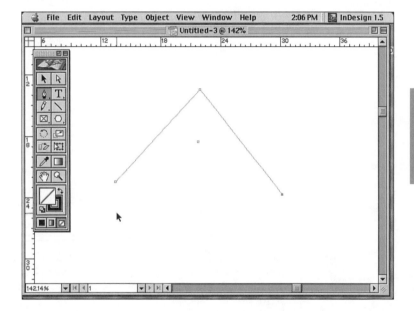

2. Click and hold on the Pen Tool in Tools palette until you see the hidden tools. Select the Point Conversion Tool (it looks like an upside down, tilted V).

3. Click the point you want to change. In the case of Figure 10.16, it would be the anchor point at the apex of the path. Drag to make the direction lines appear. You can watch your corner point inflate into a parabola. See Figure 10.17.

If you didn't like the parabola, make sure the Point Conversion Tool is selected, and simply click on the smooth point. It will turn back into a corner point.

> For you keyboard shortcut fans out there, if the Pen Tool is active, holding down the Option key (on the Macintosh) or the Alt key (on Windows) turns the cursor into the Point Conversion Tool.

▼

FIGURE **10.17**
Our angular path has put on weight, thanks to the Point Conversion Tool, and is now a lovely parabola.

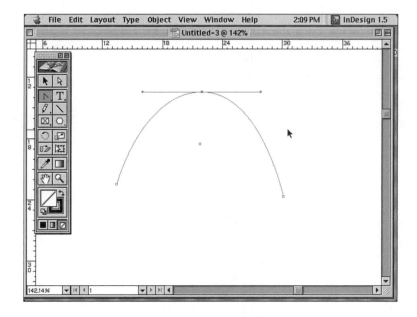

So why would you want to do this? Many reasons. It's a way of editing paths, giving you control over your drawing tools. But here's one thought, and hopefully this will help eliminate any confusion over corner points versus smooth points.

I am creating an illustration of, say, a hand. Why a hand? Who knows? Why not? I'm not a skilled illustrator (I have a hard time drawing a straight line with the shift key held down), so I quickly get out the Pen Tool and draw a bunch of paths connected by corner points, like Figure 10.18.

It's more of a hedgehog than a hand, right? Well, I can take my Point Conversion Tool and turn those sharp spines into fingers, ending up with Figure 10.19.

I can then add some more anchor points and further make it look like a proper hand.

FIGURE 10.18

A quickie "rough" path that I can clean up using the Point Conversion Tool.

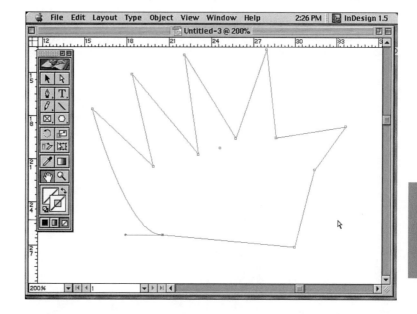

FIGURE 10.19

It's still not going to win any illustration awards, but it is distinctly more hand-like.

10

Adding and Deleting Anchor Points

In addition to moving around existing anchor points, you also can add and remove them. Remember, if we think of anchor points as dots in a connect-the-dots puzzle, the more anchor points we have, the more detail in our path. By the same token, you may end up with an anchor point in a place you don't want one.

So, you can use two tools hidden under the Pen Tool to add or delete anchor points. To access them, click and hold the Pen Tool in the Tools palette. See Figure 10.20.

FIGURE 10.20

The additional path editing tools hidden under the Pen Tool.

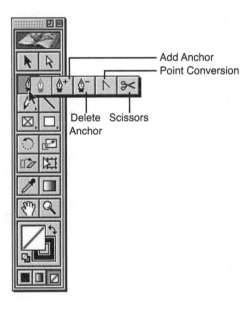

The Add Anchor Point Tool (the "pen plus" tool) enables you to add an anchor point. Just select the path and click where you want to add the point. (To add a new smooth point, click and then drag to extend the direction lines.)

The Delete Anchor Point Tool (the "pen minus" tool) lets you remove an anchor point. First, select the path so that you can see the anchor points, and then select the Delete Anchor Point tool and click the anchor point you want to remove.

Cleverly enough, the Pen Tool gives instant access to the other three tools when it is selected and you have a path selected. When you hover the cursor over a path segment, it becomes the Add Anchor Point Tool; if you click, a point will be added. When you hover the cursor over an anchor point, it becomes the Delete Anchor Point Tool; if you click, you'll delete the point. And as we saw earlier, you can also access the Point Conversion Tool by holding down the Option (on the Mac) or Alt (on PCs) key when the Pen Tool is selected.

Adding Length to an Open Path

After creating a path, you can add to either end of the path (provided, of course, it's not a closed shape, which doesn't have a beginning or an end). Here's how to do it.

To Do: Adding to a Path

To add to a path, follow these steps:

1. Create a simple path, and select it with the direct selection tool. (Selecting the path isn't required, but it makes it easier to see the anchor points.)

2. With the Pen Tool selected, bring the cursor near the last anchor point in your path. The cursor—which will be the Pen Tool with an "x" to the right of it—will turn to a pen with a slash (/) next to it. That slash indicates that when you click, you'll make the endpoint active and can connect additional anchor points.

▲   3. Click or click and drag to create new anchor points.

To create a new, separate, path on top of an existing end point without adding to the existing path, hold down the Shift key when you click the existing end point.

Advanced Techniques for Paths

This hour has covered the basics of working with paths, but there are some interesting advanced options. They include joining and splitting paths and creating compound paths. You can also create paths out of text, which we'll look at in Hour 11, "Combining Text and Graphics." You can also create clipping paths around images, which we will also look at in Hour 11.

Joining Paths

While you are creating a new path, you can add that path to the end of an existing path. Instead of clicking to create a new anchor point, click on top of the end point of an existing path. You'll notice that the cursor changes from the pen to a pen with a connector icon. This shows that you are attaching the new path to the existing one.

10

To Do

Splitting a Path

You can also split a path. If the path is closed, splitting it creates an open path. If the path is already open, splitting it creates two separate paths.

Say we have the path in Figure 10.21. It is a hand.

FIGURE 10.21

A sample path that we want to split.

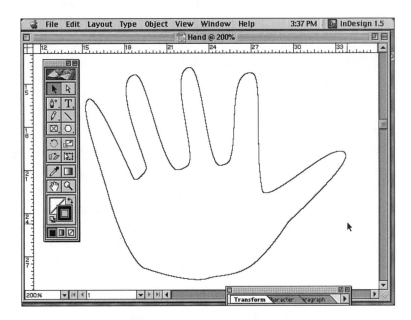

There are many reasons why we might want to split it. To do so, we would select the Scissors Tool (which, as we saw, is under the Pen Tool), and then click the path at the point where you want to split it. In this case, to split a closed path in half, we would need to split both the top and bottom portions. This will give us two half hands, which could be used for something like Figure 10.22.

Working with Compound Paths

You can combine two or more paths to create a compound path. To create a compound path, select two closed paths. Then select Object, Compound Paths, Make. The compound path that's created makes a hole wherever the top path overlaps the bottom path. It's like subtracting one path from the other. (You can also undo a compound path by selecting Object, Compound Paths, Release.)

FIGURE 10.22

We split the path to create two half hands and added a text frame in the middle. Again, it's not going to win any awards, but you get the idea.

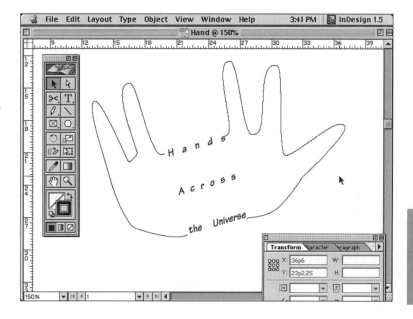

Compound paths can be used when you are doing illustrations to knock out portions of images. Figure 10.23 shows a basic example of the effects of compounding a path.

FIGURE 10.23

The figure on top comprises two filled circles that overlap slightly. Selecting each circle and making them into a compound path, knocks out the area where they overlap— the bottom figure.

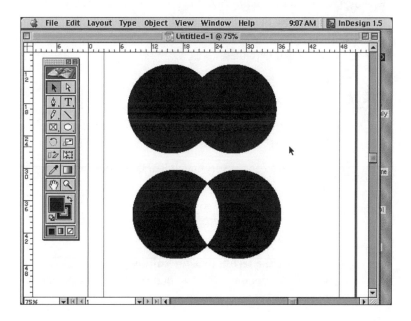

You can also combine paths to add two shapes together, such as to make a snowman out of three circles. To combine paths in this way, you reverse the top path in the compound path. Select a point on the top path (in the compound path), and then select Object, Reverse Path.

Summary

If you have no skills as an illustrator you may be inclined to give the drawing tools in InDesign a miss. I can sympathize, believe me, but even if you have no artistic skills at all, you can still get a lot out of them. Especially as these tools also let you adjust page layouts. Colored bars, backgrounds, shapes, etc., are common page elements in documents, and where do they come from? From the drawing tools.

Workshop

Drawing tools, and the idea of paths in particular, make a lot of people nervous. In fact, they made me nervous some time ago, when I would avoid Pen Tools in any program like the plague. I used to make our art director do all my clipping paths for me because I just could not get the hang of direction lines and moving anchor points. But, I forced myself to sit down one afternoon, and figure it all out, and now I love paths. The biggest obstacle is understanding how the different permutations of the Pen Tool vary from each other—and what the heck the Direct Selection Tool does. Hopefully, we have explained it well enough that you understand the basic principles. Now is your chance to start noodling around with these tools.

Q&A

Q You didn't say anything about the Rectangle/Ellipse/Polygon Frame Tools. What gives?

A These tools behave very much like the corresponding tool we discussed in this hour. The Rectangle/Ellipse/Polygon Frame Tools were covered in the last hour, and are used to import graphics into, or to act as layout placeholders. However, nothing prevents you from importing graphics into the shape tools we do cover in this chapter.

Q Can I use the techniques for editing paths (i.e., the Direct Selection Tool, as well as the "pen plus" and "pen minus" tools) to clean up shapes I drew with the Pencil Tool?

A Absolutely. In fact, you can use the Direct Selection Tool and all the permutations of the Pen Tool to edit any path—or any shape—created in InDesign. This includes not only paths you create "freehand" with the Pencil Tool, but lines created with the Line Tool, rectangles, ellipses, polygons—even text frames. You name it, you can edit it.

Q **I still don't know why I would want to convert a smooth point into a corner point, or even vice versa.**

A Well, look, you know, not everyone is going to want to use every tool and every feature in InDesign. Basically, it's a way of editing a path, and when you're creating illustrations or doing clipping paths, often you will need this sort of feature.

10

Quiz

1. To draw a circle, you do which of the following?
   a. Click and drag with the Polygon Tool.
   b. Shift+click and drag with the Line Tool.
   c. Shift+click and drag with the Ellipse Tool.

2. To move an anchor point, you:
   a. Click and drag with the Pen Tool.
   b. Select the anchor point with the Direct Selection Tool, and then click and drag.
   c. Select the path with the Selection Tool, and then copy and paste.

3. Which of the following cannot be accomplished with the Free Transform Tool:
   a. Scaling
   b. Rotating
   c. Editing anchor points

4. The Scissors Tool is used to do which of the following?
   a. Copy and paste
   b. Join paths
   c. Split paths

Quiz Answers

1. c. You can shift+click and drag with the Ellipse Tool to draw a perfect circle. And, technically, you could also use the Polygon Tool with the number of sides set sufficiently high.

2. b. Clicking and dragging anchor points with the Direct Selection Tool moves those points. Clicking and dragging with the Pen Tool only changes the direction lines, altering the shape of a curve.

3. c. You cannot edit anchor points with the Free Transform Tool.

4. c. The Scissors Tool is used to split paths.

Exercises

InDesign's drawing tools provide you with lots and lots of options. Let creativity be your guide as you experiment, but be sure to try at least these tasks:

- Experiment with the various drawing tools. Try freehand drawing with the Pencil Tool. Experiment with the Line Tool and the different options in the Stroke palette. Often you need to create dashed lines and arrow-headed lines. Practice how to do it.

- Create some paths and modify them by adding and removing anchor points, and converting anchor points from corner to smooth or vice versa. Use the Pen Tool to clean up paths you create with the Pencil Tool. Use the Pen Tool to edit the paths of such shapes as rectangles and ellipses.

- Try splitting and joining paths with the Scissors Tool. Create a hand illustration (like the one we saw earlier). Snip it in half—then see if you can put it back together again.

HOUR 11

Combining Text and Graphics

In previous hours, you learned how to create and import text into InDesign documents, and you also learned how to create graphics in InDesign and import graphics from other programs. Document and page elements don't exist in a vacuum (unless you're creating pages in space, which may be possible in the near future), so in this hour you learn how to make text and graphics interact with each other. This enables you to add special effects and have dynamic looking pages. Specifically, you learn:

- How to anchor graphics in a text frame
- How to wrap text around a graphic
- How to create and use clipping paths
- How to use text as a frame for other text and graphics
- How to use the new Eyedropper tool to apply colors and styles
- How to create text on a path

Anchoring Graphics in Text

By now, you've seen how you can create text in InDesign, and how you can place graphics on a page. Usually, when you add graphics, they exist by themselves; that is, they stay in one portion of a page and move only when you move them. However, you might want to place images on a page in such a way that they flow with the text.

Why would you want to do this? Well, take a look at this book, for example. Each of the figures corresponds to the text directly above or below it (at least in theory…). But what happens if some ne'er-do-well author or editor decides at the last minute to add a section of text to an early portion of a chapter? This means the text will wrap forward, but the images will remain in their original positions and will have to be relocated accordingly. As you can imagine, that can be a pain, especially when you have a lot of images to relocate.

InDesign enables you to anchor your images in a text frame. (InDesign refers to this as an *inline frame*; in QuarkXPress it is called an *anchored picture box*.) It's simple to do.

To Do: Anchoring a Graphic within a Text Frame

To anchor a graphic in a text frame, do the following:

1. Open an InDesign document. Add a text frame and fill it with a few paragraphs of text, either typed from scratch, imported from a text or Word file, or by means of the Fill with Placeholder Text command, which is accessed by going to Type, Fill with Placeholder Text.

2. Import a graphic using the Place command (File, Place). Put it roughly where it should appear, and resize it accordingly.

3. Now, cut the image using Edit, Cut. You also can use Command+X (on the Macintosh) or Ctrl+X (in Windows). You're not deleting it, so don't use the Delete key. You're just placing it on the Clipboard.

4. Select the Text tool, and click in the text frame where you want your graphic to go. When you see the blinking insertion point, paste the image in using Edit, Paste (or Command+V on the Macintosh or Ctrl+V in Windows).

5. Your graphic behaves roughly like text now. Add some text before the graphic. Notice that it now flows in the same position with respect to the surrounding text. If you want to center the graphic in a column, simply select it with the Text tool (as you do text) and use the Paragraph palette to center it.

To center an inline graphic, you do indeed use the Center command on the Paragraph palette. But if your graphic was inserted in the middle of a paragraph and you select Center, you'll end up centering the entire paragraph and not just the graphic. As a result, you might be better off adding an inline graphic between paragraphs rather than in the middle of them.

To delete an inline graphic, select it with the Selection tool and press Delete. You can also place the cursor to the right of the image and backspace it away, as you do text.

After you've anchored your picture frame, notice that you can resize it, but you can't move it up or down easily. To control the image's spacing, you'll need to use a combination of leading and baseline shift commands. Working with inline graphics can take some getting used to, and not everyone likes them. But they can be an easy way to save yourself work in the long run, particularly when you know that your text might rewrap in the future.

Placed graphics aren't the only objects you can anchor to text. You can also draw a rectangle, square, circle, polygon, etc., with InDesign's drawing tools and paste them inline as well. You can also anchor other text frames in the same way.

Working with Text Wraps

When you initially import a graphic into InDesign (using the Place command), it is text wrapless by default. What this means is that if you place this graphic over a column of text, it will sit on top of the text and obscure what is beneath it. See Figure 11.1.

Creating Basic Text Wraps

One way to solve this text-obscuring problem is to create a text frame above and below the graphic and simply thread the text from one frame to the next. That's kind of laborious, and if the image moves, you have to adjust the text frames. So, InDesign, like any other self-respecting layout program, enables you to add a text wrap, which offsets the text from the edges of the graphic by an amount you specify. You do this by using the Text Wrap palette. Choose Object, Text Wrap or press Option+Command+W (on the Macintosh) or Alt+Ctrl+W (in Windows). See Figure 11.2.

FIGURE 11.1

When you place a graphic in InDesign, it has no text wrap by default, and thus obscures what is beneath it. This may or may not be desirable.

FIGURE 11.2

The Text Wrap palette.

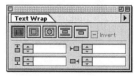

This palette has two sections: the icons along the top control how the text wraps, and the fields below the icons set the text offset from the graphic.

To Do: Creating a Text Wrap

This exercise dives right in and goes through the steps to create a basic text wrap.

1. Using techniques you learned in previous chapters, create a new InDesign document and add a text frame to a blank page. Fill it with text, either generated from scratch (if you're thinking of starting that novel you've always wanted to write), from a text or Word file, or using the Fill with Placeholder Text command.

2. Now, using the Place command, import a graphic file. Or, if you don't have one, draw a shape, let's say a rectangle. Your graphic should now be sitting on top of the text, like the graphic in Figure 11.1.

3. With your object selected, open the Text Wrap palette (choose Object, Text Wrap). You should notice that the first icon is highlighted. This is the No Wrap button.

4. Click the second icon, officially called the Wrap Around Bounding Box button. This is the straightforward wrap button and offsets the text from the picture frame. Your graphic is now offset from the text below it, but notice that by default, the wrap amount is 0p0 (or 0 in., depending on the measurement units you have set in your Preferences). This means that the text appears right up against the edges of the graphic. Design-wise, this might be undesirable, so you'll probably want to put some space between the text and the graphic.

5. Add space to all four sides of your graphic by either typing specific numbers in the fields corresponding to the top, bottom, left, and right sides of the graphic, or by clicking the up and down arrows next to each field. Notice that a blue line emerges from the sides of the graphic and effectively pushes the text away. See Figure 11.3.

For you keyboard shortcut fans, when setting your offset values you can also use the Tab key to jump from field to field, and Shift+Tab to jump backward from field to field. You can also use the up and down arrow keys to increase or decrease (respectively) the offset values.

FIGURE 11.3

You can adjust the amount that the text is offset from each side of a placed graphic.

6. For a more hands-on text wrap adjustment, you can grab the picture frame's handles and pull the frame out to displace the text. Or you can grab the handles of the wrap itself and pull to the appropriate position.

▲   Be sure to save this file for a later exercise.

Notice that as you add a wrap (as in Figure 11.3), the spacing of text can get kind of funky, particularly in narrow columns with justified text. Note those big gaps between words, and the egregious letter spacing in some of the lines. You might need to experiment with size and position to get it to look palatable. You'll often have to play with kerning, tracking, and hyphenation of the text itself.

That's your basic text wrap. You can resize the graphic and the wrap will resize with it.

Wrap and Graphic Resizing

When resizing a graphic with a text wrap, be sure to pay attention to the icon that the cursor turns into before doing the resize. If you grab a picture frame handle, and the cursor is the usual selection arrow, you will simply move the text wrap. If you want to resize the graphic, make sure the cursor has changed to the diagonal double-ended arrow. See Figures 11.4 and 11.5 for this distinction.

11

FIGURE 11.4

When the cursor displays the selection arrow, you are adjusting the text wrap applied to the graphic.

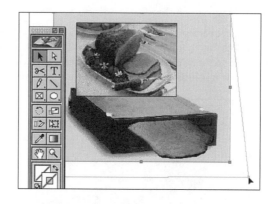

FIGURE 11.5

When the cursor displays the diagonal, double-headed arrow, you are resizing the graphic.

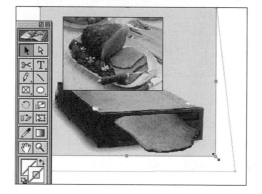

You can also apply text wraps to other text frames when, for example, you need to add a caption to an image. See Figure 11.6.

FIGURE 11.6

You can also apply a text wrap to another text frame and, by making the text offset the same amount as the graphic, you can add a caption to an image.

Setting Jumping Text Wraps

The Text Wrap palette also has a couple of other options for wrapping text around graphics. The Jump Object button (see Figure 11.7) ensures that no text appears on either side of the graphic, which is useful when you don't want text to completely surround the graphic—such as in this book, for example, where the figures do not have text (aside from captions) on their left or right sides.

FIGURE 11.7

The Jump Object button prevents text from wrapping on the left and right sides of a graphic.

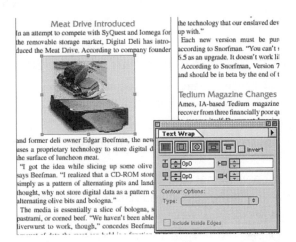

The Jump to Next Column button makes the text below the graphic jump to the top of the next column (see Figure 11.8).

FIGURE 11.8

The Jump to Next Column button, cleverly enough, causes text below the graphic to jump to the top of the next column.

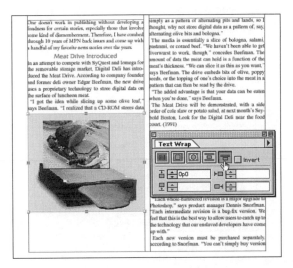

You can put text wraps around any object including EPSs and PDFs.

Wrapping Text Around Object Shapes

If you have sharp eyes, you might have noticed that the last section skipped over one option on the Text Wrap palette. That is the Wrap Around Object Shape button. This feature is based on the premise that not every graphic placed on a page is square or rectangular.

To Do: Wrapping Text Around an Object's Shape

You'll see in a bit how this feature gives you many design possibilities, but it's better to start with a simple example first:

1. Did you save your document from the last exercise? If so, make sure that it is open. If not, create a new document, create a text frame, and fill it with some sort of text.

2. Select the Circle tool on the Tools palette and draw a circle (or oval) over some portion of your text. Notice that the circle sits on top of the text (not displacing it), and that it has the usual rectangular bounding box around it.

3. Choose Object, Text Wrap to open the Text Wrap palette, if it is not already open, and select the Wrap Around Bounding Box button (the same button you clicked last time). Notice that the text wraps the same way it did last time: around the rectangular bounding box.

4. In this exercise, you want to wrap the text around the circle. So, click the Wrap Around Object Shape button, which is on the right side of the Wrap Around Bounding Box button. Your text/circle combo should look something like Figure 11.9.

FIGURE 11.9

By selecting Wrap Around Object Shape, you make the text follow the contours of the object.

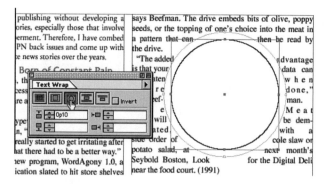

▼ 5. By default, the text is offset 0p10 (10 points) from the edge of the object. You can adjust that by clicking the up and down arrows, or entering amounts directly.

6. Just for fun, select the Invert checkbox. See what happens? This is sort of an inside-out text wrap that adds the text inside the image (see Figure 11.10).

FIGURE 11.10

By clicking the Invert checkbox, you reverse the wrap so that text flows around the inside of the object.

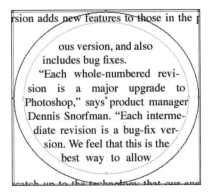

▲

Changing the Shape of a Wrap

You can also change the shape of the wrap using the Direct Selection tool. If you click on the wrap using the Direct Selection tool, you get a handle that you can click and drag. This tool warps the wrap and the text flows accordingly. For more control over the shape of the wrap, you can add more points to the wrap by clicking along it with the Pen tool. (We looked at the Pen tool in excruciating detail in Hour 10, "Using InDesign's Drawing Tools.") Each point that you add can be moved and adjusted independently (see Figure 11.11).

11

FIGURE 11.11

You can use a combination of the Pen tool and the Direct Selection tool to edit the control points that comprise a wrap.

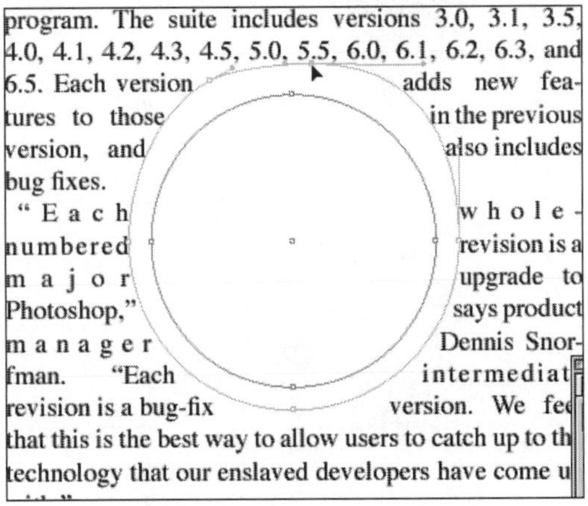

program. The suite includes versions 3.0, 3.1, 3.5, 4.0, 4.1, 4.2, 4.3, 4.5, 5.0, 5.5, 6.0, 6.1, 6.2, 6.3, and 6.5. Each version adds new features to those in the previous version, and also includes bug fixes.

"Each whole-numbered revision is a major upgrade to Photoshop," says product manager Dennis Snorfman. "Each intermediate revision is a bug-fix version. We feel that this is the best way to allow users to catch up to the technology that our enslaved developers have come u

Using Clipping Paths as Wraps

If you are good with clipping paths, you can import images containing them. By selecting the path to use in the Clipping Path dialog box, you can do some elaborate wraps.

NEW TERM A *clipping path* is essentially a mask that is applied to an image. Most commonly, clipping paths are created in Photoshop by using the Pen tool to draw a path along the contours of an image. They are often used to remove the background or extraneous bits of an image. When a clipping path is saved with an image and the image is imported into InDesign, the clipping path can be set as the graphic's frame boundary, in lieu of the usual rectangular bounding box.

Figure 11.12 shows a quickie example of how clipping paths in InDesign work. A Photoshop clipping path surrounds the devil image. The file was then saved as a Photoshop EPS. I placed it in InDesign, and was sure to select Create Frame From Clipping Path in the Import Options dialog box. With the object selected on the page, I made sure I selected Photoshop Path from the Clipping Path dialog box.

You then select the object using the Direct Selection tool. Use the arrow at the top right of the Text Wrap palette to go to the Text Wrap palette options. This enables you to select Show Options, which then adds the Contour Options to the palette. You can select Photoshop Path from the pop-up menu and InDesign will tell you which clipping paths exist in the image (files can have more than one). The result is a text wrap in the shape of the clipping path. As you saw earlier with the circle, this wrap is also editable using the Pen and Direct Selection tools.

FIGURE 11.12

A text wrap can follow the contours of a clipping path saved with a Photoshop EPS.

So you can see that you can add all sorts of funky effects to your pages using text wraps.

Creating Clipping Paths in InDesign

As mentioned earlier, clipping paths are usually created in a program such as Photoshop. For best results, you're probably better off using Photoshop. But InDesign gives you several options for creating clipping paths on-the-fly.

> As you saw in the last section, if you have a clipping path—or even an alpha channel—saved with your graphic, it can be imported into and identified by InDesign. It can then be used to wrap text.

Creating Clipping Paths Using Detect Edges

Assume the example image doesn't have a clipping path, nor do you have the time or patience to create one. InDesign can valiantly attempt to create one on-the-fly. This next exercise shows you how it works.

To Do: Creating a Clipping Path On-the-Fly

▼ To Do

11

Note that you must have a simple clipart image to complete this exercise. A photo won't cut it. You need something with clearly defined edges. The devil clipart image shown in Figure 11.9 is ideal, so if you've got something like that, make sure it is saved as a TIFF and has no clipping path or alpha channel embedded in it. if you don't have such an image, just follow along, and you can return to this section when you've got some artwork to use.

1. Open a blank InDesign document and add a paragraph or so of text, or repurpose the document you've been using for the last few exercises.

2. Using the Place command, import your image and pop it onto the page over your paragraph of text. As you expect, it just sits on top of your text.

3. Choose Object, Clipping Path. You also can press, if you have enough fingers, Shift+Option+Command+K (on the Mac) or Shift+Alt+Ctrl+K (in Windows). The Clipping Path dialog box is shown in Figure 11.13.

4. Under the Type pop-up menu, you can select your path type. If there had been a Photoshop-created clipping path or an alpha channel in the image, you can choose which one InDesign works with. If there is no path or alpha channel in the image, the Photoshop Path and Alpha Channel options will be grayed out, but you can have InDesign attempt to create a path by selecting Detect Edges. So do so. Make sure the Preview checkbox is enabled. This enables you to see what each of the subsequent controls does as it is adjusted.

▼

FIGURE 11.13
The Clipping Path dialog box.

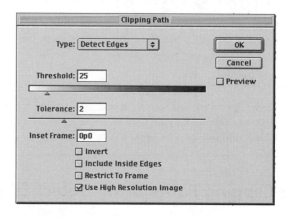

5. The Threshold slider lets you specify the darkest pixel value that will act as the boundary of the clipping path. If you simply have a white background, this value can be low, because it's not hard to have a pixel value darker than pure white. But if your background is darker than white, you might need to adjust this slider accordingly. Move it back and forth and see what effect it has. At the far right, it will select only the darkest pixels, so you might end up with a clipping path around only the absolute darkest areas of an image. In the devil image, the default seemed to work just fine.

6. The Tolerance slider controls how closely a pixel comes to the Threshold value before it is obscured by the path. The higher the tolerance, the more pixels are included. For example, you might want to define a path around a black edge. With Tolerance set to high, you'll get bits of any grayish shadow that exists. Anyway, it's harder to explain than to noodle with. Move this slider back and forth and check out the results.

7. Inset Frame tells InDesign how close to the clipping path to shrink the picture frame. A negative number in this field makes the frame larger than the clipping path. Enter some values in this field—both positive and negative—and watch what happens.

8. Invert, as mentioned in the Text Wrap section, swaps the visible and transparent portions of a path. Leave this unchecked for now.

9. Include Inside Edges includes any holes inside an image in the path. With this option selected, if you have any areas within your image that conform to the Threshold and Tolerance values, they'll be added to the path.

▼ For example, you can put a basic clipping path around a picture of a car, but if the view through the windows is the same as the background color you are removing, you can select this option to punch through the windows, and any background image you add in InDesign is visible through them.

10. Restrict to Frame creates a clipping path that stops at the visible edge of the image. It is less precise, but creates a simpler path.

11. Unless you don't mind a sloppy path, make sure that Use High Resolution Image is selected. If it isn't selected, InDesign uses a low-res screen proxy to calculate the pixel values to create the path. It's quick, but not as precise as using the high-res image.

12. If your clipping path looks okay, click OK. My path, using the default settings, is in Figure 11.14.

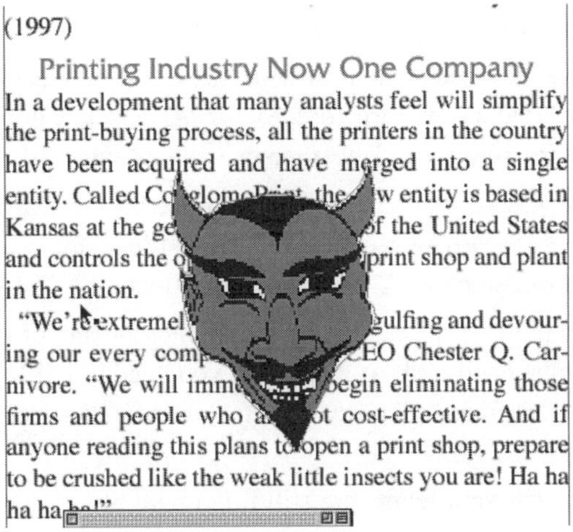

FIGURE 11.14

The clipping path created in InDesign is even more precise than the quickie path I created in Photoshop.

(1997)

Printing Industry Now One Company

In a development that many analysts feel will simplify the print-buying process, all the printers in the country have been acquired and have merged into a single entity. Called Colgloma Print, the new entity is based in Kansas at the geographic center of the United States and controls the only print shop and plant in the nation.

"We're extremely happy," said gulfing and devouring our every competitor, said CEO Chester Q. Carnivore. "We will immediately begin eliminating those firms and people who are not cost-effective. And if anyone reading this plans to open a print shop, prepare to be crushed like the weak little insects you are! Ha ha ha ha ha!"

11

▲ 13. You can now add a text wrap, as you saw earlier.

If you are creating an on-the-fly clipping path for the sole purpose of adding a text wrap, remember that you probably don't need to make it excruciatingly precise. As you probably noticed in some of my example figures, the text by nature is not going to hug the exact edge of the image, so you've got a bit of leeway when it comes to generating paths for text wraps.

Creating Frames from Text

Text wraps are nice, and they're extremely basic to many different types of layouts, but there are some other InDesign features that enable you to do a few more specialized things. InDesign enables you to combine text and graphics in an even more bizarre way: by having the text become a graphic.

Turning Text into a Text Frame

Text can also be converted into a text frame and filled with text. That sounds a bit cannibalistic, but with some experimentation, you can do some interesting things.

To Do: Creating a Text Frame Out of Text

To see how you can convert a letter or words into a text frame, try this simple example.

1. Open a blank InDesign document. Create a text frame and type a single letter or short word. As I'm doing this, I typed **FISH**.

2. With the Type tool, select all your text. Make the point size large—I used 250 points. I also used a sans-serif font, Swiss 721 Black. Choose something kind of blocky and sans-serif—say Helvetica or Arial. Make it all caps, too.

3. Choose Type, Create Outlines. This will convert your text into geometric paths and shapes. (The keyboard shortcut for Create Outlines, for you shortcut lovers out there, is Shift+Command+O on the Macintosh and Shift+Ctrl+O in Windows.)

4. Now, choose the Direct Selection tool and click on any of the letters you created. All the letters are selected. At this point, you need to tell InDesign what you want to place into this frame. Choose Object, Content and select Text from the pop-up menu.

5. You'll notice that your letters are still filled with black. You could have, at the outset, created white type, but you can just as easily go to the Colors palette (press F6) and drag the black-to-white slider all the way to the left (to white). Now, you have an empty set of letters that you can fill with text.

6. Select the Type tool and click in the first letter. You should get a blinking insertion point. Start typing, or use the Fill with Placeholder Text command. You'll see the large, hollow letters start to fill in with type. You need to make this internal text small in order to get it to flow properly, and even then it can be kind of hit or miss. Figure 11.15 shows an example.

Since the outlines you create will behave like any text frame, you can click in a letter to add an insertion point, and select File, Place to insert a Word document or text file.

FIGURE 11.15

You can take text, convert it to a text frame, and fill it with other text.

By noodling with various paragraph and character specs, you can make the text fill up letters a bit more thoroughly.

Turning Text into a Picture Frame

The previous exercise was kind of fun, but here's something even cooler: You can turn text into a picture frame and place a picture in it.

To Do: Creating a Picture Frame Out of Text

To convert text into a picture frame, follow these steps:

1. Much like you did previously, create a text frame and type some text. For example, I typed **ARIZONA**. Make it a fairly large point size. Use a thick typeface, otherwise the image you put into it won't be visible. I used Swiss 721 Black, which is kind of Helvetican but has thicker strokes.

2. Select the text you just created, and again go to Type, Create Outlines.

3. Select the outlines you just created with the Direct Selection tool and go to Object, Content. This time select Graphic.

4. Go to the Color palette (press F6) and again turn down the black.

5. Now, with the newly created picture frame still selected, import a graphic using the Place command. The image will peak out of each of the letters. You might have to do some scaling and transforming to get it to fit exactly. Figure 11.16 is what I came up with, using a digital camera capture I took of the Arizona desert.

▼ To Do

▲

11

After you have converted text to outlines, it can be scaled and transformed just like any other graphic. You don't even need to worry if your font was too narrow, or your point size too small. You can simply stretch and drag it to whatever dimensions you want. But remember: after text is converted to outlines, it is no longer editable, so make sure your text is spelled correctly *before* converting it.

Using the Eyedropper Tool

To further cement the interrelationship of graphics and text, InDesign 1.5 has added a tool that is familiar to users of Photoshop and Illustrator—the Eyedropper tool. (Adobe calls it the Eyedropper tool; I prefer to think of it as the Turkey Baster, because it has a much greater capacity than a simple eyedropper.)

Using the Eyedropper Tool to Apply Colors

If you've used the Adobe Eyedropper tool before (or similar tools in other programs), you know that it is used to pick up a color and apply that color elsewhere. The same principle applies in InDesign, but with a few special wrinkles, which I rather like.

To Do: Applying a Color from a Graphic to Text

One cool feature of the Eyedropper is that you can select a color in an imported graphic and then apply that color to text. Try the following steps:

1. Open a blank InDesign document. Using the Place command, add a color graphic—TIFF, EPS, Photoshop, whatever. Now, type some text below the image, such as a caption or headline, or just some random words.

▼ To Do

▼ 2. Select the Eyedropper (or Turkey Baster) tool. Click on a color in your graphic. You'll notice that the Eyedropper is now filled up and faces the other way. This means you can now apply that color anywhere else in your document. The color you selected, by the way, is displayed on the color chip at the bottom of the Tools palette, so there should be no doubt as to what color you are applying. Figure 11.17 attempts to show all this, albeit in black-and-white.

FIGURE 11.17

Using the Eyedropper tool to apply colors from imported graphics to text.

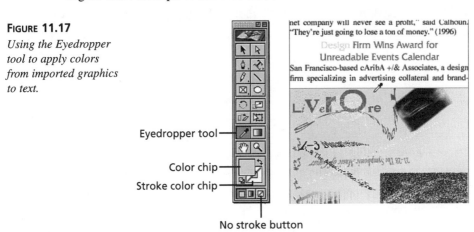

Eyedropper tool

Color chip

Stroke color chip

No stroke button

▲ 3. Click and drag the Eyedropper over your text. You'll see the text turn the color that you selected.

If you see a weird outline around your type, you might have a stroke selected. Simply click on the Stroke color chip (the one underneath the color chip at the bottom of the Tools palette) and click the No Stroke button.

If you click a full Eyedropper, it will apply the selected color to whatever is selected. If your text frame is selected, it will make the background the selected color. Using the Eyedropper tool is a good way of matching colors from different page elements. This will make a bit more sense when you get to Hour 13, "Simple Coloring with InDesign."

By the way, if you fill up your Eyedropper, but don't like what you filled it with, simply click anywhere on the tools palette to unload the Eyedropper.

Using the Eyedropper Tool to Apply Text Styles

But that's not all you can do with the Turkey Baster—er, I mean, Eyedropper. Remember in Hour 7, "Basic Typesetting with InDesign," and Hour 8, "Working with Paragraphs," when you created character and paragraph styles, respectively? Well, you can use the Eyedropper tool to suck up text styles and squirt them elsewhere.

To Do: Using the Eyedropper Tool to Apply Paragraph Styles

Here's how the Eyedropper tool sucks up text styles and places them elsewhere. Follow along:

1. Using techniques you learned in Hour 8, create one or two paragraph styles in a blank InDesign document.

2. Add a couple of paragraphs of text, either by typing it yourself, importing a Word or text file, or using Fill with Placeholder Text.

3. Apply one of your paragraph styles to the first paragraph. To see this clearly, make sure the style is discernibly different from the default paragraph style.

4. Select the Eyedropper tool and click it anywhere in the first paragraph. The Eyedropper should now fill up.

5. Click on the second paragraph. The first paragraph style is now applied to the second paragraph. Notice that the Eyedropper is still full. You can click on all subsequent paragraphs and apply that style to them all. To unload the Eyedropper, simply click the Tools palette.

As with all the tools in InDesign, you can control how the Eyedropper behaves by double-clicking its icon on the Tools palette. Figures 11.18, 11.19, and 11.20 show the three panes of options that you can turn off and on. You can cycle through the panes by hitting the Prev or Next buttons, or by using the pop-up menu at the top of the dialog box.

FIGURE 11.18

You can control what fill and stroke attributes the Eyedropper sucks up...

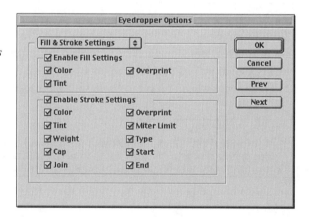

FIGURE 11.19

...as well as character attributes...

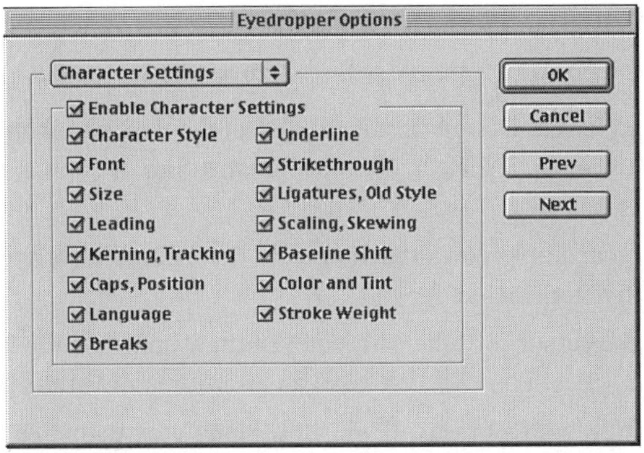

Eyedropper Options

Character Settings ◆

☑ Enable Character Settings
☑ Character Style   ☑ Underline
☑ Font   ☑ Strikethrough
☑ Size   ☑ Ligatures, Old Style
☑ Leading   ☑ Scaling, Skewing
☑ Kerning, Tracking ☑ Baseline Shift
☑ Caps, Position   ☑ Color and Tint
☑ Language   ☑ Stroke Weight
☑ Breaks

OK
Cancel
Prev
Next

FIGURE 11.20

...and paragraph attributes.

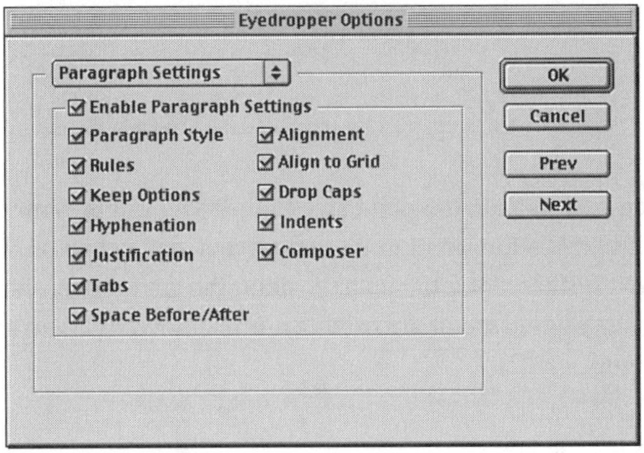

Eyedropper Options

Paragraph Settings ◆

☑ Enable Paragraph Settings
☑ Paragraph Style   ☑ Alignment
☑ Rules   ☑ Align to Grid
☑ Keep Options   ☑ Drop Caps
☑ Hyphenation   ☑ Indents
☑ Justification   ☑ Composer
☑ Tabs
☑ Space Before/After

OK
Cancel
Prev
Next

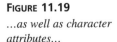

11

These panes are straightforward. Here is one caveat, though: If both Enable Paragraph Style and Enable Character Style are selected, the paragraph style will override the character style when you suck up a style and try to apply it. If you want to only suck up a character style and not have it apply to the entire paragraph, uncheck the Enable Paragraph Settings checkbox.

Text on a Path

One new feature in version 1.5 that blurs the line between text and graphics is the Text on a Path feature. This feature lets you run text along any path—either a predrawn shape like a circle or a hand-drawn shape. You have a wide variety of effects you can add, as well.

To Do: Creating Text on a Path

Try adding some text to a simple path, just to see how it works.

1. Open a blank InDesign document. Select the Pencil tool and draw a curve. It doesn't need be a perfect sine wave or anything. A simple, quickie, hand-drawn curve is fine.

2. Click on and hold down the Text tool. The Text on a path tool should pop up as an alternative tool; select it.

3. Move the cursor over the path you just drew until you see a tiny plus sign. When it appears, click. You will now have an insertion point at the beginning of the path.

4. Type a few words of text. It will flow along your path. See Figure 11.21.

FIGURE 11.21

Type flows along the path you set for it.

You can now change the point size (which you might want to do anyway, especially if it's too small to be seen), typeface, and so on. If you want to move your text further along the path, position the cursor over the leftmost In port until you get a selection arrow with a tiny "move right" icon next to it (see Figure 11.22).

FIGURE 11.22

You can shift the text further along the path.

In port

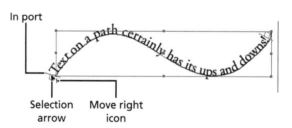

Selection   Move right
arrow   icon

When setting text on a path, your paragraph-alignment settings— left, right, centered, and so on—do apply. However, because you can only set one line of text on a single path, leading values don't apply. Rules above and below settings also do not apply.

▼

▼   5. Select the Selection tool and make sure your text is selected. Go to Object, Path
       Type and select Options. The Path Type Options dialog box (see Figure 11.23)
       enables you to apply a variety of effects to the text on a path. Make sure the
       Preview checkbox is selected, and spend some time changing various options.

FIGURE 11.23

*The Path Type Options
dialog box.*

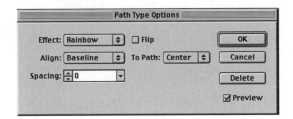

The options under the Effect drop-down box control how the type is aligned to the
path. The options are as follows:

- *Rainbow*—Keeps the center of each character's baseline parallel to the
  path's tangent. Essentially, the bottom of each letter sits flat on the path.

- *Skew*—Keeps each character's vertical edges perfectly vertical, yet allows
  each character's horizontal edges to follow the curve of the path.

- *3D Ribbon*—The reverse of skew, in a way. Keeps each character's horizontal edges perfectly horizontal while keeping each character's vertical edges
  perpendicular to the path.

- *Stair Step*—Keeps the left edge of each character's baseline on the path
  without rotating any characters.

- *Gravity*—Keeps the center of each character's baseline on the path, yet
  keeps each character's vertical edges in-line with the path's center point.

From the Align drop-down box, you can choose whether you want to align each
character's baseline, ascender, descender, or center to the path's top, bottom, or
center. You can also flip the type around the path, and you can control the spacing
of the characters.

   6. Explanations only go so far when it comes to this dialog box. Just try some
       random settings. Try using a circle, a rectangle, or other shapes as the path.

▼   Figure 11.24 shows a few of the many possible combinations.

11

FIGURE 11.24
Four sets of path type settings. Top to bottom: Rainbow (baseline aligned to path center); Skew (ascender aligned to path top); 3D Ribbon (center aligned to path center); and Gravity (baseline aligned to path center).

If you don't like your path, you can use the Direct Selection tool to edit it, and you can also use the Pen tool to add more control points to make the curve a bit more smooth, if that's what you want. By the way, if your text is too long for the path you created, you can thread text from one path to another (or from a path to a text frame, from a text frame to a path, and so on). Text is threaded from one path to another in the same way that text is threaded from one frame to another: by clicking on the red plus sign in the Out port and then clicking on another path.

Summary

So you can see that InDesign gives a great degree of control over how you can have your text work hand-in-hand with your graphics—and not simply duke it out on the page. From basic text wraps to clipping paths to using type as text frames—you can be as conservative or as creative in your treatment of graphics as you'd like.

Remember, though, that text on a path is nice, but it's one of those things that is best used in moderation. It's easy to get carried away with the tools that programs such as InDesign provide, but remember when you are designing professional documents—your pages need to be legible.

Workshop

You've just learned how you can add text wraps and clipping paths to images, as well as other ways that you can have graphics interact with text in InDesign. Check out the Q&A to find the answers to some questions you may have that might not have been covered in the chapter, and complete the quiz to test your recall of the features we covered. Finally, work through the exercises until you become a pro at working with text wraps and clipping paths.

Q&A

Q When you were talking about clipping paths, you mentioned alpha channels. What is an alpha channel?

A If you're familiar with Photoshop, you know that by default an RGB image has four color channels—one containing the red information, one containing the green information, one containing the blue information, and one containing the composite of all three. An alpha channel is an additional channel that stores mask information, thus enabling you to isolate specific portions of an image.

Q The steps you outlined for anchoring a picture frame seem a bit involved. Can't I do it directly from the Place command?

A Yes. The process is simply this: Make sure the Text tool is selected, click your insertion point in the text, and then use the Place command. Your graphic is placed inline automatically.

11

Quiz

1. In order to anchor a frame within another frame, what tool needs to be selected as you're pasting or placing?

    a. Direct Selection

    b. Text

    c. Eyedropper

    d. Magnifying Glass

2. Which of the following can the Eyedropper tool suck up and apply elsewhere in a document?

    a. Colors

    b. Character styles

    c. Paragraph styles

    d. All of the above

3. Which of the following can you use as a text wrap for an imported graphic?

   a. A clipping path created in Photoshop

   b. A clipping path created on-the-fly in InDesign

   c. Both of the above

   d. None of the above

4. When setting text on a path, which of the following type specs can you not change?

   a. Point size

   b. Tracking and/or kerning

   c. Leading

   d. Font

Quiz Answers

1. b. The Text tool is used to paste a graphic inline with text.

2. d. This is why I refer to it as the Turkey Baster tool.

3. c. You can use as a text wrap either a clipping path attached to an imported graphic, or you can add your own path in InDesign.

4. c. Since you can only set one line of text on a path at a time, you have no real need to adjust the leading, or the space between lines.

Exercises

You're at the end of the road in terms of the basics of InDesign's tools and features. The next four hours focus on color, and the five hours after that focus on getting documents out of InDesign. So this is the time to be proficient with InDesign's tools. In addition to creating sample layouts—and seeking to understand and emulate the layouts generated by professional magazine and newspaper designers—practice some special effects using the text on a path feature.

If you have a party coming up, a yard sale, or some other event, design some invites or signs—and take that opportunity to explore InDesign's tools. You can get a CD of clipart images or royalty-free photos pretty cheaply, so if you don't have many of your own graphics and images, pick up a CD or two and incorporate different types of images into your designs.

HOUR 12

Managing Objects on a Page

After spending the last few hours creating all sorts of items on your pages, it's time to bring some order to the chaos. In this hour, you learn the following:

- Grouping and stacking objects
- Aligning and distributing objects
- Locking objects so that they don't move
- Transforming and resizing objects
- Copying and duplicating objects

Grouping and Ungrouping Objects

You can combine two or more objects so that they are treated like a single object. This is called *grouping*.

Grouping your objects makes it much easier to manage complicated drawings with lots of bits and pieces. You can group together related pieces so that they are treated as one object. You can then change just the grouped object. Without grouping, you would have to select every item in the group individually.

To Do: Grouping Two Objects

Here's how to group two objects:

1. Click the first object to select it.

2. Shift-click the second object to add it to your selection. (To group lots of objects, just keep shift-clicking to add them.)

3. Select Object, Group.

Your objects are now grouped, and you'll notice that instead of bounding boxes around each selected object, you have a single bounding box around the group. See Figure 12.1 for an example.

Figure 12.1

Before grouping (left), you have multiple bounding boxes. After grouping (right), you have just one.

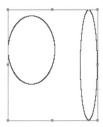

To ungroup a group, select the group, and then select Object, Ungroup.

Stacking Objects

When objects overlap on the page, they have a certain order from top to bottom. This is called the *stacking order*. The objects that are farther in front cover up objects that are farther down in the stack.

You can rearrange the stacking order by selecting an object and then changing its position in the stack.

Often, it's difficult to select the object at the bottom of the stack because the other objects get in the way. In this case, you can temporarily move the other objects to the bottom of the stack so that you can select the object you need to modify.

InDesign provides four commands that enable you to change a selected object's stacking order. You'll find them on the Object, Arrange submenu. They are as follows:

- Bring to Front—Moves the selected object to the top of the stack

- Send to Back—Moves the selected object to the bottom of the stack

- Bring Forward—Moves the selected object one level closer to the top of the stack
- Send Backward—Moves the selected object one level closer to the bottom of the stack

Figure 12.2 shows an example of the Bring Forward and Bring to Front commands in action.

FIGURE 12.2

The ellipse is at the bottom of the stack. The middle illustration shows the result of selecting the ellipse and then bringing it forward. The ellipse is now in the middle of the stack. Then, select the rectangle and select Bring to Front. The rectangle is now on top of the other shapes.

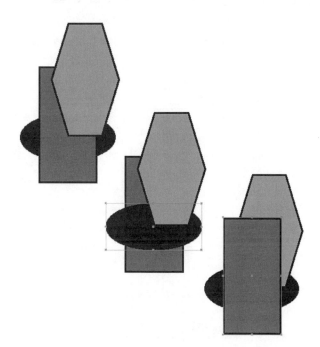

12

Aligning and Distributing Objects

InDesign's align and distribute features help you make sure that objects are arranged on the page exactly as you want them. You'll find both alignment and distribution options on the Align palette. To display it, select Window, Align.

Aligning objects means that you arrange them on an imaginary horizontal or vertical line. You can, for example, align selected objects so that all the left edges are on the same vertical line.

Distributing objects lets you arrange objects at equal distances. You can distribute objects so that there is an equal amount of space from one object to the next or so that the center points of the objects are equidistant.

To align objects, you need to select at least two objects. To distribute, you need at least three objects.

▼ To Do: Aligning and Distributing Objects

Here's how to align objects:

1. Select the objects you want to align or distribute. (You cannot modify objects within a group because the group is considered a single object.)

2. If necessary, display the Align palette (choose Window, Align), and then click the alignment or distribution option you want.

Your objects are aligned or distributed as specified. See Figures 12.3 and 12.4 for examples.

FIGURE 12.3
The selected objects are aligned to an imaginary line.

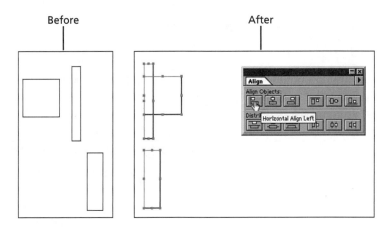

FIGURE 12.4
In this example, objects are distributed so that their center points are equidistant from top to bottom. The objects are not moved from their left/right locations.

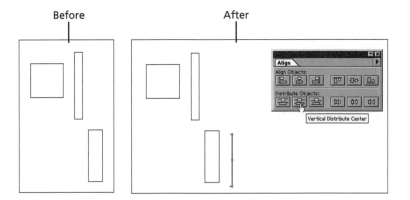

Locking and Unlocking Objects

Locking can keep an object out of the way while you modify another nearby object. When you lock the object, move commands no longer have any effect on the locked item.

Here's how to lock and unlock objects:

- To lock an object, select the object (or Shift-select multiple objects), and then select Object, Lock Position.
- To unlock an object, select the object, and then select Object, Unlock Position.

If you try to move a locked object, the cursor changes to a padlock icon.

Transforming Objects

Transforming is InDesign's catch-all term for several changes you can make to objects, including resizing, scaling, shearing (sort of a distorted tilting), and rotating them. All these features are available in the Transform palette, which is discussed in the following section.

Understanding the Transform Palette

The Transform palette (Figure 12.5) isn't very big, but there's lots going on in it.

FIGURE 12.5

Use the Transform palette to make changes to your objects.

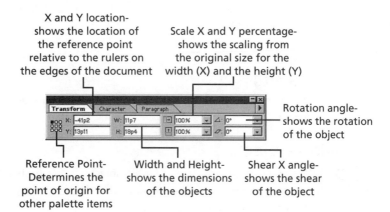

X and Y location-
shows the location of
the reference point
relative to the rulers on
the edges of the document

Scale X and Y percentage-
shows the scaling from
the original size for the
width (X) and the height (Y)

Rotation angle-
shows the rotation
of the object

Reference Point-
Determines the
point of origin for
other palette items

Width and Height-
shows the dimensions
of the objects

Shear X angle-
shows the shear
of the object

The Transform palette provides the following items:

- Reference point—Determines the point of origin for other palette items
- X and Y location—Shows the location of the reference point (relative to the rulers on the edges of the document)
- Width and Height—Shows the dimensions of the objects
- Scale X and Y percentage—Shows the scaling from the original size for the width (X) and height (Y)
- Rotation angle—Shows the rotation of the object
- Shear X angle—Shows the shear of the object

The reference point is one of nine points, either around the edges of the object or in the middle of it. The X and Y locations are measured from the reference point. If you decide to scale, rotate, or shear the object, the transformation is based on the reference point. (For example, imagine rotating a piece of paper by sticking a thumb tack into the paper to attach it to your desk, and then rotating the paper around the thumb tack. The reference point acts as a virtual thumb tack.)

Let's take a look at how you use the Transform palette to make changes to your objects.

Moving Objects

To move an object, you can simply click and drag it. But if you need more precision, you can use the Transform palette.

You can do this by typing the X and Y coordinates in the X and Y location fields (press Enter after each one). The object moves to the new location.

> Keep in mind that the X and Y location values are based on two settings: the point of origin (or 0 value) on the rulers and the object's current reference point.

Resizing Objects

To resize an object, type the new width and height values into the corresponding fields in the Transform palette.

Scaling Objects

 InDesign gives you two ways to scale objects. In the Tools palette, you can click the Scale tool, and then click and drag to scale, or you can use the Transform palette for more precise scaling.

In the Transform palette, set the reference point, and then type the X and Y values into the corresponding fields. You can scale different amounts on the horizontal (X) and vertical (Y) scales.

Rotating Objects

When rotating objects, you again have two choices. Go to the Tools palette, click the Rotate tool, and then click and drag. You can also use the Transform palette for more precise rotation.

In the Transform palette, set the reference point (the thumb tack), and then type the degree of rotation you desire into the Rotation Angle field.

Shearing Objects

The shearing feature lets you tilt and distort the selected object. Shearing is useful when you want to create a shadow for an object (be sure to shear a copy of the object) or for giving the object some perspective.

Click the Shear Tool, and then click and drag to shear the selected object.

In the Transform palette, click to set the reference point, and then type the degree of shear you desire into the Shear X Angle field. Figure 12.6 shows a shearing example.

FIGURE 12.6

To create this figure, I created the black circle. Then I copied it and sheared the copy at a 45-degree angle (using the reference point in the middle of the circle). Then I sent the sheared copy to the back and changed it to a 50 percent black color.

12

Now might be a good time to try out some shearing of your own.

Copying and Duplicating Objects

InDesign offers familiar cut/copy/paste features to help you make copies of objects and move them around. InDesign also provides a *duplication* feature, which lets you copy and paste in a single step. You can also use a special Step and Repeat feature to create lots of copies of an object and get them all lined up quickly.

To duplicate an object, select it, and then select Edit, Duplicate. A copy of the object immediately appears just below and to the right of the original.

Although I've compared duplicating to copying and pasting, it's really a different process. When you duplicate, a copy of the object is *not* stored on the Clipboard.

If you need to make several copies of an object and arrange them in a pattern, you can use Step and Repeat.

To Do: Creating Several Copies with Step and Repeat

Here's how to create multiple copies quickly:

1. Select the object you want to duplicate.

2. Select Edit, Step and Repeat. This displays the Step and Repeat dialog box shown in Figure 12.7.

FIGURE 12.7

You can make many copies quickly with Step and Repeat.

3. In the Repeat Count field, type the number of copies you want to make. (Keep in mind that this does not count the original, so if you want a total of 10 objects including the original, type **9**.)

4. In the Horizontal Offset and Vertical Offset fields, specify how far you want each copy to be from the previous one. For example, if the Horizontal Offset is 1 pica, each duplicated item appears 1 pica to the right of the previous one. See Figures 12.8 and 12.9 for an example.

FIGURE 12.8

The horizontal and vertical offsets control where your copies are positioned.

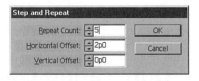

FIGURE 12.9

The copies lined up after the Step and Repeat has been applied.

Summary

With grouping, locking, and stacking features, InDesign provides you with several ways to manage the objects on the page. The transformation features let you convert simple objects into complex ones. Transformation features are available both in the Transform palette and as tools in the Tool palette.

Workshop

In this workshop, we'll review transforms, grouping, and positioning basics, then give you a chance to try out all those new tools.

Q&A

Q Can I select an object inside a group?

A Yes. Use the Direct Selection tool.

Q I'm having trouble selecting an object because other objects get in the way. What can I do?

A You can use the Send to Back command to move the troublesome objects out of the way, or you can lock them. You can also put the obtrusive objects on a separate layer and hide that layer. To learn how to do that, see Hour 5, "Using Layers and the Layout and Formatting Tools."

Q I understand that I can turn something upside down by rotating it 180 degrees, but how about a Flip command?

A You're in luck. Select the object, and then check the pop-up menu on the Transform palette (click the black triangle). You'll find Flip Horizontal, Flip Vertical, and Flip Both hiding here.

Q When I check the Transform palette, it says that my object has a 90-degree rotation. Why?

A The information displayed on the Transform palette tells you the rotation that has occurred since you created the object. You probably rotated the object earlier and don't remember it.

12

Quiz

1. To space five objects at equal distances, you use which of the following methods?

    a. Locking

    b. Aligning

    c. Distributing

2. The reference point on the Transform palette gives you what information?

    a. From what point transformations are measured

    b. Magnetic north

    c. The center of gravity for the object

3. Using the Transform palette instead of visually clicking and dragging is which of the following?

    a. Faster

    b. More precise

    c. More fun

4. How is the Duplicate feature different from using copy and paste?

    a. It's a single command instead of two

    b. The duplicated object is not stored on the Clipboard

    c. Both a and b

Quiz Answers

1. c. Locking lets you "glue" an object to a particular location and make it unselectable. Aligning lets you move objects so that they are all on the same axis. But distributing controls the space from one object to another.

2. a. The Transform palette provides you with nine reference points (in sort of a tic-tac-toe grid).

3. b. Because you can type in specific numeric measurements for your transformations, you can transform a specific amount instead of using the "eyeball" method when you click and drag.

4. c. (Both a and b). You can duplicate an object in one step instead of having to copy and then paste. But when you duplicate, the object you are duplicating is not stored on the Clipboard.

Exercises

Aligning and distributing makes it possible to create very consistent patterns with your objects. Spend some time working with those tools so you can understand how each option works. You'll also find the locking, grouping, and arrangement (Bring to Front, Send to Back) options useful in controlling which objects are moved when. Be sure to experiment with aligning grouped objects.

And while you're in the vicinity, don't forget to try out resizing, rotating, and shearing.

Here are some ideas to try out:

- Create a row of boxes that are equally spaced. Duplicate, Step and Repeat, Distribute, and Group can all be useful here.
- Create a shadow for one of the boxes using the Shear command.
- Create a drawing of a planet with rings using compound paths. Don't forget to have the planet cast a shadow.

12

PART IV
Working with Color

Hour

HOUR 13

Simple Coloring with InDesign

Up to now, you have been looking primarily at monochrome—that is to say, black-and-white—documents. Granted, previous hours have made a few tentative forays into the world of color, but usually only when discussing imported graphics. In this hour, you expand your palette, so to speak, and learn how to spice up your documents with color. Specifically, you'll learn:

- How to work with color in electronic publishing
- How to apply color to objects
- How to apply color to text
- How to create and edit new colors and tints
- How to apply colors to strokes

Electronic Publishing and Color

This hour forgoes a discussion of color theory (see Hour 15, "Trapping and Other Prepress Considerations"), but there are a few key color concepts you need to understand at the outset, especially as you go about creating color swatches.

RGB versus CMYK

The most crucial issue in any design or publishing workflow is the difference between *red, green, and blue (RGB)* and *cyan, magenta, yellow, and black (CMYK)*. You'll look at these color schemes in more detail in Hour 15, but here, it's enough to say that RGB is the color model used to display a color on a computer monitor. RGB refers to the way that colored light interacts to produce all the colors of the visible spectrum. CMYK is the color model that printing presses use to print on paper or on some other substrate. CMYK refers to the way that colorants (such as inks) interact to reproduce all possible colors on a printing press.

If your end result is ultimately going to be printed, all the colors you create need to be in CMYK. However, if what you design is ultimately going to appear on the Web or on a CD-ROM—which is viewed on a computer monitor—RGB needs to be your default color space. For now, assume that you need to stay in CMYK.

Process versus Spot Colors

To complicate matters even further, there are two basic types of colors: *process* and *spot*. Process colors are produced by the four-process inks: cyan, magenta, yellow, and black. Spot colors are single-color inks that are often used in addition to black when you don't need full-color printing, or to add color that can't be adequately reproduced with process inks.

Spot colors are selected based on a *swatchbook*—a printed or electronic collection of color patches. Each spot color is identified by a unique number, depending on the color-matching system that a printer or service bureau is using. Pantone is one of the most common, so you often see spot colors referred to as Pantone 283, for example (which is a light blue) or PMS 283 (PMS simply stands for Pantone Matching System).

In contrast, a process color is identified by percentages of its four constituent colors— C=34, M=6, Y=0, K=0, which is roughly the process equivalent of PMS 283.

All right—enough theory. You are now ready to see what the heck all this means by diving right into InDesign.

Applying Colors to Objects

InDesign makes it easy to add colors to objects, especially shapes. This is typically handled from the Swatches palette, which you access using Window, Swatches, or by pressing F5 (on both Macs and PCs). InDesign comes with a few preset swatches already created. You can create your own, which you'll get to in a little while, but for now try working with InDesign's presets.

There is also a dedicated Color palette that you can use to generate colors on the fly. You'll learn about that palette and why you use it in Hour 14, "Advanced Color Work."

Working with Fill Colors

When you fill an object—say, a circle—with a color, it is referred to, not surprisingly, as a *fill*. Fills exist independently of strokes. Coloring strokes is discussed toward the end of this hour.

To Do: Adding a Color Fill to an Object

Fire up InDesign, and follow along:

1. Open a blank InDesign document and, using techniques you learned in previous hours, draw a shape—say, a circle—anywhere on the page. You'll notice that it is by default filled with a color—probably black. Why is that?

   If you look at the Tools palette, you'll notice a color chip at the bottom (see Figure 13.1). This tells you what your default fill color is. (The hollow square just beneath it indicates what the stroke color is, which is covered later.)

FIGURE 13.1
The Tools palette shows the default fill and stroke colors.

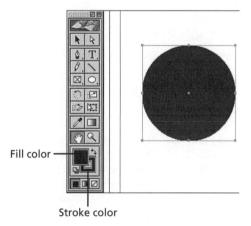

Fill color

Stroke color

13

2. Open the Swatches palette by choosing Window, Swatches, or by pressing F5. The Swatches palette appears on-screen (see Figure 13.2).

▼

FIGURE **13.2**

The Swatches palette.

3. Let's take an interactive tour of the Swatches palette. Maneuver the palette so that you can see both the palette and the object you drew. Make sure the object is selected, and click on None in the Swatches palette. You'll notice that your circle is empty and, if you have a stroke defined, has a black outline around it.

   None means that all color is removed from the object. On its swatch in the palette, you'll notice—by the little pencil icon with a red line through it—that this swatch cannot be edited.

4. Click on the next swatch down, which is Paper. You'll probably notice that nothing has happened. This is because Paper colors an object using the color of the paper on which you're printing. The default is white. If you apply None to an object and put another object beneath it, you won't see the top object. If you apply Paper to the top object, it covers the object below it.

> You can edit the Paper swatch, ostensibly to match the color of the paper stock you're using, but I advise against that. You typically use Paper in lieu of white when using reversed type—white type on black background. Although there is such a thing as white ink, when you see white text in print, what you're seeing is the color of the paper.

5. Click on Black, the swatch below Paper. This is a 100% process color black and cannot be edited.

> Notice the other swatch called Registration. This swatch specifies in what color the registration marks print. (You'll learn about registration marks in

▼

▼

> Hour 17, "Printing from InDesign.") You can edit the registration marks' color if you want to. A more important wrinkle to this swatch is that any object to which it is applied prints on every color separation—and thus appears on every printing plate. So don't use this swatch unless you want this effect.

6. Below Registration, there are a few built-in color swatches. Click on the one that suits your fancy. By default, color swatches in InDesign are named according to their CMYK percentages. So the swatch labeled "C=100 M=0 Y=0 K=0" is 100% cyan, and the swatch labeled "C=15 M=100 Y=100 K=0" comprises 15% cyan, 100% magenta, 100% yellow, and no black. That might mean nothing to you, but you can tell from the color chip next to it that it is a darkish red.

7. If you click on various swatches, you'll see that they are immediately applied to your object. If your object is not selected, you can simply grab a swatch and drag it onto the object.

▲

Applying a Fill Color to Text

In much the same way as you can apply colors to objects, you can apply colors to text. You use the same Swatches palette, and the same color swatch definitions.

All you would do is select the text with the Text tool, open the Swatches, select the color swatch—say, the dark red—and deselect your text. Your text will thus be red.

If you remember Hours 7, "Basic Typesetting with InDesign," and 8, "Working with Paragraphs," you know that you can make a color part of a character or paragraph style. You do this in the Character Color pane of the Style Options dialog boxes. This pane is a replica of the Swatches palette and you can set whatever swatch you want as a default character color.

Touring the Swatches Palette

There are a few other notable features on the Swatches palette covered here. You'll notice that most of the swatches have an icon or two on the right side of the Swatches palette. These icons indicate what type of color space is being used (RGB or CMYK) and whether it is a spot or process color.

For example, look at the swatch in Figure 13.3, C=75 M=5 Y=100 K=0.

13

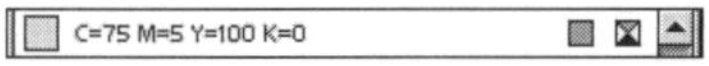

FIGURE **13.3**

A process color,
CMYK color swatch.

On the right side of each swatch are two square symbols. The one on the left, the solid gray square in Figure 13.3, indicates that it is a process color. The symbol on the right, the four triangles—which on your screen appear as cyan, magenta, yellow, and black— indicate that it is CMYK.

Contrast that with the swatch in Figure 13.4, Pantone 283 CVC.

FIGURE **13.4**

A spot color swatch.

The leftmost symbol is now different. The square with the gray circle indicates that it is a spot color, and the four triangles again indicate that it is based on a CMYK color model.

And now look at the swatch in Figure 13.5, which is red.

FIGURE **13.5**

An RGB color swatch.

The rightmost symbol is now different. Those three bars (which on your screen you see as red, green, and blue) indicate that this color swatch is in the RGB color space.

There is also one additional color space that you can use with InDesign, although you probably won't need to very often. See the swatch in Figure 13.6, L=28 A=60 B=-103.

FIGURE **13.6**

L=28 A=60 B=-103

A Lab color swatch.

The rightmost symbol has again changed. Those eight tiny color bars in Figure 13.6 indicate that this swatch is in the Lab color space. The Lab color space is used primarily in color theory and color management for making colorimetric measurements. You'll learn about the Lab color space in somewhat greater detail in Hours 15 and 16, "Color Management with InDesign."

As you have seen with other palettes, there is a Swatches palette menu, which you can access by clicking on the arrow at the top right of the palette. See Figure 13.7.

The Swatches palette menu contains basic controls for creating new types of swatches. Notice in the center of the menu the options for changing the appearance of the Swatches palette. By default, you view the swatches by name. You can choose to view only by swatch—and large or small swatch at that. Alternatively, you can choose to view by name, albeit in a much smaller space (the Small Palette Rows command).

FIGURE 13.7
The Swatches palette menu.

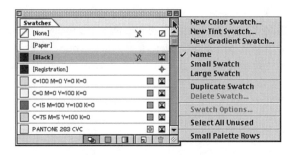

Regardless of what view you select, you can click and drag your swatches and put them in any order. So if you have one swatch you use all the time, you can put it near the top. The Swatches palette menu also enables you to delete and duplicate swatches. You might duplicate a swatch when you want to change only one or two things on it—such as make a process color into a spot color with the same CMYK values.

Creating and Editing Swatches

Unless you have a limited repertoire, chances are you'll want to create and edit your own color swatches. This also is easy to do.

To Do: Creating a New Color Swatch

You can create your own color swatch from scratch by doing the following:

1. Make sure you have the Swatches palette on-screen. In the Swatches palette menu, select New Color Swatch. The New Color Swatch dialog box appears, as seen in Figure 13.8.

FIGURE 13.8
The New Color Swatch dialog box.

13

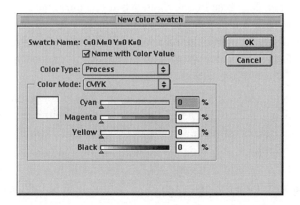

▼

▼   2. By default, the swatch inherits the name of the constituent color values. By unse-
       lecting the Name with Color Value checkbox, you can create your own name. For
       example, if you are creating a color for a certain page element, you can name it
       accordingly.

    3. Under Color Type, you determine whether you want to create a spot or a process
       color. What you choose here determines how your color plates separate when you
       send your file to a service bureau. As you saw earlier, a process color prints with
       four separations. A spot color prints with only one—itself. Leave this setting on
       process unless you want to create a spot color.

> There is a better way to specify a spot color, which involves InDesign's built-
> in swatch libraries. You'll learn about swatch libraries in Hour 14.

    4. Under Color Mode, you determine whether you want your swatch to use CMYK,
       RGB, or Lab. You'll probably want to stick with CMYK unless you're designing
       something for the Web or a CD-ROM, in which case select RGB.

    5. Here's where it gets fun. The four sliders (or three sliders, if you chose RGB or
       Lab under Color Mode) enable you to set your individual color values. So that
       you're starting on the same page, make sure all four sliders are dragged fully to the
       left (so that each color value is 0% as shown in Figure 13.8). The square on the left
       shows you what your color swatch is. At this point, it should be white.

    6. Here's what's cool about this dialog box: Drag the Cyan slider all the way to the
       right. You'll notice that as you move the slider, the color gradients beneath all the
       other sliders change. This shows you the changes made to the swatch when you
       move that slider.

       For example, under the Magenta slider, the gradient now runs from pure cyan on
       the left to a deep blue on the right. When you move the Magenta slider all the way
       to the right and add more magenta to the cyan, your swatch turns deep blue.
       Similarly, the Yellow slider runs from cyan on the left to green on the right. If you
       move the Yellow slider all the way to the right, your swatch turns green. Drag the
       Yellow slider all the way to the right.

    7. Notice how the sliders have again changed. Spend some time now moving the slid-
       ers back and forth to get a feel for how adding the different inks in different per-
       centages affects a swatch. Go ahead, knock yourself out. I'll wait.

    8. Wasn't that fun? It's a cool approach to creating swatches. Alternatively, you can
       enter the color values directly, if you know them. Enter the following values in the
▼   percentages (you can press Tab to jump from field to field, by the way): Cyan: 45,

▼   Magenta: 100, Yellow: 10, Black: 13. You should have a darkish lavender. Make
           sure the Name with Color Value box is checked, and press OK.

     9. You now have a new color swatch in your Swatches palette. Draw an object on the
▲   page and apply the swatch you just created to it. Save it for the next exercise.

After a swatch is created, you can duplicate it, delete it, or edit it. If you select Delete
Swatch from the Swatches palette menu after you have applied the swatch to an object,
you get the error message seen in Figure 13.9.

FIGURE **13.9**

*This is what happens
when you try to delete
a swatch that is in use.*

To Do: Editing a Color Swatch

Uh oh. Your art director called. She hates the color you've chosen for some page element
or other. You can change it by doing the following:

  1. Start with the swatch and swatch-colored object you created in the last exercise.
      Make sure the lavender swatch is selected in the Swatches palette. Go to Swatch
      Options in the Swatches palette menu. Alternatively, you can double-click on the
      swatch.

  2. You get the Swatch Options dialog box, which is essentially the same dialog box as
      the New Color Swatch dialog box. Move the Cyan slider to 0 and press OK.

  3. You'll notice two things. The name has changed in the swatches palette (if you still
▲   have Name with Color Value checked), and your object is now the new color.

This is a quick way to globally change a color that you have used throughout a document.

Creating Tints

You can also create tints that are based on particular swatches. What are tints and why do
you use them? A *tint* is basically a color that is not reproduced at its full strength. For
example, if you wanted to create a gray, you might use a tint of black, such as in Figure
13.10.

13

FIGURE **13.10**

This square on the left is full black. The square on the right is filled with a tint comprising 20% black, which appears in the swatches palette with the percentage indicated on the swatch.

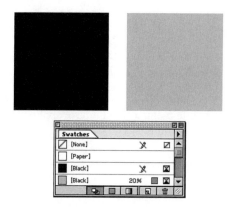

You use tints, for example, when you want to include colored or gray backgrounds for text, such as you often see in magazine sidebars or on the chapter numbers in the margins of this book. That gray box is simply a tint of full black.

Tints are created in InDesign by first selecting a color swatch you want to base the tint on (such as black) and selecting New Tint Swatch from the Swatches palette menu. You'll get the New Tint Swatch dialog box (see Figure 13.11).

FIGURE **13.11**

Creating a new tint swatch.

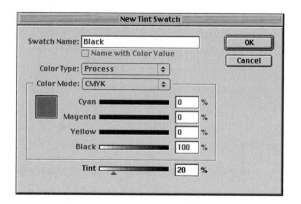

Notice that everything except the Tint slider is grayed out. This slider adjusts the strength of the tint, and you can see as you move it how dark or light your swatch becomes. If you want black text to be readable over your swatch, you might need to go down as far as 20% or even 15%, depending on the color.

Working with Colored Strokes

A stroke is akin to a border, in that it is a line drawn around the edge of an object. You've worked with strokes and the Stroke palette before in Hour 10, "Using InDesign's

Drawing Tools," but in the context of drawing and editing lines. The principle here is the same; a border is really just a line that surrounds something else. Lines, borders—they're all strokes. We saw earlier how to change the thickness of a Stroke. Now it's time to add colors to strokes.

Adding Colors to Strokes

Strokes are pretty easy to create and edit. As you might recall, stroke characteristics such as weight, miter, and corner shape are controlled from the Stroke palette, which is accessed by selecting Window, Stroke, or pressing F10 (on both platforms). The easiest way to change the color of a stroke is to use a combination of the Swatches palette and the stroke color chip on the Tools palette.

To Do: Coloring a Stroke

Begin by coloring a simple stroke around a drawn shape:

1. In InDesign, select the Rectangle tool and draw a rectangle anywhere on the page.

2. With the object selected, open the Swatches palette.

3. You've seen how the fill color chip on the Tool box indicates the fill color swatch you're using. The hollow square beneath it indicates the color of the stroke. By default, it is black. Click on the stroke color chip to bring it to the foreground. Figure 13.12 shows how this looks.

FIGURE 13.12

If you click on the stroke color chip, it comes to the fore-ground. You can change its color by clicking on a swatch in the Swatches palette.

4. Click on the swatch of your choosing in the Swatches palette. Notice that the stroke changes to the color you select.

There is a double-headed arrow on the Tools palette that points to both the fill color chip and the stroke color chip. If you click on it, you'll swap the fill and stroke colors.

13

That's the easiest way to color a stroke. Of course, it doesn't make a great deal of sense to make the stroke the same color as the fill—you might as well just set the stroke to none.

Summary

So you can see that the Swatches palette is sort of "command central" for all your color work in InDesign. We'll see in the next hour how you can create custom colors on-the-fly using the Color palette (among other things), but just about all color work comes back to the Swatches palette.

Workshop

You've just learned how you can create colors and tints, and how to add those colors to page elements. Check out the Q&A to find the answers to some questions you may have that might not have been covered in the chapter, and complete the quiz to test your recall of some of the stuff we covered. Finally, work through the exercises until you are a pro with the color swatches in InDesign.

Q&A

Q If I create a tint based on a swatch, and then edit the original swatch, will my tint change as well?

A Yes. Why tints are so dependent upon the parent swatch is a mystery, but at least it's easy to create them. Just be careful to check for any dependent tints when you do change a swatch. Also, if you delete a parent swatch, you have to assign a new parent to your dependent tint.

Q I hate the default fill and stroke colors that InDesign has. Can I change them so that every document I create has my own defaults?

A Yes. As you'll see in Hour 22, "Customizing InDesign," you can set defaults by changing settings while no document is open. So to change any of your stroke or fill settings—such as color and weight—simply close any open documents and select the specifications you want. Whenever you create a new document, your new defaults will be in effect.

Q I'm confused by that whole spot versus process color thing. If a spot color is just one ink and one plate is made, why does it have CMYK amounts? What's up with that?

A Spot colors are often defined in terms of CMYK, not because spot colors are made from individual four-color inks, but because you often need to match a process color to a spot color. By using process color equivalents, you can attempt to match a spot and a process color closely. However, because the two types of inks are different in composition and on-press behavior, it is often nearly impossible to get an exact match. But you can try.

Quiz

1. Four-color printing is also called _____ color.

   A. Process

   B. Spot

   C. Typographic

   D. Local

2. Which of the following aspects of a color is not instantly apparent by viewing its swatch in the Swatches palette?

   A. Whether it's RGB or CMYK

   B. Whether it's spot or process

   C. What its individual color values are

   D. Whether it's used in a document

Quiz Answers

1. A. In fact, four-color printing is often called *four-color process printing*. In the printing industry, it's not uncommon to find more than a few terms that all mean the same thing.

2. D. Okay, that was actually kind of a trick question. Answers A and B are instantly apparent by the icons on the swatch that indicate the color model and type. Answer C is instantly apparent if you have the Name with Color Value box checked. Answer D is not *instantly* apparent because you need to choose Select All Unused from the Swatches palette menu in order to see which swatches are not used in the document.

Exercises

By now, the whole InDesign puzzle should be nearly filled in. You know how to create documents, import graphics, add text, and now you know how to add color to your graphics and text.

Try experimenting with different color models—RGB, CMYK, and, heck, even try Lab and see what that's about. See how they differ from each other.

13

So go back through any old exercises you have saved from previous hours and add color to them. Define swatches and apply them to different page elements. If you have any magazines handy, such as *Time*, *Newsweek*, or *Micro Publishing News*, see how colors are used as design elements, both for text, as well as for things like rules and section/department heads. As always, try to emulate those designs, but put your own unique spin on them. Any decent professional designer will tell you that looking at other people's designs for inspiration and ideas is important. And it's the best way to learn how to do something: to try to emulate another's work. (Just make sure it's truly your own work before you try to sell it or publish it!)

HOUR 14

Advanced Color Work

Now that you have a basic understanding of how to create and apply colors
in InDesign, you can focus on more advanced techniques and other color
tricks. Specifically, in this hour you'll learn:

- How to create colors on-the-fly
- How to borrow colors from imported graphics
- How to create and apply gradients
- How to use swatch libraries

Creating Colors On-the-Fly

Recall that most of your colors are created in the Swatches palette, which
remains the best place to do your color mixing. However, InDesign also
gives you another way to create colors. You read about the Color palette in
passing in Hour 13, "Simple Coloring with InDesign," but you look at it in
more detail here.

Working with the Color Palette

Access the Color palette by choosing Window, Color, or by pressing F6 (on
either platform). The palette is shown in Figure 14.1.

FIGURE 14.1

The Color palette.

It seems simple and straightforward. Basically, the Color palette enables you to create a quick color on-the-fly and apply it to any page object, including text. Its default color is based on the default document or application color; you can determine from the color chip at the bottom of the Tools palette what you'll be starting with. You can change the default color by choosing a starting color from any color that can be mixed in either the CMYK or RGB color spaces.

Take a look at how this works.

To Do: Creating a Color On-the-Fly

Here's how you create a quick color for an object:

1. Open an InDesign document and draw a object on the page—say, a circle.
2. Open the Color palette by choosing Window, Color or pressing F6.
3. In its most basic form, the Color palette has a No Fill chip on the far right—it is the white square with a red line through it. Click on it. Your fill color chip now indicates that there is no fill color. If your object was selected, it will now be blank.
4. If you move the mouse pointer over the gradient in the Color palette, it turns into an eyedropper. Wherever you click along that gradient, the eyedropper sucks up that color, which then appears in the fill color chip. Click somewhere near the left end of the gradient. If you are working from a black default, you now have a gray color chip. If you are using some other color, you now have a tint of that color.
5. There's more to this palette than meets the eye. Try mixing your own colors. As you have probably surmised by now, there is indeed a Color palette menu, which you access by clicking on the arrow at the top right of the palette, just like in any other palette. See Figure 14.2.

FIGURE 14.2

The Color palette menu.

6. There aren't many choices here. Basically, you have your choice of color spaces. Select CMYK. The gradient in the Color palette now shows the whole CMYK spectrum. If you click on the eyedropper anywhere along that gradient, you'll suck up the corresponding color. So pick a general color area—say, blue—and click on it. Your color chip becomes a shade of blue.

▼ 7. That might seem woefully imprecise, so you can fine tune this quite easily. Go
       back to the Color palette menu and select Show Options. You get a somewhat
       familiar set of sliders. See Figure 14.3.

FIGURE 14.3

*You can refine your
color using the sliders
in the Color palette.*

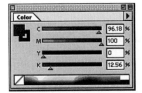

As you might recall from the New Color Swatch dialog box that you looked at in
the last hour, you can move each of these color components to the left or right, and
the gradient beneath each slider tells you exactly what you'll be doing to the color.
If you don't like your starting point, you can go back to the full spectrum and click

▲ the eyedropper on some other primary color.

> You can see from the Color palette options that InDesign enables you to
> specify an ink percentage with an accuracy of hundredths of a percentage.
> This is all well and good, but it's far more precise than is visible or printable.
> Therefore, take any numbers to the right of the decimal point with a grain
> of salt.

You now have a custom color. If your object was selected while you were doing your
mixing, it is now filled with the new color. However, if the object *wasn't* selected, be
careful not to select any other swatch or object, or you'll lose the color. Colors created in
the Color palette are fleeting things. To apply the color to an unselected object, simply
grab either the color chip on the Tools palette or the color chip in the Color palette and
drop it on the object.

Making a Swatch from a Custom Color

Using the Color palette is a good, quick way to try out different colors without labori-
ously going through the process of defining, editing, and deleting a swatch. If you decide
you like a color, you can make a swatch out of it.

14

> Recall that colors created in the Colors palette are fleeting things. If you are
> defining colors this way, be sure to save them as swatches or you'll lose
> them. Another more important caution with regard to the Color palette is

that you cannot define spot colors in it; any colors you create become process colors (or RGB, which is usually bad juju). If you need a spot color, you need to make a process-color swatch and turn it into a spot.

To Do: Adding a Custom Color to the Swatches Palette

Adding a color that you have created via the Color palette to the Swatches palette is easy.

1. Using the techniques you just learned, create a custom color using the Color palette.

2. Open the Swatches palette by choosing Window, Swatches, or pressing F5 (on either platform).

3. Click on the New Swatch button at the bottom of the Swatches palette (see Figure 14.4).

FIGURE 14.4

Clicking on the New Swatch button after creating a custom color enables you to add the color to the Swatches palette.

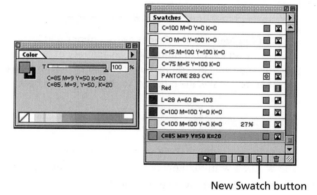

New Swatch button

Alternatively, you can select New Color Swatch from the Swatches palette menu, if you want to edit or rename your swatch. Dragging the new color chip from either the Color palette or the Tools palette to the Swatches palette also creates a new swatch.

Your color now appears in the Swatches palette and you can use it whenever you want.

Notice what happens to the Color palette when you add the swatch to the Swatches palette. The sliders are replaced by ink percentages. This indicates that your color is "frozen" and can be edited only through the Swatch Options in the Swatches palette menu. This is a good thing.

What you can do is use the Color palette to make a tint on the fly without needing to specifically create a tint as a separate swatch, as you saw in Hour 13. Simply move the slider at the top of the Color palette to whatever percentage you want. If you have an object selected, your tint is applied to that object. If not, you can drag the color chip onto an object to apply it. You can also make a tint into its own swatch by using the New Swatch button, as you saw a moment ago.

Making a Swatch from an Imported File

You can also make a color swatch from a color found in a placed graphic, be it a TIFF, EPS, or PDF. You might want your text to match a certain color in an imported graphic, or perhaps you want to match a specific logo color with the name of a company repeated throughout the text of a document. This is easily done.

You can use the Eyedropper tool to grab a color from a placed TIFF or EPS file and apply it to another object.

When you use the Eyedropper to suck up a color, that color's color values appear in the Color palette.

You can then open the Swatches palette and click on the New Swatch button to make a new color swatch out of it. Your sampled color is now a swatch that you can use elsewhere in your document.

If you work with imported Illustrator or EPS files, often after doing a Place you will see some new swatches in your Swatches palette. These are spot colors that have been defined in Illustrator and are carried along with the file. When you import them into InDesign, the defined color swatches are automatically imported with the image. However, this doesn't happen with process colors, just spot colors. Also, you will be unable to alter them in InDesign.

Working with Gradients

The last type of color you can create is what is known as a *gradient*. A gradient is essentially a gradual (or even abrupt) transition from one color to another. The most basic gradient is the grayscale, as seen in Figure 14.5.

FIGURE 14.5
A grayscale is a simple gradient.

14

Notice that the grayscale in Figure 14.5 is not completely smooth—you can see the discrete steps that comprise the transition from white to black. This phenomenon is called *banding*, and it happens because there are not enough gray values (or color values) in a particular color space. This means the output device cannot make the transition effectively.

Creating Gradients

As with other color swatches, you can create gradients in two ways: as a gradient swatch in the Swatches palette or as an on-the-fly gradient in the Color palette. Take a look at the gradient swatch option first.

To Do: Creating a Gradient

Try creating a simple red-to-blue gradient to begin with.

1. With a blank InDesign document open, open the Swatches palette. Select New Gradient Swatch from the Swatches palette menu. The New Gradient Swatch dialog box appears, as shown in Figure 14.6.

FIGURE 14.6

You can set up your gradient swatch in the New Gradient Swatch dialog box.

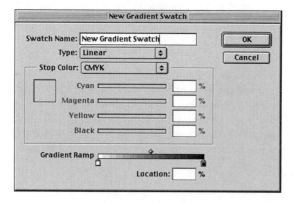

2. The first thing you can do is name your swatch. For example, you might want to indicate what colors you transition from and to, such as Red-Blue.

3. The next option, Type, enables you to set a linear or radial gradient. A *linear gradient* starts with red on one side and transitions in a straight line to blue. A *radial gradient* starts with red in the center of a shape and transitions to blue in all directions out from the center, like ripples emanating from where a pebble was thrown into a pond. Set it to linear for now, and when you get to the exercises at the end of this hour, you can see what the radial gradient does.

▼ 4. Stop Color simply refers to the color space that InDesign uses for the *stops*, or the starting and ending points of the gradient. The choices are RGB, CMYK, LAB, or Named Color. The default is CMYK. Named Color enables you to use a swatch from the Swatches palette. Leave CMYK as the choice for now.

5. You'll notice that the sliders are grayed out. This is because you need to select a color stop before you can start mixing the colors. The Gradient Ramp at the bottom of the dialog box enables you to set the specs of your gradient. To set the left color stop, click on the little icon at the far left of the Gradient Ramp. The sliders should become active and a black arrow should appear over the color stop you just clicked.

6. These sliders should seem familiar. To set the leftmost color stop to red, drag the Magenta slider to 100%. Notice that when you drag Yellow to the right, you get a darker red. Do so. My starting color is C=0 M=100 Y=75 K=0.

7. Click on the right color stop, the little icon at the far right of the Gradient Ramp. Make sure the Stop Color says CMYK and not Named Color, and create the blue. My ending color is C=100 M=90 Y=0 K=0.

8. You should now have a gradient. The Gradient Ramp creates a gradient from red to blue. You can now determine where the gradient starts, where it ends, and where the midpoint falls. Click on the left color stop and drag it toward the right. Notice that your gradient starts with solid red. The gradient will actually start much further along the space where you place the gradient. The Location field tells you where specifically the midpoint falls.

   For example, if you add the gradient to a rectangle and drag the left color stop to 25%, the first 25% of the rectangle will be solid red. The same goes for the right color stop. If you move that left, you stop the gradient that much sooner.

9. The little diamond hovering over the center of the Gradient Ramp tells you where the exact midpoint of the gradient falls, or where the color that is the average of the transition colors appears. In this case, the midpoint color is pink. You can also move this midpoint indicator left or right to determine where the midpoint falls with respect to the two end points. It's easier to experiment and see what this does than to read about it, so move the two end stops and the midpoint indicator around and see what they do.

10. When you are finished setting up your gradient, press OK. Save this gradient for
▲   the next exercise.

Your gradient now appears on your Swatches palette. Well, it might, depending on what you have the display set to.

See those three buttons at the bottom of the Swatches palette? They are View All Swatches, View Color Swatches Only, and View Gradients Only. See Figure 14.7.

14

FIGURE 14.7

With View All Swatches, you can intermingle solid colors and gradients. With View Color Swatches Only, you can see only solid color swatches. And you guessed it, with View Gradients Only, you can see only gradients.

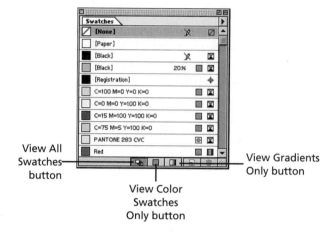

You can also select your gradient and edit it using the Swatch Options command from the Swatches palette menu.

Creating Multiple-Step Gradients

You can also create multiple-step gradients. You do this in either the New Gradient Swatch or the Gradient Options dialog boxes.

To Do: Creating a Multiple-Step Gradient

▼ To Do

Using the same document you just created, do the following:

1. Click on the gradient swatch you created and select Swatch Options from the Swatches palette menu. This should be familiar.

2. If you click anywhere along the bottom of the Gradient Ramp between the two color stops, an additional color stop is added. Click somewhere under the first half of the Gradient Ramp. See Figure 14.8.

FIGURE 14.8

You can click beneath the Gradient Ramp to add additional color stops.

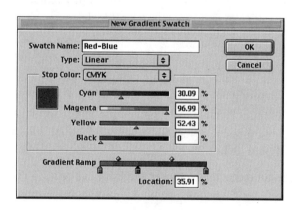

▼

▼

3. Click on the new stop you just added, and you can move the color sliders to make it whatever color you want. Make it a green. My green is C=85 M=0 Y=65 K=25. Notice that your gradient now transitions from red to green to blue. (Also notice that for each new color stop you create, you get a new midpoint to adjust.) If you

▲

like that better, you can change the name accordingly and press OK.

You can add as many additional color stops as fit in the space beneath the Gradient Ramp. To remove a color stop, simply click and drag it downward off the dialog box.

Applying Gradients to Page Elements

There are several ways to apply a gradient to an object. The first is to simply select the object, and then select the swatch in the Swatches palette. Whoomp! There it is. The same process goes for text.

To Do: Applying a Gradient to Text

To apply a gradient to text, do the following:

1. Make sure you have a gradient swatch defined. With any luck, you saved the ones you created in previous exercises.

2. Create a text frame and type a word or two of text.

3. Select the text with the Text tool and open your Swatches palette. Select the gradient.

▲

4. Deselect the text. You should have a gradient applied to your type. See Figure 14.9.

FIGURE 14.9

A gradient applied to text. It might look like gray, grayer, and grayest here, but it is actually a red, green, and blue gradient.

Red, Green, and Blue

As with your other color swatches, you can add gradient swatches to character and paragraph styles via the Character Color pane of the Character/Paragraph Style Options dialog boxes.

Using the Gradient Palette

14

As you saw earlier this hour with solid color swatches, you can use the Color palette to create gradients on-the-fly. As with many features in InDesign, there is more than one way to accomplish roughly the same thing, which gives you a lot of flexibility.

In this case, you use the Color palette in conjunction with the Gradient palette, which is accessed by choosing Window, Gradient. There isn't a keyboard shortcut for this palette, but it lives one tab over from the Color palette, so you can simply press F6 and then click on the next tab over. The Gradient palette is shown in Figure 14.10.

FIGURE 14.10

You can use the Gradient palette to edit gradients on-the-fly.

This palette contains the Gradient Ramp and enables you to reposition the color stops and midpoint. You can also toggle between linear and radial gradients, and if you click on the Reverse button, you can reverse the red-to-blue gradient and make it go, in this case, from blue to red. If you click on the Reverse button again, you restore the original direction.

You can edit your stop colors, as well. The process is essentially this: click on a stop, and then click on the Color palette. You have your usual set of sliders. (If you don't, go to the Color palette menu and select CMYK). You can then adjust your stop color accordingly. Click on the Gradient palette again, click on the next color stop, and go back to the Color palette and adjust the second stop accordingly.

You can add additional color stops and edit those colors as well. If you want to save this gradient as a swatch, simply click on the color chip in the Gradient palette and drag it onto the Swatches palette. The Location field lets you set a numerical midpoint, if you want, while the Angle field lets you set how far from the horizontal the gradient makes its transition—in other words, if you add the gradient to a rectangle and set the Angle to 45 degrees, the gradient will run from the lower lefthand corner to the upper righthand corner, rather than straight across the rectangle.

> If you are doing a lot of gradient editing this way, you can tear off either the Gradient or Color palettes and place them side by side for easier access. Just click and drag the palette tabs onto the page.

Working with Fills, Strokes, and Gradients

Now that you've learned not only how to use fills and strokes but also gradients, you are ready to look at the color controls on the Tools palette (see Figure 14.11) and learn how you can further streamline your work in InDesign.

FIGURE 14.11
The color tools on the
Tools palette enable
you to apply fills,
strokes, and gradients.

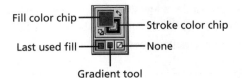

Fill color chip —
—— Stroke color chip
Last used fill ——
—— None

Gradient tool

As you've seen before, the fill color chip shows you the active fill color. If a gradient has been selected, the fill color chip shows it. Nestled beneath the fill color chip is the stroke color chip, which shows you the active stroke color. You can click on the stroke color chip to bring it to the front, and any colors you select in either the Swatches palette or the Color palette are then applied to strokes. If you create a gradient as a stroke, that gradient is visible on this chip as well.

Below the color chips are three tiny color chip buttons. The left one shows the last used fill. The center button shows the last used gradient. By clicking on the center button, you move it to the fill color chip, and any objects you draw are filled with the gradient. The right button is the None button, which clears the active color chip, or gives it a fill (or stroke) of None.

Using the Gradient Tool

There is one last means of applying gradients. This is using the Gradient tool, which you can see in Figure 14.11. Double-clicking on it brings up the Gradient palette, which you can use in conjunction with the Color palette to customize a gradient. (You can also select the Gradient tool by pressing the G key.)

To Do: Adding a Quick Gradient with the Gradient Tool

Try this quickie exercise to see how the Gradient tool works:

1. Using techniques you've learned in this hour, create a new gradient using the Gradient palette in conjunction with the Color palette. Notice that the fill color chip takes on the characteristics of your new gradient.

2. Click on the None button to clear the color chip. Make sure you have a stroke defined, though.

3. Draw an object of your choosing on the page. Say, a rectangle. Make sure it is selected.

4. Select the Gradient tool. The cursor changes to a crosshair icon.

5. Position the crosshair icon anywhere on the left frame of the rectangle. Click and drag across the width of the rectangle. For now, keep the line perfectly horizontal.

6. When you get to the right edge, release the mouse button. The rectangle fills with your gradient.

▼ To Do

14

You can drag across the rectangle in any direction you like, and see some interesting effects. Try dragging from corner to corner, top to bottom, or between two random points. You can also drag the Gradient tool over text.

 The Eyedropper tool can also suck up a gradient and apply it elsewhere.

Working with Swatch Libraries

Finally this hour, you learn about swatch libraries. You'll look at libraries in more detail in Hour 23, "Using InDesign in a Mixed Environment," but because you're dwelling on the concept of swatches, it's a good time to learn about swatch libraries.

Using InDesign's Built-In Swatch Libraries

A *swatch library* is essentially a preset collection of swatches stored in a central location (the InDesign application folder), accessed from InDesign, and imported into a specific document—either in toto or on a swatch-by-swatch basis.

InDesign's swatch libraries are accessed using Window, Swatch Libraries. Figure 14.12 shows the set that comes with InDesign 1.5.

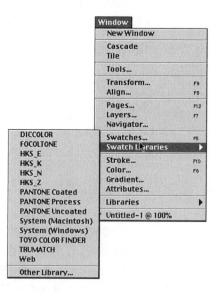

These are some industry standard international colors, both spot and process. DIC and Toyo are Japanese color models; Focoltone is a European spot-color model; Trumatch and Pantone are two popular American spot and process color models; and Web is the Web-safe palette.

For now, you'll probably want to stick with Pantone. Note, however, that it is up to your printer to tell you which color matching systems they use.

Here's how you use a swatch library. Say you want to add a spot color. You open your Pantone library, and you get a palette chock full of all the Pantone colors. You find one you like, select it, click on the Pantone Library palette menu, and select Add to Swatches.

> After you bring a Pantone (or other library) swatch into your own Swatches palette, it becomes editable. However, don't edit it! Editing a Pantone color swatch defeats the point of the Pantone Matching System.

Snatching Colors from Other InDesign Documents

You can use the Swatch Libraries feature to access colors from another InDesign document. For example, say you have defined a bunch of color swatches in a document, and you suddenly realize as you are creating another document that you want them. Not a problem. You simply choose Windows, Swatch Libraries and scroll down to Other Library. Selecting Other Library opens your usual navigation window. You simply navigate to the document that contains the colors you want. Select Open, and a new Swatches palette having the name of the file you selected appears. See Figure 14.13.

FIGURE 14.13

You can snatch the colors you want from another InDesign document.

The Colors We Want	
C=100 M=0 Y=0 K=0	
C=0 M=0 Y=100 K=0	
C=15 M=100 Y=100 K=0	
C=75 M=5 Y=100 K=0	
C=100 M=90 Y=10 K=0	
Red	
C=100 M=100 Y=0 K=0	
C=100 M=100 Y=0 K=0	27%
C=15 M=100 Y=100 K=0	31%
C=0 M=37 Y=0 K=0	

14

You can then drag the colors you want from the imported Swatches palette to the document's own Swatches palette.

After you have done this, this document is added to the Swatch Libraries pop-up menu and can be accessed whenever you want. And adding swatches from libraries when no document is open makes them available for every document in the default Swatches palette.

 If you are proficient in Illustrator, you can use the Illustrator color swatch libraries in InDesign. They use the same format.

Summary

Well, you learned a lot this hour, but a combination of this and the previous hour should have you well on your way to using color in InDesign. In the next few hours, you'll look at color in a much more technical way, including trapping and color-management issues. Although not as much fun, these subjects are important. They help you understand how to provide trouble-free output, which is, after all, the goal of any printed design work.

Workshop

Now that you've learned how to create colors on-the-fly and work with gradients, you've learned all the essentials of working with colors in InDesign. Now check out the Q&A to see if there are any residual questions you might have. Then take the Quiz to see how good your powers of recall are. Then work through the exercises to become truly proficient at creating and applying colors and gradients.

Q&A

Q You mentioned a printed Pantone swatchbook. What is it, why might I want one, and where do I get one?

A The Pantone Matching System is a system for specifying spot colors using a unique identification number. When you specify Pantone 183 to a printer, everyone involved is on the same page and you probably won't get any unpleasant surprises. A *swatchbook* is a collection of color patches that lists the Pantone identification numbers and their CMYK constituents. Pantone swatchbooks can be purchased at most commercial art stores, sometimes through a commercial printer, or you can go to http://www.pantone.com for information on ordering one or more. They typically range from about $50–$100. A printed swatchbook has value over an electronic one because, by virtue of the fact that it is already printed, you know how a particular color looks on paper.

Q Can I create my own swatch library?

A InDesign does not let you create your own swatch library per se, as you will see in Hour 23. However, there are ways to create a swatch library without actually creating one. You can create a general library (covered in Hour 23) and add a shape to it that uses the colors you want. The color information is stored with the library and you can add those colors to any new documents.

Quiz

1. Which of the following is not a way to apply color to an object?

   A. Using the Swatches palette

   B. Using the Color palette

   C. Using the Stroke palette

   D. Using the Eyedropper tool

2. You can only create a gradient that involves two colors.

   A. True

   B. False

3. If you create a document using only one spot color, how many color plates do you end up with?

   A. 0

   B. 1

   C. 2

   D. 4

Quiz Answers

1. C. The stroke color is controlled from the Color or Swatch palettes. The Stroke palette is used solely to change the weight, corner, and miter of the stroke.

2. B. You can add as many color stops to the Gradient Ramp as you like.

3. B. A spot color is a single ink, unlike a process color, which is made by combining four inks on press. Most commonly, however, a spot color exists in addition to black, for a total of two plates.

Exercises

What can I say? Practice what you learned in this hour. Define some colors using the Color palette and apply them to page elements in documents you created in previous hours. Create and add some gradients. I mentioned earlier that you would check out the radial gradient, so take this opportunity to do so. Create different shapes using the draw-

14

ing tools you mastered in previous hours, and use the Gradient tool to add different types of gradients at different angles. You can achieve some cool effects with gradients. But focus on the Swatches menu, and practice creating, editing, and applying color swatches.

Finally, go to your newsstand and pick up several types of magazines. Try some high-quality art or food magazines, a rock-and-roll magazine or other publication geared toward young adults, a national weekly news magazine, and maybe a sports magazine. Notice how they handle various design elements—and especially color—differently. Notice how they handle some things similarly. *Tiger Beat* will have a different design than *National Review*, and only one will include pin-ups of William F. Buckley. Try to replicate those designs—but hopefully not the pin-ups of William F. Buckley—in your own documents.

HOUR 15

Trapping and Other Prepress Considerations

In the past two hours, you learned how you can define, modify, and apply colors to objects in InDesign. There is more to color than simply clicking on a swatch in a palette, however. Especially when the document you create is going to be printed on an offset printing press, there are certain considerations you have to, well, consider.

That is where the service bureau comes into play. Hour 18, "Getting Ready for the Service Bureau," takes a more detailed look at the role of the service bureau.

In this hour, you'll learn:

- How to work in different color spaces and color models
- How to set up InDesign to perform on-host trapping
- How to create trapping styles
- How to use overprint settings as faux traps

Working In Various Color Models

Regardless of whether you are sending your InDesign files to a service bureau, or preparing them for a computer-to-plate system, or even going out to a direct digital press, there are a number of considerations you need to worry about. And chief among them is the thorny issue of color space.

As we saw in the previous two hours, there are a variety of color models out there, but for your purposes, you only need to be concerned with two of them. They are our old friends RGB and CMYK.

RGB versus CMYK

Although we've seen these before, perhaps a little of the theory behind these two color spaces will help you understand why RGB versus CMYK is such a crucial issue in prepress. Color is produced in two ways. The first is called *additive* and the second is called *subtractive*. You can use two "desktop" examples to illustrate the difference: the color monitor and the color printer.

Additive color is the way color is produced by means of light. There are three primary colors in additive color mixing: *red, green,* and *blue.* The interaction of these three colors in seemingly infinite combinations is responsible for producing all the colors of the visible spectrum. When all three colors are combined in equal proportion, you get white. This color space is called, not surprisingly, *RGB.* Your color monitor is an RGB device. Depending on your video card, your monitor combines red, green, and blue light to display hundreds, thousands, even millions of colors on your screen.

But an inkjet printer or a printing press doesn't combine light. It combines colorants—either dye- or pigment-based ones—which brings you to subtractive color mixing. Whereas additive color refers to the intermixing of colored light, subtractive color refers to the mixing of colored pigments to produce color. There are also three primary colors in subtractive color mixing: *cyan, magenta,* and *yellow.* As a result, this color space is referred to as *CMY.* It is more commonly called *CMYK,* which I'll explain in a moment. The combination of these three primaries in various proportions yields the full range of printable colors. When all three are present in equal proportion, the result is black, at least in theory; in actual practice, it's more of a dark brown.

Printing devices add a fourth color—black—to the three primary colors typically to improve color density and as an ink-saving measure. Most text is black and printers don't want to monkey around with combining cyan, magenta, and yellow inks to yield black text.

Although you will usually want to use black ink for black text and solids, you don't necessarily have to. In InDesign, and in other graphics programs, you can create what is known as a *rich black*, or a black that is defined as the sum of cyan, magenta, and yellow. You might want to add black to the mix to keep the color from getting muddy and brownish.

CMYK refers to the four colorants that comprise it—cyan (C), magenta (M), yellow (Y), and black (K). K is short for black? Actually, K stands for key. In process color printing, the black plate is called the *key plate* because it is the ink that is usually printed first.

15

If you have a color inkjet or laser printer, you probably installed four ink or toner cartridges for it. (Or, you might also have installed a black cartridge and a color cartridge, the latter of which probably had CMY colorants.)

Surpassing the CMYK Gamut

These days, you are not limited to four-color printing. One of the problems with four-color process printing is that its *gamut*—the range of reproducible colors—is extremely limited, much more so than the RGB color space. Various attempts have been made to expand the gamut of process color printing. Inkjet printers, proofers, and large-format devices often print in six colors (sometimes more), adding a light cyan and light magenta to standard four-color inks to widen the gamut.

There is also a process called *HiFi Color printing*, which adds additional process colors such as green and orange. Setting up your InDesign files to print in HiFi Color is a bit beyond the scope of this book. Suffice it to say that it is an option that might be available to you. Check with your printer or your service provider if you want to investigate this option.

You Will Convert!

This RGB versus CMYK dichotomy creates problems for electronic publishing and prepress workflows. Scanners, digital cameras, and monitors display colors in the RGB color space (for obvious reasons), but a printer or printing press uses the CMYK color space. Therefore, when you prepare your document for print, you need to ensure that all your colors are in the CMYK color space.

Hour 16, "Color Management with InDesign," addresses some of the specific problems the conversion process can cause. For now, assume that none of this is going to cause you any output problems.

As you saw in Hour 13, "Simple Coloring with InDesign," you can use the Swatch Options dialog box in the Swatches palette to switch from CMYK to RGB (or vice versa). You also saw how you can use the Color palette to create colors in different color spaces. Now you know why paying attention to these settings is important.

There is one caveat with regard to converting from one color space to another, and that is that the conversion from one space to another is not a 100-percent accurate one. For example, notice in Figure 15.1 that we have a defined color of C=100, M=100, Y=0, and K=20.

FIGURE 15.1

A color defined in the CMYK color space.

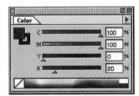

If we then select RGB, converting the color to the new color space, we can see the RGB values (see Figure 15.2).

FIGURE 15.2

The CMYK colors converted to their RGB equivalents.

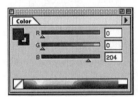

Now, without touching a single slider, I will convert back to CMYK. Look at what happened (see Figure 15.3).

FIGURE 15.3

The CMYK colors now have different percentages than they started with.

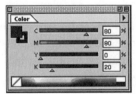

The C and M percentages have dropped to 80 percent each. This is because when you convert from one color space to another, you are changing the color values—sometimes slightly, sometimes quite dramatically.

You'll notice that each of the four colors can be specified as a percent. This is how process colors are defined—as percentages of the constituent inks.

> Recall that there was a third color space in the Colors palette: Lab. *Lab* describes a particular color in terms of three values: a lightness or darkness value (L), a red-green value (a), and a yellow-blue value (b). It's often used in colorimetry, and is beyond the scope of much of what you'll be doing with InDesign.

Ensuring that the colors we create in InDesign are in the correct color space is important, but the more serious problems come with linked color images. Hour 18 dwells on this in greater detail when I nag you about making sure your linked TIFF and EPS images are in CMYK rather than RGB.

Understanding Trapping

You finally get to the purported subject of this chapter: *trapping*. As you might remember, process color printing is done by laying down four different inks one after the other. One common problem involves registration. *Registration* refers to the extent to which each color is laid down in alignment with each other. Colors that do not align properly are said to be *out of register*. You've seen out-of-register printing, I'm sure. Sometimes, for example, when you get your Sunday paper, you'll notice color photos or comic strips in which the inks are out of alignment. The result looks sort of like images that can be viewed in 3D with those special glasses.

Registration can be tricky, but a skilled pressman can adjust the press during *makeready* so that misregistration is not a serious issue.

NEW TERM *Makeready* is a collective term for all the processes involved in setting up a printing press for a print run. This includes adding ink, adjusting the amount of ink, feeding the paper through properly, and making sure that registration is accurate. Makeready is done so as not to waste paper after the run has started in earnest.

Registration can be a serious issue when solid colors abut. Figures 15.4 and 15.5 aim to represent—in a black-and-white book—the problems certain page elements can present.

FIGURE 15.4

The way you want your page to look.

FIGURE 15.5

The way your page might come out.

Figure 15.4 shows the adjacent colors. There are a number of reasons why it would probably come off press looking something like Figure 15.5 (which is admittedly an exaggeration). The big reason you get gaps that you could drive a truck through between adjacent colors has to do with the fact that paper is a flexible substrate. Paper can expand or contract as it is printed, as temperature and humidity change, and so on. Some substrates—newsprint, for example—absorb more ink than others. Ink absorption also affects the extent to which colors align.

Trapping refers to the means by which you can attempt to compensate for potential misregistration before you go on press. In the dim and distant past, this was done photographically, using a slight enlargement and reduction technique referred to as *spreads and chokes* (or fatties and skinnies, if you want to be less politically correct about it).

InDesign gives you the capability to position objects on a page with staggering precision. You can zoom in and get those color squares to abut with almost molecular precision. But this is far more precise than can probably ever be printed.

Setting Up In-RIP Trapping

In InDesign 1.0, the burden of trapping was left to a technology referred to as *Adobe In-RIP Trapping*. Basically, the point of this strategy was to remove the trapping process from the desktop, and put it in the hands of the service bureau or CTP department. In-RIP Trapping is a feature of some raster image processors (RIPs), the devices that convert PostScript code coming from the application to the map of pixels (dots) that an imaging device—be it one that produces film, prints, or plates—can output. RIPs also perform a number of other prepress functions, such as color management, and, well, trapping.

In-RIP Trapping was designed to help you avoid setting traps manually. It works in tandem with the trapping engine built into a RIP, and automatically applies traps by detecting the edges of contrasting colors and then spreading a lighter color into a darker color, which is typically the preferred means of trapping. The color overlap created by the trap is less visible if the lighter color has overprinted the darker.

In-RIP Trapping is easy enough to set up; as you can see in Figure 15.6, it is a pop-up item in the InDesign 1.0 print dialog box.

FIGURE 15.6

In InDesign 1.0, you easily set up In-RIP Trapping through the Print dialog box.

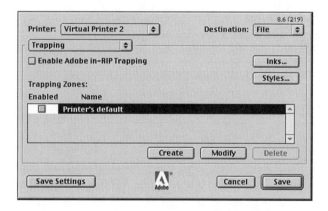

You select Trapping, and then click on the Enable In-RIP Trapping checkbox.

If you're not connected to a printer that supports In-RIP Trapping (such as a desktop inkjet printer), you'll get a warning, and you will not be able to enable it. Needless to say, unless you have a PostScript 3 RIP in your office or home, this will need to be a service bureau task.

You can also specify your trapping zone. By default, it is the entire document range, but if you know what pages you need to trap, you can define those either individually or as ranges of pages.

You can also specify your inks by pressing the Inks button, as you can see in Figure 15.7. This button lets you define what inks your document will be printed with, as well as their neutral densities.

FIGURE 15.7

You can define your custom inks and their neutral densities.

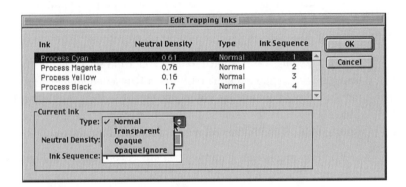

Typically, you do this only when you are working with specialty inks. You can also rearrange the inks if you know that your printer's press will lay them down in a specific order that differs from the default.

Needless to say, this is a printer decision.

How to Set Up Your Own Trapping

Adobe's rationale in leaving out user-defined trapping in InDesign 1.0 was that, as any printer can tell you, trapping can do more harm than good in the hands of a novice. But, after InDesign 1.0 appeared, there was much clamoring and gnashing of teeth about the limited trapping capabilities. Not everyone was fond of In-RIP Trapping, nor had access to a PostScript 3 RIP, much less one that supported In-RIP Trapping.

In InDesign 1.5, Adobe has added built-in trapping capabilities. These new features are accessed in the same way, through the Print dialog box, except that you now have three options (see Figure 15.8).

Your options are Off, which seems self-explanatory; application built-in, which you'll get to in a moment; and In-RIP, which Adobe still prefers above all else.

Built-in trapping, also called on-host trapping, enables you to set up various trapping styles, much like you can set up printer styles (which we'll see in Hour 17, "Printing from InDesign"). See Figure 15.9.

FIGURE 15.8

In InDesign 1.5, you now have the option of using built-in trapping, rather than In-RIP Trapping.

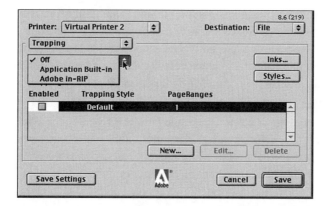

FIGURE 15.9

In InDesign 1.5, you can set up trapping styles if you work on different documents that require their own trap settings.

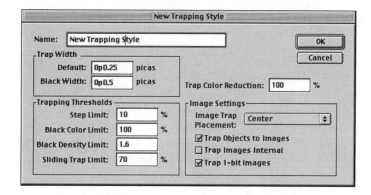

15

The Trapping Styles are accessed by going to the Print dialog box by choosing File, Print or pressing Command+P (on the Mac) or Control+P (in Windows). Select the Advanced Page Control pop-up menu. Scroll down and select Trapping. On the right side of the Trapping dialog box, click on the Styles button. In the Trapping Styles dialog box, click on the New button to create a new trapping style. The View Trap Style dialog box that you saw in Figure 15.9 appears.

There's a lot of stuff in this dialog box. Here are the highlights:

- *Trap Widths.* The default trap width determines how much InDesign overlaps neighboring colors. This number applies to all your colors with the exception of black. The default is 0.25 point. If you increase the trap width, you run the risk of making a more pronounced third color as the result of the mixing of the two colors you're trapping.

- *Black Width.* This is typically twice the amount of the trap width of the other colors. You can get away with a larger black width because mixing other colors with pure black doesn't create a noticeable difference.

- *Trapping Thresholds*. First set a Step Limit, which is basically the difference between two adjacent colors, in a percentage. By entering a number here, you are telling InDesign to ignore adjacent colors that are within that percentage. For example, 10 percent is the default, which means that InDesign ignores all colors that differ from each other by less than 10 percent.

- *Black Color Limit*. This limit tells InDesign when it should start considering dark gray as black when deciding to treat it with the Black Width setting you made earlier. This number typically depends on the paper you are printing on. When printed on papers that absorb a larger-than-usual amount of ink, dark grays can come out looking like 100-percent blacks.

- *Black Density Limit*. This setting tells InDesign what to do about dark colors—such as a dark blue—that end up printing like black. InDesign uses this number to evaluate the ink densities that define various colors, and determines at what point they should be trapped like black. Pure white is specified as 10, and pure black is specified as 0. As a result, 1.6 is the default.

- *Sliding Trap Limit*. This value controls how much one color is spread into another. The greater the difference between two colors, the greater the distortion that occurs when those two colors combine to create a third color. Therefore, this value refers to the difference in ink density between two adjacent colors. At 70 percent (the default), when the difference in ink density between the two colors is 70 percent or more, the darker color does not spread quite so much into the lighter color. If you change this to 100 percent, the entire trap width is used.

- *Trap Color Reduction*. At 100 percent, both colors being trapped are reproduced in the *trap zone* at 100 percent, which can cause any third color created in the trap by their mixing to be dark and unpleasant. Reducing this number lowers the strength of each color in the trap zone.

- *Image Trap Placement*. In this field, you need to decide whether you want an imported bitmap image to overprint the solid color by the amount specified in Trap Width (Spread) or whether you want the solid to overprint the image (Choke). Alternatively, you can have them meet halfway (Center).

- *Trap Objects to Images*. Unselect this checkbox to turn off any trapping between bitmapped images and solid objects.

- *Trap Images Internal*. Be sure to unselect this checkbox, which traps individual colors within a bitmap. This is good only for computer screen grabs and other images that have few gradations and more large solid areas of color.

- *Trap 1-bit Images*. Selecting this checkbox traps any black-and-white-only bitmap images to any adjacent objects, which keeps the black areas from having a white shadow if misregistration occurs.

15

Once you've made all your selections and you press OK, your new trapping style appears in the Styles list. Press OK to return to the general Trapping section of the Print dialog box.

> If you don't intend to print with your new trapping style(s) right away, be sure to press the Save Settings button before pressing Cancel, otherwise your newly defined styles will be lost.

Needless to say, trapping is one of those areas where a little knowledge is a dangerous thing. Consult with your service bureau, production department, and/or printer before noodling with these settings. Incorrect settings can make the solution worse than the initial problem.

Depending on the complexity of your print job and the traps it needs to contain, the trapping process can add some time to your output process.

Working with Overprint Settings

All that said, you might not even need to go through the trapping process. InDesign has a variety of overprint settings, some of which are the default. These are designed to obviate the need for trapping.

For example, InDesign automatically overprints objects to which you have applied black (in the Swatches palette). As a result, all your black type, lines, strokes, and solids overprint. What does this mean? This means that when you type black on, say, a light blue, the black prints on top of the blue. If you turn off the Overprint Black option by choosing Edit, Preferences, General (see Figure 15.10), the black knocks out the light blue.

FIGURE 15.10

The Overprint Black option is a checkbox in the General Preferences dialog box.

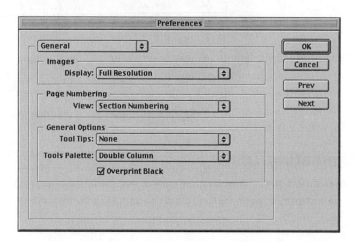

In other words, with Overprint Black off, the light blue will have blank spaces where the black ink goes. As you can imagine, this can be a registration problem in the making. Overprinting the black is the default, and it makes sense to use it unless you have a specific need to disable it.

Here's another way to look at the difference between overprinting and knocking out. In Figure 15.11, the dark gray circle knocks out the portion of the black circle with which it overlaps. If you took the dark gray circle away, you would have a sort of crescent shape.

FIGURE 15.11
When one object knocks out another, any portion of an image beneath the top object ceases to exist.

However, if you use overprint, as you can see in Figure 15.12, the area where the two images overlap becomes a combination of the two colors from the two overlapping objects. You can use this principle to simulate traps manually.

FIGURE 15.12
When one object is set to overprint, the area where they overlap becomes a mixture of the two overlapping objects.

Simulating Traps

You can use a stroke to simulate a trap. If you have two adjacent process colors, you can create a stroke between them that acts as a trap. To do this, create a stroke that is about twice the expected trap width. First determine how wide your trap needs to be, and then create a stroke that is twice that size.

To Do: Using a Stroke to Simulate a Trap

Assume you have two design elements that abut each other, and you want to apply a stroke to simulate a trap between them. To follow along with this example, download and open the InDesign file labeled strokeTrap.indd (see the instructions on how to download example files from Macmillan's Web site). Then, follow these steps:

1. Open the document (strokeTrap.indd).

2. Using the Magnification tool, zoom into the join between the two colored rectangles so that you can see the full height of it on-screen.

3. On the Toolbar, select the Line tool, which can be found by holding down the button for the Pen tool, or by simply typing the backslash (\) character. Draw a line that covers the seam between the two rectangles.

4. Without deselecting the line, open the Stroke palette (choose Window, Stroke or press F10).

5. Enter the weight of your desired stroke. Remember from the Trapping Styles setting that 0.25 point was a good default trap width. So, enter .25 in the Weight field.

6. Without deselecting the line, click over one tab to the Color palette.

7. Click on the arrow at the top-right of the palette and select CMYK.

   Now you need to enter the CMYK values you want your line to have. For reasonably good results, each C, M, Y, and K value should be the greater of those values possessed by the two adjacent objects.

8. To get the CMYK values for each rectangle, select each one in turn and click on the solid color chip in the Color palette. You'll find that the blue rectangle has values of C=80, M=60, Y=40, and K=20. The red rectangle has values of C=20, M=80, Y=60, K=10. Thus the line should be C=80, M=80, Y=60, K=20.

9. Making sure the line is still selected and the Stroke color chip has been clicked, enter the color values you calculated above, as per Figure 15.13.

10. Click over to the Attributes palette and click on Overprint Stroke.

11. Zoom up to the maximum (4000 percent) to ensure that the line is placed exactly between the two rectangles. If you zoom back to 100 percent, your stroke is barely visible.

▼

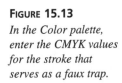

FIGURE **15.13**
In the Color palette,
enter the CMYK values
for the stroke that
serves as a faux trap.

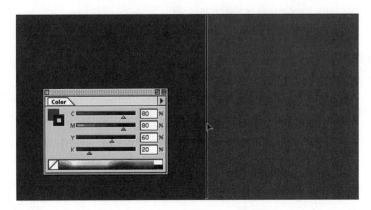

▲

This strategy is a kludge at best, but it can work if you're desperate.

To Trap or Not to Trap...

That is the question. And the answer will depend. (Big help, right?) Some design guides (and the InDesign manual) will tell you to avoid designing a document in which traps are necessary. Well, that's not a good solution. Is software your tool or are you its tool? If you can conceive a design, shouldn't your tools be able to cope? And if not, doesn't that mean you need new tools?

Let the philosophers ponder that one. For now, keep in mind that the decision to trap is one that's made after discussions with your service bureau and printer. As mentioned earlier, different presses, substrates, and inks affect how much or how little trapping is required. InDesign is flexible enough that it can bend to whatever your needs are.

Summary

During this hour, you've learned about some of the issues that prepress folks are concerned with regarding color, namely proper color spaces and trapping. You've also learned that trapping is something you might want to avoid, or at least foist onto someone else. From here, you'll explore some more color issues, namely, color management. (Oh, this should be fun.) In other words, the next hour attempts to answer that age-old question, "Why doesn't the print match my monitor?"

Workshop

You've learned about many of the prepress considerations that designers need to think about when creating their documents. Specifically, we've looked at color spaces and trapping issues. There's not a lot in the way of exercises that can be recommended here. But do check out the Q&A for any lingering questions you may have, and take the brief Quiz to see how much of the preceding hour you've retained.

Q&A

Q Does the line screen at which a page is printed affect trapping values?

A Yes. Generally, printing on glossy coated stock at 150 line screen requires a trap of .003 inch. Printing on glossy coated stock at 133 line screen requires a trap of .004 inch. And so on.

Q You made those numbers up, didn't you?

A No, I did not. They are from *The Complete Guide to Trapping*, published in 1996 by Hayden Books, a division of Macmillan Computer Publishing.

Q Do I need to trap Web-based pages?

A Unless you're applying ink directly to your monitor, the answer is no.

Q Should I perform my own trapping?

A Only if you are experienced enough to do so. Always consult with your service bureau, printer, and/or CTP department before doing any sort of trapping, be it manual or automatic.

Quiz

1. In CMYK, K stands for _____.

   A. Kill

   B. Kangaroo

   C. Kodak

   D. Key

2. Spot colors use the same inks as process colors.

   A. True

   B. False

3. When using an overprint stroke as a faux trap, each CMYK value should be the greater or lesser of the two adjacent colors?

   A. Greater

   B. Lesser

4. Which of the following is not a form of trapping supported by InDesign 1.5?

   A. In-RIP Trapping

   B. Host-based trapping

   C. Fur trapping

Quiz Answers

1. D. The black plate is referred to as the key plate because it is printed first.

2. B. Spot inks are opaque, whereas process inks are somewhat transparent. This is why process colors can be overprinted to yield a wide range of colors, whereas spot inks cannot.

3. A. Essentially, you want to create a third color trap that is as close chromatically to one or both of the colors you are trapping. In fact, you're almost creating a gradient, as way of segueing from one color to another somewhat seamlessly.

4. C. If you answered A or B, the PETA folks are going to be mighty upset.

HOUR 16

Color Management with InDesign

You learned about some of the basic issues with regard to color in the last hour—namely, process versus spot, CMYK versus RGB, and trapping. This hour attempts to answer the age-old question, "Why doesn't my finished print look the way it did on my monitor?"

There are many reasons for this discrepancy, and those reasons provide the basis for what is loosely called *color management*. The first and most basic reason is that monitors display images with light, whereas printers reproduce images with colorants such as inks. A color inkjet printer will print much differently than an offset press, and even offset presses differ from each other. Add digital cameras and scanners into that mix, and you have a whole slew of color hoops to jump through from input to output.

This hour briefly looks at those obstacles, and then shows you how to use InDesign to overcome them.

So, in this hour, you'll learn:

- How color management works
- How to create a color profile for your monitor

- How to enable color management in InDesign
- How to set Document Color settings in InDesign
- How to calibrate imported images

Understanding Color Management

Of course the first question you might be asking is, "Do I even need color management?" It depends. (You're going to hit me at some point, aren't you?) It really does depend on how meticulous you need to be about color reproduction.

If you are producing a clothing catalog, for example, you need to ensure that a green shirt appears in print the exact same color as the actual item. Otherwise you'll be in deep trouble with irate—and badly dressed, as it happens—customers. But, conversely, you might have fairly lax color requirements; some workflows rely solely on default settings with minimal tweaking, and everything works out just fine.

In the current realm of the diverse graphic arts, there are two parallel attitudes toward color management. The first is from high-end designers and publishers who use high-end spectrophotometers and expensive color-management systems to ensure that every pixel is matched from input to output. At the other end—typically those who do quick-turnaround, on-demand jobs at print shops using direct digital presses—is a reliance on "good enough" color management. Which means unless something is truly ghastly, no one is particularly concerned.

But, there is a third road you can take: keep some color profiles, use ColorSync, and pretty much do what we're about to do, but not get too involved with expensive spectrophotometers. It's really up to you which of the three roads you want to take.

Color Management Systems and Profiles

Basically, color management has two components:

- Color-management system (CMS)
- Color profiles

A color-management system (CMS) is responsible for coordinating all the color profiles coming into the computer from scanners, cameras, color images, and other sources. The CMS looks at the colors you have defined in InDesign (or other programs) or have imported, compares them to your monitor and printer settings (from the profile), and adjusts the colors accordingly. Basically, if you import an image that contains a color that the monitor cannot display, the CMS will recalibrate it to a color that is its closest equivalent. Similarly, if your destination printer does not support a color that's viewable onscreen, it will recalibrate it to a close equivalent.

There are several CMSs out there. If you are on the Macintosh, there is ColorSync, Apple's operating system-level color management system. On Windows, there is the Integrated Color Management (ICM) system.

ColorSync is not the panacea that many think it is, but it does help. There are also third-party CMSs, such as Heidelberg's LinoColor CMM (Mac only) and Kodak Digital Sciences ICC CMS (Windows only). Alternatively, you can use the default Adobe CMS, which is a good way to go when you're in doubt.

NEW TERM Color management works by using profiles. A *profile* is a file that stores information about how a device represents color. It includes information about the color gamuts (the range of colors a device can reproduce) and models the device supports.

There are two ways to profile your components—you can use the profiles that come with InDesign (and InDesign has many), or you can create your own profiles. The disadvantage to using the built-in profiles is that they are based on a standard and might not account for idiosyncrasies in your own set up. The downside to creating your own profiles is that to profile a printer, scanner, or digital camera, you need to invest in color-management hardware and software. For example, a spectrophotometer might be needed. A *spectrophotometer* is an instrument that reads reflectance or transmittance of light at various intervals throughout the visible spectrum.

To profile a color printer, you need to print a *test target*—a set of color squares whose exact color values have been scientifically measured and are known quantities. You then use the spectrophotometer to measure the color values of these squares. The data gleaned by the spectrophotometer is then used to determine how that device reproduces those colors. This information forms the basis of the color profile.

One other acronym you need to be aware of is ICC, which stands for International Color Consortium, and is a standard way of describing color characteristics. What you're after is an ICC-compatible profile, because it will allow any ICC-compliant CMS—which any self-respecting CMS should be—to use the profile in the same way. Remember, standards are good things.

The best way to see how all this works is to actually go ahead and do it. So the first step in creating a color-managed workflow is to set up profiles for your various components. Try this quick-and-dirty monitor profile.

16

To Do: Setting Up a Monitor Profile

There are several ways to create a monitor profile. Apple's ColorSync is one of the best, but is not supported in Windows (doh!). Adobe ships the Adobe Gamma control panel with InDesign, so let's use Adobe Gamma to profile the monitor for this example.

> If you already have a color-managed workflow, and everything is profiled and calibrated, please ignore this example. I certainly don't want you to screw up your system. After all, if it ain't broke...well, you know.

To create a monitor profile using the Adobe Gamma control panel, follow along with these steps:

1. Open the Adobe Gamma control panel, which on the Mac is under the Apple menu under Control Panels. In Windows, it is in Settings. You'll get the opening screen (see Figure 16.1).

FIGURE **16.1**

The Adobe Gamma opening screen.

2. Here, you will create a profile—ICC compliant—that is compatible with both ColorSync (Mac) and ICM (Windows). This is a good thing. At this point, you can stampede straight to the control panel, or go through the process step by step. Let's go through it step by step, so select that option, and click Next.

3. You can now see the profile you are starting from, as shown in Figure 16.2. This is useful if you screw something up; you can simply start from scratch. If you want to load a different starting point, you can click the Load button and select an alternative.

FIGURE 16.2
The starting point for creating your new profile.

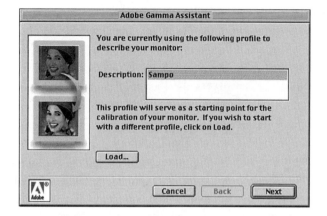

16

4. Click Next to adjust the brightness and contrast of the monitor so that the control panel knows where you're starting from. You have to do this because, no matter how sophisticated a CMS might be, it is impossible for it to determine your brightness and contrast settings since these are set manually using knobs on the display. The calibration box (see Figure 16.3) is a grayish black square surrounded by a white frame.

FIGURE 16.3

Adjust the brightness until the gray box becomes almost—but not completely—black.

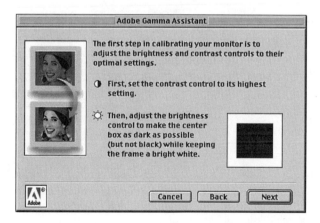

Follow the instructions and turn the contrast all the way up. Adjust the brightness until that dark gray square is as dark as it can be without being black. And remember to make sure that the white box remains bright white. When you're done, click Next.

5. Now the panel asks about your phosphors. You probably have no idea what red, green, and blue phosphors your monitor is using. I don't either. Stick with the

▼ default unless you know what you've got. The options are listed in the pop-up menu in the center of the dialog box. See Figure 16.4.

FIGURE **16.4**
Picking your phosphors.

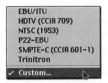

NEW TERM Click Next to set the gamma. *Gamma* is a numerical value that attempts to quantitatively specify monitor contrast. Without getting too involved, gamma is the slope of a curve that compares input and output. When related to monitors, a higher gamma indicates a darker display.

6. Notice in Figure 16.5 that there are three squares roughly like the one you saw a few screens ago when setting the brightness. (This is a black-and-white book, but these squares are actually red, green, and blue.) If you don't have three squares on your screen, make sure the View Single Gamma Only checkbox is deselected.

FIGURE **16.5**
Setting the gamma.

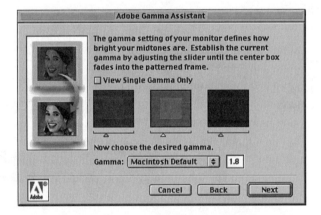

Move the sliders for each square until the square in the center melds as seamlessly as possible into the background.

When setting the gamma, it's best to try to focus your eyes on a point in front of the display, that is, blur your vision slightly so that the screen is out of focus. It's kind of like trying to see those MagicEye 3D posters—you can get a better sense of when the one square is disappearing into the other.

▼

▼ Do this for each of the three squares, and then set your desired gamma. Unless you have some compelling reason not to, use the standard that corresponds to your platform. On the Mac, the standard gamma is 1.8. On a PC, it is 2.2. (Toggle between the two and see what effect that has.)

Essentially, what you are doing in this screen is setting up how your monitor *is* displaying color and then telling it how it *should be* displaying color. The CMS can then compare those two values and correct for the difference.

7. Click Next. You are prompted to set the *white point* (see Figure 16.6). White point is essentially a measure of color temperature, and is measured in "degrees Kelvin (K)."

16

FIGURE **16.6**

Setting the white point.

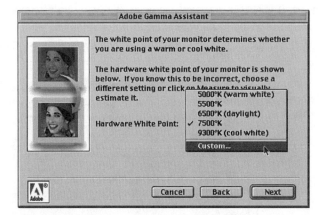

You can either accept the default (which comes from the profile you started with) or you can measure the white point. If you click Measure, you are presented with a black screen and three gray squares. You then select the square that appears to be the most neutral gray—the one that has no remnants of any other color. Doing this sets a new white point.

Most monitors manufactured in the last few years can adjust their color temperature internally, which is a much more accurate and stable method than what we're outlining in step 7. If your monitor lets you set the hardware white point to D50 (5000K) using the monitor's controls, you're better off doing that than applying a white point with software. In other words, just click Next.

▼

If you are measuring your white point, it is best to turn off all your lights and close your drapes or blinds so that your room is as dark as possible. External illumination can skew the onscreen display. It also wouldn't hurt to hit your Degauss button (or turn your monitor off and on if you monitor has automatic degaussing).

8. If you think you made a mistake, you can always try and try again. When you're done, click Next. You can choose to work in a different white point if you prefer (depending on your monitor, it might be more pleasing to you). Alternatively, you can keep it the same as the hardware by choosing that option. It's kind of a silly option. It is best to stay with Same as Hardware unless your monitor's hardware white point really hurts your eyes.

9. Finally, the control panel will show you your handiwork (see Figure 16.7).

FIGURE 16.7

*You can see a before-
and-after comparison
of your calibration
adjustments.*

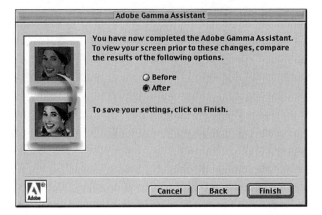

10. Click Finish to save your profile. Be sure to save it in the same folder as your other profiles—or at the very least with the default ones. That way, when you select this profile in InDesign, you know where it is.

If you are using Windows, you have to save the name of your profile using DOS naming conventions—eight characters and a three-character extension (in this case, .ICM). Adobe Gamma does not support long filenames, for some bizarre reason.

It is also a good idea to stay with only one calibration method. For example, if your monitor settings are made through the Mac OS's Monitors & Sound control panel, and then again with the Adobe Gamma control panel, you'll have two different settings loading at startup, which will give you skewed monitor calibration results. Pick one utility or the other and stick with it.

If you are serious about color management, you need to invest in a cali- brated monitor. A *calibrated monitor* includes a special display, as well as integrated software and system extensions that constantly monitor that dis- play. Monitor set up is done by attaching a colorimeter or spectrophotome- ter to the monitor (in carefully controlled lighting conditions) and measuring white, black, red, green, and blue values. These systems—from vendors such as Barco, Mitsubishi Display Products, and Radius (now sold by Miro)—can be very expensive. This doesn't include the spectrophotometry equipment you need to calibrate the images correctly in the first place.

Another new option for those on a budget is the Apple 21-inch Studio Display, which includes internal calibration hardware that constantly mea- sures and corrects calibration of the monitor. It does it automatically and without any additional equipment. At around $1500 there is nothing else in its price class that does this. It's very accurate and works with the Mac System software when connected with a USB cable. The Studio Display is also compatible with Windows PCs. However, the 17-inch Studio Display does not include internal calibration hardware; only the 21-inch model comes with it.

Calibrated monitors are best used in carefully controlled lighting conditions, which is not always possible in small graphics shops or home offices. And because your ambient lighting will affect the display, you might not get the full benefit of the calibration. But, then again, you'll get closer than ever before.

A middle ground between the quick-and-dirty Adobe Gamma "calibration" and a high-end calibrated monitor is the use of software packages designed for color management from such companies as Monaco Systems (www.monacosys.com), X-Rite (www.xrite.com), Gretag-Macbeth (www. gretagmacbeth.com), Aurelon (www.aurelon.com), and others. These all vary widely in price, ease, and efficacy, but are worth looking into if you're interested in color management.

16

Working with InDesign's Color Management

The profiles you create either through ColorSync, ICM, Adobe Gamma, or some other CMS, can be accessed by InDesign. This section shows you how to set up color management in InDesign.

Enabling Color Management

There are two stages to setting color management in InDesign. The first is to set the application defaults. The second is to set the specific document color settings, which is accomplished by two sets of dialog boxes in the Color Settings submenu of the Edit menu.

To Do: Enabling Color Management in InDesign

To turn on color management and set the application defaults in InDesign, follow these steps:

1. Open the Application Color Settings, which is under Edit, Color Settings. You'll get a dialog box that looks like Figure 16.8.

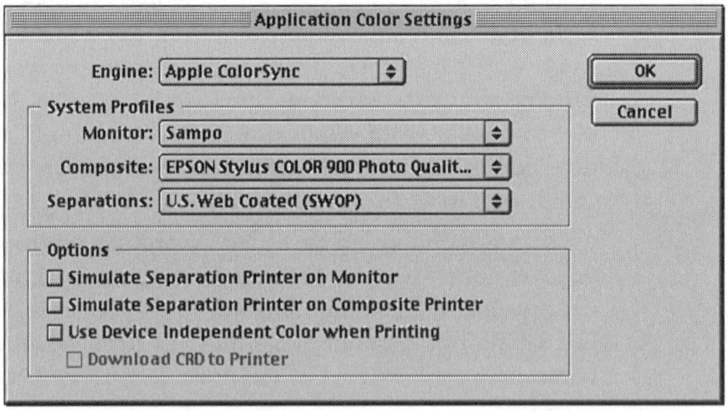

FIGURE **16.8**

The Application Color Settings dialog box.

> **Application Color Settings**
>
> Engine: [Apple ColorSync ▢]   [OK]
>
> ┌─ System Profiles ──────────────────┐   [Cancel]
> │ Monitor: [Sampo   ▢]   │
> │ Composite: [EPSON Stylus COLOR 900 Photo Qualit... ▢] │
> │ Separations: [U.S. Web Coated (SWOP)   ▢] │
> └─────────────────────────────────────┘
>
> ┌─ Options ──────────────────────────┐
> │ ☐ Simulate Separation Printer on Monitor │
> │ ☐ Simulate Separation Printer on Composite Printer │
> │ ☐ Use Device Independent Color when Printing │
> │   ☐ Download CRD to Printer │
> └─────────────────────────────────────┘

This box lets you tell InDesign what profiles to use when displaying pages, when printing composite pages, and when printing separations. Composite pages have all four process colors on the same sheet, and might be used when sending output to a color printer or proofer.

2. You'll first need to determine what engine you need. This simply is the CMS you want to use. You have a choice of Apple ColorSync (Mac only), Heidelberg (formerly LinoColor), CMM (PC only), and Adobe CMS (both platforms). Select the one that you want or can use. When in doubt, choose Adobe CMS.

▼   3. Now you select your system profiles. For Monitor, click the pop-up menu to find
         and select the profile that corresponds to your monitor. If you just created one in
         the last example, find it from the list and select it.

> If InDesign was open while you were going through the Adobe Gamma pro-
> filing set up, you need to quit InDesign and relaunch it so the new profile
> appears here.

     4. For Composite, select a profile that corresponds to your color proofer or printer. In
         my case, I have an Epson Stylus Color 900 that I use for color proofing, and I use
         inkjet media. So I select the profile that corresponds to this device. If a profile for
         your device isn't here, you can select Adobe InDesign Default RGB (or CMYK,
         depending on whether your printer is an RGB or CMYK device).

> You can find these profiles on the Mac in a subfolder called ColorSync
> Profiles, found in the System folder. In Windows, they are usually in a Color
> subfolder found in the main system folder. They are either included with the
> operating system, or are added when installing printers.

     5. For Separations, you need to select the profile that most closely matches the output
         device that will produce the color separations. It's not surprising if you have no
         idea what this device is. It will probably be a RIP, imagesetter, platesetter, or some
         other high-end service bureau or print shop device. You can always select Adobe
         InDesign Default CMYK when in doubt.

         Or, if you know generally what sort of printing press you're going to be printing
         on, and what type of paper that will be used, you can select the various offset print-
         ing standards. These include US Web Coated(SWOP), which is coated paper run
         through a web offset press; US Web Uncoated, which is uncoated paper run
         through a web press; and US Sheetfed Coated and US Sheetfed Uncoated for the
         coated and uncoated papers run through sheetfed presses. These are based on
         SWOP (Specifications for Web Offset Publications) standards.

> By the way, SWOP is a set of color-proofing standards developed by a joint
> committee of many trade associations and other printing industry groups.
> SWOP standards are designed to ensure that colors are reproduced consis-

▼

▼

> tently among different publishers and publications. The SWOP standards
> focus on the ability of a particular printer to accurately evaluate and repro-
> duce a color proof on-press. This is aided also by the use of standard SWOP
> inks. When setting up output profiles for documents that will be printed on
> a Web press, you can always use a SWOP standard profile. Check with the
> specific printer, though, if you have questions.

6. There is also a series of option checkboxes in the Application Color Settings dialog
   box. The first checkbox, Simulate Separation Printer on Monitor, attempts to display onscreen how colors will reproduce on the device you chose for your
   Separations profile. Checking this is a good idea, although remember to take all so-
   called accurate monitor color displays with a grain of salt. If you are designing for
   the Web, PDF, CD-ROM, or other screen-based use, be sure to leave this option
   unchecked.

7. The second checkbox, Simulate Separation Printer on Composite Printer, makes
   InDesign attempt to print colors on your composite device (a printer or proofer) the
   way it thinks they will print on your Separations device. If you have no other
   proofing software or hardware, you can check this. It won't hurt that much,
   although it will slow printing. If you have a better proofing set up—be it something
   like Epson's Stylus Pro 5000, the Imation/Hewlett-Packard Inkjet proofing System,
   or even Adobe's PressReady, it's better to use those proofing systems than check
   this box.

8. The third checkbox, Use Device Independent Color when Printing, keeps InDesign
   from converting colors. Instead, InDesign simply uses the options that are selected
   in the Monitors pop-up menu or stored in an imported image's color profile. It is
   up to the output device to do its own color adjustments.

   Beware though: The output device must support PostScript device-independent
   color, otherwise the effect is akin to disabling color management entirely. It's best
   to leave this unchecked. If you do check it, you can make InDesign send the printer
   a Color Rendering Dictionary (CRD) based on your Separations profile selection
   (just click the Download CRD to Printer box). But again, your output device (and
   service bureau) must support these features in order for them to do anything but
   screw up your files.

9. If you're happy with your settings, click OK to set them. If you're scared, remember that you can override these settings in a specific document.

▲

Most graphics programs enable you to set up and use profiles in much the same way that Adobe Gamma and InDesign do. Not surprisingly, Adobe products tend to operate consistently. In Photoshop, for example, you use File, Color Settings, Profile Setup to set up your profiles. It is important to create and use the same profiles in all your graphics programs. InDesign uses color profile information that comes into it from an imported image. To keep everything managed nicely, you'll therefore need to ensure that your profiles are consistent from one program and file to the other.

16

Now that you have set up your application defaults, you are ready to set up the specific document defaults.

Configuring Document Color Settings

The Document Color Settings dialog box is under Edit, Color Settings, Document Color Settings (see Figure 16.9).

FIGURE **16.9**

The Document Color Settings dialog box.

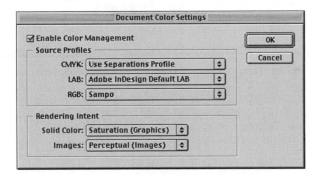

Don't worry too much about this dialog box, because as you'll see shortly, you can change these settings on an object-by-object basis. You do need to set some basic defaults here, though. The first thing you should do is check the box that says Enable Color Management, otherwise all this will be for naught.

You're also going to use the Separations profile for your CMYK images. So you can click on the pop-up menu and scroll down to select the device profile you have been using for your Separations (see the last example concerning the application color settings).

You don't need to worry about any LAB profiles. If you import a lot of images that are in the Lab color space, you can investigate this further, but for the most part, you can leave this as the default with impunity. You will probably want to use your monitor setting for the RGB profile, unless you are printing to an RGB device.

The Rendering Intent selections might sound kind of daunting, but they aren't too bad (see Figure 16.10). The following list discusses each option in more detail:

Figure 16.10

Rendering intent choices.

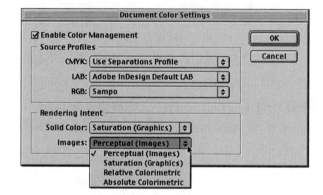

- *Perceptual (Images)*—When an image is imported, InDesign attempts to balance the colors when converting from its original color range to that of the output device. This is a good option for photographs or other continuous-tone images.

- *Saturation (Graphics)*—Attempts to print vivid colors when converting, and goes for the flashiest option over an exact match. This is a good option for transparencies and other types of eye-catching graphics, or those cases in which you want punch rather than an accurate color match.

- *Absolute Colorimetric*—Makes no changes to colors whatsoever, and allows the output device to take all the blame for the output.

- *Relative Colorimetric*—Like Absolute Colorimetric, but it shifts all the colors to take into account the white point setting of the monitor (based on the monitor profile you created or imported).

For standard images, the best bet is have Perceptual (Images) as the default. For solid colors, you'll probably also want Perceptual (Images) but you can probably get away with Saturation (Graphics) which is not as accurate but can be more vivid.

Calibrating Imported Images

When you import an image into InDesign, the default settings from the application color settings or document color settings are applied. However, you can change those defaults on an import-by-import basis, either before or after the fact.

To Do: Calibrating an Imported Image

To change the calibration settings of an imported image, do the following:

1. Create a bitmap image—preferably a color one, otherwise what's the point?—in Photoshop or some other image editor. Save it as a TIFF or other bitmap format that can be imported into InDesign. If you don't have Photoshop or a bitmap image you can use for this exercise, you can just read along.

2. Create a new InDesign document. Letter size is fine.

3. Select the Place command, either by choosing File, Place or pressing Command+D (on the Macintosh) or Control+D (on PCs).

4. In the Place dialog box, make sure that Show Import Options is checked, find your image file, and then click Choose. You should get a familiar dialog box (see Figure 16.11).

FIGURE 16.11

The Import Options dialog box.

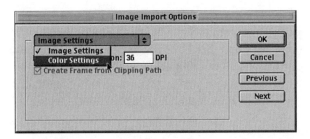

5. Click the Image Settings pop-up menu and then select Color Settings from it. You'll get a dialog box that looks like the Document Color Settings dialog box. See Figure 16.12.

FIGURE 16.12

The Color Settings portion of the Import Options dialog box.

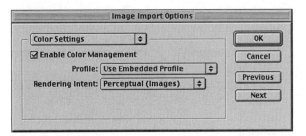

6. If Enable Color Management is not checked (it should be), check it.

7. If there is already a color profile attached to this image—as there indeed is in this case—you can use it by selecting Use Embedded Profile. This option won't exist if there is no profile embedded in the image, so if you get the option, you have an embedded profile. If you are unaware what it is—you didn't consciously put it there—you might want to choose a different profile—one that you are familiar with.

One thing you'll notice if you click the Profile pop-up menu is that the profile options match the color space of the image you are importing. For example, if your image is an RGB image, you'll only have profiles for RGB devices. By the same token, if the image is CMYK, you'll only have CMYK device profiles.

8. You just learned what rendering style means, so select Perceptual (Images) since you are importing a bitmap.

9. Click Choose, and voilà, your calibrated image is placed.

You can always go back and change the image color settings after you have placed an image. With the image selected, go to Object, Image Color Settings or press Shift+Option+Command+D (on the Macintosh) or Shift+Alt+Control+D (on PCs). This brings up the Image Color Settings dialog box—the same dialog box you saw in Figure 16.12. You can change your profile, your rendering style, or disable color management for that image. You can also use this dialog box to add a profile to an imported image even if you declined to apply one when you imported the image.

The Image Color Settings can also be accessed via a contextual menu, which you can bring up if you Ctrl-click (on the Macintosh) or right-click (in Windows) on the graphic and select Graphic, Image Color Settings... from the menu that pops up.

You can also quickly tell what profile an image is using by choosing Link Information from the Links palette.

Summary

This hour hasn't even begun to realize the subject of color management, which is an unwieldy topic. To keep this lesson under an hour, I have focused on InDesign's native approach to color management. If you want further reading on the subject, *The GATF Practical Guide to Color Management*, published by the Graphic Arts Technical Foundation, provides a good overview.

The key point to remember if you are going to go the color-management route is that you need to calibrate every link in your workflow chain—color is only as accurate as your least-calibrated device.

Color management takes a lot of effort to work truly effectively. But it's not out of the reach of the average user.

16

Workshop

Color management can be a tough subject to get one's head around. We're going to eschew formal exercises in this hour, but the Quiz should hopefully reinforce some of the concepts we've looked at in this hour.

Although we won't give you any exercises, you are welcome to experiment with InDesign's color management features. Try importing images with color management on and with it off and note any differences. If you have a color printer, print out some images and compare them to what you see onscreen, both with color management on and with it off. As you work with color images more and more, both onscreen and in print, you'll be able to instinctively determine how printed colors will differ from what you see on your monitor.

Q&A

Q How do I reconcile the fact that my service provider probably doesn't use the same color profiles that I do?

A There are a variety of ways to keep your color-management consistent even when outsourcing. The first is to provide your service provider with your color profiles. Alternatively, if you have color-profiling hardware, you can simply have your provider output an IT8 test target, have a proof made, and measure the proof. That way you've got a profile of your service bureau's equipment.

Q Tell me truthfully: Do I really need color management?

A The opinion on this will differ from expert to expert. All I can say is evaluate your own workflow and the final quality of your own work. Do your scans look like the slides or prints you scanned them from? Do your in-house color prints resemble what you see on the monitor? If you print jobs at a printer, are you surprised by how bad (or how good) the printed colors look? If you're having minor problems, invest in an inexpensive proofing system. If you're having serious problems, look into more expensive and meticulous color solutions.

Quiz

1. Which of the following is not a color-management system (CMS)?

    a. ColorSync

    b. ICM

    c. ILM

2. Which of the following does not need to be calibrated in a true, color-managed workflow?

    a. Monitor

    b. Scanner

    c. Printer

    d. None of the above

3. InDesign does not support ICC color profiles.

    a. True

    b. False

Quiz Answers

1. c. ColorSync is the Mac's CMS, ICM is Windows' CMS. ILM is Industrial Light & Magic, and does special effects for movies.

2. d. Remember, a color-managed workflow is only as strong as its least-calibrated element.

3. b. If you answered a, you might want to reread this chapter.

PART V

InDesign Output

Hour

Hour **17**

Printing from InDesign

In previous hours, you learned about certain InDesign features for creating documents. It is now time to get your documents *out* of InDesign, so in this and the next four hours, you learn how to actually get your InDesign documents into a variety of "external" forms.

In this hour, you learn how to print your InDesign documents. Not only does this introduce you to the Print dialog box and all its myriad functions, but it also teaches you how to set up your document (and your computer) for printing to a desktop laser or inkjet printer.

During this hour, you learn the following:

- How to work with printers and printer drivers
- How to work with InDesign's extensive Print dialog box
- How to create and use printer styles

Working with Printers

Chances are good that the InDesign document you are creating is not designed to be printed by a desktop printer. In other words, you are most likely creating your document for printing-press output somewhere down the line. Some people do, however, use InDesign as a word processor, and it is not uncommon to use programs like InDesign to create party invites and other one-page flyers that are printed from laser printers.

NEW TERM The primary reason you might print to a local printer is for *proofing*—both for text proofing and for color/graphics proofing. As a result, getting good results from your desktop printer is a good predictor of the kind of results you'll likely get when you get your film or proofs back from the service bureau or CTP department.

Know Your Printers

This chapter doesn't dwell too long on the myriad printing and imaging technologies that are out there. There are many competing types, so this section includes a rundown of the three you'll most likely come across. And, sure, there are probably still a few dot-matrix printers out there, but you won't get decent results if you print to them from InDesign—or any program, for that matter.

Laser Printers

The laser printer is probably the most familiar type of printer. Essentially, a laser printer uses a laser to create an electric charge in the image areas of a metal plate. Oppositely charged particles of toner adhere to these image areas, which are then transferred to the paper and fused to its surface by means of heat and pressure. Laser printers are available in black and white or four color.

Advantages: Smooth, high-resolution output. Fast, especially on black-and-white, text-only pages. Easily made PostScript-compatible. Prints on plain paper extremely well.

Disadvantages: Expensive, especially when PostScript-compatible.

Inkjet Printers

There are several types of inkjet printers, but generally they all print by firing tiny droplets of a liquid ink on to the paper or other substrate.

Advantages: High resolution. Vibrant color output. Inexpensive. Easy to generate accurate color proofs.

Disadvantages: Slow. Usually require special paper, which can be expensive. Inks can also be expensive. PostScript compatibility can be hard to come by.

Dye-Sublimation Printers

Dye-sublimation printers use a *sublimable dye* (a solid colorant that, in the presence of heat, turns directly into a gas without first becoming a liquid) imprinted on a carrier sheet to transfer images to a receiving sheet. Dye-sublimation printers (or, colloquially, *dye-subs*) are often used for cheap photoprinters as well as for expensive high-end color proofing systems. They are starting to be eclipsed by high-quality inkjets as proofing systems.

Advantages: Long-lasting output. Great for color proofing. Easy to find PostScript-compatible versions.

Disadvantages: Consumables (inks and media) can be pricey. The devices can also be expensive.

An area of promise in the industry now is getting inkjet printers to a point where they can be used for accurate color proofing. And that brings you to the next subject: PostScript.

PostScript versus Non-PostScript Printers

17

You read about PostScript, the page description language, in previous hours, but here is where it starts to become important. If you intend to print from InDesign to your printer, your printer needs to be PostScript-compatible.

Basically, this means that the printer you are using has a raster image processor built into it.

New Term   A *raster image processor*—often called a *RIP*—contains hardware or software that can read the PostScript code coming from an application such as InDesign. When you press Print, the program sends a page as a long stream of PostScript code that describes where everything on the page is. A RIP processes this code and converts it into a pattern of dots, which a particular output device can then print. This pattern of dots is called a *raster image*, hence the device's name. The word RIP has become a neologism in the graphics industry, and is also used as a verb, as in "The file won't RIP" or "We spent hours RIPing that file."

In a desktop printer, a RIP is more commonly called a PostScript interpreter, but it's basically the same thing.

> Actually, the main difference between RIP and a PostScript interpreter is that the latter is limited in its functionality. It processes PostScript code and that's it. A RIP proper, however, usually has many more features—such as your old friend In-RIP Trapping, which you saw in Hour 15, "Trapping and Other Prepress Considerations," as well as various color management utilities, color separation tools, imposition software, and many other functions.

Although a PostScript upgrade to a printer can be an expensive option, it's worth it because of PostScript's device independence. What this means is that the same document will print just about the same way on any PostScript-compatible device. It was this aspect of PostScript that enabled desktop publishing to become viable in the first place.

Device independence is possible with PostScript files, but up to a point. If someone sends you an InDesign file but you do not have the fonts that were used in the document, you will find an unpleasant font substitution—usually Courier—when you run over to the printer and get your output. This becomes a serious concern when you are going out to film or direct to plate, as you'll see in Hour 18, "Getting Ready for the Service Bureau."

PostScript compatibility is also important for a much more prosaic reason: InDesign won't print to anything else. When you try to print to a non-PostScript printer, you get the error message shown in Figure 17.1.

FIGURE 17.1

The rather terse error message you get when you press Print in InDesign while connected to a non-PostScript printer.

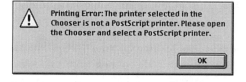

Printing Error: The printer selected in the Chooser is not a PostScript printer. Please open the Chooser and select a PostScript printer.

OK

You might recall that with other programs, such as QuarkXPress and PageMaker, you can print to a non-PostScript printer, but you get unpredictable results, especially with regard to fonts and imported EPS files.

Adobe has recently released *PressReady*, a software RIP for inexpensive and mid-range inkjet printers. PressReady is easy to install and not only is a PostScript RIP, but also has color profiling features for generating fairly accurate color proofs. Its only drawback is that it supports a small number of printers, but Adobe is working on adding more.

For more information on PressReady, as well as a list of supported printers, visit Adobe's Web site at www.adobe.com.

Windows-based InDesign users do have the luxury of printing to some non-PostScript inkjet printers using those printers' native drivers. The InDesign Read Me file contains a list of supported printers. And for Mac OS users, there is now a free download on Adobe's Web site (www.adobe.com) that gives InDesign 1.5 support for certain non-PostScript printers. The Non-PostScript Printing Update for Adobe InDesign 1.5 is still only a beta version, and is only available in English-language versions. For now.

Installing Drivers and PPDs

As you can imagine, to print to any kind of device, you need to install its drivers.

NEW TERM A *driver* is a small piece of software, usually a system extension, that tells the operating system how to recognize and print to a particular device. Using the proper driver is crucial to not only taking advantage of InDesign's printing features, but also yielding good printed results in general.

17

InDesign 1.5 requires the latest Adobe PostScript printer drivers. You need Adobe PostScript driver version 8.6 on the Macintosh, version 4.3.x on Windows 98, or version 5.1.x on Windows NT 4.0. If you are running Windows 2000 (and if so, this is probably the least of your problems), you can use the Windows PostScript driver version 5.0, unless you are printing over a Windows NT 4.0 network or to a Windows NT print server, in which case you need the AdobePS 5.51 driver. If the moon is full, you need to sacrifice a goat.

The proper print drivers are supplied on the InDesign CD and you have no doubt already installed them. If not, take this opportunity to do so. Follow the instructions Adobe supplies for your operating system. Go ahead; I'll wait.

If for whatever reason you are installing or reinstalling older software, be careful that you don't override a newer print driver with an older version of the same one. Double-check the documentation that comes with your software to find out what specifically it is installing. If you are in danger of overriding a newer extension, try to do a custom install and omit the older drivers and extensions.

All printers differ in how they are installed, and all systems themselves vary. As much as I'd love to guide you through the installation of your printer—and believe me, sometimes that can be even more complicated than learn-

ing a program like InDesign!—please refer to the documentation that came
with your specific model for installation instructions.

Using the Print Dialog Box

It's time to walk through the Print dialog boxes and actually start printing some documents.

Setting Up the Page

Printing from InDesign, as with most other programs, actually begins with a visit to the
Page Setup dialog box. Choose File, Page Setup. You can also use Shift+Command+P
(on the Mac) or Shift+Control+P (in Windows). You can see the Page Setup dialog box
in Figure 17.2.

FIGURE 17.2

The Page Setup dialog box in InDesign.

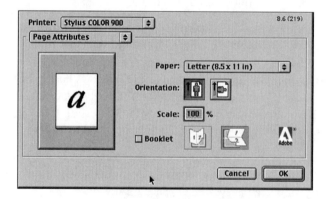

You're probably familiar with most of this dialog box. The printer is listed up top. It also
includes the pop-up list of paper sizes, the scale amount (to print at a size other than
100%), and the orientation (to print in landscape or portrait).

In other applications, Page Setup is an important dialog box. However, InDesign moves
most of its functionality to the Print dialog boxes, so the only thing you need to worry
about in Page Setup is your page orientation. You'll come back to this later on this hour.

Pressing Print

Okay, you have a document open, you press Print, and you get myriad dialog boxes.
Where to begin?

Well, oddly enough, the dialog box that comes up first in InDesign is Advanced Page
Control (see Figure 17.3).

FIGURE 17.3

*The dialog box that
appears when you
press Print.*

8.6 (219)

Printer: [Stylus COLOR 900 ↕]   Destination: [Printer ↕]

[Advanced Page Contr... ↕]

┌─Pages──┐
│ ● All Pages   │
│ ○ Ranges: [1   ] ☑ View Section Numbering │
│ ○ By Section: │
│   Prefix   Section Numbering   Section Folio Style │
│   [Sec1   1 – 1   1 – 1]   │
│   │
│   Options: [Both Pages ↕]   ☐ Reader's Spreads │
└───┘

[Save Settings]   **A** Adobe   [Cancel] [Print]

Despite the dialog box's name, it's straightforward, and it actually supersedes the
General Print dialog box (which you'll get to). Technically, you can use only this dialog
box and print just fine. As you can see, you can print all the pages in a document. Or,
you can enter individual page numbers when you want to print a single page.

Printing Ranges of Pages

One of the beauties of InDesign that it inherited from PageMaker is the ability to print
noncontiguous sets of pages. For example, if you have 15 pages in your document and
you only want to print pages 1, 3, 4, 6, 7, 8, 9, 11, and 15, all you have to do is enter
those pages in the Ranges field, separated by commas. You can also separate contiguous
pages by hyphens, rather than enter each page number, which you do in the following
example.

To Do: Printing Noncontiguous Sets of Pages

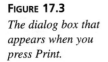

To print noncontiguous sets of pages, follow these steps:

1. Create a new InDesign document, preferably with a page size of 8 1/2×11 inches
   (letter size). In whatever way you can, make it 15 pages. You can import a long
   Word document, or simply create 15 pages, put linked text frames on each one, and
   fill the lot with Greek text using InDesign's Fill with Placeholder Text feature
   (Type, Fill with Placeholder Text). The choice is yours.

2. Open the Print dialog box by selecting File, Print or pressing Command+P (on the
   Mac) or Control+P (in Windows). You should be in the Advanced Page Control
   dialog box.

3. Make sure your printer is on, connected, and ready.

17

> If you don't want to waste paper with this exercise, you can use the Virtual Printer that is installed with the AdobePS driver. If you click on the name of your printer at the top of the Print dialog box and hold it down, you'll see a pop-up menu. (See Figure 17.4). Select Virtual Printer. This enables you to simply "print" your virtual document to a PostScript file that you can delete when you are done. You also can create a PDF using Create Adobe PDF, and then open the PDF to ensure that the correct pages have been printed.

FIGURE 17.4

To avoid wasting paper, you can print this exercise to a Virtual Printer or, in other words, a PostScript file that you can later delete.

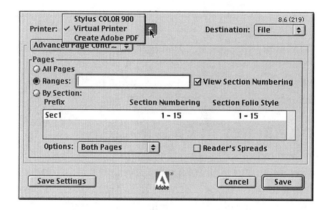

4. In the Range field, enter the pages you want to print. Use the sets you specified previously: 1, 3, 4, 6-9, 11, 15. (See Figure 17.5.)

FIGURE 17.5

Enter your page ranges or sets.

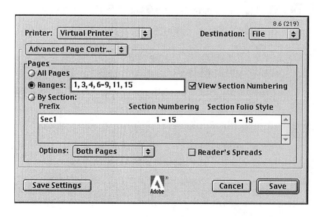

You don't need to enter spaces after the commas if you don't want to. You do need to enter commas, however.

5. If you are printing to a Virtual Printer or to a PostScript to PDF file, you'll notice, like in Figure 17.5, that instead of the usual Print button, there now is a Save button. That's because you're printing to a file. If you are printing to an actual printer, it will indeed say Print. But whatever it says, click on it.

6. You'll either start printing to your printer, or, again, if you are printing to a Virtual Printer, you'll get the Save As dialog box. You can cancel the save if you want. If you entered incorrect values or syntax in the Ranges box, you get an error message.

Keep your 15-page InDesign document open for the next exercise.

Printing Sections

As you saw in Hour 4, "Managing Pages," you can divide your InDesign document into different sections that are paginated differently. The Print dialog box lets you specify which pages within each section you want to print. You can, in the Print dialog box, see how the section and/or absolute numbering for the document have been set up in the Pages palette.

Try the following exercise to see what that specifically means.

To Do: Printing Pages in Different Sections

To print individual pages and ranges of pages that are in different sections within an InDesign document, follow these steps:

1. Hopefully, you still have your 15-page document open from the last exercise. If not, create another one.

2. Open the Pages palette (choose Window, Pages or press F12) and double-click on Page 4.

3. Click on the arrow at the top-right of the Pages palette and scroll down to select Section Options.

4. This will start a new section on page 4. Let's give it a distinctive numbering style. Click the Style drop-down box and scroll down to select A,B,C,D. This will label the pages from page 4 onward with letters.

5. Under Page Numbering, click the Start at 1 radio button. Figure 17.6 shows how the Section dialog box should look.

17

FIGURE **17.6**

The new section.

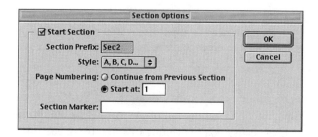

6. Press OK. If your pages were set up as two-page spreads, you'll notice that page A (the former page 4) is now on a right-hand page. Don't worry about that.

7. Open the Print dialog box by choosing File, Print, or pressing Command+P (on the Mac) or Control+P (in Windows). You should be in the Advanced Page Control box. Notice that the section you just created appears in the Section field in the center of the dialog box. (See Figure 17.7.)

FIGURE **17.7**

You can now print one or both sections.

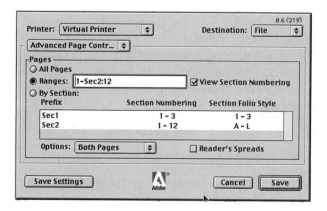

8. If you click the By Section radio button, you can print whichever section you highlight. Highlight Sec1, and press Print (or Save, as the case may be).

9. You're not done yet. Try printing only a couple pages from each section—say, pages 1 and 2 from section 1, and pages 1 and 3 from section 2. Reopen the Print dialog box.

10. In the ranges field, enter **1,2, Sec2:1,3**. (See Figure 17.8.) After the section number, you need to enter a colon, followed by the corresponding page numbers in that section.

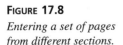

FIGURE **17.8**

Entering a set of pages from different sections.

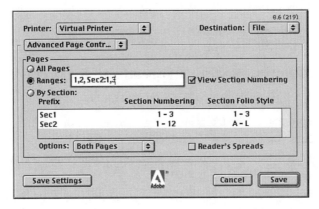

11. Press Print (or Save). You now print the four pages you specified. Keep the 15-page document open for the next exercise.

You can toggle between section numbering and absolute numbering using the View Section Numbering checkbox. If you leave section numbering on, Section 1 becomes pages 1-3 and Section 2 becomes pages 1-12. If you turn it off, you will see Absolute Numbering, which shows Section 1 as pages 1-3 and Section 2 as pages 4-15. By using these pagination features as a reference, you can enter your ranges in shorthand. For example, instead of entering **Sec2:1** you can simply enter **4**.

For much of your basic desktop print work with InDesign, the Advanced Page Control dialog box is all you need to use.

But, as you can imagine, InDesign gives you a great many more printing tools. Most of those are covered in succeeding hours as you need them, so this chapter runs through some of the other things you can do with the Print dialog box.

Printing Reader's Spreads

Before you leave the Advanced Page Control dialog box, notice the Reader's Spreads checkbox in the bottom-right corner. Basically, this option enables you to combine two-page spreads on a single sheet. You might do this to show clients mockups of designs, determine how a spread will look in print, or save paper while printing. Printing spreads properly is a tricky proposition—or it can be.

The best way to approach it is to print at 100%. This means that if your pages are 8 1/2×11 inches, you can print spreads full-size on 11×17-inch paper.

But often, you only have 8 1/2×11-inch paper available, yet you want to print spreads. How do you do it?

To Do: Printing Reader's Spreads on 8 1/2×11-Inch Paper

▼ To Do

To print a set of reader's spreads, follow these steps:

1. Return to the 15-page document you created in the earlier exercises. Using techniques you learned in Hour 4, create an 8 1/2×11-inch document that has a two-page spread. You can fill it with whatever content you want, or use InDesign's Fill with Placeholder Text feature.

2. Open the Page Setup dialog box by choosing File, Page Setup, or pressing Command+Shift+P (on the Mac) or Control+Shift+P (in Windows).

3. Make sure your paper size is letter (8 1/2×11 inches), and then click the landscape button so that the page prints lengthwise (see Figure 17.9).

FIGURE 17.9

Make sure landscape orientation is selected.

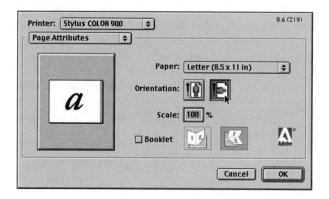

4. Because you're trying to print two 8 1/2×11-inch pages on one 8 1/2×11 inch sheet, you naturally have to scale the pages to fit. However, despite what you might think—and what has been the case in the past—the Page Setup dialog box is not the place to do this. In fact, check out the haughty error message you get when you try to change the scaling in Page Setup (see Figure 17.10).

5. Press OK, and then choose File, Print to open the Print dialog box.

▼ 6. In the Ranges box, enter two pages that correspond to a spread—say, 2-3.

FIGURE 17.10
Well, la-di-dah. I guess you won't try changing the scaling in Page Setup again.

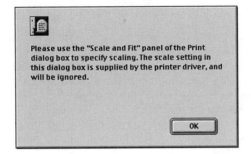

Please use the "Scale and Fit" panel of the Print dialog box to specify scaling. The scale setting in this dialog box is supplied by the printer driver, and will be ignored.

OK

In typical publication design, a left-hand page—called the *verso*, by the way—is an even-numbered page, whereas the right-hand page—the *recto*—is an odd numbered page. When you create pages in InDesign, notice that page 1 typically stands alone and that the first spread comprises pages 2–3.

17

7. Check the Reader's Spread checkbox.

8. Click on the Advanced Page Control drop-down box and scroll down to select Scale and Fit.

9. This portion of the Print dialog box gives you more control over how you scale images to fit on a sheet. Select the Scale to Fit radio button, and you'll see that the two-page spread needs to be shrunk to 57.8%. For the sake of aesthetics, let's center the spread in an imageable area—or, in other words, on the paper. (See Figure 17.11.)

FIGURE 17.11
You can let InDesign calculate how much the spread needs to be reduced to fit on a sheet.

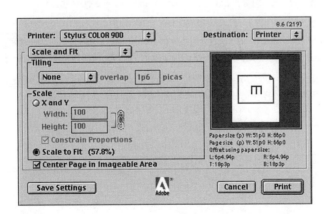

▼   10. Press Print, and the spread will print.

> If your document contains single pages (such as the opening and perhaps
> the closing page), InDesign reduces these pages less than the two-page
> spreads. As single pages, they don't need to be as small as two-page
> spreads. If it's crucial that these pages be the same size as your spreads, print
> them separately, and manually enter the reduction amount that InDesign
> had calculated for the spreads.

▲

Printing Printer's Marks

Often when printing proofs of pages, you need to print some combination of printer's or page marks. Figure 17.12 shows the major types of page marks, and where they fall on a page.

The primary types of page marks include:

- *Registration marks*—Appear on all four edges of a sheet, and appear on each color plate. They enable the pressman to determine whether the registration marks of each of the four colors are lining up on the press sheet.

- *Crop marks*—Appear at each corner of the sheet. Instructs the printer or bindery where the sheet should be trimmed. These correspond to the page size specified in the Document Setup. The crop marks are often accompanied by *bleed marks*, which are just beyond the crop marks. They indicate the bleed margin.

- *Density control bar*—Appears (usually) at the top of a sheet, and is a scale of gray values from black to white. Used as a quick reference during printing to determine whether the black and gray ink densities are correct.

- *Color control bar*—Appears (usually) at the top of the sheet, near the density control bar, and is used as quick reference to determine how the color reproduction is coming along and how consistent it is over the course of the run.

- *Filename and save date/time*—Indicates the name of the file and when it was saved. Used to determine where and when something came from.

You might need to print one or more of these marks on your prints or proofs.

Figure **17.12**

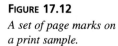

*A set of page marks on
a print sample.*

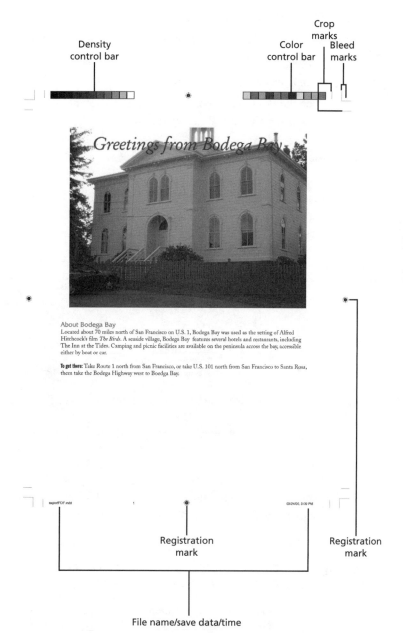

To Do: Printing Page Marks

To set up the Print dialog box InDesign to automatically add page marks to a sheet, follow these steps:

1. Open a document in InDesign.

2. Open the Print dialog box by choosing File, Print, or by pressing Command+P (on the Mac) or Control+P (in Windows).

3. Click on the Advanced Page Control drop-down box, and scroll down to select Page Marks.

4. You can see from Figure 17.13 that you have the usual suspects to choose from—crop marks, page information, registration marks, color bars, and bleed marks. You can set them individually, or turn them on en masse. Click the All Printer's Marks checkbox.

FIGURE **17.13**

InDesign's Page Marks region of the Print dialog box.

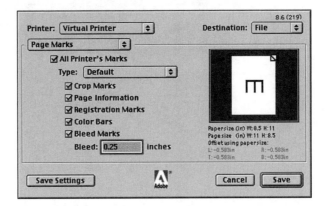

5. You might have noticed that your page marks probably don't fit on the sheet. Therefore, you need to go to the Scale and Fit region of the Print dialog box and click on the Scale to Fit radio button in order to get all the marks on the sheet.

> If you want a 100% proof of your page with crop marks, you need to use paper that is slightly larger than the document size, especially when you want your bleeds to be represented. Often, mid-range inkjet or laser proofers and printers support paper sizes up to 13×19 inches, which are called *full-bleed tabloid pages*. This means you can comfortably print two-page 8 1/2×11-inch spreads (or one 11×17-inch tabloid page) with all your bleeds and marks in living color (or in living black and white as the case might be).

▼

▼　6. Now press Print (or Save, if you've been using the Virtual Printer or Create Adobe PDF).

▲　You should now have a page that has a cornucopia of page marks.

Creating Printer Styles

One last trick you can do in the Print dialog box is create *printer styles*. You learned how to create character and paragraph styles in Hour 7, "Basic Typesetting with InDesign," and Hour 8, "Working with Paragraphs," respectively—and trapping styles in Hour 15—as a way to save oft-used settings for reuse.

The printer styles option lets you save groups of commonly used print settings. You can create a bunch of them, such as when you work on several recurring projects that require different settings.

In the next exercise, you create a printer style so you can apply it to a specific job.

To Do: Creating a Printer Style

To set up a printer style, follow these steps:

1. Go to the File menu and scroll down to Printer Styles. Select Define. This brings up the Define Printer Styles dialog box. Notice in Figure 17.14 that the only style currently available is *Current*—these are basically the default settings you have been using all along.

FIGURE 17.14
The Define Printer Styles dialog box.

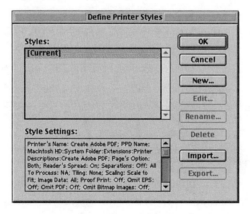

2. Click New to create a new style.

3. You'll be prompted to name the style, so give it a distinctive name, perhaps reflecting either the job, client, or printer it is designed for. Press OK. InDesign opens the Page Setup dialog box followed by the sundry Print dialog boxes. But you first get

▼   a brief explanatory note from InDesign (see Figure 17.15). This just tells you that
         you're going to see the Page Setup box first, and then Print dialog boxes, and to
         save the style, press Print, which saves the style without printing. If you are creat-
         ing many styles and don't want to be pestered by this message every time, check
         the Do Not Show This Message Again checkbox.

FIGURE 17.15
InDesign tells you
what's about to
happen.

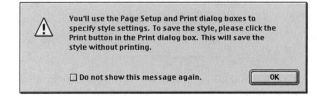

You'll use the Page Setup and Print dialog boxes to specify style settings. To save the style, please click the Print button in the Print dialog box. This will save the style without printing.

☐ Do not show this message again.   OK

 4. Well, you were warned about changing the scaling in the Page Setup dialog box.
    Here, though, you want to set the printer this is designed for, using the pop-up
    menu at the top of the box. I'm going to make it my Stylus Color 900 color printer,
    because I am going to use this style to print two-page color spreads.

 5. And, as you saw earlier in the section on printing spreads, you might need to be in
    landscape orientation. Because my document is 8 1/2×11, I indeed need to set
    landscape as the orientation. My printer supports only letter-size paper so I need to
    leave the paper size at letter.

 6. Press OK, and you return to your old stomping ground, the Advanced Page Control
    dialog box.

 7. The first thing you might notice is that you cannot print a range of pages, which
    only makes sense. You can set all the options you have seen in this hour already.

 8. If you want this style to print spreads, check the Reader's Spreads checkbox.

 9. You also need to go to the Scale and Fit region of the Print dialog box and make
    sure that you have checked the Scale to Fit option so you don't get chopped
    spreads.

10. If you want to show all the page marks, go to the Page Marks region of the Print
    dialog box and enable All Printer's Marks.

11. You can set many more options, but this is all you need for this style. Press Print,
    and you can see (in Figure 17.16) that your new style now appears in the Styles
▼   menu.

FIGURE 17.16
*Your new style is now
ready.*

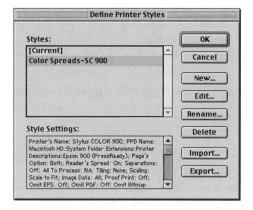

17

As you learn about additional printing options in successive chapters, you can incorporate them into various printer styles.

To use a printer style, you no longer need to use the Print command. Instead, use File, Printer Styles. You'll see, as per Figure 17.16, that the new style—and any other styles you create—are available there. Simply scroll to the style you want and select it. The Print dialog box with your preset settings appears, and you can enter all the usual info—such as page ranges and so on. You can also change your default settings, which do not affect the saved style. This enables you to use every feature of the style except one (or more).

Summary

So, you've seen how to print basic documents, ranges of pages, and sections, as well as how to print spreads, and how to add page marks to printouts. You've also seen how you can create printer styles as a time-saving feature. You'll see some of these options again—and other aspects of the Print dialog box—in the next hour, when you bundle documents for transmission to a service bureau.

Workshop

You've just learned how InDesign works with printers and printer drivers (in particular those of the PostScript variety), and how InDesign's extensive Print dialog box gives you a great deal of options for printing to printers or to files. You've also learned how to create and use printer styles. Now, read the Q&A to find the answers to some lingering questions you may have, and complete the quiz to test your recall of what we covered. Finally, work through the exercises until you know the Print dialog box inside and out.

Q&A

Q I don't have a PostScript-compatible printer, nor do I have PressReady. Am I out of luck?

A Not at all. Although it's true that you cannot print native InDesign files to your non-PostScript printer, you can export your document as a PDF and print from Acrobat or from Acrobat Reader.

Q When I am sending my files to a service bureau, do I need to include the drivers or PPDs for their output devices?

A No, and it's best if you don't even try to create Print settings for your service bureau. When they get your files, they will configure their own Print dialog box to print to their own equipment. You'll see this in the next hour. Trying to do the service bureau's job does more harm than good.

Q Can I share my own (and others') printer styles?

A Absolutely. Check out Figure 17.14 again. You'll notice two buttons in the bottom-right corner: one called Import and one called Export. If you click on Import, you can import the printer styles from another InDesign Document. If you define a style and click Export, you can export your printer style for others to use.

Quiz

1. You change the page scaling using the Page Setup dialog box.

    a. True

    b. False

2. Which of the following is not a type of page mark?

    a. Crop circles

    b. Color control bars

    c. Bleed marks

3. If you have a letter-size document and you want to print reader's spreads at 100%, what size paper do you need?

    a. Letter size (8 1/2×11 inches)

    b. 11×17 inches

    c. 13×19 inches

Quiz Answers

1. b. Remember the haughty message you got? The place to change page scaling is in the Scale and Fit region of the Print dialog box.

2. a. Unless you're doing a die-cut job, or design work for extraterrestrials, I guess.

3. b. However, if you want page marks, you need a size larger than 11×17.

Exercises

Take some time and print some documents. If you have been saving the exercises you've been working on throughout this book, open them back up and print them. Experiment with print settings. See what the Page Marks are all about. Practice printing spreads. If you have a color printer, even better. Go back to the exercises you did in the color chapters and print some of them out. Print out individual cyan, magenta, yellow, and black separations if you want to get a look at how color separations work. And, as you have seen, if you don't want to waste any more paper or kill any more trees, print to PostScript and/or PDF files.

17

HOUR **18**

Getting Ready for the Service Bureau

You saw in the last hour how to print your documents from InDesign using the various options in the Print dialog boxes. You also noted that a desktop printer was probably not the final destination of your document.

Chances are you need to send your InDesign documents somewhere else for output. Where you will be sending them can vary, depending on what it is you actually do. But, generally speaking, when sending your InDesign files out, the same considerations and issues apply.

In this hour, you'll learn:

- How to format InDesign files for service bureau output
- How to troubleshoot and correct imported TIFF and EPS files
- How to use InDesign's preflighting and packaging features

Working with Service Bureaus

In this hour, we will be using the term "service bureau," which is a generic term for the number of different options you have for outputting your files.

Here are likely candidates for output:

- Service bureau for film output
- Computer-to-plate department of a publication or printer for direct-to-plate output
- Service bureau or quick print shop for direct digital printing on a Xerox, Indigo, Agfa, or Xeikon digital press

There are of course differences among all three destinations, but the same basic issues remain. This chapter keeps matters relatively simple by sticking with the term *service bureau*.

Setting up your files properly is of crucial importance. In this hour, you'll learn about the issues you need to keep in mind when you send your files out. This way, you won't get panicky calls from your service bureau clamoring for missing fonts or missing images, complaining about pages that won't output, or worse, stating that the film is unusable because an image was left in the RGB color space rather than CMYK. Film output is expensive, and only when the service bureau makes an error do they do it over for free. It also takes at least 24 hours to turn around four-color film. Rush jobs can be expensive. And if you are using a "direct-to" technology such as CTP or digital printing, you often don't see errors until you get your job back.

Although I have been carping on the fact that your images need to be in CMYK rather than RGB before being sent to a service bureau, there are some occasions when RGB is more appropriate. For example, some digital presses support composite color images—RGB. And if you are getting into large-format output, high-end photoprinters such as the Cymbolic Sciences LightJet or the Durst Lambda require RGB images. Double-check with your service bureau if any doubt remains.

At the end of this hour, you will learn about the process of preflighting and collecting InDesign files using InDesign's Packaging feature for output.

Understanding Service Bureaus

Basically, a service bureau is a company that takes your InDesign documents and outputs them on film, using high-end output devices (such as imagesetters) that most designers and publishers are not likely to have in-house. This film can either be a single black plate—if you're going to be printing a black-and-white document—or four-color separations. In order for your film to output correctly, your files need to be set up properly.

The process is essentially this. Assume that you are sending out a single, four-color InDesign page—a color flyer, for example—and you want a set of film back. You need one sheet for the cyan plate, one for the magenta plate, one for yellow, and one for black. This is common. If everything is set up correctly, you make a copy of your InDesign document, as well as of every image you have imported—bitmaps and EPS files. You also copy all the fonts used in the document, as well as any fonts included in imported EPS files. You then copy the lot to a Zip, Jaz, CD-R, or other type of removable media.

If you and your service bureau have high-speed Internet access (such as T1 or DSL), you can transfer files by means of an FTP (file transfer protocol) site, or as email attachments. If your files are large, this might not be a viable option, however.

When the service bureau gets the files, they open the page in InDesign, and set up the Print dialog box using settings and drivers that correspond to their raster image processor (RIP) and output device. The RIP processes the files and prints them to the film. If you are doing a four-color job, you will usually want to get a color proof—typically a *Matchprint*. This is a color proof that is generated from the film itself, and is the best way of ensuring that all your page elements have been processed correctly. By the way, you should also print a proof yourself—preferably a color one—and supply a copy of it to the service bureau. This shows them that your file indeed outputs properly, at least by some type of device.

The process can be more complicated than that, but you get the idea.

Be sure to determine, before sending jobs to a service bureau, that they do in fact support InDesign. As a program, InDesign is less than a year old, and despite the great deal of hype surrounding the program, it isn't as ubiquitous as PageMaker or QuarkXPress, both of which have been around since the 1980s.

The following sections introduce you to the three basic stages of preparing your files for the service bureau:

- Formatting
- Preflighting
- Collecting

18

Formatting Files for the Service Bureau

By formatting, you ensure that all your images are imported correctly into InDesign, and that there are no page elements that will likely cause trouble upon output. A discussion with your service provider helps resolve any problems and makes the whole process go more smoothly. Never be shy about asking them what they prefer. Generally, though, the considerations you need to pay close attention to involve:

- Bitmap images
- EPS images
- Fonts

Double-Checking Bitmap Images

Once again, there are several considerations with regard to imported bitmap images.

The first involves file format. As you have seen, InDesign gives you the capability to import native Photoshop files—complete with layers—into your layouts. However, if you send this format to a service bureau, you're going to have trouble. Your best option for bitmap images is *TIFF*.

 TIFF stands for Tagged Image File Format and is a standard file format—and a cross-platform one at that—for bitmap images. Although the Macintosh version differs somewhat from the PC version (the differences are not worth going into here), they tend to open fairly readily from one platform to another.

Yes, sure, there are probably service bureaus that can RIP native Photoshop files, but why take that chance? You can't go wrong with TIFF. If you need your Photoshop layers present until the last possible moment—in case you need to edit something at the eleventh hour—you can always convert in Photoshop and relink just prior to sending your files out.

 Always check with your service bureau before attempting to send them any file format other than TIFF or EPS. All RIPs are different; some can handle a wide variety of file formats, some cannot.

Another bitmap issue is color space. You've been down this road before. For most purposes, you need to ensure that your bitmaps are in one of two color spaces—CMYK or grayscale.

If you are printing a four-color page, your bitmaps need to be in CMYK mode. This is easily accomplished in Photoshop, and it is here that the integration between InDesign and Photoshop comes in handy.

To Do: Correctly Formatting a Bitmap Image for Output

InDesign enables you to get information about your imported image, and to edit the original image via Photoshop. For this exercise, you need to have Photoshop 5.X installed on the same hard disk as InDesign. If you don't have Photoshop, you can just read along. To follow along with this example, download and open the InDesign file labeled cnvrtBitmap.psd (see the book's introduction for instructions on how to download example files from Macmillan's Web site). Then follow these steps:

1. In InDesign, create a new document. Letter size is fine.

2. Place the bitmap cnvrtBitmap.psd by choosing File, Place or pressing Command+D (on the Mac) or Control+D (in Windows). Place it anywhere on the page, at whatever size you like. (To save time while downloading, the file has been saved at 72 dpi.)

3. You can easily determine most of the salient details about an imported image using the Links palette. Open the Links palette by choosing File, Links, or pressing Shift+Command+D (on the Mac) or Shift+Control+D (in Windows). The placed image should be listed in the Links palette.

4. Select the image and click on the arrow at the top of the Links palette. Scroll down to select Link Information (see Figure 18.1). Alternatively, you can simply double-click on the name of the link in the Links palette.

FIGURE 18.1
The Links palette.

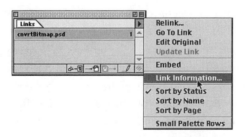

5. Link information tells you whether the imported image will give you any problems when output (see Figure 18.2).

FIGURE **18.2**

Link information.

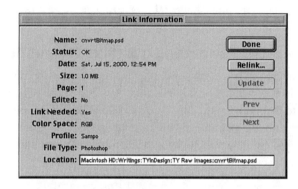

6. The following information is included on the Link Information dialog box:

- *Name*—The name of the file.

- *Status*—Tells you whether InDesign knows where the file is. If it has moved to a different folder or disk, you'll see "Missing" here.

- *Date*—The date and time the imported bitmap was last saved.

- *Size*—How large the image file is. This tells you whether it is suitable for reproduction at the size you specify in InDesign. (For example, at 1MB, you cannot go very large with this image.)

- *Page*—What page the image is on. In documents having many pages, it is easy to lose track of the images. Using this information, you can easily find out where the image is.

- *Edited*—Whether you have used InDesign's tools to edit the imported bitmap.

- *Link Needed*—This tells you whether the file needs to remain linked in order to output properly. Images almost always need to remain linked. The reason this field is here is that InDesign treats imported text and Word documents as links. However, text and Word files are stored within InDesign, so InDesign doesn't need an external link to those files. As a result, you don't need to supply a service bureau with linked Word files in order to output.

- *Color Space*—This tells you if you are in RGB, CMYK, grayscale, or some other color space. You can see in Figure 18.2 that you are in RGB, which is one problem you need to fix.

- *Profile*—This tells you what color profile you are using to control the color display of this image, which is usually a variety of sRGB. As you saw in Hour 16, "Color Management with InDesign," sRGB is not a desirable color

▼ profile for higher-end workflows, so I am using the profile I created for my monitor.

- *File Type*—This tells you what the file format is. Notice that you are in Photoshop native format, which is another problem you have to address.

- *Location*—This tells you the file path of the image, in case you need to find it.

7. I flagged a couple of things you need to fix. InDesign can open the original link. Go to the arrow at the top of the Links palette and scroll down to select Edit Original. If you have Photoshop 5.X on the same hard drive as InDesign, InDesign launches Photoshop and opens the linked image.

8. So, you can now change the two things you need to change. (This isn't a tutorial on Photoshop, so I'll assume you know how to do this.) Change the color space from RGB to CMYK (and notice that you'll have to flatten all the layers in the image first, which is fine), and save the file as a TIFF. If you are on the Windows platform or are using a file extension (such as .PSD), Photoshop will rename the file with the proper extension. Alternatively, if you're not monkeying with file extensions, you can replace the original. Either way, you have to relink in InDesign, so it's up to you.

Before you replace any original RGB or native Photoshop file, be sure you either have a backup or are absolutely certain you will not need it again. Remember that if you are designing for print but will be repurposing for the Web later on, you will need an RGB file. And after you convert to CMYK, you can convert back to RGB, but you'll be stuck with the limited color gamut of CMYK. In other words, your Web image will look blechy.

9. Now, go back to InDesign. If you resaved the corrected image with the same name, you'll see a warning icon in the Links palette. Double-click on the link, and InDesign will tell you that the image has been modified. Click on the Update button to reimport a preview of the corrected image.

10. If you saved the corrected image with a different name, click on the arrow at the top of the Links palette and scroll down to select Relink. You'll then get a Link To dialog box; press Browse to look for and select your corrected image.

11. If you go back to your Link Information dialog box, you'll notice that the changes you made have been recognized by InDesign—you are now in CMYK mode, and ▲ you have imported a TIFF file.

You can use the Edit Original feature to change imported text or Word files. Sure, you can simply make changes to text in InDesign without bothering with the original. But if you have Word, InDesign will launch it and open the linked file. Make your corrections, and save out the file again. Back in InDesign, be sure to update your linked Word file. You have simultaneously corrected the text in InDesign and in the original Word file.

Resolving Resolution

The quality of a bitmap image is a function of its *resolution*, or how many dots per inch comprise the image. The optimal resolution depends on a couple of factors, most importantly (for print output) on the line screen your printer can support.

NEW TERM *Line screen* is a term that dates back to the days of photographically producing halftones. A printing press can't print continuous-tone images; photographs and other such images need to be broken into a bunch of small dots, each of which is some level of gray. Naturally, the more dots, the better the image replicates the original continuous-tone image. Pick up a magazine or newspaper if you have one nearby and closely inspect a photograph. Chances are, you'll be able to discern the tiny halftone dots. The number of halftone dots per inch is called the *line screen*, and line screen is a function of the printing press and the paper you are printing with.

Web presses printing on newsprint, for example, can reproduce an 85-line screen, and not much more. A typical, good-quality, middle-of-the-road line screen for many publications—such as magazines—is 133-line screen. Higher-end presses printing fine-quality glossy magazines can go up to 150-line screen.

What does this mean in terms of image resolution in InDesign? Use this rule of thumb: your image resolution should be double your line screen. There is some debate about the true efficacy of this rule, but generally speaking, you can't go wrong. This means that if you know your printer's press will support a 133-line screen, your images will need to be at least 266 dpi. Most graphics pros routinely make all images 300 dpi (which goes up to a 150-line screen), regardless of what the actual line screen is. That also is a good rule of thumb.

Working with EPS Files

EPS files have their good points and bad points, like most file types. EPS is typically used for line drawings, logos, and other images that involve vectors, in whole or in part. EPS is often preferred over a bitmap because vectors, as you have seen in past hours, can be scaled to various sizes without pixellation. EPS files tend also to be small, at least without any placed bitmap graphics within them.

Like TIFF, EPS is a widely supported file format that few output devices have serious problems with. But, there are a few caveats about EPS files. The first and most important involves *nested* EPS files. This means that an EPS file contains an EPS file that has been placed within it. And that EPS file contains an EPS file within it, and on and on. As you can imagine, this will drive a RIP crazy, and you can run into serious output problems. If you can control the creation of the EPS file, keep it as simple as you can.

Another problem involves the same old bugaboos you saw earlier—wrong color spaces. If you are accepting EPS files from external sources, be sure to open them in Illustrator or FreeHand to make sure that all the colors are CMYK (if that's what you need them to be). Sometimes, designers or illustrators will specify a Pantone spot color in an EPS file—and the chances of this outputting properly are slim to none.

A third problem that graphics pros working with EPS files encounter involves fonts. As managing editor for a trade publication, I see this all the time. For whatever reason, people designing logos, ads, or other elements in programs such as Illustrator seem to think that you don't need to supply any fonts you use. Always make sure you either supply the fonts you use in your EPS files to your service bureau, or convert all your text to *paths*, a feature of Illustrator, FreeHand, and any other self-respecting illustration program. It is also a feature of InDesign.

Fonts

Oy gevalt—don't even talk about fonts. Well, actually, you do need to consider font issues. Fonts comprise one of the biggest headaches in all the graphic arts. Fonts were tricky enough when there was just PostScript, but, alas, someone decided that the world needed TrueType, which confused matters even more.

Probably the biggest thing to remember in terms of sending files to a service bureau is to supply your fonts. Granted, most service bureaus have a font library of their own, but how do you know that their version of Garamond is the same as yours? All Garamonds are not created equal, as you'll find out when you use the wrong version and all your text reflows.

It's good also that you cannot create artificial bolds and italics using the Style palette like you can in most other applications. That was always a no-no.

Another caveat regarding fonts to be wary of is fonts from small foundries or individuals. Obviously, I'm not suggesting you not use them, but some of these can conflict with other fonts you have. Using a font-management program such as Diamondsoft's FontReserve (my favorite), Extensis' Suitcase, Alsoft's MasterJuggler Pro, or Adobe's own ATM Deluxe, helps you spot trouble even before you start using fonts in InDesign.

> **Fonts and the Law**
>
> One other troublesome area regarding fonts is legally supplying them to an outside vendor. Although fonts are not copyrightable, foundries license fonts like software programs. Under the terms of the license, you can get into trouble if you install them on more than the allowable number of workstations. So, technically, if you supply fonts to a service bureau, you are committing software piracy.
>
> However, most type foundries understand the necessity of providing an output service bureau with fonts, so they have turned a blind eye. Implicit in this tacit understanding is that the service bureau will delete the supplied fonts as soon as the job is done (and they usually do). So honor is served, the jobs get output, the end user will not end up in prison, and everyone is happy.
>
> However, one vexing wrinkle is that many files are now being sent directly to printers' CTP departments rather than service bureaus. The users are supplying their fonts, as they always have. Printers, however, are starting to refuse to accept fonts, for fear of violating the license agreements. Designers are instructed to only use fonts that the printer has in its library. Well, as you can imagine, that's unacceptable to designers. So, often printers accept *locked-in* files such as TIFF/IT, PDF, or native PostScript, in which the font information is embedded in the document file and doesn't exist as a font file per se.
>
> As you can tell, this is a complicated issue. It is many years away from a solution that will satisfy everyone involved. If you are concerned, check with your printer, service bureau, or whomever you are sending your files to.

Preflighting Documents

Now that you've seen what some of the issues are, you are ready to learn how InDesign can help you spot trouble before you send files out. This is known as *preflighting*.

 Preflighting is essentially the process of checking your page layout files, as well as your linked bitmaps, EPSs, and other files, for any problems that can result in poor—or no—output. This includes issues such as color spaces, missing or damaged fonts, incorrect resolutions, incorrect file formats, and so forth.

There are several programs out that will preflight documents. One of the best is Markzware Software's FlightCheck, perhaps the de facto standard for preflighting page files. (A testament to this is that preflighting is often called FlightChecking.) By the time you read this, Markzware will have released an update to FlightCheck that is compatible with InDesign. FlightCheck also works with QuarkXPress, Illustrator, PageMaker, FreeHand, and many other file formats. It is one tool that belongs in the graphic designer's toolbox.

If you don't want to splurge on FlightCheck, you can take advantage of InDesign's built-in preflighting utility that can be used to check for potential output problems. When your document is ready to go, choose File, Preflight.

The Preflight dialog box comprises several panes. Take a look at what you'll find when you preflight a document.

Using InDesign's Preflight Dialog Box

The first pane is the Summary pane. This sums up what the Preflight utility has found. See Figure 18.3.

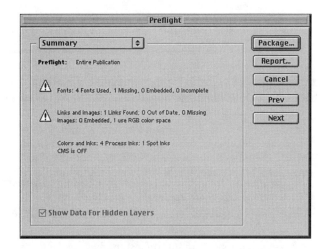

FIGURE **18.3**

The Summary pane of the Preflight dialog box.

This pane gives you three areas of information:

- *Fonts*—You can see that you are using four fonts in the document, and you are missing one. You'll have to fix that.

- *Links*—You have one link, but it is in the RGB color space. You'll have to fix that.

- *Colors*—This tells you what colors you will be printing or, in other words, how many plates can be made from this. InDesign didn't see this as a problem, but notice that you are set up to print four process inks and one spot ink. The spot ink is a mistake. You'll need to fix that as well.

You click on Next to get to the Fonts pane. This gives you a bit more information about the font situation. See Figure 18.4.

FIGURE **18.4**

The Fonts pane of the
Preflight dialog box.

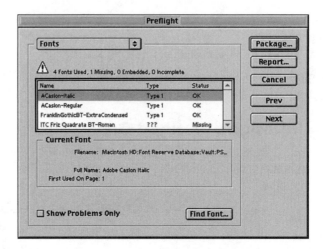

You get the font name, its type (a PostScript Type 1, TrueType, or other), and its status.
Notice that the Friz Quadrata is missing. It has apparently been moved or turned off in a
font management program.

> If your missing font is simply the result of it having been deactivated in a
> utility such as Suitcase or FontReserve, be sure to activate it and re-preflight
> to make sure there isn't really a problem with it.

If you do get a missing font warning, InDesign gives you the opportunity to substitute
the absentee font with one it knows exists. To do so, click on the Find Font button at the
bottom of the Fonts pane. You get a dialog box that determines where the missing font is
used and gives you the opportunity to replace it. See Figure 18.5.

FIGURE **18.5**

You can get more
information about your
fonts, and suggest
replacements for those
that are missing.

You can click on Next to get to the Links and Images pane, which gives you more information about problems associated with linked images. See Figure 18.6.

FIGURE 18.6

The Links and Images pane of the Preflight dialog box.

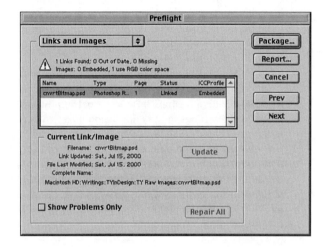

This pane lists your links and gives you information as to what file format it is (notice that it is a Photoshop document rather than a TIFF; that might be a problem). It is also not in the CMYK color space. It also tells you that the image is linked; if it were not, you can relink to it, much like you saw in the Links palette earlier.

18

You click on Next to get to the Colors and Inks pane. This pane tells you what your colors are and what line screen they are set up for. See Figure 18.7.

FIGURE 18.7

The Colors and Inks pane of the Preflight dialog box.

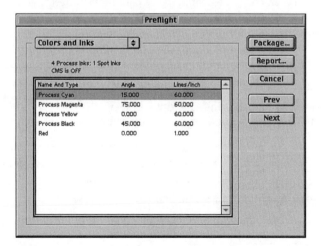

Notice that you're set up for a 90-line screen. That might need to be changed (you'll learn how to do that in Hour 21, "Exploring Other Export Options," so don't worry about it right now). Notice also that you have a spot color defined. That is not good, and you do have to fix that. You'll look at how specifically to do that in Hour 21, but suffice it to say here that you can go to the Print dialog box, go to the Color pane, and click on All to Process, which will convert any non-process colors to process colors.

If you're wondering where InDesign is getting this information, the Preflight tool uses the settings in the Print dialog boxes. In particular, the Colors and Inks pane is based on data in the Color pane of the Print dialog box, which you will look at in more detail in Hour 21. It's not necessary to worry about these preflight preferences, because if you are sending your files out to a service bureau, you likely don't have the equipment the service bureau has. Consequently, you do not have the printer drivers and PPDs needed to set up the Print dialog boxes in the same way that your service bureau does. And you shouldn't try.

You might also have noticed something in Figure 18.7 called Angle. This refers to screen angle, and I point this out only to advise you never try to change it. Basically, this refers to the angle at which the rows of halftone dots are printed so to minimize the visibility of the dots. The defaults are the angles that printers have been using since color halftone printing was invented, and monkeying with them even slightly can cause *moiré*, which is an undesirable interference pattern that appears in color images printed with incompatible screen angles.

Finally, you can click on Next to go to Print Settings, and see what the Print dialog box settings are. This is all the information that InDesign was basing its preflight on. It's not that necessary to pay too close attention to this, because the service bureau will change the Print dialog box to use their own equipment, equipment drivers, and PPDs.

If you want, you can produce a report, which is saved as a text file. It's always a good idea to hold on to reports, because they can be used to absolve oneself of blame if film comes back with problems. By saving the InDesign preflight report, you can demonstrate that the files were correctly set up before they were sent out.

At this stage, you can automatically have InDesign package all the files.

Packaging Your Files

Packaging files is usually called *collecting for output*—I suspect Adobe doesn't use that term because that's what QuarkXPress's similar feature is called. Be that as it may, you can have InDesign automatically gather up all the linked files that are needed for output.

To do so, simply choose File, Package. InDesign performs another preflight before it is packaged, and if there are problems, you'll get an error message (see Figure 18.8).

Possible problems were detected during Preflight. View Preflight information or continue with Packaging?

Continue | View Info

If you click on View Info, you'll go through the Preflight panes. Or, you can throw caution to the wind and package anyway.

After you do so, you'll be prompted to fill out an instruction sheet, or a sort of job ticket. See Figure 18.9.

18

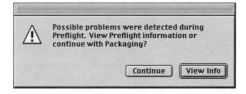

Printing Instructions

Filename: Instructions.txt

Contact: Harold Moist

Company: Giant Tongues, Inc.

Address: 6666 Liquid Way

Ballston Spa, NY

Phone: (518) 555-1235   Fax:

Email: moist@tongues.com

Instructions: Four-color negs, emulsion down, right reading

133-line screen

Matchprint

Continue | Cancel

This has all your contact information and specific instructions—such as what specifically to output, and so on. (Things you'll look at in a few minutes.) This form is saved as a text file as part of the package. You're better off using the specific job ticket supplied by your service bureau, which will have information specific to their equipment and services.

After that, you tell InDesign what specifically you want to collect. See Figure 18.10.

FIGURE **18.10**

The Create Package Folder dialog box.

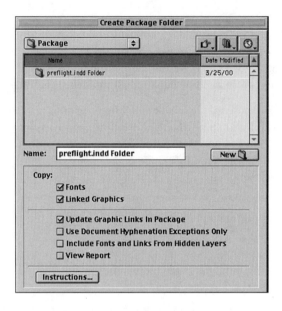

This dialog box gives you several options. You can specify whether you want to package images or fonts. Remember the Coffee Break on the legality of collecting fonts? If you decide you want to package fonts, here is what InDesign says about it (see Figure 18.11).

FIGURE **18.11**

Adobe's position on the subject of collecting fonts for service bureaus.

Other options in the Create Package Folder dialog box include whether you want to update links as they're being packaged. This means that InDesign updates any links that are missing or have been modified before packaging them. Leaving this unchecked results in an incomplete package, as InDesign cannot package missing or modified links.

If you are using Layers in your InDesign document, you can also collect the items that are on your hidden layers using the Include Fonts and Links from Hidden Layers option. You can thus have InDesign package all the stuff you

> need at one time without needing to go back, turn on the other layer(s), and re-package. You can also preflight stuff on hidden layers.

New in version 1.5, you can also package your hyphenation exceptions so you won't have any odd text reflows when you get your film back.

You can view your preflight report, if you want, as well as edit the instruction sheet by clicking on the Instructions button.

And that's all there is to packaging. After you pick a spot, you'll get an organized folder. See Figure 18.12.

FIGURE 18.12

InDesign packages your document, your links, and your fonts in a neat, organized folder with subfolders.

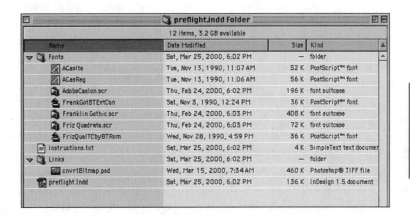

All that remains to be done is to copy the lot onto a Zip or Jaz cartridge, burn a CD, or use a high-speed file transfer system like WamNet to your service bureau or printer.

Summary

It doesn't make too much sense to dwell on film output, because, as computer-to-plate and direct digital printing become more cost effective and prevalent, film output might not be the standard much longer. But regardless of the workflow, the same basic issues that you've looked at in this hour will remain. And new technologies such as PDF are simplifying the process. Well, they're actually simplifying the process in some ways and making it more complicated in others.

Close attention to proper file formatting and especially font issues ensures that no matter where you send your files, you won't get any unpleasant surprises when you get your pages back.

18

Workshop

You've just learned how to set up your files for delivery to a service bureau, and you've also learned how to use InDesign's native Preflight and Packaging features. You may have some further questions, so do check out the Q&A, and complete the quiz to test your recall of the issues we dealt with.

Q&A

Q When sending my files to the service bureau, should I set my pages up as reader's spreads?

A Absolutely not. Without going into the process of imposition, suffice it to say that when publications are printed, they are not printed in contiguous pages like spreads. They are printed in 8-, 12-, and 16-page units called *signatures*, and only in the case of the center spread are adjacently printed pages actual adjacent pages. The service bureau or printer will likely import your InDesign file(s) into a special program for imposition that automatically places each page where it needs to be.

Even if your printer strips a publication manually rather than using software-based imposition, you still want each page output separately.

Q Can I send a service bureau PostScript files rather than an InDesign document? Wouldn't that be easier?

A Yes, but that's not a great idea. The reason is that when you print a document to a PostScript file, it remains pretty uneditable, unless someone at the service bureau is willing to wade through the acres of PostScript code to fix something. So if there is a problem, it can't be easily fixed. And unless you have the correct device drivers and PPDs for the service bureau's equipment, you'll be making PostScript files that are unusable.

Quiz

1. A good rule of thumb regarding the resolution of bitmapped images is that they should have a resolution that is _____ the line screen at which they'll be printed.

    a. The same as

    b. Twice

    c. 100 times

2. Which of the following should you supply to a service bureau with your InDesign file?

    a. The fonts you used

    b. Any Word files that you imported

    c. Any linked images

    d. a and c

Quiz Answers

1. b. An image resolution of twice the line screen is generally a good rule of thumb. Or, if your line screen is 133, your image resolution should be 266 dpi.

2. d. Fonts and images are the only things you need to send to your service bureau. You do not need to supply Word files.

18

HOUR 19

Preparing Acrobat Output with InDesign

Adobe's Acrobat first appeared in 1993, and was originally designed to facilitate the concept of the paperless office. Well, you know how that concept has fared, but Acrobat and PDF have become major players as a file format for prepress, proofing, and other aspects of the graphic arts, and are becoming increasingly suited to solve a great many workflow problems.

As you can imagine, Adobe gives Acrobat and PDF a major role in InDesign. In this hour, you'll look at the symbiosis between the two.

In this hour you'll learn:

- Why you would want to create a PDF from InDesign
- How to export a PDF from InDesign
- How to create, save, and reuse a PDF style
- How to create a PDF using the Print command

What Is Acrobat?

Acrobat is a suite of programs that creates, edits, reads, and indexes PDF files. You've no doubt seen PDF files before—especially if you own graphics hardware or software because documentation is routinely supplied as PDFs. A PDF is a file distilled from PostScript code. It contains all the text, graphics, and page formatting from the original document—whether that be an InDesign file, a QuarkXPress document, a Word file, and so on. If it is created properly, it also has all the fonts from the original document embedded within it. The result is a file that you can open and read on any computer, regardless of the platform you are running, the programs you have (although you need Acrobat Reader, naturally), and the fonts you have.

Acrobat also does a million other things, it seems. Version 4.0 added extensive annotation and forms features. There are a variety of plug-ins available for Acrobat, both for the graphic arts, as well as for other areas in which Adobe is positioning Acrobat. For example, there is a Web Capture plug-in that can capture an entire Web site and save it as a PDF, which is good for creating portfolios.

How Suite It Is

The Acrobat 4.X suite comprises the following separate yet related programs:

- *Acrobat*—Called Acrobat Exchange in earlier versions, but is now just called Acrobat. Acrobat is the program in which you open, read, edit, and annotate PDFs.
- *Distiller*—Distiller is the application that takes a document's PostScript code and distills it into a PDF. In a nutshell, Distiller is the PDF creator.
- *Reader*—Reader is the freeware component of the suite, and is freely distributed so that people can read PDF files without needing to pay for the full version of the suite. It is a small enough application that it can be easily downloaded from Adobe's Web site. It is also provided on CDs that contain PDFs.

There are also other elements that enable you to catalog and index PDFs, but the previous three elements constitute the holy trinity of the Acrobat suite.

In order to create a PDF in the past, you typically needed to first create a PostScript file (via an application's Print to Disk command), and then launch Distiller and distill the PostScript into a PDF. Now, many if not most programs give you the option of exporting directly to a PDF, which might render Distiller passé in a short period of time.

Why Acrobat?

PDF is a hot file format, for a number of reasons. The first is that it is a great format for *soft proofing*—proofing a document on-screen rather than using hard copy. With careful attention paid to monitor calibration and rudimentary color management, your PDF can be a pretty close rendering of how your colors will output. Version 4.0 supports embedding ICC color profiles in a PDF (remember Hour 16, "Color Management with InDesign"?), which means that it is easy to incorporate PDF in a color-managed workflow.

PDF also has a great many annotation features, which not only enable you to proof using PDF, but also to mark up the file and send the PDF back to its creator. PDFs are usually small enough to email conveniently, thus facilitating the concept of remote proofing. *Remote proofing* is done some geographical distance from where design and production actually takes place.

> At *Micro Publishing News*, we often use the advantages of PDF to facilitate remote proofing. Often, when editors are on the road, we email PDFs of page layouts for sign-off. And our collateral materials and media kits are designed in California, but need to be okayed by our corporate office on Long Island. FedEx won't want to hear about this, but we always do our proofing of these files by emailing PDFs.

PDF is also becoming a standard file format for several computer-to-plate workflows. A couple of years ago, Adobe came up with the Extreme workflow, which essentially involved PostScript 3 RIPs, PDFs, and computer-to-plate systems generating press-ready plates directly from PDFs.

The capability to edit and preflight PDFs—using plug-ins such as Enfocus Software's PitStop or Adobe's own InProduction system—is also making PDF a much more attractive way of getting files from the content creator to the printer. Other plug-ins designed to color-separate PDF files as well as impose multi-page documents also make PDF useful for print production.

So the answer to the question of "Why Acrobat?" might well be "Because it's there." It is solving a great many workflow problems in many areas of the graphic arts.

19

Exporting PDFs from InDesign

You saw in Hour 9, "Using Graphics from Other Programs," that you can import PDFs into InDesign. Now, you learn how to export an InDesign document as a PDF.

There are several ways of doing this. You learned in Hour 17, "Printing from InDesign," that you can select Adobe PDF as a printer from the Print dialog box. However, a quick-and-dirty way to create a PDF from InDesign is using the Export command. (You'll learn about the differences between them in a bit.)

To Do: Exporting a PDF

If you already know how to create PDFs, you're ahead of the game here. At any rate, it's pretty easy. To export an InDesign document as a PDF, follow these steps:

1. Create an InDesign document—whatever you like. Add some text and graphics. It can be greek text, a placeholder graphic, whatever. Make it a single page. Save the InDesign file.

2. Choose File, Export, or press Command+E (on the Macintosh) or Control+E (on PCs). You'll see the Export dialog box shown in Figure 19.1.

FIGURE 19.1

The Export dialog box.

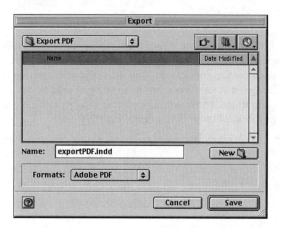

3. Make sure the Formats pop-up menu at the bottom of the box says Adobe PDF. (You'll learn about the other options in a later chapter.) Click on Save.

4. You'll get the Export PDF dialog box, which comprises several frames, as shown in Figure 19.2.

5. This set of boxes is roughly analogous to the Job Options setting in Acrobat Distiller. Set the options in the first pane—the PDF Options dialog box:

   - *Style*—At the top of the box, you can select a PDF style (you'll learn how to create PDF styles in a bit). Keep it on the default (Custom) for now.

   - *Subset Fonts*—Subsetting fonts is a way of keeping PDF file sizes small. Subsetting means that only those characters (which Adobe calls *glyphs*) that physically appear in a document are embedded in the PDF. This setting is a percentage of the entire font. So, for example, if you set this to 50% and 50% or fewer of all the characters in a font are used in the document, only those characters are embedded. If you use more than 50% of the characters in a font, InDesign embeds the entire character set. The default is 100%, which is somewhat confusing. However, notice that the bottom of the dialog

▼

box says "All fonts used in publication will be embedded." Somewhat counterintuitively, this refers to subsetting. To make sure you always embed all fonts—and not subsets—set the Subset Fonts Below field to 0%.

FIGURE **19.2**

The Export PDF dialog box.

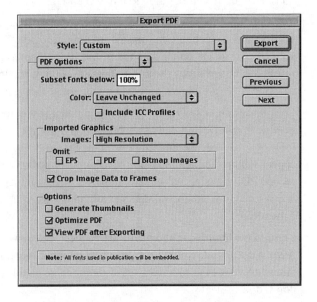

The reason subsetting can be dangerous is that some Acrobat plug-ins, such as Enfocus Software's PitStop, enable you to edit text in a PDF. However, if you have subsetted a font, you cannot add any characters that did not appear in the original document. (Actually, you can add characters, but they appear in a different font.)

19

- *Color*—You have three options. The first is Leave Unchanged, which is the best option when you have preflighted your InDesign document and you know all your images are in the correct color spaces. Your other options are CMYK and RGB. Choose wisely. If you have color management enabled (in the Document Color Settings; see Hour 16), you can embed the ICC color profiles in the PDF. If color management is disabled, this option is grayed out.

- *Imported Graphics*—This set of options controls how your imported graphics are handled. High Resolution means that all available image data is included. So, if you have a 300 dpi image, it is imported at 300 dpi. Low Resolution means that a screen-resolution (72 dpi) version of the image is included. If

▼

you plan to print the PDF to a high-resolution output device, pick High Resolution. If you are doing on-screen viewing or soft proofing, Low Resolution is the better option. The resulting PDF will be smaller, which is a consideration if you're going to email the PDF.

You can also choose to omit any of your imported images if you are using an OPI system. Selecting Omit makes InDesign include the OPI comments for an imported image rather than the image itself. The keeper of the high-resolution image needs these comments to replace the low-resolution version in the PDF. Omit images only when you are in fact using an OPI workflow.

- *Crop Image Data to Frames*—This means that if you have imported a graphic into InDesign, but are using only a portion of it (you've cropped it), InDesign discards the unused portion, or the bit of the image that doesn't appear within the picture frame. Selecting this option is a good way to reduce PDF file size. Make sure, however, that your service bureau or printer doesn't need the additional data in case additional image editing or bleeding is required.

- *Create Thumbnails*—Thumbnails are reduced preview versions of the pages in your document, which help you check content, organization and layout. If you want your PDF to have a set of thumbnails, enable this option. If you don't, don't select it.

- *Optimize PDF*—This is a good option only when your PDF is being downloaded one page at a time from a Web server. Essentially, this option reduces the file size of the PDF by including repeated page elements—backgrounds, headers and footers, and so on—only once, and by adding pointers to the original wherever it needs to be repeated.

- *View PDF after Exporting*—This option automatically launches Acrobat or Acrobat Reader after the export is complete. This is a useful timesaving feature when you do in fact want to double-check a PDF after you create it (which is always a good idea).

6. Click on the Next button, and you come to the Compression pane (see Figure 19.3). How images and line art are compressed can significantly alter the quality of the PDF you create. There are three issues to consider: downsampling, subsampling, and compression.

- *Downsampling*—You can choose to reduce the pixel dimensions of an image. If, for example, you are only doing on-screen proofing, you can downsample to 72 dpi, which is all you need. If you are going to use the PDF for final output onto film or plates, don't downsample. You can choose No Sampling Change here, and, because you selected High Resolution in the earlier pane, all your image data will be intact.

▼

FIGURE 19.3

The Compression pane of the Export PDF dialog box.

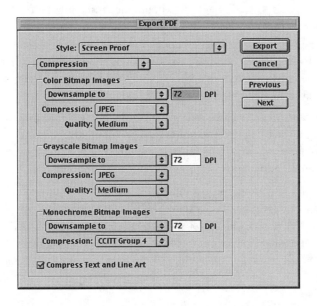

Notice that if you play with the pop-up menu in the Compression dialog box, you can either downsample or subsample. They are two different means of accomplishing the same thing. *Downsampling* essentially takes a sample area of the image, averages the pixel values, and replaces all the pixels in that area with that average value. *Subsampling* chooses a pixel in the center of a sample area and replaces all the pixels in the sample area with that value. Subsampling is faster than downsampling, but the quality is not as good.

19

- *Compression*—Your choices for color and grayscale bitmap images are JPEG and Zip. Both have their trade-offs. Zip compression is best for line art or bitmap images with large areas of single colors or repeating patterns, such as screen grabs. JPEG is best for photographs and other continuous-tone images. Each type of compression has varying degrees of quality. Zip has 4-bit and 8-bit. 8-bit has the greater potential to be lossless, whereas 4-bit Zip compression tosses out data in images that are greater than 4-bit.

Remember that an 8-bit image is one that has 256 colors or shades of gray. Photographs and other such images are usually much greater than 8-bit.

JPEG has Minimum, Low, Medium, High, and Maximum—referring to the *quality* of the compressed image. Maximum means the highest quality, and the lowest amount of compression. It's easy to get confused and think that this refers to the amount of compression—that maximum means the maximum amount of compression—especially because earlier versions of Acrobat did in fact set compression that way. It was redesigned in Acrobat 4.0 to conform to Photoshop's way of specifying JPEG compression.

Medium might well be a happy medium, but depending on your end use, you might want High or Maximum quality. Alternatively, you can select None in the Compression pop-up menu. You can also select Automatic, which means InDesign determines the best compression option for your images.

For Monochrome Bitmap Images—such as black-and-white line art (essentially 1-bit images)—you have several CCITT compression options. CCITT Group 4 compression works well on most black-and-white line art. CCITT Group 3 compression is an international standard for data compression and transmission typically used in fax machines. Run Length is a lossless compression algorithm that's good for black-and-white images with large areas of solid black or solid white.

7. Select the settings you want based on your end result. Because this is only a practice exercise, downsample to 72 dpi and select minimum quality JPEG compression. Then click on Next.

8. If you've been through Hour 17, this Pages and Page Marks pane should look somewhat familiar. See Figure 19.4.

FIGURE 19.4

The Pages and Page Marks pane of the Export PDF dialog box.

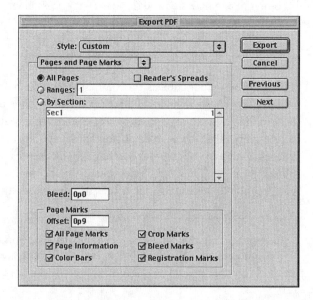

▼ This is where you decide what pages you want to include in the PDF. Notice that you can create reader's spreads, if you want to see how your two-page spreads look. You can also set your bleed amounts and add any page marks (see Hour 17 for an explanation of page marks and why you need them). Usefully, InDesign automatically enlarges the page size of the PDF to fit the page marks, so you don't have to noodle with scaling.

9. Because this is only a one-page test sheet, you don't have many page or section options. But turn All Page Marks on to see what that will do. When you're ready, click on Next.

10. The final pane is the Security pane, where you add password protection to a PDF. See Figure 19.5.

FIGURE **19.5**

The Security pane of the Export PDF dialog box.

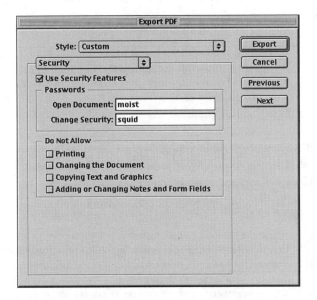

This might seem overly paranoid, but in many situations you might want to give various readers and users the capability to look but not touch. Notice that you can prevent users from printing the PDF, changing the PDF, copying text and graphics from the document, or adding notes and annotations. You can enable these in any combination, and when opened in Acrobat, the prohibited options are grayed out.

Be sure to note the two password types. The password specified in Open Document simply opens the PDF. You still cannot do any of the things you have prohibited users from doing—such as printing and editing. The password specified in Change Security enables users to override the security prohibitions you set here.

▼ Essentially, this is the owner or creator's password.

19

If you try to open a password-protected PDF in Photoshop, you are confronted with an error message instructing you to disable protection before you can open it. See Figure 19.6.

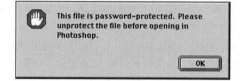

This file is password-protected. Please unprotect the file before opening in Photoshop.

OK

If you try to place a password-protected PDF in InDesign, you are also prompted to enter a password. Other programs such as Illustrator will also give you grief about it.

Be careful—if you do not enter a Change Security password, no one—not even the creator—can print or edit the document. You'll have to re-export the PDF to access it.

11. If all your settings are to your liking, go ahead and click on Export. If you have the View PDF after Exporting option checked, your computer will launch Acrobat (or Acrobat Reader) and you can see what you have done.

You saw in Hour 17 that InDesign will only print to a PostScript printer or to certain non-PostScript printers. So what to do if you don't have a PostScript printer or one of the anointed non-PostScript printers? One solution is to export your InDesign document as a PDF and print it from Acrobat. Acrobat has no restrictions on what type of printer you must have.

Creating PDF Styles

As you've seen in a few past hours, you can set a bunch of styles for various aspects of InDesign. You can set paragraph and character styles for text, set printer styles for assorted print jobs, and set trapping styles if you want InDesign to do your trapping for you. Not surprisingly, you can also create PDF styles.

One of the best additions to Acrobat Distiller 4.X is the capability to set and save different job options, such as one set for screen-resolution PDFs, another set for high-resolution PDFs to output proofs on a desktop printer, and yet another set for high-resolution PDFs suitable for print output at a service bureau or CTP department.

InDesign's PDF styles are similar, and setting up PDF styles is remarkably like setting up all the other types of styles you've seen.

To Do: Setting Up a PDF Style

To set up a PDF style, follow these steps:

1. Choose File, Define PDF Style. You'll get the Define PDF Styles dialog box, as shown in Figure 19.7.

FIGURE **19.7**

The Define PDF Styles dialog box.

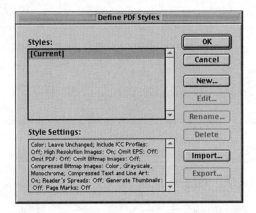

2. If you have defined no other PDF styles, this dialog box contains just the default. Like other boxes of its ilk, it tells you, in stream-of-consciousness text, the specs of the default style. Notice the Import button; you can import PDF styles from other InDesign documents. For now, though, click on New to define a new style.

3. You'll get the same set of dialog boxes you got when you exported your PDF, so I don't go through them in detail here. Define a style suitable for on-screen proofing. Figure 19.8 shows you the settings you'll use in the PDF Options pane.

    Basically, you're setting up this style to create a PDF suitable for email. Notably, you'll set your imported graphics to export at Low Resolution. You'll also omit thumbnails, because they can make a PDF larger than it needs to be.

4. Click on Next, and you can set your compression. Figure 19.9 shows the settings to use for compression.

19

FIGURE **19.8**
These PDF options are suitable for screen-resolution proofing.

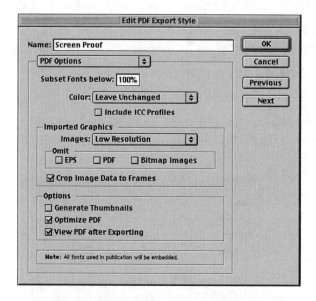

FIGURE **19.9**
These compression settings are suitable for on-screen proofing.

In the fictitious scenario you are setting up for this style, you produce one-page flyers or brochures with a minimum of images, and they are bitmaps. You can therefore leave everything at Medium JPEG. You can then generate a sample PDF of a typical document and check the size. You do need to downsample everything to 72 dpi, though.

5. Click on Next, and you come to the Page and Page Marks pane. Notice that, not surprisingly, you can't include specific page ranges in the PDF style. You can, however, decide whether you want to include Reader's Spreads or Page Marks in this style. Don't include spreads, but do include all page marks; see Figure 19.10.

> There is a known glitch involving page marks in PDFs exported from InDesign, the result of which is that page marks will not be visible except to users of the full version of Acrobat, and unless the exported file is fixed using the full application. In other words, those who view these documents using just Acrobat Reader won't see page marks. A bit of a limitation. If this is a serious issue for you, the problem and workaround details are included in the Adobe Support Database, Document #323712, found at www.adobe.com/support/techdocs/1c71e.htm.

FIGURE 19.10

Specifying page marks in your PDF Export Style.

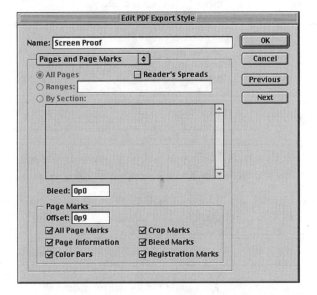

6. Click on Next, and you'll notice that you're back at PDF Options. You can't set security in your PDF style, which is probably just as well. You can always add security options when you export an actual file.

7. Now press OK; your new style becomes available in the PDF Styles palette. Press OK again, and you're back in your document.

8. To use this style, open a simple InDesign document. I'm using a one-page, letter-size document with a couple of fonts and a single bitmap.

▼   9. To export a PDF using the style, choose File, Export, or press Command+E (on the Mac) or Control+E (on PCs). You'll get your usual InDesign Save As box. Pick a location and a name, and then press Save. You'll then get your Export PDF options. To use the style you created, select it from the Style pop-up menu at the top of the Export PDF dialog box (see Figure 19.11).

FIGURE 19.11

Selecting the PDF style you want to use.

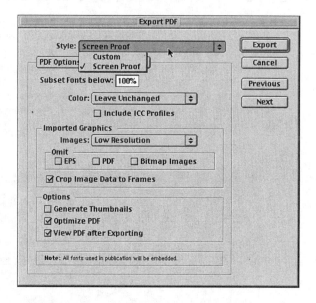

10. Click on Export, and InDesign will do its thing. If you left View PDF after Exporting checked, Acrobat will launch and you can double-check your PDF.

▲

You can also change any of your style settings on a per-job basis. You can go back and create other PDF Export Styles for your desktop printer, or for your service bureau, if you're going to be sending them a PDF file for output.

Although PDF is a good file format for output these days, it is not yet prevalent, especially because it requires PostScript 3 RIPs, which not everyone has upgraded to. Be sure to check with your service provider before sending a PDF file.

Printing to PDF Using the Print Command

The Export PDF option is a quick-and-dirty way to generate PDFs from your InDesign documents. However, if you have the full Acrobat suite and are experienced with

Distiller, you know that Distiller gives you a lot more control over how your PDFs are created, especially for high-end applications. You can use InDesign's Print command to tie into Distiller, as well as use the extensive features in the Print dialog boxes to produce PDFs.

Basically, the procedure is this. Choose File, Print or press Command+P (on the Mac); Control+P (on PCs). From the Printer pop-up menu, you can select Create Adobe PDF (see Figure 19.12).

FIGURE 19.12

Using the Print dialog box to create a PDF from InDesign.

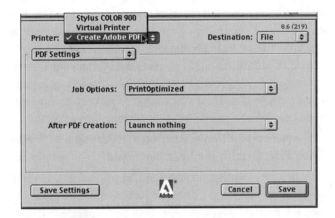

Selecting this option brings up the PDF Options pane. If you have Acrobat Distiller, this pane ties into your Distiller preferences, and whatever job options you have created in Distiller can be set here. InDesign will then use these options to distill your PDFs. You can also use the various Print dialog box options that you saw in Hour 17. You'll be learning more about these options in Hour 21, "Exploring Other Export Options."

Summary

So now you know how to export PDFs from InDesign and the various issues involved in doing so. Whether PDF is the future of publishing is anyone's guess. But if you find yourself suddenly plunged into a PDF-based workflow, now you know how to cope with it.

Workshop

You've just learned how you can export PDFs from InDesign, and all the issues involved with creating PDFs that are suited to whatever application you are creating it for. Now, to see if any lingering questions have been addressed, check out the Q&A. And complete the quiz to test your recall of what we covered. Finally, work through the exercises until you become a pro at creating and working with PDF files.

Q&A

Q I'm unclear on the concept of embedding and subsetting fonts. What do they mean?

A When you create a PDF, you have the option of embedding your fonts. This means that whomever you send the PDF to doesn't need to have the fonts you used. Always embed your fonts—unless you need to make the PDF very small. Subsetting means that only the characters you use in a specific document are embedded. For example, if you created a PDF in which only the word "moist" appeared in, say, Adobe Caslon Bold, only the letters m, o, i, s, and t are embedded in that font. As a result, if you wanted to add text in Adobe Caslon Bold, you would only be able to add text that contained those letters.

Q Is there any real difference between exporting a PDF and using the Create Adobe PDF through the Print command?

A The latter uses Distiller and the Distiller job options. If you have used Distiller, you know all the things it lets you control—many more than what you can set using the Export command. So if you are preparing PDFs for final output, you will probably want Distiller's options. Of course, you'll need to buy the Acrobat suite (which includes Distiller) to use this option.

Quiz

1. If you were creating a PDF for soft-proofing on-screen, what is the best choice for compression?

    a. None

    b. Low quality

    c. Maximum quality

2. You cannot embed ICC color profiles in PDFs.

    a. True

    b. False

3. Which of the following is not a use for a PDF file?

    a. Soft proofing page layouts and documents

    b. IRS tax forms

    c. Hardware and software documentation

    d. None of the above

Quiz Answers

1. b. Low quality means high compression, which is a good choice for screen-based viewing.

2. b. Yes, you can indeed embed ICC color profiles in PDFs, as of Acrobat 4.

3. d. It's true. You can download tax forms as PDFs from the IRS's Web site. Think of it as the first time a PDF ever compressed the user—or the user's bank account, that is.

Exercises

Spend some time exporting PDFs from InDesign documents with various combinations of settings, especially compression settings, and view the results, both on-screen and by printing the PDF. The best way to get a feeling for these settings is to go ahead and change them.

19

HOUR 20

Creating Web Content with InDesign

I should point out right off the bat that InDesign was not designed to be a Web tool. There are a kajillion Web programs out there, and if you want to get seriously involved in Web site design and development, you're better off with a program specifically designed for Web site creation. This doesn't mean that you can't use InDesign. You certainly can, and there are certain cases when it might be simpler to use (especially if you're on a budget, where having to buy only one program is a nice option).

You do have to invest in an HTML editing program at some point if you are serious about putting your pages on the Web. Despite Adobe's best intentions, InDesign isn't even the only program you can use for print publishing. How many designers can live without Photoshop?

So, all that said, in this hour you'll learn:

- How designing for the Web differs from designing for print
- How to work with color, images, and fonts with regard to Web design
- How to create HTML from an InDesign document

Taking It to the Web

Before we delve into the specifics of how to create Web content with InDesign, there are a few basic terms and issues we should tackle briefly at the outset.

NEW TERM   *HTML* stands for *Hypertext Markup Language*, and is the standard language used to create Web pages and other hypertext documents. An HTML document creates text, as well as codes corresponding to linked files. These linked files can include graphics, video, audio, or others. One important feature of HTML is its ability to code hyperlinks—the blue underlined text you find on Web sites—which take you to a different page when clicked.

There are two basic ways to generate Web page content: design it from scratch or repurpose it from another source, such as print. Not a staggeringly original observation, but there it is.

Print versus Web

There are many design considerations that need to be taken into account when going from print to the Web (and vice versa). Since this is not a book on Web design, it's beyond the scope of this hour to deal with them all. Instead, we'll focus on a few of the more concrete considerations that pertain to working with InDesign. Namely, color, images, and fonts. In other words, all the things you need to worry about when designing for print. *Plus ça change, plus c'est la même chose!*

Color

With regard to color, Web designers have a slightly easier time of it than their print counterparts. As you have seen, the biggest problem that print designers have is that colors produced by a printing press are completely different than those produced by a monitor. So trying to preview on-screen what will come off press is a nettlesome problem. The Web, however, keeps everything on the monitor. The medium *on* which you are designing is the same as the medium *for* which you are designing. This makes it easier to match colors.

But problems still remain. Part of the problem is that, as you saw in Hour 16, "Color Management with InDesign," different monitors display differently—sometimes dramatically so. Compounding the problem is that most browsers only display using a palette of 216 colors. This is far less than the true 24-bit, millions-of-colors palette used in most image-creation and editing processes. If you keep your images in 24-bit RGB color, you will have color shifts and loss of detail in gradients and shades. Fortunately, most image-editing programs let you convert to what is called a *Web-safe palette*—the standard 216 colors that browsers can display. InDesign has a built-in Web-safe swatch library, a fragment of which appears in Figure 20.1.

FIGURE 20.1

InDesign has a Web-safe swatch library.

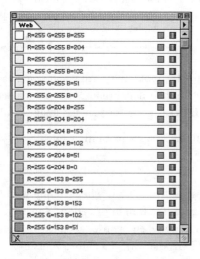

Although you can come pretty close to generating "standard" colors using the Web-safe palette, you still might get wildly different colors from monitor to monitor. Remember, everyone's monitor is different. The best bet is to preview any pages you design on as many different systems as you can. Any self-respecting Webmonkey should have both a Mac and a PC. Still, the Web-safe palette is a good place to start. If you are working in both print and Web, Pantone's ColorWeb Pro comes with swatchbooks to match up printed colors with their approximate Web-safe version(s).

Images

When designing for print, as you've seen, you have a few standard image file formats you can use—TIFF, EPS, and PCX. However, on the Web, you can use only two—GIF and JPEG.

Each of those two image types has its place. GIF is a good format for images that don't have a lot of detail—uncomplicated bitmaps, spot art, and navigational buttons. The advantage of GIFs is that they are extremely small and load quickly. They can also be animated.

20

Remember, as you probably know from experience, small graphics are better than large graphics on the Web. How large an image is determines how long it takes users to access that page. And I'm sure you know that people tend to give up after a while.

Some images, such as photographs, look pretty bad when saved as GIFs, so an alternative is JPEG. JPEG images retain their detail (and 24-bit color), and can be downsized with increased compression. JPEG is good for scanned images and photos.

You'll read more about optimizing images in a little while.

Fonts and Text

This is another tricky issue—as it invariably is when dealing with fonts. When you export HTML text, you can export the font information. However, when that page is opened, it displays in that font only when the user actually has the font. (Assuming you are not embedding fonts in HTML the way you embed fonts in a PDF.) The page can take advantage of the user's font only when the user's browser supports fonts.

Users can set their default fonts in their browser preferences. Usually, you are given the option of a proportional-width font and a fixed-width font. Proportional-width means that each letter and character is only as wide as it needs to be. An "i" is narrower than an "m." Default proportional-width fonts in most browsers are Arial and Times. A fixed-width font means that every letter and character is the same width—an "i" is as wide as an "m." Courier is the archetypal fixed-width font.

In terms of other character attributes such as size and paragraph formatting, you can export this information to HTML, but the users might not be able to view it as you intended. In terms of point size, newer browsers support more of them, but not everyone uses newer browsers, so there might be some resizing going on at the viewing end.

In terms of paragraph formatting—left-, center-, right-alignment, justification, indents, and so on—you're pretty much at the mercy of the browser. You can export paragraph formatting to HTML, but the extent to which it is implemented depends on the browser. Again, the more recent the browser, the more faithful the display.

You might be muttering under your breath that people should update their browsers, but not everyone does unless forced to. Therefore, although you want to add lots of bells and whistles to your page, you should be mindful of the lowest common denominator. Pretend you work in Hollywood.

This variable text display also means that you cannot create carefully constructed text wraps. C'est la vie.

Think of it this way. Print has been around for almost 600 years. The Web hasn't even been around for a decade. Naturally, there are more options and standards with print. Think of the Web as a work-in-progress.

Creating Web Pages in InDesign

Most layout programs worth their salt let you create at least rudimentary Web pages.

Regardless of how good you think your page looks, you will almost always want to export the HTML page to a dedicated HTML editor. It'll do a better job, because that's what it's designed to do.

Exporting HTML

Here's what's ironic. It is actually simpler to create Web pages from scratch in InDesign than to repurpose material from a print-based document. You'll see why that is in a bit, but for now, try designing a simple page and exporting it in the following exercise.

To Do: Exporting HTML

To create a simple page and export it to an HTML file, do the following:

1. Create a simple one-page InDesign document, but with the following parameters. Set all margins to 0. Make sure you turn off Facing Pages; you only want single pages.

2. Import an image of some kind and place it on the page. Add a text box or two— one short burst of text (or placeholder text) below the image, and one box with Navigation items on the left side of the page. See Figure 20.2 for a sample.

3. When you have your page set up the way you want it to look, you're ready to export. Choose File, Export or press Command+E (on the Mac) or Control+E (on PCs). You'll get the Export dialog box. Select HTML from the Formats pop-up menu at the bottom of the box. Click on Save.

4. Remember from Hour 19, "Preparing Acrobat Output with InDesign," that when you exported to PDF, you had several panes worth of settings to adjust. Same deal here—you have four of them. Start on the Documents pane, as shown in Figure 20.3.

To Do

20

▼

FIGURE 20.2

A sample Web page set up in InDesign. Note the navigation aids on the left. Using an HTML editor, you can make these hyperlinks to other pages.

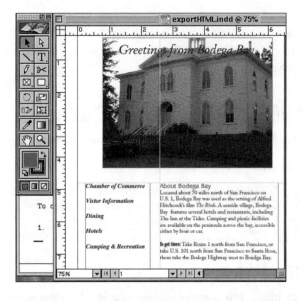

FIGURE 20.3

The Documents pane of the Export HTML dialog box.

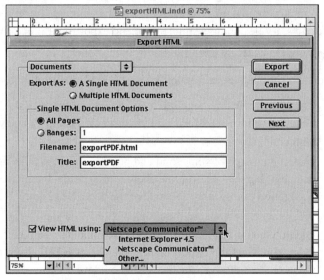

You have several options here. The first is whether you want to save the file as a single HTML document or as multiple documents. In this example, you only have a single page. If you have more than one page in the document, you can export each page to a separate HTML file; the dialog box would look something like

▼   Figure 20.4.

FIGURE 20.4

Exporting multiple HTML pages.

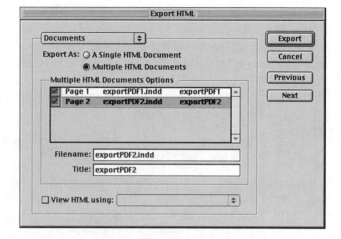

This is a useful option because sometimes you'll want separate pages to export separately, such as when you have separate Web pages in the same InDesign document. Sometimes you'll want a range of pages to export to the same file, such as long text boxes that continue onto separate pages.

> If you have lots of text, you're better off creating one single text frame, and getting all your text to fit in it, even if you have to drag the bottom of the text frame onto the pasteboard (or even onto subsequent pages) or reduce the size of the text. This is because InDesign adds line breaks where the pages break.

Note that you can change both the filename (what you call the page) and the title (what appears at the top of the Browser window).

Finally, you can determine whether you want a browser to launch—which can be, by default, Netscape Navigator, Microsoft Internet Explorer, or some other browser of your choosing. It's always a good idea to review what you've done, but if you are going to be exporting a number of pages and documents, you might want to leave this unchecked until the end.

20

5. Click on Next and you come to the Formatting pane. See Figure 20.5.

This is where you set the text and page background settings. There is one default you need to override in this box, and that is the Maintain Non-Standard Text setting. The default is Appearance. There is a wrinkle to this. If you leave this as the default, the entire page is converted to a bitmap image—but only if your text contains "non-standard" text attributes such as an applied gradient, a text frame back-

▼ ground or stroke, inline graphics, and so on. Sure, all your fonts and such are pre-served, but the browser won't be able to change margin settings and sizing. This causes the page to look bad and to take a long time to download. It will also be uneditable in an HTML editor. Change this option to Editability.

FIGURE 20.5

The Formatting pane of the Export HTML dialog box.

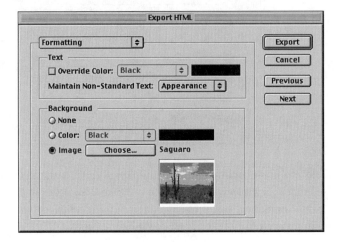

Note that you can also set an Override Color for text. This converts all the text in an exported document to one color. This is useful if you color code text for various proofing and editing purposes. However, if you have deliberately colored text as part of your design, you might not want to select this option. Any unwanted text colors that get through can always be corrected in an HTML editor.

Finally, you can set your page background. You can choose from None, a color of your choosing, or a JPEG or GIF image. Just for fun, this example chooses a JPEG. This looks silly, at least with this page, so I'll turn this off before actually exporting. The image you choose will repeat across and down the page like tiles.

6. When you're ready, click on Next and you come to the Layout pane. See Figure 20.6.

The first option, Positioning, has two choices: CSS-1 and None. CSS stands for Cascading Style Sheets, and essentially enables accurate representation of the page in the browser as you specified it. The other option, None, leaves it up to the browser, which means InDesign exports the text frames sequentially. This means that the navigation aids are above or below the descriptive text, not off to the left.

As far as margins are concerned, Maintain keeps the margins set in InDesign, whereas None uses the InDesign margins as the page boundary.

The Navigation Bar option is kind of pointless. With this option, InDesign creates its own Prev and Next buttons. You have no way of determining what they look

▼

▼ like, so unless you are way too lazy to create your own buttons, this isn't a good option. Most browsers have their own Back and Next buttons anyway, so you're better off setting this to None.

FIGURE 20.6
The Layout pane of the Export HTML dialog box.

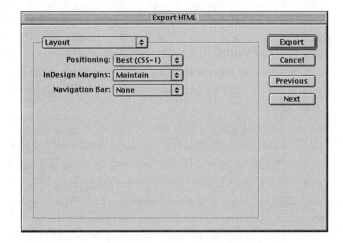

7. When you're ready, click on Next. You come to the Graphics pane, as shown in Figure 20.7.

FIGURE 20.7
The Graphics pane of the Export HTML dialog box.

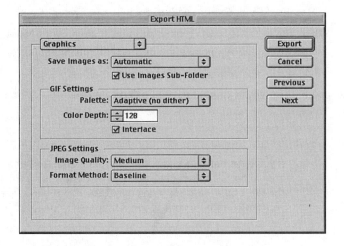

20

Here is where you tell InDesign what to do with your graphics.

The first option is Save Images As. You can set it to Automatic, JPEG, or GIF. Automatic lets InDesign determine which option is best. It's the best option, unless you have a compelling reason for making everything either a JPEG or GIF. Also, if
▼ you check the Use Images Subfolder checkbox, InDesign stores the converted

▼ images in a subfolder of the folder in which you are saving your HTML. Otherwise, the images are saved in the same folder as the HTML file. It's up to you.

You can then adjust the GIF and JPEG settings. Under GIF Settings, you can choose between several palettes for GIF image conversion. Adaptive is the best bet, although you can also specify the Web-safe palette here, if you want. It's up to you. Color Depth is a value between 2 and 256—2 is black-and-white whereas 256 is full 8-bit color. In other words, the higher the number the more faithful the color reproduction, but the slower the download time. The default is 128—a reasonable middle ground.

Interlace lets GIF images load into a browser in several passes of increasing resolution. With this unchecked, the users see nothing until the image has completely downloaded. Most people like to look at something while waiting for the rest of it to load, so check this option unless you want to keep users in suspense.

Under JPEG settings, you set the quality—Low, Medium, High, and Maximum. Medium is usually a happy medium, but experiment with different settings to determine the best tradeoff between quality and download speed.

Finally, you can set whether you want Baseline or Progressive JPEG. This is the JPEG equivalent of the GIF Interlacing option that you just read about. Select Progressive if you want the image to load in several passes of increasing resolution or Baseline if you want to wait to show the image until it's completely loaded.

8. When you're ready, press Export and you'll create your HTML file. You can check out what you did by opening the exported file in Navigator or Internet Explorer.
▲   Figure 20.8 shows the page you just created as opened in Internet Explorer.

You need to open your exported page in a dedicated HTML editor, if only to add hyperlinks. You might also want to clean some things up, as well.

 If you have both Navigator and Internet Explorer, open the page you created in both. You can get a good sense of how different browsers handle the same basic data in varying ways. You might even want to try different versions of each browser to see if they display pages differently.

FIGURE 20.8

This probably won't win any awards for Web site design, but it does show that you can easily export Web pages from InDesign.

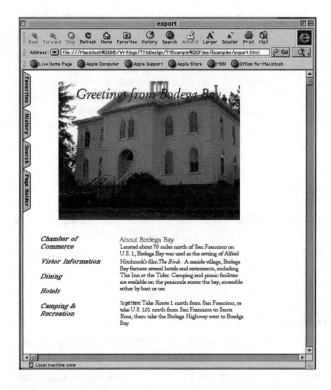

Repurposing Print Content

You might think that it would be easier to simply repurpose a print layout and export it as HTML than to start a page from scratch. Well, that's not necessarily true. If you are porting an issue of a magazine, you have to take out all the ads, repaginate the text, and undo all your columns—unless you want to keep your print column grid on-screen, which is not a great idea. And so on. The point is, if you are planning to repurpose your print documents, you are better off taking your original graphics and text files and laying out your page either from scratch in InDesign, or in a Web-specific program such as Dreamweaver or GoLive.

20

Very often, text exists only in a page layout file, not a Word or text file, especially in newspaper and magazine publishing. For example, although stories are likely to be in Word files, captions and other "spot text" here and there might not be. You can easily export these as text files using the Export Text feature that you'll look at in the next hour.

If you are serious about getting involved in Web development, you also need to worry about image optimization for the Web. There are a lot of tools out there that dither your GIFs and compress your JPEGs, all with varying degrees of quality. Adobe has ImageReady, which is now bundled with Photoshop 5.5. (Some argue that ImageReady should actually be a part of Photoshop itself.) Other programs include Ulead's PhotoImpact, which does a nice job, too. There is also Macromedia' Fireworks, and Adobe's own ImageStyler.

Summary

This has been a brief look at the issues involved in designing pages and documents for the Web versus print and how you can use InDesign to create HTML. It is hard to get a sense of how this truly works without going into far more detail about Web imaging than fits in the scope of this book. Suffice it to say that you know enough to be dangerous.

Workshop

You've just learned how to generate HTML from an InDesign document, and you've seen how that HTML is read by Web browsers such as Navigator and Internet Explorer. Now, read the Q&A to find the answers to some lingering questions you may have, and complete the quiz to test your recall of the features we covered. Finally, work through the exercises until you understand many of the nuances of generating HTML from InDesign.

Q&A

Q When I repurpose my print pages, do I have to convert my images back to RGB from CMYK?

A Yes, images on the Web are, by virtue of being monitor-based, RGB images. However, you might not want to convert the CMYK images. As you have seen in previous hours, CMYK is a much more limited color space than RGB, so you discarded color data when you initially converted the files. If you convert back to RGB, you do not get any data back. But this might not be a big deal. Your images will look on-screen the same in both RGB and CMYK (remember, your monitor can only display in RGB, so you're only getting an RGB approximation of CMYK). For instance, if you are working with an outdoor photograph, you'll notice that when you convert to CMYK your clear blue sky will get a bit murkier and muted. CMYK is not as vivid as RGB. My point with all this is that you might want to save an RGB version of your images and swap out the CMYK version when you create the Web page.

Q You mentioned dithering. What is that?

A Dithering is a way to reduce the number of colors in an image, such as when going from 24-bit (millions of colors) to 8-bit (256 colors) or to the 216-color Web-safe palette. Essentially, you end up with undesirable color patterns when colors have been dithered. This is why Web designers prefer the Web-safe palette. Those colors are defined as non-dithering because they are not (deliberately) changed by a browser.

Quiz

1. In which of the following programs can you *not* add hyperlinks to a Web page?

    a. InDesign

    b. Microsoft Word

    c. Microsoft FrontPage

2. The Web-safe palette colors look the same on every system that views them.

    a. True

    b. False

3. The GIF file format is better suited for which of the following?

    a. Small, uncomplicated graphics

    b. Scanned images and photos

4. The JPEG file format is better suited for which of the following?

    a. Small, uncomplicated graphics

    b. Scanned images and photos

Quiz Answers

1. a. In fact, it's hard not to add hyperlinks in Word documents! Just typing a URL turns it into a link, which can drive editors crazy.

2. b. As you have seen, all monitors tend to display colors differently.

3. a. Because of its limited color palette, GIFs are more suited for small uncomplicated graphics.

4. b. JPEG is better suited for scanned images and photos.

20

Exercises

Take some of the documents you created in previous hours and export them as HTML, exploring the different options you saw in the Export HTML dialog box panes. Open up the resulting HTML document in the Web browser you typically use, be it Navigator or Internet Explorer. If you have both, open up your HTML in each of them and note the differences. Practice creating HTML with different types of documents, each containing different page elements—bitmap images, vectors, and so on. How does each document type or page element appear when converted to HTML and opened in your browser?

HOUR 21

Exploring Other Export Options

So far, you've looked at the Print dialog box in general, so you can print your InDesign proofs to a desktop laser or inkjet printer (Hour 17, "Printing from InDesign"), how to prepare files for service bureau output (Hour 18, "Getting Ready for the Service Bureau"), how to export PDFs from InDesign (Hour 19, "Preparing Acrobat Output with InDesign"), and how to create Web pages from InDesign Documents (Hour 20, "Creating Web Content with InDesign").

Now it's time for a little cleanup, and time to consider all the other export options InDesign gives you. You'll also look as some of the "lost panes" of the Print dialog box. You'll find out what they are and why you might use them.

So, in this hour you'll learn:

- How to export InDesign documents as EPS files
- How to export InDesign documents as prepress-ready PostScript files
- How to export text from InDesign

Using the Export Command

The first place to find additional export options is—not surprisingly—using the Export command, which is accessed by going to File, Export. Figure 21.1 shows you the Export options.

FIGURE 21.1

InDesign's export options.

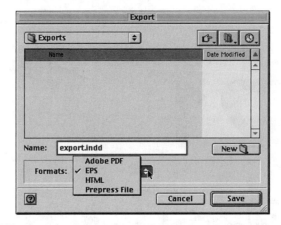

You've looked at Adobe PDF and HTML already, but you haven't seen EPS yet. You should know what an EPS file is, though, and how to place one in an InDesign document. Now you can learn why you would export an InDesign document as an EPS and how you would go about doing it.

Exporting EPS Files

You've seen in an earlier chapter that EPS—which stands for Encapsulated PostScript—is a standard file format commonly used for vector-based graphics. Not only can you import EPSs into InDesign, you can also save an InDesign page as a self-contained graphic that can then be imported—like any other EPS file—into another illustration or page layout program such as Illustrator, FreeHand, QuarkXPress, and even InDesign. Why would you want to export an InDesign page as an EPS and then bring it back into InDesign? Isn't that kind of like a snake eating its own tail?

In a way, yes, but there are several reasons you might do this. The first is because you create documents in InDesign—such as ads—just because you absolutely love InDesign. However, the publication running the ad might not support InDesign. This way, it's win-win. You get to use InDesign, and the recipient of your ad can use the document you create.

Another reason is that you can create a simple, single graphic that, when set up correctly, can be sent from place to place as a single self-contained unit, rather than as an InDesign page with lots of disparate elements all ready to be shifted out of alignment.

Yet another reason is to replicate an InDesign page elsewhere in a publication. For example, if you design a magazine cover in InDesign and want to run a smaller version of it on the letters to the editor page, or want to use it in a marketing piece, you don't need to rescale every page element. You simply export the page as an EPS, and then you can resize the entire page en masse to whatever dimensions you want.

Using the Export EPS Feature

As you saw in Hour 19, you can create a PDF through the Export command. Likewise, you can create an EPS in the same way.

Although the PostScript Options pane of the Print dialog box seems to let you use the Print command to print to an EPS, Adobe would prefer that you use Export, and InDesign will not let you print to an EPS.

To Do: Exporting an EPS

To export a page as an EPS, follow these steps:

1. Create a single, letter-sized page in InDesign, in whatever way you want. If you still have one you used in a previous hour, by all means use it.

2. Be sure to save your page as a regular InDesign document. Then choose File, Export or press Command+E (on the Mac) or Control+E (on PCs). You'll get the Export dialog box, which you should be intimately familiar with by now.

3. Select EPS from the pop-up menu at the bottom of the box. Press Save, and you'll get the Export EPS dialog box. See Figure 21.2.

4. The first pane (there are two, by the way) gives you the basic file setup options. You have a few options here:

   • *Encoding*—ASCII or Binary are the options here and in most cases it's six of one, half-dozen of the other. ASCII has the advantage of being editable (meaning someone who is familiar with PostScript code can edit it, if need be), but will produce a larger file. It's asking a lot for someone to edit a PostScript file, so you can select Binary here.

21

FIGURE 21.2

InDesign's Export EPS dialog box.

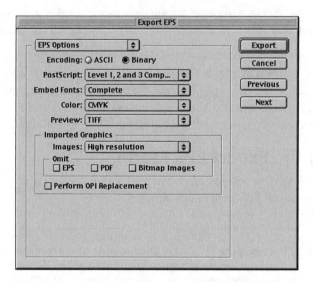

- *PostScript*—As you might know, there are three levels of PostScript currently in use. You can choose Levels 1, 2, and 3 Compatible, which works with whatever PostScript device exists. However, you'll have a larger file, and you might have banding problems in gradients. (There's no winning, is there?) Level 2 is currently the most prevalent version of PostScript, so you're safe with that option. PostScript 3 is the newest, and has yet to become ubiquitous, but supports more options. Be sure to check with your service bureau before using PostScript 3.

- *Embed Fonts*—You've seen this option before in connection with PDF. The options are None (no font embedding), Subset (only those specific characters used in the document are embedded), and Complete (all fonts). Your best bet is to select Complete, whereby the EPS can be edited after the fact. For example, a typo in an ad can be corrected by well-meaning ad production folks.

- *Color*—The options here are CMYK (for print production), RGB (for on-screen display), Device-Independent (the burden of color is on the output device), and Grayscale (for black-and-white images). As you know by now, your best bet is CMYK. (If you are using spot or Pantone colors, use Device Independent so your spot colors are not converted to process colors.)

- *Preview*—When you import an EPS into another program, a bitmap file that represents the data contained in the EPS is used as the preview page. (Vectors can be represented as bitmaps only on a computer screen). You can select None (if you are going direct to output with the file) or TIFF (if you want to be able to see what the graphic is when you import it into another program).

- *Imported Graphics*—You've also seen this before. Choose High Resolution if your EPS is designed for print at some point. Choose Low Resolution if your EPS is intended only for on-screen viewing.

> Even if you are exporting the EPS for use in a CD-ROM or Web page, you might want to select High Resolution if the page containing the EPS will eventually be printed at some point, such as on a laser printer. Documentation, technical drawings, and figures display fine at low resolution on-screen, but if someone prints the page, it will look pretty bad.

- *Omit*—If you are using an OPI workflow, you can omit an imported graphic that will have a high-resolution version swapped in by the OPI server. And, if this is indeed the case, be sure to check the Perform OPI Replacement checkbox.

5. When your settings are done, click on Next. You come to the Pages pane, as shown in Figure 21.3.

FIGURE 21.3

The Pages pane of InDesign's Export EPS dialog box.

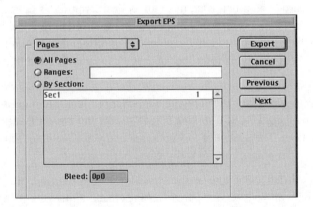

This pane should also look familiar. It's straightforward; simply indicate which pages (or range of pages, or sections) you want to include. You can also specify a bleed. Sadly, you cannot add page marks, which would have been nice.

▼

By the way, InDesign on the Mac saves the EPS with the .indd filename extension. You might want to add the .eps file extension if you're working in a cross-platform or Windows-only environment. Conveniently, the Windows version adds the proper file extension.

6. When you're ready, press Export.

   If you want to see how your EPS file came out, you can launch Illustrator or FreeHand and open the EPS. Alternatively, you can simply do a place and bring it into your InDesign document.

▲

Exporting a PostScript File

Alternatively called a *prepress* file, or *prepress PostScript*, this option saves an InDesign document as a PostScript file. Now, why on Earth would anyone want to do this? There are a couple of reasons.

Some folks prefer to send PostScript files rather than application files to service bureaus. In the Q&A for Hour 18, you learned a bit about this idea. If you do your own imposition, you might have little choice but to send PostScript files.

Another reason you might want to supply a PostScript file is to ensure that no changes to your document are made, either on purpose or inadvertently. Also, it's a good way of ensuring that your own trapping settings are implemented. Additionally, you don't have to worry about supplying fonts, because you can embed all the fonts in the PostScript file.

However, the drawback to supplying a PostScript file is that it needs to be formatted correctly. It's asking a lot of a service bureau to edit and correct PostScript code—if anyone there even can. The upshot of this option is that you should not send your service bureau PostScript files unless you are well-versed in file creation.

If you're worried about your application files getting changed, effective and open communication with your service bureau ensures that nothing gets changed without your permission. Remember, service bureaus are on your side.

To create a PostScript file via the Export command, it's pretty much the same deal you've just seen. Go to Export (you should know how to get there by now) and select Prepress from the pop-up menu. You'll get the Export Prepress File dialog box. See Figure 21.4.

FIGURE 21.4

*InDesign's Export
Prepress File
dialog box.*

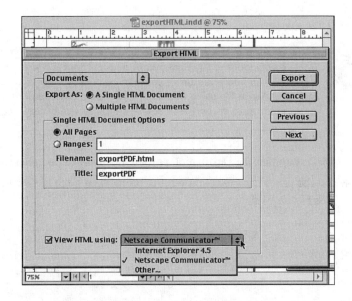

Most of these options should look familiar to you by now. What you do need to remember is that because this is a prepress file, everything needs to be high-resolution and in CMYK.

If you click on Next, you'll get to the second pane of this export box, the Pages and Page Marks dialog box. Unlike the EPS rendition, you can actually set page marks when saving a PostScript file. This is a good thing, because printers and service bureaus usually need page marks, especially crop marks.

Printing to a PostScript File

Alternatively, as with PDF, you can create a prepress PostScript file using the Print command. This is a good option when you want more control over how the PostScript is created.

To Do: Printing a PostScript File

To create a PostScript file using the Print command, follow these steps:

1. As you have done so many times before, create an InDesign document. Save it, tweak it, and get it to a point where it can be printed.

2. Go to the Print dialog box. Select the Printer you'll need.

21

Under the Printer pop-up menu, make sure that you are using the PPD that corresponds to the final output device. Chances are you do not have the PPD for whatever device your service bureau is using. If you create your PostScript file using the PPD for your own desktop printer, your file might not output properly—or at all—on the service bureau's equipment.

3. Make sure that the Destination pop-up menu says File rather than Printer.

4. Set the pages or ranges you want to print. Then go to the PostScript Options pane. See Figure 21.5.

FIGURE 21.5

The PostScript Options pane of the Print dialog box.

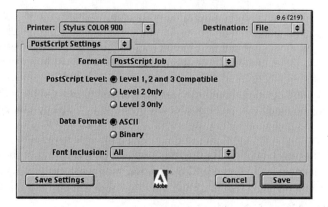

5. This gives you some of the same options you saw in the Export Options dialog box. Make sure PostScript Job is selected under format.

6. Set your appropriate PostScript Level. You saw the differences in the previous section on exporting.

7. Set your ASCII or Binary option. As you might recall, ASCII generates a larger file, but at least it can be edited.

8. Set your Font Inclusion. Here, you have some different options. See Figure 21.6.

   You have the obvious choices of None and All, and also have All But Standard 13. This last option embeds all the fonts except for the 13 "standard" fonts—Helvetica, Palatino, Times, your dear friend Courier, and others. Chances are that you are using fonts other than these standard ones. You can also select All but Fonts in PPD File. The PPD for an output device contains information as to which fonts the output device has built-in. Processing time of PostScript files can be increased if you embed fonts that the device already has. However, you might be using a differ-

▼ ent version of the same basic font, or you might have custom kerning, tracking, or other values. So, in a nutshell, you're usually better off embedding all fonts.

FIGURE 21.6

Font inclusion options.

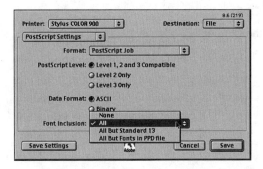

> Some service bureaus use a special font downloading utility with their RIPs, so it might be counterproductive to embed your fonts. You might still want to supply your fonts separately. Be sure to check with the service bureau before you choose either option.

9. When you're ready, press Save. You'll be prompted with a Save dialog box. Rename the file if you want (InDesign will automatically append a .ps file extension on the name). InDesign will then create the PostScript file.

▲

There are a couple of ways you can check out the PostScript file you just created. The first is to open it in Word. Be forewarned: It will be a long file, and it will likely make no sense to you. The single page I created for this exercise (which had a couple paragraphs of text, three fonts, and one placed bitmap) was 572 pages long. This is something strictly for the curious; unless you know how to read PostScript code, it will be gibberish.

Another quick and easy way you can check your PostScript file is to use Acrobat Distiller. Launch it and distill the PostScript file you just made. You don't need heavy-duty, print-optimized settings. Basically, you just want to ensure that everything embedded correctly. If your PDF looks okay, chances are your PostScript file will output properly.

21

Revisiting the Print Dialog Box

When you enter the hoary netherworld of prepress files, you need to be more cognizant than usual about how your print settings are created. The last exercise took a basic look at how to create a PostScript file using, for the most part, default settings. This section covers some of the "lost panes" of the Print dialog box and discusses your options for high-end output.

Setting Colors

If you go back to the Print dialog box and choose Color from the pop-up menu, you'll see the dialog box shown in Figure 21.7.

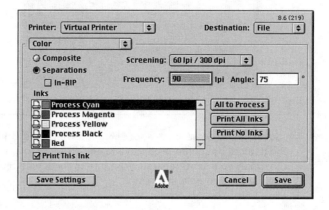

Notice that the first thing you need to set is whether you want to print a Composite Print—all colors on one sheet, as from a color desktop printer—or Separations. If you click on Separations, you can choose which ink(s) print. If you are setting up files for a service bureau, you need to click on Separations.

Now, notice that your inks are listed in the box in the center. If you are printing a four-color job, there should only be four inks. Notice that here you have a problem—you have something called Red. This is a stray color that has been defined as a spot color rather than as a process color somewhere in the document.

The best way to correct it is to go back to the Swatches palette, find the offending color, and convert it to a process color. See Figure 21.8.

There is another way, however. The Color pane contains a button called All to Process. If you click on it, all the colors are converted to process colors. Notice that when you do so, you have the option of converting the Red back to a spot color. See the Revert to Spot button in Figure 21.9.

This All to Process setting only affects the printing; the original Red still remains a spot color as defined in the Swatches palette. If this is indeed an error, you are better off correcting it at the source—in the Swatches palette.

FIGURE 21.8

Correcting an inadvertent spot color.

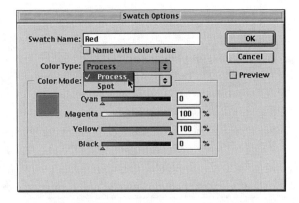

FIGURE 21.9

You can now revert to the spot color.

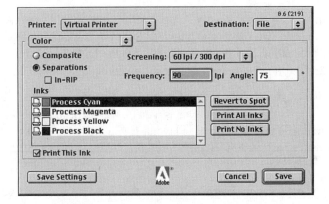

What would happen if you sent this file—uncorrected—to the service bureau? You'd get five plates—one of them a red that your printer couldn't use. Anything that used that red color definition wouldn't get printed.

Other options in this pane include printing only selected inks, which is useful when you want to provide a set of separation proofs to the service bureau—you can print each color as a separate print. You can also set your line screen (Frequency) here. The default is 60 lpi, but check with your printer to see what line screen you should set.

Recall from previous hours that you should not touch the Angle settings, otherwise you'll print with an unpleasant moiré pattern.

Settings Graphics Settings

One last pane of the Print dialog box that you should worry about is the Graphics pane. See Figure 21.10.

21

FIGURE 21.10

The Graphics pane of the Print dialog box.

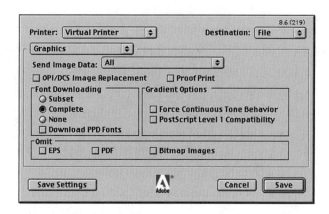

First off, unless you are strictly doing proofing, you should select All under Send Image Data. The other two options—Optimized Subsampling and Low Resolution—are designed for proofs that don't necessarily need to be high-resolution. For final output onto film, you'll need all the image data you can get.

Alternatively, you can check Proof Print. This outputs no graphics, just empty picture frames with Xs through them. This is a quick way to print proofs in which the primary consideration is text or basic page layout. If you are using an OPI system and your service bureau or printer has the high-resolution versions, select OPI/DCS Image Replacement.

Here is where you can determine the font downloading, as well. You know what Subset means: only those characters that are used are sent to the printer. This is a good option when you are printing to your desktop printer. Check Complete if you are sending your files out.

You also have a Download PPD Fonts option. PPD fonts are the fonts that the printer already has in memory. If you check this, you will download fonts that the printer already has.

If you are creating PostScript files to supply to your service bureau, check with them to see what sort of font downloading options they prefer. You don't want to conflict with a system they already use.

Under Gradient Options, you have two choices. You can Force Continuous Tone Behavior, which you might need to do if you know that the output device in question has problems with banding. This option forces the output device to treat the gradient like a photograph. There is PostScript Level 1 Compatibility, which should be checked only when you are printing to a PostScript Level 1 device.

You've seen the Omit options—omit those images that your OPI server will be replacing later.

Saving Your Settings

You saw in Hour 17 that you can create printer styles in InDesign—essentially preset collections of settings. Naturally, you can add the Color and Graphics panes to any style you create.

Exporting Text

It's time to take a step back in terms of complexity and look at exporting text from InDesign. Why would you want to export text? There are a few reasons. For example, if you write something wholly within InDesign, you might want to open it in Word or use it somewhere else.

If you select the Text tool and click on a text box, you can go to the Export dialog box, and notice that there are three additional Export options. You saw Adobe InDesign Tagged Format in Hour 20, but note the other two: Rich Text Format and Text-Only. See Figure 21.11.

FIGURE **21.11**

More Export options.

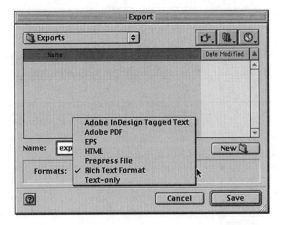

 The difference between ASCII and rich text is that Rich Text Format (RTF), a text format developed by Microsoft, saves the text, plus some basic formatting, such as the font, point size, and some basic font styles (bold, italic, and bold italic). RTF can be read by most word processors and page layout programs. Text only, also called ASCII text, saves just characters with no formatting.

21

To Do: Exporting Text

To Export text, either as straight ASCII text or as Rich Text, follow these steps:

1. Open an InDesign document, create a text frame, and fill it with text. If you're feeling creative, type something. You can also use InDesign's Fill with placeholder Text feature. Add some formatting—use a couple of different fonts, point sizes, and styles. Save it as an InDesign file.

2. With the Type tool, click anywhere in the text frame you want to export.

3. Go to the Export dialog box, and select Rich Text Format from the pop-up menu at the bottom of the box. Give it a name (use the file extension .rtf).

4. Click on Export.

5. Repeat steps 2-4, selecting Text-Only from the Format pop-up menu. Keep the same name, but use the .txt file extension instead.

6. If you have Word or some other word processor, open each file you created to see the differences. (Alternatively, create a text frame in InDesign and place each text file you created.)

▲

Figure 21.12 shows the text frame you created in InDesign. Figure 21.13 is the RTF file opened in Word, and Figure 21.14 is the Text-Only file opened in Word. You can't see this in this black-and-white book, but the red InDesign text also appears red in the RTF version.

FIGURE 21.12

The original text in an InDesign text frame.

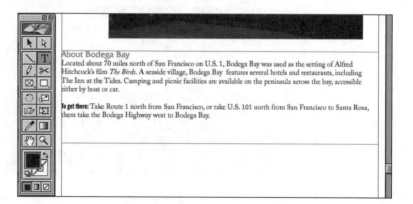

The RTF version of the Exported text in Word. Needless to say, Word does not handle typography nearly as well as InDesign.

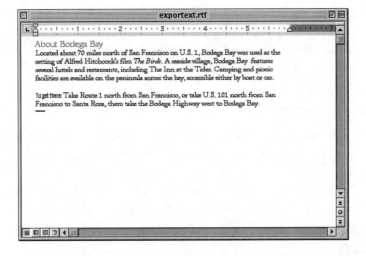

The text-only version of the Exported text in Word.

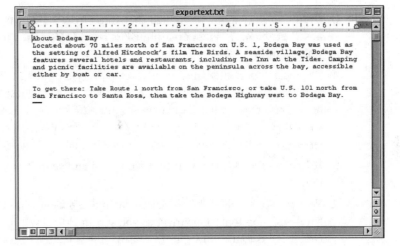

Summary

So, you have seen, in this and previous hours, that there are a wealth of options for getting elements and pages out of InDesign into other forms you need to use—be it paper, film, PostScript files, EPSs, PDFs, HTML, or text.

With the end of this hour, you should be adept at all the myriad ways of getting objects and graphics into InDesign, as well as getting everything back out—the entire InDesign

21

digestive tract, if you will. In the remaining few hours, you will look at more advanced subjects, such as using plug-ins and scripting to customize your workflow, working in a cross-platform environment (that should be fun), as well as using InDesign in the "real world," which is far from all the ivory tower speculation here.

Workshop

You've just learned how you can export a number of different file types from InDesign. Specifically, EPS files, PostScript files, and text. Any questions? Of course there are. So check out the Q&A. And even if you don't have any questions, we do, so complete the quiz to test your recall of the features we covered. Finally, try out the exercises to learn the ins and outs of the various export options.

Q&A

Q Didn't you say a few hours ago that EPSs were kind of tricky, or that they posed problems? When creating EPSs from InDesign, what issues do I need to worry about?

A The most important goal is to try to keep everything simple. If you are exporting an EPS from InDesign, try to make sure that that page doesn't have any sub-EPSs on it. This creates what are known as *nested EPS files*, which can snarl some RIPs when they are output. Although today's RIPs are more powerful than those of yesteryear (or quite literally yesterday, now that I think about it), why take chances?

Q If I create an EPS from an InDesign page and send it out, do I need to supply fonts?

A Yes! Yes! Yes! This is the biggest problem that people who receive EPS files have—missing fonts. One trick, as you saw in Hour 11, "Combining Text and Graphics," is to use InDesign's Create Outlines feature to convert all your fonts to independent paths. The drawback is that you can't edit your text, but at least you won't get any nasty phone calls from those on font scavenger hunts. Another trick is to open the EPS in Photoshop and save it back out as a high-resolution TIFF. It'll probably print the same as an EPS, but it will cause fewer headaches.

Quiz

1. Prepress PostScript files can be easily edited if there's a problem.
    a. True
    b. False

2. Encapsulated PostScript (EPS) files can be easily edited if there's a problem.

    a. True

    b. False

3. Which of the following cannot be exported from InDesign?

    a. EPS files

    b. PostScript files

    c. Formatted text

    d. TIFF images

Quiz Answers

1. b. Wading through PostScript code and attempting to edit it is not for the faint of heart.

2. a. EPS files can be edited in Illustrator, FreeHand, or even Photoshop.

3. d. At least not natively as TIFFs.

Exercises

As exercises for this hour…we'll, export stuff. Take some of the documents you've created in previous hours and practice exporting them as EPSes. Import them back into InDesign to see how changing different options changes how they import. Also have a go at creating PostScript files, both via the Export command as well as the Print command. There's not much you can do with the finished files, but if you have Acrobat Distiller, distill the PostScript files you create into PDFs. You'll then be able to see how changing the various PostScript options changes the file you end up with.

21

PART VI

Advanced InDesign

Hour

HOUR 22

Customizing InDesign

There are several layers to customization, especially in terms of InDesign.
You can start at the most basic level—customizing the tools in InDesign.
This involves keyboard shortcuts and other little time-saving techniques. The
next level involves InDesign's modular plug-in approach. Need a special tool
but don't want to wait for Adobe to build it into InDesign? Well, you can
either create the tool yourself as a plug-in or explore the vast array of third-
party plug-ins.

In this hour, you'll learn:

- How to customize InDesign's keyboard shortcuts
- How to customize InDesign's palettes
- How to work with plug-ins

Using Shortcuts

There are two schools of thought on the subject of keyboard shortcuts. Most
people like them; they can simplify the process of getting to a command or
dialog box. Most people pick them up—either deliberately or by force of

habit—after a while. But then some people find the process of trying to remember keyboard shortcuts a colossal headache and refuse to make the effort.

What is even more of a headache is not so much the concept of the keyboard shortcut itself but the fact that they can vary from program to program. For example, when trying to place objects in InDesign, I still routinely get the Export dialog box, because after many years of using QuarkXPress, I'm used to pressing Command+E to get images and text.

Customizing Keyboard Shortcuts

In InDesign, you can customize all your keyboard shortcuts, or you can use the defaults. Alternatively, and this is an interesting idea, InDesign also lets you use the QuarkXPress shortcuts, eager as they are to get Quark users to switch to InDesign.

To Do: Applying QuarkXPress Keyboard Shortcuts in InDesign

To eschew the InDesign keyboard shortcuts and use Quark's, follow these steps:

1. Choose Edit, Edit Shortcuts. You'll get the large Edit Keyboard shortcuts dialog box. See Figure 22.1.

FIGURE 22.1

The Edit Shortcuts dialog box.

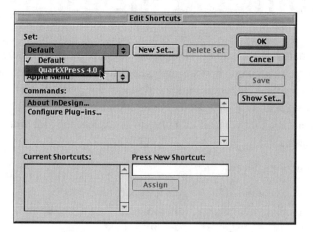

2. Click on the Set pop-up menu and select QuarkXPress 4.0.
3. You can see if this is what you want. Click on the Product Area pop-up menu and go to File menu, where you can see its list of commands. By single-clicking on Place, you can see that it is now associated with Command+E. So no more getting the Export dialog box when I want to import. See Figure 22.2.

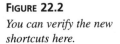

FIGURE 22.2

You can verify the new shortcuts here.

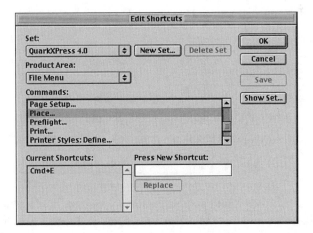

22

Of course, after all those chapters on Export options, I now know that Command+E is Export, so switching to the QuarkXPress set now might make my head explode or force me to crawl under my desk and whimper. Remember that keyboard shortcuts are supposed to be a time-saving technology, not one that causes irreparable psychological damage.

4. To get a list of the shortcuts, click on the Show Set button. This will open a text file that lists all the keyboard shortcuts, which you can then print out and tape someplace convenient. Alternatively, you can cut the list into flash cards and have friends and co-workers quiz you.

5. If you want to use the QuarkXPress keyboard shortcuts, press OK. If you don't, switch back to Default, or just press Cancel.

Some people think that resorting to Quark keyboard shortcuts is just a colossal case of denial. But whatever makes you comfortable with new software can't be bad.

If you are a PageMaker user, many of the default InDesign shortcuts will be familiar to you, because they are based on PageMaker's shortcuts.

However, perhaps you have your own idea of how you want to remember certain shortcuts. Well, InDesign lets you customize your own set as well.

To Do: Creating Your Own Shortcuts

To create your own customized keyboard shortcuts, follow these steps:

1. Choose File, Edit Shortcuts.
2. Click on the New Set button. You are prompted to name your new set. See Figure 22.3.

FIGURE 22.3

Step one in creating your customized keyboard shortcuts.

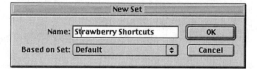

3. Let's start with what I suspect could very well be most useful shortcut for the obsessive/compulsive InDesign user. Click on Product Area and select Edit Menu.
4. Scroll down the Commands list until you come to Edit Shortcuts. I'm guessing you'll want a shortcut for this. You can enter the key sequence; in this case, use Control+Option+Shift+E. InDesign then tells you that that sequence is currently unassigned, which means you can use it with impunity. See Figure 22.4.

FIGURE 22.4

Entering the new keyboard sequence.

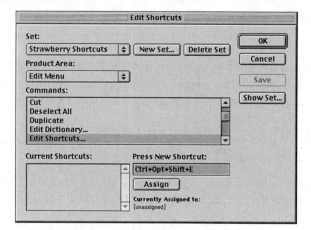

5. Click on Assign to set the shortcut.
6. You can then change any other shortcuts you want, and press OK when you're done.

   What if you pick a key sequence that is already assigned? As you can see from Figure 22.5, when you try to assign Command+E to Edit Shortcuts (and send me completely off the deep end), InDesign tells you that that sequence is already

▼ assigned. You do have the option of replacing it, which will of course strip Export of a shortcut.

FIGURE **22.5**

When a key sequence is spoken for, you can choose to usurp it if you want.

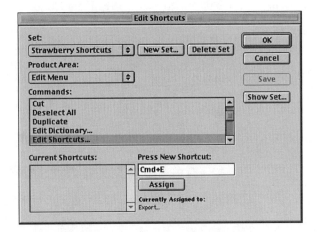

▲

What's fortunate is that InDesign doesn't let you modify the Default set because, as you can tell, it can be easy to screw up your keyboard shortcuts to the point where the chances of ever remembering them are slim. Suffice it to say that you don't want to change your keyboard shortcuts so often that recalling them becomes an exercise in futility.

One other consideration is whether you work with others, or especially whether others use your computer. If you use a whacked-out set of bizarre shortcuts, communicating tasks to others can become a bit of a problem. If anyone tried to use keyboard shortcuts on your computer, their chances of getting anything productive accomplished are likely to be nil.

One other caveat regarding keyboard shortcuts is that if you use an extended keyboard, the numeric keypad numbers cannot be used for custom keyboard shortcuts. Custom shortcuts can be assigned to the numbers on the main keyboard, however.

And if you have any doubt about what a particular keyboard shortcut is, InDesign's default set is listed on the tear-out card at the front of this book.

Customizing Tools

InDesign also gives you the capability to customize tools in a variety of ways. In version 1.5, you can control how the Tools palette appears on-screen, and you can more easily dock your palettes.

Setting Your Tools Palette Display

You've seen the Preferences dialog box before, but in the General preferences, you can set how you want the Tools palette to display. See Figure 22.6.

FIGURE 22.6

In General Preferences, you can set how you want the Tools palette to display.

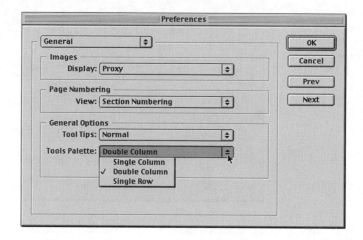

You can leave the default, which is the familiar double-column format (see Figure 22.7)...

FIGURE 22.7

The double-column Tools palette.

You can, for some hideous reason, use a Microsoft Office-like single row (see Figure 22.8)...

FIGURE 22.8

The single-row Tools palette for those who don't hate Office.

Or, you can use a single vertical column (see Figure 22.9).

FIGURE 22.9
A single-column Tools palette.

A minor convenience, but it's there, nonetheless.

Minimizing and Docking Palettes

If you have been using InDesign for any period of time, you know that there are a slew of palettes. Granted, you don't always need them all open at one time (unless you happen to be writing a book on InDesign). Therefore, InDesign gives you a few options for maximizing screen real estate.

To Do: Minimizing Palettes

To minimize a palette, do the following:

1. Open a new InDesign document. There should be a couple of palettes on the screen already. Pick one. In this case, I chose the Character palette. Double-click the name tab of the palette.

2. The palette should be minimized. For example, the bottom options have been removed and you have a simple Character palette.

3. Double-click on the palette title tab again. Now you see the tab floating alone on-screen. If you double-click on the tab again, the entire palette pops back out. See Figures 22.10, 22.11, and 22.12 for the sequence of events.

▲ To Do

Figure 22.10
The Character palette in all its glory.

Figure 22.11
A slightly reduced Character palette after one double-click.

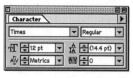

Figure 22.12
The Character palette is reduced to a floating head sailing over the landscape after two double-clicks.

 If you double-click on the gray bar at the top of the palette or click on the minimize button on the top-right side of the palette window (as is standard on the Mac OS), you will collapse the palette to an unidentified gray bar, which isn't particularly useful. So always double-click on the palette's tab.

New in version 1.5 is the ability to dock palettes in a variety of ways. InDesign by default combines several separate palettes into one large tabbed megapalette, but if the default megapalette doesn't comprise a logical set for you, you can split each palette off separately and dock the ones you want.

To Do: Docking Palettes

To dock two or more palettes together into one big megapalette, follow these steps:

1. Open a new InDesign document.
2. Press F12 to get the Pages palette. By default, this comes attached to the Layers and Navigator palettes. Click on the Pages title tab and drag it to a new position. Release it, and you now have a standalone Pages palette.

▼   3. Repeat this process with the Layers palette. You now have three standalone palettes. Shrink or close the Layers and Navigator palettes.

    4. Assume you want to combine the Pages and the Character palettes. Choose Type, Character or press Command+T (on the Mac) or Control+T (on PCs) to bring up the Character palette. Notice that it comes attached to the Paragraph palette. Assume you don't want the Paragraph palette. Detach it and move it to a new position on the desktop.

    5. Click and drag the tab for the Character palette into the Pages palette. You'll see an outline form within the inside of the palette you are dragging into. Don't release yet; drag the Character palette toward the top of the Pages palette. When you see a black line running horizontally along the top of the Pages palette, release the mouse.

    6. You'll now see that the two palettes are docked vertically. See Figure 22.13.

FIGURE 22.13

The Pages and Character palettes are docked vertically.

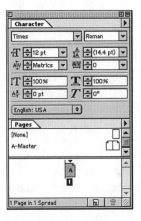

    7. Detach the two palettes. Try docking them again. This time, drag the Character palette toward the center-left side of the Pages palette. You'll see a vertical line running down the left side of the Pages palette. Release, and you'll now have the two palettes docked horizontally. See Figure 22.14.

    8. You can now add the Paragraph palette, either horizontally or vertically.

FIGURE 22.14

The Pages and Character palettes are docked horizontally.

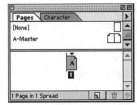

▲

Anyway, you get the idea. Try playing around with the docking and minimizing to find a screen arrangement that suits you.

> Some folks often get a second monitor and attach it to their systems. They keep all their palettes on the second monitor and keep just the document they're working on displayed on the first. Check the documentation of your computer or video card to see whether you can take advantage of this approach if you need to.

Advanced Customization Options

What you've looked at so far in this hour—keyboard shortcuts and docking palettes—is just plumage. It's cosmetic, despite how much more efficient it makes the workspace. But now it's time to turn to a higher-powered customization option—plug-ins.

Working with Plug-Ins

The concept of plug-ins began with Photoshop many years ago. Photoshop's extensible architecture enabled many third-party developers to come up with special effects, filters, and tools that users can add—often inexpensively—rather than waiting for Adobe to incorporate such filters into new versions. This approach spawned an entire cottage industry of plug-in developers, and was likely one of the reasons that Photoshop became the de facto standard for image editing.

The plug-in approach spread to Illustrator and PageMaker, and ultimately to QuarkXPress. A smaller but just as vital clutch of XTensions developers (Quark calls its plug-ins *XTensions*) create specific solutions for XPress.

With Acrobat, Adobe started to move toward a more modular approach to application development. With InDesign, Adobe has taken the plug-in approach even further toward its logical conclusion. Most of InDesign exists as some plug-in or other. The core application is actually very small. This makes it easy to correct various bits of InDesign, or to update it.

> You might want to periodically check out www.adobe.com for updates and fixes to various portions of InDesign.

InDesign is still pretty new, so there isn't a large volume of plug-ins available just yet. But they're getting there. There are already a bunch of plug-ins that extend InDesign's functionality. Some of the highlights are as follows:

- *A Lowly Apprentice Production* (www.alap.com)—ALAP has made its name with Quark XTensions, many of which are absolutely crucial. Two of their XTensions have made the move to InDesign. Imposer lets users create printer's flats or impositions from InDesign documents. Shadowcaster lets users add drop shadows to objects.

- *Extensis* (www.extensis.com)—Extensis makes plug-ins for Photoshop, XTensions for QuarkXPress, and brought over its Preflight Pro to InDesign for enhanced preflighting capabilities.

- *LizardTech* (www.lizardtech.com)—LizardTech created an InDesign plug-in for its MrSID Portable Image Format. MrSID is a graphics file format that allows lossless compression of images for easy storage and transport. With MrSID, files can be compressed to three percent of their original size.

- *Managing Editor* (www.maned.com)—Managing Editor has an InDesign plug-in that complements its MagForce publication layout program, an excellent way of laying out a publication. The InDesign plug-in, like its Quark counterpart, allows production run-up information to be used to place ads and editorial in an InDesign layout. Digital ads can automatically be incorporated.

- *PowrTools Software* (www.powrtools.com)—PowrTools has PowrTable, a plug-in that lets you create tables in InDesign.

- *ShadeTree Marketing* (www.borderguys.com)—ShadeTree's Fraemz PS comes to InDesign from its days as a PageMaker plug-in, and lets you add a variety of custom PostScript-compatible borders to picture frames, pages, and more.

- *Virginia Systems* (www.virginiasystems.com)—Recognizing the lack of an indexing feature in InDesign, Virginia Systems has Sonar Bookends InDex, a plug-in for InDesign that enables you to, well, index.

There are others from companies such as Cascade Systems (www.cascadenet.com), Em Software (www.emsoftware.com), HexMac Software Systems (www.hexmac.com), Mapsoft Computer Services (www.mapsoft.com), Ultimate Technographics (www.ultimate-tech.com), and more.

When you purchase a plug-in, you install it the way one typically installs a program. They typically come with installers or Install Wizards, and away you go.

If you look in the Plug-Ins folder in your InDesign folder, you'll see that all the assorted plug-ins are sorted into subfolders by category—Filters, Graphics, Layout, Prepress, and so on. There is also a Required folder that contains all the plug-ins that InDesign needs to function.

If you are used to the old days of QuarkXPress 3.3 and its way of handling XTensions, you know that to enable or disable an XTension, you physically dragged it out of the XTensions folder. (This changed in 4.0, but how many people got used to the XTensions Manager?) Never ever do this to InDesign plug-ins. By virtue of InDesign's modular approach, dragging plug-ins in and out of the plug-ins folder is a recipe for disaster. Use the new Configure Plug-ins dialog box to activate and deactivate your plug-ins instead.

If you have used a lot of XTensions in QuarkXPress, you might remember that when they were all enabled at once, you had a seven-day waiting period before the application launched. This is because of the fact that plug-ins, not surprisingly, take up memory. And, logically, a lot of them take up a lot of memory.

New in version 1.5 is the Configure Plug-ins dialog box, which is found in the Apple menu (on the Mac) or under Help (on PCs). Using this dialog box, you can determine which plug-ins are active. So, for example, if you have many third-party plug-ins, you can deactivate the ones you aren't using until you actually need them. For example, if you have an imposition plug-in, you probably don't need it if you are just starting to create a document. And by the same token, if you have a drop shadow creation plug-in, you probably don't need it if you are starting to create your impositions or PostScript output files.

In the Configure Plug-ins box (see Figure 22.15), you can see which plug-ins you've got, which plug-ins are required, and which are optional or third-party plug-ins.

You can create various sets of plug-ins. Notice in the Sets pop-up menu that you can choose to view only the required plug-ins. See Figure 22.16.

You can also highlight a plug-in and get information about it. See Figure 22.17.

FIGURE 22.15

The Configure Plug-ins dialog box.

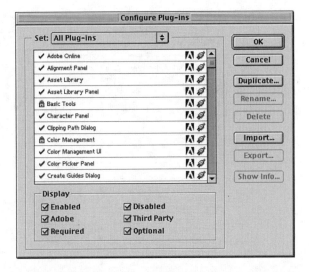

22

FIGURE 22.16

You can view only the required plug-ins.

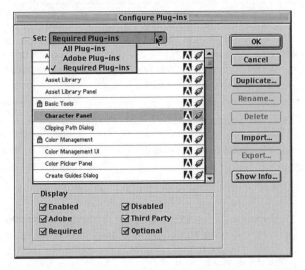

You probably will never need to know half the information provided here. It does tell you whether the plug-in is required, and whether it is dependent on any other plug-in to work. If you are having problems with plug-ins—and if you start activating and deactivating them and adding more, chances are you will—check out these boxes to determine whether you are missing a dependent plug-in or whether there was an error loading a plug-in. Sometimes files get corrupted.

FIGURE 22.17

*The Plug-in
Information box.*

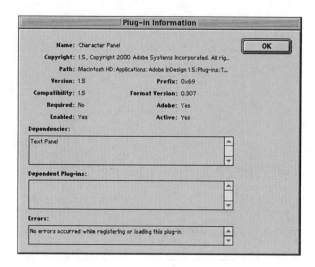

Adobe was smart here, as it was with keyboard shortcut sets. You cannot modify the All Plug-Ins set (the default). You are forced by InDesign to create a duplicate set and modify that. This is a good thing, in case you screw things up seemingly irretrievably. You can just go back to All Plug-Ins and save yourself the heartache.

You can also import and export plug-ins sets. This is useful when you are working with groups of people who all need to have the same sets. (You'll look at this in more detail in the next hour.)

If you use third-party plug-ins for certain tasks, you might need to have the plug-in in order to work with, output, or even open the document. This is fine if you are the only one working on the file. But if you send your file out to the service bureau, they might not be able to do anything with it. You thus need to ensure that you supply the plug-in you used to create it. Also keep in mind that, like the font issue you read about in Hour 17, "Printing from InDesign," copying and sharing third-party plug-ins is not unlike software piracy.

22

Summary

You've seen the various ways you can customize InDesign to your liking, be it in simple ways such as keyboard shortcuts and docking palettes, or through third-party plug-ins. Now it's time—in the next hour—to see how well InDesign plays with others.

Workshop

You've just learned how you can customize your workspace in InDesign. Be sure to read the Q&A for some provocative questions about InDesign and customization. Complete the quiz to test your recall of what you learned in this hour. Finally, work through the exercises until you have configured your workspace exactly the way you want it.

Q&A

Q I've noticed that not everything in InDesign comes with a default keyboard shortcut. Is there a reason for this, and can I add my own?

A If something shows up in the Edit Shortcuts dialog box, it can be a candidate for a keyboard shortcut. Just make sure you give it a shortcut that makes mnemonic sense to you (otherwise it's a wasted effort) and doesn't override another shortcut you also want to use.

Q Third-party plug-ins can get expensive. How do I know if I need them?

A Like Quark XTensions, InDesign plug-ins can often be "demoed" free of charge, either for a limited period of time, or in a sort of hobbled version (you can use the plug-in, but not print or save a document that uses them). Most of these demos can be downloaded from the vendor's site. If you come across a plug-in that sounds enticing, see if you can check out a demo first before purchasing it.

Q You made no mention of this, but does InDesign support scripting?

A Scripting is a very powerful customization option that many programs, including InDesign, support. Basically, it involves writing small programs in a scripting language (AppleScript on the Macintosh and Visual Basic in Windows) which automate certain tasks. Scripting is not for everyone, and although it doesn't require a degree in programming to learn and use effectively, it can be very complicated, and as such is beyond the scope of a beginner's book like this one. If you're interested in delving into the hoary netherworld of scripting, InDesign comes with a 250-page scripting guide that's actually pretty good. It's a PDF on the installation disc. Additionally, there are several titles on both AppleScript and Visual Basic, depending on what platform you're on. Specifically, Greg Perry's *Sams Teach Yourself*

Visual Basic 6 in 21 Days is a good place to start if you're on the Windows plat-form.

Quiz

1. Which of the following is not customizable in InDesign?

    a. Keyboard shortcuts

    b. Toolbar layout

    c. Menu items

2. You can use QuarkXPress's keyboard shortcuts in InDesign.

    a. True

    b. False

3. Which of the following is the best way to activate and deactivate plug-ins?

    a. Manually moving them out of the Plug-Ins folder

    b. Using the Configure Plug-ins palette

    c. Telekinesis

Quiz Answers

1. c. Unless you hack into the InDesign code, menu items are not customizable.

2. a. If you're a longtime Quark user and want to feel at home in InDesign, you can indeed configure InDesign to use Quark's keyboard shortcuts.

3. b. Although if it existed, c wouldn't be a bad option.

Exercises

Spend some time exploring the customization options. By now, you've explored most of the features in InDesign. Take this opportunity to add any keyboard shortcuts you desperately wish you had. Practice docking and undocking the palettes; creating your own custom megapalettes can be a great conveniences.

Hour **23**

Using InDesign in a Mixed Environment

However much you "vant to be alone," the truth is that you likely will be collaborating with others, probably in some sort of network or workgroup.

Sharing resources and working with others involves several issues that you'll consider in this hour. The first is basic networking and other means of connecting computers together. A second issue is cross-platform file sharing. You'll see that it's not as big a deal as it used to be. There is also the issue of sharing specific InDesign files and resources.

In this chapter you'll learn:

- How to transfer InDesign files in a cross-platform environment
- How to work with fonts in a cross-platform environment
- How to share character and paragraph styles, printer and PDF styles, and color swatches with others
- How to create and work with libraries

Resolving Cross-Platform Issues

Despite those who still take sides in the tedious Macintosh versus Windows debates, it is quickly becoming a cross-platform world. It is also becoming easier and easier to keep Macs and PCs on the same network or within the same workgroup. That said, if you are working on a regular publication, you are better off using one platform or the other, at least for all your primary design and production workstations. This minimizes any problems that might crop up as a result of platform incompatibilities.

It might also be less expensive to get one site license for one platform's version of an application than to get two site licenses—one for Mac and one for Windows.

Be that as it may, you often do encounter more than one platform in a workflow. For example, writers and editors, as well as sales, advertising, and administrative people, often have PCs, whereas designers and production folks normally use Macs.

Most major applications these days are cross-platform in nature. For example, the Mac version of Photoshop has no problems opening graphics files created by the Windows version of Photoshop, and vice versa. Similarly, the Mac version of InDesign has no trouble reading files created by the Windows version, and vice versa. When creating files for cross-platform use, there are a few things to bear in mind that will make the workflow as painless as possible.

Naming Conventions

The first issue you need to consider is that of naming. Each platform has its own file-naming conventions.

On the Mac, you are limited to 31 characters, and you can use any character you want except for a colon (:), which the OS uses to designate file paths. You can also use word spaces in filenames to separate words. A word space at the start of a filename moves it to the top of a folder. A bullet (•) at the start of a filename puts that file at the bottom of a folder. These are useful ways to organize files within folders. Filenames on the Mac are not case-sensitive. Therefore, *FileName*, *FILENAME*, and *filename* are all treated as the same file. So, on the Mac, an InDesign document is simply called *InDesign document*.

On Windows, you are limited to 250-character filenames (please don't use all 250 characters). Windows filenames can use any character except for slashes and vertical lines (/, \, |), colons (:), asterisks (*), double quotes ("), less than and greater than symbols (<, >), and question marks (?). Like the Mac, Windows filenames are also case-insensitive, and can include word spaces.

InDesign will automatically add the necessary Windows file extension. In this case, it's a four-letter string separated from the rest of the filename by a period. This extension indicates to the operating system what type of file it is.

So, on a PC, an InDesign filename is *InDesigndocument.indd.*

So when working in a cross-platform environment, be sure to name your files in a neutral way. For example, keep to the Mac minimum character limitation, and be sure to use the file extension when saving on the Mac. They need to be the standard file extensions (otherwise, what's the point). Here are some of the most common file extensions for graphics-related files:

23

.AI	Adobe Illustrator file
.BMP or .RLE	Microsoft bitmap
.DOC	Microsoft Word document
.EPS	Encapsulated PostScript file
.GIF	Graphics Interchange Format
.INDD	InDesign document
.INDT	InDesign template
.JPG or .JPEG	JPEG file
.PCT	PICT file
.PCX	PC Paintbrush file
.PDF	Acrobat PDF file
.PNG	Portable Network Graphic
.PS	PostScript file
.PSD	Photoshop file
.QXD	QuarkXPress document
.SCT or .CT	Scitex CT format file
.TGA	Targa file
.TIF or .TIFF	TIFF file
.WMF	Windows metafile

When opening InDesign files on one platform that were created on another, you might not be able to double-click on the file to open it. As a result, you need to use the Open command within InDesign. This is not a complete tragedy.

Macs and PCs: Playing Well Together

If you are connecting Macs and PCs directly using a network, it is fairly simple to get files from one computer to the other. If you are sneakernetting, or get files on floppies, Zips, Jazes, or other removable media, you might have a problem getting them to mount. But there are solutions in place that allow each platform to mount the other's media.

On the Mac, there is a system extension called PC Exchange (or File Exchange in OS 8.5 and greater) that, when activated, will mount PC media—floppies, Zips, CDs, and so on. PC Exchange comes with the Mac OS. There is also DataViz's MacLinkPlus (www.dataviz.com), which uses its own translators to mount PC media on Macs. On PCs, you need to invest in a third-party alternative. One excellent solution is MacDrive 98 from Media4 Productions (www.media4.com). This is an expensive program that, when installed, allows Windows 98 and NT 4.0 to mount and read Mac-formatted media. There is also a new version that is compatible with Windows 2000. DataViz also has Conversions Plus, the PC version of its MacLinkPlus.

Fonts

If ever there were an argument for picking one platform for production and sticking with it, font compatibility is it. As you have seen in previous hours, fonts are troublesome enough when confined to a single platform—never mind when they are transferred from one platform to the other.

Things have gotten better with regard to fonts, though. Several years ago, cross-platform workflows were not a chief consideration of users and font vendors, so incompatibilities abounded. Now, however, most vendors make Mac and PC versions of their fonts, and although differences still exist, it is not as dire a situation as it once was.

 It can become expensive to buy PC and Mac versions for all the fonts you use—another good reason to stick to one platform.

Some of the cross-platform problems related to fonts include different internal font names. As a result of these names, if you open a Mac-created InDesign document on a PC you get an error message indicating that a particular font is not loaded on your system. To get around this, you have to use the Find Font command and replace the old name with the new one. This means that when your Mac users reopen the document, they get the same error message you just got. They will not be happy with you.

Another font-related problem involves tracking, kerning, and other font metrics information, which can vary from platform to platform. As a result, you can experience text reflows.

Another problem is that symbols, especially diacritical marks and other special characters, don't always translate. You need to proof your text closely to ensure that you don't have bizarre characters appearing in the middle of your text.

In InDesign, you can get around this symbol problem by using the Insert Special command, rather than using the Option/Alt keyboard choices.

You can use a program such as Macromedia Fontographer to translate fonts from one platform to another and keep everything consistent.

23

Sharing InDesign Resources

Take a break from platform differences so you can see how to share your various InDesign resources. You'll come back to the issue of platforms and learn which InDesign elements cannot be shared across platforms later in this chapter.

Sharing Paragraph and Character Styles

You learned in Hour 7, "Basic Typesetting with InDesign," and Hour 8, "Working with Paragraphs," how to create character and paragraph styles, respectively, in order to save time when formatting text in a document. You can also easily copy your styles from document to document, so if you need to use the same typographic specifications in one document that you used in another, it is an easy matter to grab the ones you want.

To Do: Borrowing Type Styles

To import the type styles you created in one document into another, follow these steps.

1. Create a new document in InDesign or reopen a preexisting one.

2. Using techniques you learned in previous hours, create a few character styles and a few paragraph styles.

3. Save the document.

4. Open a second document or create a new one.

5. Choose Type, Paragraph Styles, or press F11 to get the Paragraph Styles palette.

6. Click on the arrow at the top-right side of the palette. The option called Load Paragraph Styles enables you to import styles from another document. If you go to the Character Styles palette, you see an option called Load Character Styles. Notice (see Figure 23.1) the option called Load All Styles as well. If you select the load

▼ all option, you can import both the paragraph and character Styles. So go ahead and select Load All Styles.

FIGURE 23.1

The options for loading styles from another document.

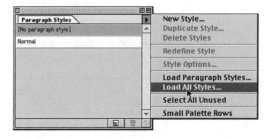

7. You'll be prompted to find the document you want to import styles from. Find the document you just created, and then click on Open. Your styles should now be imported.

▲

> If you load styles while no document is open, the styles are imported into your default settings, and every new document you create contains those styles. This is a useful shortcut when you are creating several documents that use the same character or paragraph styles. However, previously saved documents do not incorporate these styles, so you have to grandfather those styles in using the Load command.

If others in your workgroup need these styles, all you have to do is give them a file containing the styles.

Sharing Printer/PDF Styles

You've learned in previous hours how to create printer and PDF styles to save time when printing and creating PDFs. You can also trade these styles back and forth with others in your workgroup. It's a similar process to importing character and paragraph styles, but with an extra step involved.

To Do: Lending and Borrowing Printer Styles

To trade printer styles with other people in your workgroup, follow these steps.

1. Choose File, Printer Styles and select Define.

2. If you have defined a printer style that differs from Current, click on it. If you have not defined a style, create one using techniques you learned in a previous hour.

Printer and PDF styles are stored in InDesign's Defaults file, which means they are available in all your documents, unlike character and paragraph styles, which are specific to certain documents (unless they are imported into the Defaults file). As a result, your own printer and PDF styles are always on hand, unlike your own character and paragraph styles, which you may have to reload from other documents.

3. With the printer style you want to export selected, click on the Export button.

4. You are prompted to save your printer styles someplace. Pick a central location, such as on a network file server. If you are not on a network while doing this exercise, just save them somewhere on your hard drive. Press Save.

5. You'll be returned to the Printer Styles palette. Click on Cancel.

6. If you are on a network and have in fact saved the printer style to a central server, go to another workstation and launch InDesign. If you are not networked or only have one computer, you can still follow these steps.

7. Choose File, Printer Styles and select Define.

8. Click on the Import button. You are prompted to look for the printer styles file you want to import. Find the file you just exported, which should look something like Figure 23.2.

FIGURE 23.2

Importing printer Styles.

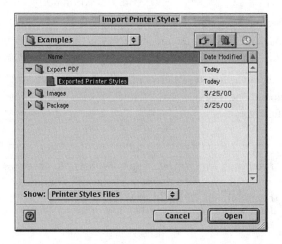

▼   9. When you've found the file, click on Open. If you are on the same computer that
          exported the file, just click on Cancel, because you already have these styles.

▲   The printer style should now appear in the Printer Styles palette.

 The same procedure works for PDF styles as well.

Sharing Color Swatches

You learned in a previous hour how to create a color swatch. You have several shortcuts
for using a defined color in another document. For example, if a logo or other design element uses a specific color, you might want to include that color in a number of other
documents.

To Do: Adding a Swatch to Another Document

 To add a color swatch used in one document to another document, follow these steps:

1. Create a new InDesign document or reopen one you have been working on.

2. Choose Window, Swatches, or press F5 to get the Swatches palette.

3. Using techniques you learned in Hour 13, "Simple Coloring with InDesign," create
   a unique color swatch, say C=50, M=80, Y=10, K=0.

4. Open a second InDesign document—either create one anew or open a previously
   created one. This second document serves as the document you want to copy the
   swatch to.

5. Click on the swatch you just created and drag it anywhere in the window of the
   second document. The new swatch now appears in the swatches palette of the sec-
▲ ond document.

 If you work with libraries, you know that you can't copy a swatch to a
library. However, if you create an element—such as a colored circle or polygon—that uses that color swatch, the swatch specs are saved along with
that element. You can create a sort of swatch library containing colored
shapes.

Sharing Libraries

One good way to share resources of all sorts is to create libraries. Libraries can be easily
shared by putting them in public folders. Libraries can also be easily shared across

platforms. You can store commonly used graphics such as logos or other recurring images as well as text in a library. As you saw in the last section, you can also create colored shapes that function as a sort of ersatz swatches library.

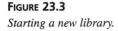

To Do: Founding Your Own Library

1. Choose Window, Libraries and select New. See Figure 23.3.

23

FIGURE 23.3
Starting a new library.

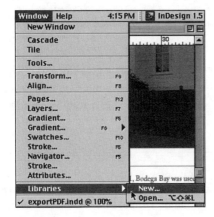

2. You are prompted for a place to store the library. If you want others to share it, pick a central location. If you are by yourself, simply pick a place on your hard drive.

3. You now have the Library window on-screen. See Figure 23.4.

FIGURE 23.4
The new library.

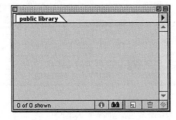

4. Note that there is nothing in it yet. Your first task is to start making deposits. Open a document that has graphics and text, if you have one. If you don't have one on hand, spend some time creating one. It's okay; I'll wait.

▼ 5. There are several options for adding items, as you can see from Figure 23.5.

▼

FIGURE 23.5
Library options.

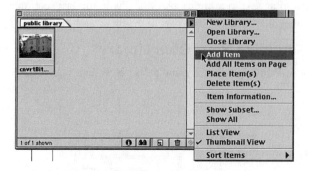

6. If you highlight a page element, such as a graphic, and click on Add Item, that item is deposited in the library. Alternatively, you can simply drag a page element into the library window—be it a graphic or a text frame—to deposit it. You also can select Add All Items on Page.

 If you select Add All Items on Page, the entire page is stored as a single library element, instead of each page element being saved as a separate element. Use this option only when you want to save an entire page as is.

7. Double-click on an element in the library, such as a graphic, and you'll get the Item Information dialog box. See Figure 23.6.

FIGURE 23.6
The Item Information dialog box.

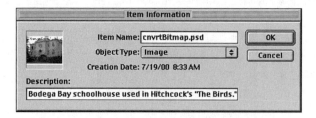

Here you find some basic information about your item, such as the filename, file type, and creation date and time. You can also add some description or keywords. Go ahead and enter a brief description of the item and press OK.

8. Add as many page elements as you wish.

9. Now, you probably don't have a great many things in your library at this point, but if you and your co-workers make extensive use of it, it can get quite large. Adding descriptive text and keywords aids in finding items in the future. Click on the

▼

▼ arrow at the top-right side of the library and scroll down to select Subset. (Or, you can click on the binoculars icon at the bottom of the Library window.)

10. You can now search the library via the Show Subset command in the Library palette menu, based on various criteria, as you can see in Figure 23.7.

FIGURE 23.7

Searching the library.

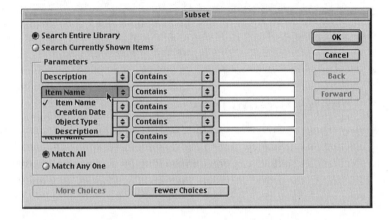

You can search by Item Name, Creation Date, Object Type, and Description. Notice that if you keep pressing the More Choices button, you can search on multiple criteria. Select Description in the top row and enter one of the keywords you entered in the Description for one of your library items. Press OK.

11. This displays a subset of your library with all the items that fit your search criteria. You can go to the arrow at the top-right side of the window and choose Select All to view your entire library.

12. Now assume that you want to use the object you found in the Library. Insert a new blank page in your document and go to it.

13. Highlight the library item you found and click on the palette options arrow.

14. Select Place. (Alternatively, you can click and drag the object from the library onto the page.)

Your library object is now on the page.

▲ You can also sort your objects by various criteria, and you can adjust the view—as thumbnails or as a list.

Beyond the Library

The library feature is a basic example of what has been a hot industry category called *digital asset management*. The bloom is off the asset management rose these days, but a few years ago there was a flurry of activity. There are still many programs out there—

ranging from small, desktop programs such as Extensis Portfolio or Canto Cumulus (my personal favorite), to high-powered hardware and software combos that can cost tens of thousands of dollars. They all serve the same basic purpose: to store, organize, and retrieve your digital assets, be they graphics, text documents, audio, video, and so on.

As you can imagine, they do much more than the simple InDesign library, and many can integrate with other programs. They become a sort of database for digital assets. If you accumulate a lot of graphics files that you need to hang onto and organize, you might want to look into an asset-management program.

Sharing Dictionaries

Any changes you make to spelling and hyphenation dictionaries can also be shared. Dictionaries are stored in the Proximity subfolder of the Dictionaries folder. The Dictionaries subfolder is stored in the Plug-Ins folder, which is stored in the InDesign folder. (So the path is InDesign, Plug-Ins, Dictionaries, Proximity.) Figure 23.8 shows a portion of the dictionaries.

FIGURE 23.8

Some of the dictionaries available in the Plug-Ins folder.

The filename corresponds to the nationality/language of the dictionary. The file extension indicates what type of dictionary it is:

.LEX is a basic spelling dictionary.

.HYP is the basic hyphenation dictionary.

.UDC refers to spelling exception dictionaries—words you add or remove via the Edit Dictionaries command.

.NOT refers to hyphenation exception dictionaries.

These dictionaries can be copied and shared by simply copying the dictionary files (and you really need to copy only the exception dictionaries because everyone has the base dictionary by virtue of having InDesign).

Sharing Keyboard Shortcuts

You can also copy your keyboard shortcuts. They live in the Shortcuts Set subfolder, which is in the InDesign folder. If you have created a custom set, simply copy it and give to your co-workers. Keyboard shortcuts are not cross-platform, however.

23

Viruses

Here is one thing you absolutely don't want to share with your colleagues: viruses. There is no shortage of them, and no platform is safe from them (except maybe Linux, but give it time...). True, there are very few Mac viruses, at least compared to the ones the PC folks had to fend off.

But boy was the graphics industry in for a shock in mid-1998 when a virulent and dangerous strain of Mac viruses tore through the industry. These were known as the *9806 Autostart Worms*, and they invaded Mac systems primarily through Zip disks. After these viruses got on your system, they quickly started destroying data. There were horror stories of entire hard disks being corrupted.

So don't take viruses and the threat thereof lightly, especially if you use Windows. If you share files or download files from the Web or from other outside sources, be certain that you have an effective antivirus program. Dr. Solomon's Virex and Symantec's Norton Antivirus are two that I use regularly on various systems, both at home and at the office, and there are others. Virus descriptions are usually updated monthly, and are often available as a free download from the vendor's Web site. Be certain to scan every disk and file you come into contact with. We still are getting Zip disks with the Autostart Worms on them, and we do occasionally get Word files with macro viruses—which are cross-platform. And as the recent "Love Bug" debacle pointed out, it pays to be vigilant. If you do get an infected file, be sure to tell the person who gave it to you. They might not even know they're infected.

Sharing Elements Across Platforms

Most things in InDesign can be copied from platform to platform. You've already seen that InDesign files are easy to copy and open from Mac to Windows and vice versa. Graphics are also readily moved back and forth, especially TIFF, PCX, and EPS. And of course PDF is as portable as its name indicates.

So, essentially, the pieces of your InDesign pages are easy to transfer, but what about things like style sheets, dictionaries, and shortcuts?

The following list shows items that are indeed capable of being copied from Mac to Windows (and vice versa):

- Color swatches (when copying to Windows add the file extension .AI)
- Style sheets
- Dictionaries

The following items are not transferable:

- Keyboard shortcut sets
- Color profiles
- Scripts

Also, if you are using third-party plug-ins, you need to have both platforms' version of the plug-in in order to take advantage of the plug-ins' features.

Summary

So, you've seen the issues involved in sharing InDesign resources, files, and other elements with others, both on the same platform, as well as on other platforms. You can now get yourself networked and transfer files back and forth.

Workshop

You've just learned how to share resources with others in your workgroup, as well as create custom libraries of elements that you may want to reuse from document to document. Now, check out the Q&A to find the answers to some lingering questions you may have, and complete the quiz to test your recall of the features we covered.

Q&A

Q You didn't mention templates. Aren't they useful?

A Of course they are. The only real difference between a template and a proper document is that when you open a template, you can't press Save. You always have to save it as something else, so as not to overwrite the original template. Templates are useful when documents use the same basic page elements from job to job. Templates can also be shared across platforms.

Q **When I copy a graphic into a library, does the entire graphic get copied, or just the link, like in InDesign proper?**

A All that is imported into the library is a preview and a path to the original graphic file. If the file is moved, you lose the link to it. InDesign will ask you to relink it.

Quiz

1. Which of the following is not capable of being shared across platforms?

    a. InDesign documents

    b. TIFF graphics

    c. Keyboard shortcuts

2. Character and paragraph styles cannot be added to InDesign default preferences.

    a. True

    b. False

Quiz Answers

1. c. Because Macs and PCs have somewhat different keys, it doesn't make sense that they would be cross-platform, now does it?

2. b. Character and paragraph styles can be added to the default preferences. Simply create the styles you want while no document is open, and those styles will be available in every document you create and open.

23

Hour **24**

Deploying InDesign in the Real World

You've seen throughout this book all the tools that InDesign puts at your disposal for creating documents. All this is nice, and it is a great program, but you do need to be conscious of the fact that InDesign does not exist in a vacuum. Graphics users have been using other programs, such as QuarkXPress and PageMaker, for years.

This is not to say that users are unwilling to switch, but there is more to converting a workflow than simply buying a new program and reading a book like this. A great deal of investment—both time and money—has gone into preexisting workflows.

So in this, the final hour, you will:

- Learn about roadblocks that can impede adoption of InDesign
- Review solutions that can make the switch somewhat painless

Meeting InDesign's System Requirements

One of the big complaints that I have heard from various corners of the graphics industry involve the prodigious minimum system requirements that InDesign needs.

Knowing Your Mac System Requirements

To run on a Mac, the big requirement is that you need at least OS 8.5 (preferably OS 8.6, as 8.5 is not without its problems). That might not seem like a problem, but OS 8.5 and greater need a fairly hefty set of system resources to run. Depending on your extensions and utilities, you need *at least* 24MB just to run the OS. (I just checked my own system and my OS—8.6—is using about 44MB of RAM.) You also need a few hundred megabytes of hard disk space to install the system. Not everyone wants to upgrade their OS. I was happy with 8.1. (Of course, I was happy with 7.5, but I suppose I can't remain mired in the past.)

The InDesign documentation says you can get by with a PowerPC 604 chip. Well, I've tried this, and yes, you can *get by,* but allow six to eight weeks for launching. Make no bones about it: You need at least a G3, be it a proper G3 or an older PowerMac that has been retrofitted with a G3 processor. You also need 48MB of RAM with virtual memory on; if you don't like virtual memory, you need 96MB of built-in memory. You also need at least 120MB of hard disk space to install InDesign.

This doesn't take into account the fact that you might be running programs like Photoshop, Illustrator, and Acrobat at the same time. So you'll need to boost your system resources by the amount that *those* programs require. That's a lotta do-re-mi.

Knowing Your Windows Requirements

Windows 95 won't cut it here; you need at least Windows 98, a Windows NT 4.0 work-station with Service Pack 4, or Windows 2000.

In terms of processor, you need at least 300 MHz, although Adobe says you can get by with a Pentium II. Adobe also recommends at least 64MB of RAM. Don't forget that, again, you might want to run Photoshop, Illustrator, or Acrobat simultaneously. How aggravating would it be to keep launching and quitting applications? If you're like me, you've done that, and ended up running down to CompUSA to get more RAM.

So before you decide to upgrade to InDesign, make sure that your system—and the systems of those you'll be working with—can handle it.

Working with Service Providers

Not all service providers support InDesign yet. Until the end of March 2000, there was only the 1.0 version, and not everyone likes working with 1.0 versions of programs. But service bureaus have reported that they have yet to see an influx of InDesign-related jobs, so everyone is still at the learning stage with this program. This will change as the program becomes more widely adopted. It sounds like the chicken and the egg dilemma. Which comes first: user or service bureau acceptance? Service bureaus respond to what their clients want. So as more users adopt the program, service bureau support will not be far behind.

Switching from QuarkXPress

There are two issues to consider when deciding to convert from QuarkXPress to InDesign. The first is how easily your Quark documents can be converted to InDesign documents. The second is how easy it is to adjust to the InDesign interface.

24

Opening Quark Files in InDesign

One of the most basic conveniences that Adobe added to InDesign is its capability to faithfully open QuarkXPress documents. There have been various utilities in the past that purported to let you convert Quark documents to PageMaker, and vice versa. But, let's face it, none of them worked well, and it was often more time-consuming to fix things than to create the document from scratch.

InDesign does a great job of opening Quark documents, and it's simple.

> The following exercise is based on the premise that you have and know QuarkXPress. If you don't, you can simply follow along or skip to the next section.

To Do: Converting a QuarkXPress Document to InDesign

To convert a QuarkXPress 3.3 or 4.X document to an InDesign document, follow these steps:

1. Create a simple, one-page QuarkXPress document. Add a graphic and sample text. For added fun, create some character and paragraph style sheets, and a custom color. Save it as a native Quark file. Figure 24.1 shows my (by now) excruciatingly familiar example document in QuarkXPress 4.1.

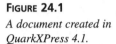

FIGURE 24.1

A document created in QuarkXPress 4.1.

2. Launch InDesign and choose File, Open or press Command+O (Mac) or Control+O (in Windows).

3. Find the Quark file you just saved and click on Open.

   InDesign tells you that it is converting various things, and that it takes a minute. If it encounters anything problematic, it will notify you.

Depending on your document, you should have a pretty clean and faithful rendition of your original Quark document in InDesign. As you can see in Figure 24.2, my example opened pretty flawlessly, right down to the paragraph and character style sheets.

Although you can't see this in this black-and-white book, the red "About Bodega Bay" text was also imported with its appropriate color swatch, which now appears in the Swatches palette.

Conversion Hits and Misses

One new feature of InDesign 1.5 is that it supports text on a path. Because of this, you can convert text on a path from Quark to InDesign. For example, Figures 24.3 and 24.4 show how this works.

FIGURE 24.2

The Quark document opened in InDesign.

FIGURE 24.3

Text on a path created in QuarkXPress 4.1.

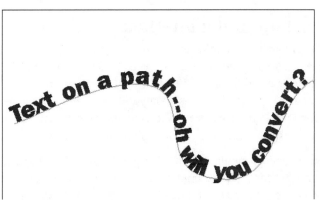

FIGURE 24.4

The same document opened in InDesign 1.5. The text is fully editable.

Other features that convert readily include master pages, along with all guides, items, and content. Even a Bèzier picture box converts to a Bèzier picture frame in InDesign.

That all said, some features don't convert very well, if at all. For example, clipping paths created in Quark do not.

 Of course, if an image is listed as missing or modified in Quark's Picture Usage dialog box, it cannot make the jump to InDesign. So be sure to update all your links before converting.

Images that have been embedded in QuarkXPress documents, created with third-party XTensions, or imported using OLE or Publish and Subscribe also cannot make the jump to InDesign.

The decision of whether to convert a Quark document or create a document from scratch in InDesign is of course yours. But it's pretty easy to see how this decision should be made. It takes very little time to perform an import, so import the document and quickly flip through it. If everything looks okay, stick with it. If it looks completely out of whack, abandon it and start over. But even in the best of cases, opening a Quark document in InDesign is merely a starting point.

Adjusting to the Interface

This is probably going to be more a function of your personality than anything. Some people take to new programs quite easily. Others—not so much. If you are familiar with the Photoshop and Illustrator interfaces, InDesign will not be all that foreign to you. (Then again, even if you are used only to Quark, you will probably not find InDesign all that foreign.) If you have been following the exercises throughout this book sequentially, you are no doubt used to the InDesign interface by now.

There are enough similarities in InDesign that it will not seem strange. Picture boxes and text boxes become picture frames and text frames. The difference is that, in InDesign, you don't need to create a frame before you can put anything on the page. In fact, as you've seen, in InDesign you can just drag graphics and text files from the desktop onto the page.

Different Toolsets

Probably the biggest thing to get used to is the different toolset. In Quark, you have the Move tool, which enables you to move objects around the screen, and the Content tool, which enables you to enter or edit text and import or edit images. In InDesign, as you have seen, the Selection tool functions much like the Move tool. In InDesign, the Type tool, used to enter and edit text, and the Direct Selection tool, used for working with graphics, take on the functions of the Quark Content tool.

Perhaps the toughest thing to get used to is the Page Grabber Hand tool. In Quark, regardless of whether you have the Move or Content tool selected, you can always Option+drag to use the Page Grabber Hand to move the page around the screen. In InDesign, you can get the Page Grabber Hand if you hold down the spacebar and drag, but only when the Selection tool is selected.

Hybrid Text Flow

Another major difference is the way InDesign flows text, which is kind of a Quark/PageMaker hybrid approach that combines the best of both worlds. In Quark, you need to create a text box and click on the Text Chain tool to flow from one text box to another. In InDesign, you don't need to create a frame first, although you can if you want. You can simply click on the overflow text indicator (the red + sign at the bottom of a text frame) and drag the new text to the area you want to place it. It's PageMaker-like, and actually reminds a lot of more seasoned people of the way that manual paste-up used to be done.

There are other petty little things as well. Suffice it to say that they are part of the adjustments you need to make when you try something new.

24

Switching from PageMaker

Users who have called PageMaker home for most of their careers will have few problems adjusting to InDesign, because InDesign is not that different from PageMaker. This is not to say that it's the same program; it's very different in many ways. But the interface is familiar, which is not surprising because the two Adobe versions of PageMaker (6.0 and 6.5) attempted to make it congruent with other Adobe products.

Opening PageMaker Documents

As you saw recently with QuarkXPress, converting a PageMaker document to an InDesign document is simply a case of opening the PageMaker file in InDesign.

The following exercise is based on the premise that you have and know PageMaker 6.5. If you don't, you can simply follow along or skip to the next section.

To Do: Converting a PageMaker Document to InDesign

▼ To Do

To convert a PageMaker 6.5 document to InDesign, follow these steps:

1. In PageMaker, create a simple one-page document. Add a graphic, some text, maybe a style sheet and color swatch. Save it as a native PageMaker document. For our final exercise, in the interest of variety, let us leave the lovely yet ornithologically doomed seaside town of Bodega Bay. In Figure 24.5, we have a page with graphics and text, this time in PageMaker.

FIGURE 24.5

A simple document created in PageMaker.

2. Launch InDesign, and choose File, Open or press Command+O (on the Mac) or Control+O (in Windows).

3. Find the PageMaker document you just saved, and click on Open. InDesign tells you what it is converting, and if there are any problems, it will notify you.

   You should now have a pretty clean and faithful representation of your PageMaker document in InDesign. See Figure 24.6.

▲

By virtue of their basic similarities—and by virtue of their both being Adobe products—PageMaker documents should open fairly reliably in InDesign. Because there are also numerous differences, not everything will convert reliably. So, as with Quark documents, think of a converted PageMaker document as merely a starting point. Repair work might be required.

FIGURE 24.6

The sample PageMaker document opened in InDesign.

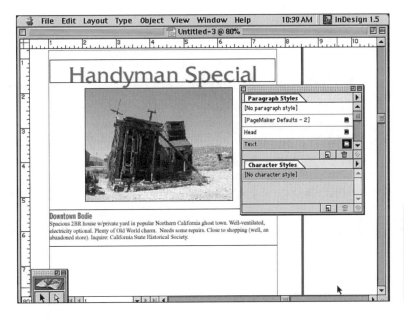

Adjusting to the Interface

The InDesign interface is reminiscent of PageMaker's—except you have a whole slew of additional tools and features. But the basic approach is still there. You have picture frames, but you don't necessarily have to use them. You can place graphics or text wherever you want.

Another beneficial change is that to place a keyline around an image, you don't have to go to the clunky Keyline plug-in; you can just add a stroke in InDesign.

Story Editor

Another adjustment that some folks are not fond of is the lack of a story editor à la PageMaker. Not everyone likes to proof text on-screen in layout; they would much rather go to a dedicated text editor. This was a big complaint in version 1.0, and when 1.5 came out, many users bemoaned its continued omission. Well, suffice it to say that Adobe is on top of that and has announced a story editor for InDesign called InCopy. It is slated to be available in the last quarter of 2000 through the Adobe systems integrator channel. Pricing will be based on the particular installation. As you can probably tell, this is a higher-end editorial tool, so for now, editors have to get used to proofing text in the layout.

Lack of Control Palette

Another point of disorientation is the lack of the Control palette along the bottom of the screen. (Quark users might also feel this.) You can use the Transform, Character, and

Paragraph palettes in its place, if you prefer. There are other differences, most of which you have probably picked up on by now.

Playing Well with Others

InDesign is not designed to be the only program you use to create documents. Specifically, it is designed to work in tandem with Photoshop and Illustrator (and Acrobat) as an integrated graphics package. You've seen in previous chapters how this integration works. Not only can native Photoshop, Illustrator, and PDF files be imported easily into InDesign, but InDesign can also easily launch those other programs to facilitate editing. Even non-Adobe products work in tandem with InDesign. For example, you have seen how you can launch Word from the links palette to edit placed Word documents.

Summary

So you've seen the issues involved in working with InDesign in the real world, and some of the possible barriers to its widespread adoption as a page layout tool. You've been through the exercises in this book. Is it the twenty-first century publishing tool that it was touted as? I can't answer that for you. A program can only be as good as the extent to which it solves a particular user's problems.

You now have an intimate familiarity with InDesign, and are well-situated to begin using it in earnest—if you haven't been already. I can only show you how to use the program; I can't make you like it. Hopefully, you do.

Workshop

So you've seen the issues involved in converting a workflow to InDesign, as well as basically becoming acclimated to the program. Probably the best way of becoming acclimated is to just keep using InDesign. Before adopting it completely, start using it for small, extraneous, or personal projects. Using it on a regular basis is a good way to get acclimated to it.

Q&A

Q Because InDesign doesn't use font styles (such as bold, italic, and so on) like other programs such as Quark or PageMaker do, what happens to those styles if I convert?

A Well, first of all, you should never use the styles for italics and bolds. Bad bad bad. Actually, InDesign does something smart, or tries to. It attempts to convert the faux bold or italic to a real bold or italic, if you have the font. If not, you'll just get plain text. And it serves you right, because that's what you'd get if you tried to RIP it.

Quiz

1. Which of the following features will not convert from Quark to InDesign?

    a. Style sheets

    b. Clipping paths

    c. Text on a path

2. Which of the following programs can't be launched from InDesign?

    a. Acrobat

    b. Photoshop

    c. Word

    d. None of the above

Quiz Answers

1. b. Or at least clipping paths created in Quark.

2. d. InDesign lets you launch many of the native programs you used to create elements that you imported into InDesign.

24

INDEX

X-Z